REWRITING HISTORY

The Life and Times of Pandita Ramabai

UMA CHAKRAVARTI

zubaan

An Imprint of K

Rewriting History: The Life and Times
of Pandita Ramabai

First published in 1998
Second impression 2000
Second edition 2006

Zubaan
K-92 Hauz Khas Enclave
New Delhi - 110 016

© Uma Chakravarti 1998

Cover design: Uzma Mohsin

ISBN 81-85107-79-3

Typeset in India by Scribe Consultants
B4/30 Safdarjung Enclave, New Delhi 110 029

Printed at Raj Press
R-3 Inderpuri, New Delhi - 110 012

For
my grandmothers Alamelu and Lakshmi,
who experienced the routine humiliations of 'adult'
widowhood, dependence, and a reluctant maintenance from
their sons
my aunt Parvathi, who was
– married at twelve, mother at fifteen,
deserted by her husband in her twenties
– widowed at thirty-four
– mortified eleven years later by the painful death from
consumption of her eldest daughter, condemned to replace her
as an unpaid domestic drudge for the twenty-four remaining
years of her life
my father, P.S. Doraswami, who, even at the age of ninety,
suffered the guilt that some sensitive men have felt at not
being able to do enough to prevent the anguish caused to
the widows in their families
my mother, Saraswathy, her sister Vijayalakshmi,
and their father P.V. Aghoram,
who resisted and broke with the oppressive practices
of Brahmanical patriarchy so that I and my sisters and our
daughters could have a better today
and
for the named and unnamed widows
who feature in this book

Acknowledgements

The Nehru Memorial Museum and Library for the grant of a Fellowship that enabled me to do the bulk of the work on this book; the British Council for financial assistance that made it possible for me to use the India Office Library; Miranda House for the grant of leave relieving me of my teaching duties; and the Haven's Center, Madison, for providing me with an opportunity to present some of this material at seminars; Madhu Malti Deshpande and Sudhanwa Deshpande for generous help in translating material from Marathi to English; Geetanjali Gangoly for accessing material for me from various archives in Bombay; Kumkum Sangari for academic support over many years and especially for extensive suggestions on the first draft of this work; Ram Bapat, G.P. Deshpande, Gail Omvedt, Prem Chowdhry, Svati Joshi, Tanika Sarkar, Sumit Sarkar, Aijaz Ahmed, Kumkum Roy, Rajul Sogani, Indira Gupta, Patricia Uberoi, Sudesh Vaid, C.V. Subbarao and my colleagues at Miranda House for creative academic interaction which has helped to shape this work when it was in the making; Antoinette Burton, Tanika Sarkar, Inderpal Grewal and Edith Blumhofer for sharing their work in manuscript form and providing useful references; Mrinalini Sardesai for introducing me to her mother Madhu Malti Deshpande who not only generously gave of her time but enthusiastically got into the spirit of the work and identified completely with the travails of the nineteenth century women whose writings in Marathi she translated for me; my brother Anand Doraswami who began by finding the time from his over-stretched schedule to edit this work but went on to be so moved by the anguish of the widows that the work is now as much his as it is mine; Prem Chowdhry for especially creating the evocative painting reproduced on the cover; Urvashi Butalia for patiently and, for the most part, good-humouredly watching this work grow alarmingly in size; Ritu Menon, Jose,

Elsie, and Jaya for making me feel so much at home at Kali For Women; Juhi for preparing the index; Anuja for unfailing support in preparing this manuscript and bailing me out from every imagined or real crisis at home and outside during the last five years; Siddhartha for sharing his experiences of working towards a redefined masculinity; and finally to Anand Chakravarti for a lifetime of shared interests and concerns.

Contents

Prologue / vii

1

Caste, Gender and the State in
Eighteenth Century Maharashtra / 1

2

Caste Contestation, Class Formation,
Nationalism and Gender / 43

3

Law, Colonial State and Gender / 121

4

Men, Women and the Embattled Family / 200

5

On Widowhood: The Critique of Cultural
Practices in Women's Writing / 246

6

Structure and Agency: A Life and a Time / 301

Bibliography / 351

Index / 362

Prologue

Why has the life and work of Ramabai and, more importantly, her critique of society been marginalised from mainstream history[1] which otherwise is more than generous to the great men (and occasionally women) school of history? Ramabai had all the elements required for a 'great' character: she was articulate, learned, confident and forceful — a woman who got considerable media attention when she first burst upon the public arena in the 1870s. Men of the nineteenth century, both reformists and traditionalists who had been waxing eloquent on the 'glorious' position of women in ancient India, suddenly found an embodiment of such womanhood in the person of Ramabai. Welcomed and feted in Calcutta in 1878-79, Ramabai was soon honoured with the title of 'Saraswati' for her learning and eloquence, not just in any 'vernacular' but in Sanskrit (from which women had been traditionally excluded) — an apt title that was soon to become ironic. The goddess Saraswati is associated with learning but also with *vac* (speech or voice). Unfortunately, as Ramabai was to discover, unless this voice or speech tied into what men wanted to hear and what they themselves were saying, it was regarded as dissonant. Ramabai's critique of Brahmanical patriarchy and her decisive break with its oppressive structure through her conversion to Christianity were too much for those riding the high tide of history and for whom nationalism was synonymous with Hinduism. Ramabai became at best an embarrassment and at worst a betrayer. Her marginalisation then is not the mere consequence of gender bias in history, although that certainly accounts for a part of it. It is not merely an obscuring, an invisibilising, as is commonly the case with women, but a *suppression*. Our task then is not just to retrieve forgotten histories but to explore the histories of suppression.

That Ramabai's absence from dominant history is not a case of forgotten history but a case of suppression is evident from accounts of Annie Besant, whose life and work invariably find mention in any history of modern India. In many ways Annie Besant's life was a counterpoint to that of Ramabai and was probably perceived as such. Before Annie Besant came out to India she had been an active member of the women's suffragette movement.[2] Once she was in India she threw herself into the task of the spiritual and national regeneration of the country. The nation's regeneration itself was inextricable from a revival of Hinduism. Within a few years of her arrival in India Annie Besant established herself as an outstanding revivalist of Hinduism in south India as she held forth vigorously on the 'glories' of ancient and modern Hinduism. What is significant is that reform itself was irrelevant in her national and spiritual revivalist agenda.[3] Hindu culture was 'blessed' in her view and needed no major changes. The chief target of her ridicule, especially in the late nineteenth century, was the social reformers whose influence she regarded as 'debilitating.' The impact she had was tremendous, the more so because here was a cultivated European woman outlining the virtues of Hinduism in all its facets as she besought Hindus to avoid the pitfalls of so-called western advancement and revere their own culture.[4] The newly constituted English- educated elite fraught with ambivalent feelings about themselves and their society found it most reassuring that a member of the ruling race was vigorously defending Hindu society. Annie Besant's defence of Hindu society and civilization enabled this class to exorcise any sense of guilt they might have especially in relation to the low status of women in their own families and in the wider community. Further, as she idealised many controversial practices, including celibate widowhood by a refusal to sanction widow marriage, her sex, her eloquence, her antecedents and her nationality,[5] all worked together to undermine the basis for social reform which a section of the educated elite had begun to recommend.

Over the years Annie Besant revised her position on reforms to some extent[6] but continued to speak and write fervently about Hinduism, with nationalism and Hinduism being intertwined in her social and political agenda. Her approach to women's issues remained cautious and in her later years she concentrated her energies on building up the Theosophical Society and on the Home Rule Movement. Despite the changes in her position on the need for reform Annie Besant continued to be associated in the minds of men with her pleas for a revival of Hinduism and for the foundation of nationalism as lying in Hinduism — 'Without Hinduism there is no future for India,' as she put it.[7]

An important facet of Annie Besant's career both in England and in India is that like Ramabai's it was deeply controversial. But what needs to be noted is that unlike Ramabai, in the final analysis, the controversies around Annie Besant were not of the kind incapable of being accommodated within the dominant nationalist discourse in history, whereas in the case of Ramabai this appears to have been impossible. Ramabai crossed two *Lakshman rekhas*: first, she mounted a scathing critique of Brahmanical patriarchy at a time when even contemporary male reformers were shying away from confronting its structure; second, as a high-caste Hindu widow herself, she 'chose' to become a Christian, 'betraying' her 'religion' and thereby her 'nation' in the eyes of nineteenth century Hindu society. Not just that, she had led other high-caste Hindu widows to do likewise. Ramabai's choice represented an audacious challenge to men: a widow was regarded in nineteenth century Maharashtra as someone who should retreat into the dark spaces even within the confines of the home. That such women could *choose* to accept a new religion and make a break with the faith of their kinsfolk was seen as outrageous. Henceforth Ramabai symbolised a threat to the moral and social order of the kind of nationalism being forged by Hindu nationalists. It was not without reason that Ramabai was regarded as having betrayed the nation; such a label masked the power relations which determined what the political and social agenda within nationalism should be. It was not an agenda which could include a critique of patriarchy, or of Hindu social institutions and religious practices, when it was voiced by a woman publicly and one who had opted out of the faith and customary practices of her ancestors.

The difference in the way in which Ramabai and Annie Besant have figured in historical writing in both the late nineteenth and early twentieth centuries as well as now indicates that there has been an easy conflation not only of nationalism with Hinduism but more importantly of Christianity with colonialism. There is a latent assumption that in opting for Christianity Ramabai and others had accepted the religion of the rulers and had therefore become 'compradors' and were complicit with the colonial presence. Such an assumption is both simplistic and motivated. The mere existence of a relationship between Christianity and colonialism is not enough to treat Christianity automatically as the handmaiden of colonialism. That there were some shared ideological positions is evident but it needs to be noted that there were also major moments and points of tension between the colonial administration and the Christian missionaries. More importantly, for those who were potential or actual 'converts' were Christianity and colonialism the same thing? Did acceptance of Christianity mean acceptance of the colonial relationship or of western dominance over indigenous people? There is no reason to accept such assumptions without an analysis, which has hardly been undertaken, of the many facets of Christianity in India. It is unlikely that such a lacuna is likely to be filled in the near future given the obsession with 'colonial discourse' which is currently dominating historical scholarship. Practitioners of discourse analysis are unwilling to explore pre-colonial structures or to dismantle colonialism itself into its constituent elements. In practice, therefore, such a view ties in with the agenda of Hindu nationalists both in the past and in the present.

In locating Ramabai in the history of the nineteenth century, and in exploring her conceptualisation of Brahmanical patriarchy and her search for alternatives to it, we find such a paradigm highly restrictive. Gender history forces us to recognise that it is not enough to use methodologies which focus essentially on men, even as they make a passing gesture to gender by writing about the feminisation of the colonised male in relation to the colonising male, thereby reducing gender to a representational phenomenon rather than a material and ideological arrangement. Further, studies using the framework of Said's *Orientalism* treat the colonised and colonisers as homogeneous entities.[8] Such an approach ignores the power relations and hierarchies within the colonised, and is unwilling to concede the different histories of social groups and their relationship to each other in pre-colonial times as well as to their experience of colonialism.[9]

I intend to make a modest beginning in this work to provide an alternative framework of analysis for studies of gender: by treating Ramabai's controversial life as an entry point I shall explore the relationship between gender, class, and nation in the nineteenth century. More specifically this will enable me to outline the links between structure and agency in the context of women's lives. And since the nineteenth century saw important transformations in the relationship between gender, caste, class, and the state, I consider it useful to begin my exploration of the larger context of gender in the pre-colonial period to understand the nature of change in the nineteenth century following the establishment of colonial rule. The eighteenth century thus forms the proper starting-point for this work. To facilitate the outlining of the diverse themes covered by this work the book is in three parts: Part One provides an overview of the structure of society in eighteenth and nineteenth century Maharashtra; Part Two with issues of gender; and Part Three with the relationship between structure and agency in the specific context of gender as played out in the life and work of Pandita Ramabai.

NOTES AND REFERENCES

1. The social history of the nineteenth and twentieth centuries in India has dwelt at considerable length upon the socio-religious reform movements of the period. Descriptions and analyses of such movements have featured in all the standard text-books and form a part of historical learning from the school syllabi upwards. The centre of this reform movement is admittedly the reforms relating to women's status. Yet the focus of almost all the writing on the nineteenth century is on men — men who spearheaded it and men who resisted it. Ramabai, who spent the better part of her life working for women in general but more specifically on the most powerless section within upper-caste society — the widow —, gets only a passing reference in discussions on reform and no mention at all in any discussion on the 'making of modern India'(see for example G.P. Pillai, *Representative Indians*, London, Thacker and Company, 1902, where all the representative Indians are men; T.V. Pavate, *Makers of Modern India*, Jullunder, University Publishers, 1964, where all 25 of the makers of modern India except one are men — characteristically the only woman is Annie Besant; H.N. Verma and Amrit Verma, *Hundred Great Indians Through the Ages*, Campbell, California, G.I.P. Books, 1992, which lists some women among its 'great' Indians such as Mirabai, Ahilyabai, and Andal, but not Ramabai).
2. Arthur H. Nethercot, *The First Five Lives of Annie Besant*, Chicago,

University of Chicago Press, 1960, p. 1. Nethercot writes that by
the age of forty, in 1885, Annie Besant was a Fabian socialist,
feminist, and freethinker. Soon after, she was also a union organiser
and strike leader. But all these dimensions of her work were left
behind when she came out to India where she was transformed into
a spiritualist and a revivalist and finally into a fiery nationalist.

3. C.H. Heimsath, *Indian Nationalism and Hindu Social Reform*,
Princeton, Princeton University Press, 1964, pp. 255, 312, 315.

4. *Ibid.*, pp. 327–28.

5. *Ibid.*

6. *Ibid.*, pp. 328–331.

7. *Ibid.*, p. 329. A survey of Annie Besant's writings over some twenty
years does reveal some shifts over the nature of Hindu society and
the need to choose between an unalloyed return to the past and a
moderate reform programme. However, her attitude to caste and
gender issues remained conservative. Unlike Ramabai, who made a
sharp critique of the Brahmanical texts including Manu, Annie
Besant believed that Manu provided the 'most orderly and perfectly
arranged code' for India (George Arundale (ed.), *Annie Besant,
Builder of New India: Her Fundamental Principles of Nation Building*,
Madras, Theosophical Publishing House, 1942, p. 22). Manu's
social organisation of caste, in Besant's view, was based on a
recognition of 'different types of human beings.' Even though she
came to believe that India no longer needed it she went so far as to
explain endogamy as a way to ensure that the Aryan minority was
not swamped by the aboriginal majority: heredity was a means by
which specific types of individuals were built up (Annie Besant,
*Birth of New India: Collection of Writings and Speeches on Indian
Affairs*, Madras, Theosophical Society, 1917, p. 223). Her writing
on women is informed by a dualism. She might occasionally
recognise that the status of women in India was low and 'men were
selfish' but she wrote that even though women's 'utter sacrifice' was
apt to increase masculine selfishness, nonetheless it was in their
self-sacrifice that the salvation of India lay (*Annie Besant, The Builder
of New India*, p. 26).

Annie Besant's understanding of what must be done for women
and how different this was from Pandita Ramabai's understanding
of the women's question is evident in a lecture she gave on 'The
Education of Hindu Girls,' published also as a pamphlet in 1904.
She advocated the launching of a 'national movement of girls'
education' on 'national lines', which should not be dwarfed by the
modern view. Women were to be thought of as mothers, wives, or
'Brahmavadinis' of the older days. Education was not to make

women think of themselves as rivals and competitors of men in all forms of outside or public employment as was becoming prevalent in the west. The west, in Besant's view, had created an artificial problem between the sexes. The distinction between the public and private domain and a sexual division of labour was thus to be continued to avoid the creation of an 'artificial problem'. The 'natural' function of women was to be wives and mothers. Education was to socialise and spiritualise them such that 'we could bring back the Gargis and Maitreyis of yore' (Annie Besant, *Speeches and Writings*, Madras, Natesan and Company, no date, pp. 72–80). Consistent with her position on caste and gender was the framework within which Annie Besant understood the different institutions prevalent in India: it was its spirituality that was the main characteristic of India. The greatness of India's past had been that everything was done for a spiritual purpose, every act was a *religious service*. The essence of the Aryan type was spirituality and high morality (*Annie Besant: Builder of New India*, pp. 19–22 and *Speeches and Writings of Annie Besant*, p. 128).

8. The limitations of the new cultural studies using Said's framework have been succinctly but effectively dealt with by Tanika Sarkar recently ('Rhetoric Against Age of Consent: Resisting Colonial Reason and Death of a Child Wife', *Economic and Political Weekly*, Vol. 27, No. 36, 1993, pp. 1869–1878).

9. It is also unfortunate that studies that carefully outlined the institutional and legal changes affecting women and were published in the seventies and eighties, such as Lucy Caroll's paper on 'Law, Custom and Statutory Social Reform: The Hindu Widows Remarriage Act of 1856' (in J. Krishanamurty (ed.), *Women in Colonial India: Essays on Survival, Work, and the State*, Delhi, Oxford University Press, 1989, pp. 1–26), have not been followed up with similar studies in other areas. The most crucial lacuna is in studies which explore what was happening to gender within a larger set of relations during the nineteenth century. A beginning has now been made by some feminist historians (see for example Kumkum Sangari, 'Relating Histories: Definitions of Literacy, Literature, Gender in Nineteenth Century Calcutta and England', in Svati Joshi (ed.), *Rethinking English: Essays in Literature, Language, History*, Delhi, Trianka Publishers, 1991, pp. 32–123; and Prem Chowdhry, 'Customs in a Peasant Economy: Women in Colonial Haryana', in Kumkum Sangari and Sudesh Vaid (eds.), *Recasting Women, Essays in Indian Colonial History*, Delhi, Kali For Women, 1989, pp. 302–336).

PART ONE

Ramabai's critique of a patriarchal system as the locus of women's oppression, embodied in the title of her book *The High Caste Hindu Woman*, highlighted Brahmanical patriarchy as it prevailed in all parts of India but more specifically in Maharashtra. To understand the structure that Ramabai attempted to analyse, break with, and contest through her work, it is necessary to outline those factors, material and ideological, which provided the basis for a specific set of cultural practices. In Chapter One I shall explore the relationship between caste, gender and the state, and the manner in which gender codes, a crucial component of cultural practices prevalent in the eighteenth century, were upheld, reinforced and reproduced in a patriarchal and hierarchical society backed by the coercive power of the Peshwa state. In Chapter Two I shall examine the extent to which the relationship between caste, gender and the state was transformed by the establishment of colonial rule and the impact of this transformation on cultural practices in the nineteenth century. Further, the manner in which the processes of caste contestation, class formation and the emergence of nationalism shaped issues of gender will form a central aspect of the analysis in Chapter Two.

1

Caste, Gender and the State in Eighteenth Century Maharashtra

I

Peshwa rule in eighteenth century western India is unique in recorded and documentable history for its combination of secular and ritual power in the hands of the Brahmanas. Although Brahmanas have been among the dominant groups of society all over traditional India, in Maharashtra they held a position of unrivalled prestige under the Peshwas.[1] Their importance in the eighteenth century was noticeable even in the time of Shivaji. Although a Maratha himself Shivaji, like earlier Indian kings, staffed his administration with Brahmanas, who came to be prominent in the Maratha judicial system and in the collection of land revenue, crucial functions of any state. In 1713 Shivaji's grandson appointed a Chitpavan Brahmana as Peshwa. Thereafter the Peshwas accumulated such prestige and power that the office became hereditary in their family and they became the de facto rulers of Maharashtra. The Peshwas ruled from Poona while the nominal Maratha dynasty sank into insignificance at Satara.

Shivaji had used Brahmanas but had ensured that the balance of caste forces was so maintained that power was not concentrated in any one caste or sub-caste.[2] His political system was also an attempt to bridge the gulf between Maratha-Kunbis and the Brahmanas, and knit the conflicting elements into an integrated society while at the same time establishing centralised control over the Deshmukhs, non-Brahmana landed chiefs with extensive powers left intact under Muslim rule.[3] As his control expanded he installed Deshastha Brahmanas (who would be joined to him by ties of interest and sentiment and would, therefore, remain loyal to him) in his administration as a counterpoint to the traditional Deshmukhs. When the Peshwas began to wield authority they in turn realised the value of a loyal constituency and appointed the Chitpavans in important positions.[4] The initial employment of the Chitpavans in the Peshwai was not so much as clerks but as messengers and spies. In course of time Chitpavan power was consolidated; crucial factors in this process were that, in addition to the possession of literacy and a measure of prestige that they shared with all Brahmanas, the Chitpavans demonstrated great industry and assiduousness and a perfecting of strategic generalship.[5] Their militarisation was recalled with pride by one of the prominent nineteenth century Chitpavan Brahmanas, Vishnu Shastri Chiplunkar:

Those people who traditionally were priests and are now clerks threw away in that century (the eighteenth) their priestly functions and pens and became Kshatriyas. Some became kings, some became soldiers. This was an unprecedented and remarkable change in which people of Parshurama's land demonstrated their bravery all over the country.[6]

With this militarisation in the eighteenth century the Brahmanas came to combine secular power with sacerdotal status and attained a unique authority (as symbolised by the term Maratha-Brahmana) scarcely rivalled in other parts of India. The terms Poona, Deccan, and Maratha-Brahmana came to be regarded as synonyms of the Chitpavan Brahmanas and also of those other Brahmanas who had followed the Chitpavan example of combining political activity with the traditional pursuits of the Brahmanas.

Success in military and political activities was interlinked with economic prosperity and various kinds of privileges for the Chitpavans. Their clerks and writers (who had a virtual monopoly of all the secretariat or *daftar* offices) were able to have their goods exempted from customs duties and ferry charges when they imported grain and other goods from places outside the territories of the Peshwas.[7] By far the most important economic advantage was the establishment of control over land.[8] The Brahmanas adopted various strategies for this. For example, in the seventeenth century, the Deshastha Brahmana family of Moroba Gosavi founded a lineage at Cincvad in the vicinity of Poona where the establishment of a site sacred to Ganesh also meant extending land control over several villages surrounding Poona, particularly after Ganesh became the patron god of the Peshwas.[9]

Brahmana power in general and Chitpavan power in particular has been summed up thus for Maharashtra:

Of the significant concentrations of power in society, namely the institutions of religion, the administration, and the ownership of land, the Chitpavans virtually controlled all three. Their status in the scale of caste assured their supremacy over the institutions of religion; their ties with the Peshwas secured for them a monopoly over the administration; and finally the ties of caste once again encouraged the Peshwas to create a landed aristocracy which was recruited from Brahmana families and on whose loyalty they could rely in all circumstances. This is not to altogether deny the existence in Maharashtra of landlords, or administrators, or soldiers who were non-Brahmanas. This is merely to assert that the privileges enjoyed by the Chitpavans through their special ties with the Peshwas enabled them to dominate the rest of the community.[10]

The principal *watandars* had also been invariably drawn from the two dominant communities, high-caste Marathas and Brahmanas. But because it was the Brahmana watandars who rose to such high positions under the Peshwas, it is not surprising that the Peshwai was called *Brahmanya raj*.[11] The Brahmanas, particularly the Chitpavans, thus became a constituent element in what Gokhale has termed the military-bureaucratic elite. A section of the Chitpavans have been characterised as the 'aristocratic' power-brokers in eighteenth century Poona since they had elevated themselves, through dynasty formation, to the status of an aristocracy. Apart from them there were also the 'money-movers', prominent banking families who constituted an important segment of the elites, many of whom had earlier been holders of the lucrative offices of Khot, Mahajan and Kamavisdar through which they accumulated capital. With this they began money-lending. The Peshwa's family married into both the military-bureaucratic elite and the financial elite, cementing their common Chitpavan background and their mutual dependence. There was thus a close nexus between banking, administration and military power and the rural-urban continuities in eighteenth century Maharashtra.[12]

The most notable feature of these developments had been the successful entry of Brahmanas into military and financial roles, both regarded as alien to their varna.[13] Even those Brahmanas who were not part of the military, financial or landed elite were privileged by virtue of their caste. The control of political and social power by the Chitpavans was best expressed through the institution of the *dakshina* which represented an informal alliance between the Chitpavans and the state.[14] The dakshina, literally a gift, was the means through which the Peshwas extended support to the Brahmanas in their role as 'custodians' of Hinduism. It involved the distribution of enormous sums of money as charity to thousands of 'scholarly' Brahmanas after they had been examined by a body of *shastris* who ascertained their knowledge of the sacred texts of Hinduism. In return for the recognition that the grant of dakshina accorded, the Brahmanas gave unstinting support to the state.[15] The support is also attributable to the general policy of Brahmana *pratipalana* (protection of the Brahmanas) pursued by the Peshwas. Throughout the second half of the eighteenth century all categories of Brahmana men enjoyed land revenue remissions, exemption from transit dues, house taxes, forced labour, death penalty and enslavement.[16]

While all Brahmanas shared certain privileges in the form of exemptions, the grant of lands, or large gifts of dakshina, they were subject to competing pulls from within the sub-castes among themselves. In this the Chitpavans had a natural advantage as kinsmen of the Peshwas but it is significant that the Peshwas could not openly treat kinship as the rationale for favouring some Brahmanas over others. Religious grants, dana, were supposedly strictly the prerogative of those Brahmanas who were qualified as *satkarmi* (technically performers of good deeds, more generally bearer of high status), as the *inampatra* (grant deed) often stated that the recipient Brahmana was a *satakarmadhikari* and thus qualified for dana. Under the Peshwai, with the Chitpavan Brahmana dominance, political considerations began to affect questions of caste purity. This impinged on the fortunes of sub-castes like the Saraswat Brahmanas. Controversy regarding their status erupted in the reign of Madhavrao I who held that they were not *trikarmi* (high status) Brahmanas and therefore of a lower order than other Brahmana sub-castes.[17] Thereafter he resumed most of the religious lands of the Shenvis around Poona (on the ground that they had had no right to receive them in the first place), and redistributed them among the Chitpavan Brahmanas.[18] The Peshwas thus played off one set of Brahmanas against another, projecting themselves as upholders of the *dharma* while reinforcing the position of, and their alliance with, their own subcaste of the Chitpavans.

In view of the high stakes that internal stratification and ranking among the various sub-castes entailed, it is not surprising that there were a number of disputes between the sub-castes among the Brahmanas, and between the Brahmana sub-castes and other high-status groups. Wagle points out that there is recorded evidence to show that the Chitpavans had disputes with the Chandraseniya Kayastha Prabhus, the Saraswats, the Pathare Prabhus, and the Shukla Yajurvedis.[19] The fact that the Chitpavans were one of the parties in all of these disputes indicates their high stakes in such contests. Clearly, purity of caste was continuously being contested and reiterated for ideological and material reasons throughout the eighteenth century.[20]

The Peshwas' usurpation of political power and the consequent Brahmanisation of the state had consequences for other social categories too. The 'alliance' between the Marathas and Brahmanas, forged in the time of Shivaji, had virtually collapsed. Shivaji's political system was less concentrated in one caste as it had been built on attempting to bridge the gap between the 'elites' and the ordinary folk, i.e., between the Brahmanas as administrators and the lowly Marathas as soldiers. The Peshwai, with its marginalisation of the Marathas, particularly of Shivaji's lineage at Satara, was a source of conflict which was postponed to the future since the balance of social forces was in favour of the Brahmanas at that point of time. Following the Peshwai's conscious process of Brahmanisation, an imperative which may be attributed to the need for self-legitimation, it appeared to nineteenth century observers that there were only two grand classes in Maharashtra: the first consisting entirely of Brahmanas and the second composed of all the inferior castes.[21] The caste structure of Maharashtra was however more complex than this: it had the Brahmanas with their various sub-castes and the Prabhus at the top; followed by the numerically largest Maratha caste, including the elite comprising 96 families who claimed Kshatriya descent such as Shivaji's lineage and the rest known as Kunbis who were 'peasants'; several artisan castes who were castes of roughly similar status as the Kunbis; and the untouchables such as the Mangs, Mahars and Dhors.[22] Maharashtra did not have its own trading caste since, on the whole, trading activity was limited. It has been argued that in the absence of an indigenous trading caste the polarisation between the Brahmanas and the non-Brahmanas has been especially sharp as it has not been mediated by another social stratum.[23] As in the case of neighbouring Gujarat, as well as in other parts of India, in Maharashtra too the residential pattern both in the towns and the countryside reflected the caste system, with the caste Hindus residing within the main village and the untouchables occupying areas outside the town or village.

II

In analysing the nature of the caste system as it operated on the ground in eighteenth century Maharashtra it might be useful to look at the attempts to establish and consolidate Brahmanic ideology and power in the region during the centuries preceding it. Brahmanism, as the dominant ideology, does not appear to have had a continuous or uncontested presence in the Deccan although there is evidence of Brahmana penetration as far back as the rule of the Satavahanas (circa first century B.C. to third century A.D.). Adopting a conscious Brahmanic position, a Satavahana king proclaimed that he had stopped the 'contamination' of the four varnas. He furthered the interest of the twice-born and patronised Sanskrit, referring to the Prakrit spoken in the area as 'gibberish' and associated with a backward people.[24] But at the same time the strength of both Buddhism and Jainism is attested to by archaeological and inscriptional evidence from the region.[25]

From the twelfth century onwards the attempts of Brahmanic ideology to establish hegemonic control are more clearly discernible. According to Kosambi, Brahmanism was the dominant ideology in the twelfth century. Hemadri, the Chancellor of the last Yadava ruler of Devagiri, who wrote the *Chaturvarga Chintamani*, was concerned in this work almost entirely with Brahmanical rites and rituals codified from earlier religious texts. But Lakshmidhara's treatise *Krityakalpataru*, written roughly at the same time, indicates certain tensions in the attempt to impose Brahmanic ideology upon a pre-existing complex of cultures. The section on jurisprudence particularly captures some of the contradictions inherent in conflicting practices wherein attempts were made to impose Brahmanical textual norms upon local custom. While it shows that common law was practised and decisions for each caste and locality were based upon particular custom, the work itself repeats Smriti doctrine without mention of the innovations in practice.[26]

The history of Brahmanism in the region was accompanied also by a simultaneous critique of it, thereby contesting its undisputed hold upon the people. This is evident in the strength and vitality of the Bhakti tradition in Maharashtra, as is recognised by historians even though a number of other questions about the Bhakti tradition are among the most controversial and hotly contested issues in the historiography of Maharashtra.[27] From the point of view of this study I shall summarise and highlight the questions as they relate to caste, Brahmanism and gender.

According to Kosambi, the reaction to increasing Brahmanisation was expressed in Maharashtra by two different groups, both oriented towards Krishna worship. The earliest was the Mahanubhav or Manbhav sect. It was founded by Chakradhara in the twelfth century and went back to the ideals of primitive tribal communal life. It was the Mahanubhavs who produced the earliest Marathi literature.[28] The use of black garments, absolute rejection of the caste system and a greatly simplified marriage ritual were some features of the sect.[29] However, the Mahanubhavs drew a sharp distinction between the householder and wandering renouncer. Their antagonism to Brahmanic ritualism and to the caste system made the sect popular with the 'untouchables'[30] (hereafter Dalit in consonance with the term used by the oppressed castes to describe themselves). The other movement, the Varkari, was built around the seasonal pilgrimage to Pandharpur, a custom which Kosambi dates back to the Mesolithic age.[31] The Varkari movement has also been described as something of a Brahmanical response to the challenge of the Mahanubhavs and was an attempt to incorporate a modified devotionalism within the bounds of caste.[32]

The Varkari tradition is attributed to a mystic named Pundalik who transformed the ritualistic worship of god Vithoba at Pandharpur into an 'interiorised adoration prescinding caste differences and institutional priesthood'.[33] It was crystallised by Jnanadev, a Brahmana who was regarded as an outcaste because he was the son of an apostate monk. The Varkari *sants* were drawn from a wide social base; Namdev was a Shimpi (tailor), Gora a potter, Chokhamela a Mahar and Tukaram a Kunbi,[34] and they all wrote in Marathi.[35] It is not easy to discern the complex position of the sants in relation to caste and the Brahmanism of their times.

Kosambi regards Jnanadev as a contradictory figure striving after the Vedic lore denied to all but the initiates, extolling the Brahmanas as veritable gods on earth while pointing out that the Kshatriya, Vaisya, Shudra and 'untouchable' retained their separate identity only as long as they had not attained god.[36] The tradition of god Vithoba as the god of the humble goes along with the persecution of the sants by Brahmanas in legends about them.[37]

The generally painful tenor of the lives of the sants reflected in accounts about them is viewed by Kosambi as evidence that they were regarded as the opposition by the Brahmanas.[38] One of the earliest of the Varkari sants was Chokhamela, born in the second half of the thirteenth century. The legends about his birth and death involve traditional Mahar village duties. Chokhamela was killed while repairing, along with other Mahars, a wall which collapsed upon them. Since his bones chanted Vitthala even after his death,[39] they were buried near the steps of the temple at Pandharpur. Other legends recall how god Vitthala helped Chokhamela perform even the lowliest duties of the Mahars. What is significant is that there is no evidence to suggest that Chokhamela ever protested against the traditional duties of the Mahar. Nevertheless some of the *abhangas* attributed to him do refer to untouchability and his anguish at his despised place in society (he was barred from entering temples despite his devotion). In one of the abhangas he cries out, 'If you had to give me this birth, why give me birth at all?' Yet another rationalises his low birth as 'this impurity is the fruit of our past'.[40] Devotionalism seems to have enabled Chokhamela to protest and question as well as accept the traditional role of a Mahar, seek succour in Bhakti and perform his obligations, finally looking forward to delivery from suffering through devotion.

In contrast to Chokhamela's location was that of Eknath, who was born in a Brahmana family of considerable fame from Paithan, a trading centre of some importance in the sixteenth century during the time of the Ahmadnagar Sultanate. Eknath's work reflects the influences of his location, living in a closed Brahmanical world and yet being in contact with the many different men around him.[41] His hagiography positions him as one who was most conscious of the presence of 'untouchables' in society and of their spiritual capabilities. Using the Bharud style, he contributed numerous drama poems meant to be enacted, many of which are written as if they are the statements of the Mahars. One of the most popular Bharuds is a conversation between a Mahar and a Brahmana in which the Mahar teaches an arrogant Brahmana the true nature of devotion, a formula reminiscent of the Buddhist Jataka tradition.[42] But again as in Chokhamela's case the aspects of conforming to caste duties, obligations in the world of everyday existence and work,[43] and of caste distinctions being attributable to *karma* are evident in Eknath's abhangas. What marked him off was his compassion and the belief that God was present in all humanity.

It was Tukaram's abhangas which ultimately came to be the most popular in Maharashtra, and the Bhakti tradition reached its zenith in the first half of the seventeenth century. Reflecting his harassment by family obligations and by the orthodox Brahmanas, his abhangas, too, carry an anti-caste theme but affirm a life in the world rather than renunciation because it gave the devotee repeated opportunity to worship God. Tukaram survived famine, and the contempt of his fellow-beings, especially Brahmanas, ultimately to drown himself in a river.[44]

There is also a rich tradition of women sants going back to the Mahanubhavs. Their poems are part of the Marathi Bhakti corpus; among them were Muktabai, the sister of Jnanadev, Bahinabai, who combined devotion with domestic responsibilities, and Janabai, a lowly *dasi*, who performed a series of never-ending tasks allotted to a menial in the house of Dama Shetty, the father of another sant, Namdev. The hardship of being a dasi and a woman are themes in her compositions. In the execution of heavy domestic labour, Vithoba was her constant companion, helping her to complete the tasks which were otherwise too burdensome.[45] As in the case of men sants coming to terms with caste, the women sants both found space and had to negotiate their roles as women within marriage (as Bahinabai records in her autobiographical account) and with their social obligations, as with Janabai.

Locating the influence of the Varkari cult in moderating the impact of caste and countering Brahmanism has been one of the major concerns of nationalist historiography, as discussed above, but it is also a deeply controversial issue. In one strand of evaluation by historians, Bhakti has been seen as bridging the divide between 'elites and plebeians', and of contributing to a unique pluralist Maharashtra dharma.[46] However, following the more radical critique of Ambedkar and the post-Independence Dalit intelligentsia the evaluation of Bhakti's democratising impact has been more guarded.[47] This view has pointed to the existence of conflicting trends within the Varkari cult containing compromise with caste as well as egalitarian impulses as outlined above. The response of the Brahmanas to the movement also contained elements of compromise. As early as the thirteenth century the Brahmana minister of Yadava rulers, Hemadri, visited Pandharpur and the Varkari cult may have received some official patronage through the visit.[48] In Pandharpur itself temple ritual remained in the control of Brahmanas whose antagonism to the 'untouchables' often appears in Chokhamela's abhangas. And finally with Ramdas, the seventeenth century Brahmana 'sant' who had no connection with the Varkari cult, the tentative Brahmana compromise was followed by more aggressive Brahmana reformulations of the sant tradition. His approach was a counter to the renunciation of political concerns by the sants and their interiorised form of devotion. Ramdas urged a strong political regeneration of religion.[49]

Perhaps the multiple strands of Bhakti, the conflicting pressures that were part of the movement through its earlier vital phase, and the resurgence of Brahmanism as the dominant ideology during the eighteenth century, shaped the way it survived in the Varkari cult's annual pilgrimage to Pandharpur from Alandi. After participating in the fifteen-day journey in the 1960s Irawati Karve wrote that the Brahmana group that she was part of sang the abhangas of Chokhamela in which Chokhamela drew attention to the inner essence of the devotee rather than his outward lowly form, along with others. They, however, cooked and ate their food separately.[50] The distinction of caste society thus remained unchanged and so the practices of caste faced no major onslaught or transformation. The caste system as a form of organising labour and surplus appropriation, which was well established by the time the Varkari cult originated, was unaffected by the cult. Since both hierarchy and obligation imposed upon the lower castes remained intact, Bhakti ideology was not fundamentally subversive of the established order and may even be regarded as representing the interests of the dominant elements in that order.[51] Zelliot's summing up of the complex strands is that while Bhakti has remained a rich reservoir of living ideas, even when it has lost its vitality, providing an ideology to be dipped into by those seeking an alternative to

Brahmanic ritual and the caste system, it has more appeal for Brahmana reformers than for Dalit radicals.[52] It is not an uncritical legacy for those who wish to transform the material location of the Dalits, and those at the receiving end of the caste system.[53]

From the point of view of this study, even if one accepts the view that at least in its heyday Bhakti helped to bridge the gap between the upper castes and the lower castes through a common devotional tradition, it must be recognised that there were other developments in religious practices with the consolidation of the Peshwai. Under them the Pandit Kavis in the Peshwa court, whose best representative was Moropant, articulated a new religious ethos incorporating Brahmanised folk cults rather than any form of worship; rituals now became prevalent manifestations of religiosity at least among the upper segments of society. Poona and the Peshwa regions witnessed a great proliferation of the Ganesh cult. The Peshwai's political and cultural needs resulted in a frenetic phase of temple-building, making for an increased patronage of Brahmanas, and therefore of increased Brahmanical control over society.[54]

III

In eighteenth century Maharashtra the Peshwai sought to recreate, at least ideologically, the Brahmanical Hindu kingdom which tried to strictly uphold the Brahmanical social order.[55] In this situation privileging Brahmanas and suppressing other castes went together.[56] In Poona, the seat of the Peshwai, for example, Mahars were not allowed within its gates after 3 p.m. as their long shadows would defile people of higher castes. They were also required to carry an earthen pot tied around their necks to contain their spittle lest it defile an unwary caste Hindu, and also to sweep off their defiling footprints. Another manuscript indicates that a Sonar who performed religious rites according to Vedic mantras had his tongue cut off for 'defiling' the sacred verses.[57]

In consolidating the sacred Brahmanical traditions the Peshwai was seeking to tighten the functioning of the caste system which may have been more flexible during the centuries preceding it when state power had been in the hands of a range of social groups and Brahmanism itself was being contested. Now that state power was in the hands of Brahmanas, 'leakages' in the functioning of the caste system were plugged and shifts in the local status arrangements were not tolerated. In this connection Fukazawa's argument that there was a close connection between the caste system and the state's enforcement of it, is relevant. In his study of eighteenth century Maharashtra, Fukazawa argues forcefully that far from the caste system being an institution which continued without any relation to the secular political powers, state power was a crucial factor in its development and diversification. He shows that the caste system in Maharashtra was not a 'spontaneous' social order of the people but very much a state order of society, controlled and protected by the state. In his view the Peshwai and its central bureaucracy sought to preserve the caste hierarchy in the areas under its control through the legal apparatus of the state.[58]

An analysis of materials available in the Peshwa daftar indicates that apart from suppressing the lower castes, the state played a decisive part in upholding the caste system in two ways. It removed and restored the caste status of individuals who had deviated from the traditional religio-social code of conduct. Further, the state often confirmed internal splits within a caste and enforced certain codes of conduct to be observed by, as well as between, separate castes.[59]

The Peshwai self-consciously functioned as a 'dharmarajya'; it privileged Shastric law over customary law, as in the case of the Yajurvedi Brahmanas of the Bassein region, who like many other pensinsular Brahmanas practised cross-cousin marriage. The practice, regarded as an aberration attributed to the laxity in the application of dharma during Portuguese rule, was banned. Those who had begun to practise it were treated as a separate caste and were fined for their improper behaviour.[60] The Peshwa government's concern as upholder of the dharma extended not only to the behaviour of the upper castes but also to the lower castes. For example, disputes about the pedigree of a weaving community were decided upon, and weavers of good pedigree were separated from those descended from female slaves; intermarriage between the two groups was banned and weavers of good pedigree had a certificate issued to them by the Peshwai. A tribute of Rs 5,000 was then levied upon them. The government thus confirmed and systematised division as the dharma pratipalana (protector of the dharma), but at the same time used every possible occasion to raise money by levying fines and tributes.[61]

The Peshwai's agenda in relation to the Brahmana caste was

twofold. The government suggested and formulated codes of behaviour for Brahmanas based on its understanding of the Shastric law. It is significant that the Peshwa state was far stricter in its upholding of caste norms for the Brahmanas than for any other community to which the transgressor might have belonged. (Fukazawa cites the example of a Brahmana who converted to Islam while he was away from his native village. After some years he returned to his village and was readmitted to his original status by his caste-fellows. However, the Peshwa government, the final authority for sanctioning readmission to a caste, overrode the decision of his caste-fellows).[62] At the same time as upholding an extremely strict code for Brahmanas, the Peshwas also ensured through various actions that the Brahmanas retained the highest status in society by expressly forbidding lower castes from imitating usages and customs only practised by the former, including wearing the sacred thread and performing certain rituals.[63] The Peshwa's unambigious upholding of Brahmana superiority over other sections of the elite is very interesting. On the complaint of the Brahmanas of Sasken district in 1790 that the Prabhus, a Kayastha caste (next only to the Brahmanas in importance because of their literacy skills), were within their houses secretly engaging in practices that were privileges only the Brahmanas enjoyed, the Peshwai commanded the Prabhus to behave like Shudras. They sent almost 200 letters to bureaucrats and representative Brahmanas all over the kingdom instructing them to ensure that the Prabhus observed the code laid down for them. The code stipulated that the Prabhus should not recite the Vedic mantras, and that they should visit only temples confined to Shudras. Even the greeting *namaskar* used by Brahmanas was denied to them. Instead, they were to use the term *dandvat* among themselves, as was customary among the Shudras. (The untouchables were expected to use a third term, *johar!*) The Prabhus were not permitted to use Brahmanas as their servants, and finally they were commanded not to oppose the remarriage of widows[64] — that supposed 'privilege' being the prerogative of the Brahmanas.

The Peshwai's privileging of Brahmanical traditions in relation to hierarchy as laid down in the most conservative Shastric texts is best exemplified in its attitude to the Bhakti traditions in Maharashtra. Pandharpur, the great centre of Bhakti worship, was brought under the totalising power of the Peshwai which ordered seven rules of worship to be executed by the officers of the state. The image in the main shrine was of Vithoba, a central figure in the Bhakti cult. As part of the attempt to democratise worship in the Bhakti movement Vithoba became accessible to the lower castes during the period of its influence. Among his worshippers was the 'untouchable' Chokhamela, and there came to be installed, north of the main shrine, a stone image of the saint which the 'untouchables' frequented for their worship. By the eighteenth century, emboldened possibly by the pro-Brahmana Peshwai, the Brahmanas complained that the place was so narrow and crowded that the visitors touched each other, thus 'polluting' the Brahmanas. The state then ordered the 'untouchables' to perform their worship of Chokhamela from a distance, or from the nearby Maharvada. They were prohibited from approaching the temple of Vithoba and were threatened with punishment if they failed to conform.[65]

Thus we see that state power was crucial in closing off the spaces sought by the lower castes in democratising access to worship even within Bhakti. Under the Peshwai the untouchable Mahars were required to demolish their huts if they were located too close to the village, as a record shows.[66] Another record shows that despite upper-caste suppression, not all untouchables were reconciled to their fate. The Mahars in the Konkan area demanded that Brahmana priests officiate at their marriages. This demand was supported by the local bureaucrat, who in his enthusiasm even attached the office of the Brahmana priests who did not do so. The Brahmana priests then appealed to the Poona government. On the advice of specialists, themselves Brahmanas, the Peshwai decided against such a practice. The government reprimanded the local bureaucrat, and threatened to deal with the 'untouchables' suitably if they continued to 'trouble' the Brahmana priests.[67] Thus the Peshwai acted effectively on behalf of the Brahmanas and against the lower orders. Sanctions were imposed on those who transgressed these injunctions. The state also ensured that the 'untouchables' would continue to occupy the lowest rungs of the social and religious ladder. What is significant is that there was a demand even among the 'untouchables' for better treatment and that it was ultimately state power that suppressed such demands and kept them in the lowest position in society.

Thus, the internal functioning of the caste rules and the maintenance of the established hierarchies were of crucial significance to the government. While a situation of contestation between the Brahmana sub-castes was manipulated according to political expediency by the Peshwas themselves, the state, the ultimate arbiter of status within the caste system, was unwilling to tolerate such contestation between the lower castes and the Brahmanas. No explicit situation of contestation appears to have been possible for the individual, especially of the upper castes in relation to the caste group to which the person belonged, because it was the Peshwai that defined what Brahmanical law was, even in such situations. It is within this background of Peshwai Brahmanism that we can locate gender and explore the workings of Brahmanical patriarchy in eighteenth century Maharashtra.

IV

The Peshwai, with its notions of Brahmanya and the rigid hierarchies of the caste system, could not but have a direct and crucial bearing on gender relations in eighteenth century Maharashtra. Apart from other things, the Brahmanya implied a certain strictly regulated code of conduct for women, differing to some extent according to caste, but always the index in fixing ranking within the caste hierarchy. Administrators and observers in the nineteenth century have noted the linkage between castes seeking and being regarded as of higher rank by adopting new ceremonial practices, the most important of which was a prohibition in the remarriage of widows.[68] Other castes lost their ranking by admitting the remarriage of widows. As noted earlier, the Prabhus whom the Peshwa regarded as unfit for the higher status they were seeking, were also prohibited from enforcing a ban on the remarriage of widows because this would establish their case for high status equivalent to that of the Brahmanas. In Brahmanical patriarchy the relationship between caste and gender is crucial: ultimately the degree to which the sexuality of women is controlled is the degree to which a caste group is regarded as maintaining the purity of blood and can thereby establish its claims to be regarded as high.[69] This is the key to understanding gender in eighteenth century Maharashtra under the Peshwas.

The sexuality of all women was closely monitored under the Peshwai although according to different norms for each caste. The Brahmanya implied that questions about women e.g., about legitimate wifehood, remarriage, ascetic widowhood without remarriage, tonsure, excommunication for lapses, and when and how women must marry, were all regulated by the community headed by the Brahmanas and then ultimately of the state's concern. Most significantly, the sexual 'offences' of women, especially widows, were punishable with imprisonment and, uniquely, with enslavement. Women lived under the continuous and combined surveillance of the community and the state. As Fukazawa pointed out in respect of caste, we might say that ultimately gender codes were not spontaneous, not merely an arrangement of society — they were extended, consolidated and reinforced by state power under the Peshwas.

Marriage and codes of legitimate sexuality of men and women, but particularly women, were major elements in the organisation of gender relations, especially of the upper castes. Elaborate rules were devised in this connection relating to prohibited and desirable factors in settling marriage alliances.[70] Proper rituals had to be completed for the marriage to be regarded as legal in the case of the high castes. Practice among the high castes of the *asura* form of marriage where bride price was taken or wives abducted was frowned upon by the Peshwai.[71] Instead, gradually the practice of dowry was gaining ground.[72] In general the Peshwai favoured textual law over customary law in the matter of the marriage of Brahmanas and forbade cross-cousin marriage as we saw above, as part of the privileging of Shastric law.

Marriage alliances, a crucial means of consolidating the exchange of women by men, were central to the functioning of patriarchy, caste and class. The best documented cases for the eighteenth century are those of the Peshwa's family where marriages were a means of establishing political and financial linkages.[73] Polygamy was an institutional way for the ruling elite to expand such political alliances. However, it is not our contention that all marriages were necessarily arranged according to political or financial considerations. Nevertheless, we can conclude that marriage alliances were part of a web of social relations for most people with varying degrees of compulsions and benefits operating within the larger context of achieving legitimate reproduction.

The most significant element in ensuring legitimate reproduction was the requirement of pre-pubertal marriages for women. As early as the second century A.D. Manu had considered eight the ideal age for the marriage of girls.[74] The need for such an age was that girls would already be the sexual property of their husbands at the time of puberty. All sexual activity would then be exclusively concentrated upon the husband and there would be less possibility of women going 'astray'. Immediately after puberty (referred to locally as *shanee*,[75] literally inauspicious, probably regarded so because women become 'dangerous' and need to be safeguarded thereafter)[76] the *garbhadhanam* ceremony would be performed,[77] thus harnessing female sexuality for the sole purpose of ensuring legitimate reproduction. The upper castes followed the practice of early marriage (in the case of the Peshwa family between the ages of five and eight) scrupulously. For most Brahmana families the age varied from five to ten. The *Yadi Dharmasthapana* of the year 1735 issued by the government to regulate the lives of Brahmanas laid down that all Brahmana women should be married between the ages of seven and ten.[78]

Severe strictures were faced by fathers who failed to perform their duty of organising the marriage of their daughters at the proper age. In case a girl began to menstruate before she was married her marriage could only be performed (if anyone was willing to marry her) after the prescribed ceremony of a penance[79] called *nirnaya sindhu*. Such was the force of the obligation that fathers must marry their daughters off before puberty that the government released a whole family of 16 prisoners since the marriages of two girls, aged 10 and 11, were pending! The government even provided clothes and ornaments worth one thousand rupees to cover the expenses of the marriages.[80] Further, the anxiety about daughters' marriages (with a nine-year-old girl regarded as far advanced in age) was a matter that has been referred to in the surviving correspondence of the period. It was treated as a venture to be given the highest priority for completion in cases where fathers had died leaving behind unmarried daughters. The Peshwai in turn did not forget its obligations to the Brahmana dharma with regard to monitoring customs relating to female sexuality even while racked by internal dissensions. At the end of the eighteenth century the government under Nana Phadnis passed 20 orders to the *mamlatdars* and Brahmanas of certain *talukas* stating that the government had come to know that the Brahmanas kept their daughters 'unmarried' after the age of nine. Brahmanas were advised to refrain from such a practice and officials were ordered to keep a close watch on them, and to impose excommunication upon those who violated the government order.[81]

From the available evidence it is clear that the Peshwai regarded the family as a key institution and took a very serious view of adultery as a violation of social norms. All castes were expected to conform to the pattern of confining sexual activity within marriage (and confine marriage within the endogamous circle) as the cases cited below show. Given the high premium on a strictly regulated sexual code for all men and women, surveillance of all categories of women, and restricted movements, amounting to virtual confinement within the private domain of the household in the case of high-caste women, formed the pattern prescribed by the texts and the customs prevalent in eighteenth century society to prevent 'illicit' sexual activity. Institutional structures designed to prevent 'illicit' sexual relations did not however fully succeed and there were a number of publicly recorded instances of adultery.[82] Kadam has pointed out that women were held to be solely responsible for such acts. The severest condemnation was reserved for such occasions with women facing public and private measures of punishment. For example, a Brahmana woman visiting her natal home was seduced and impregnated by the son of a priest. When the husband got to know of the relationship he discarded his wife and demanded that the priest arrange a new marriage for him. Fearing public criticism, the priest did so by giving the husband Rs 800 and the husband then got himself another wife. There is no indication that the priest's son was punished but the woman was soon found dead and it was widely believed that she had been murdered by the priest.[83] Socially sanctioned and enforced punishment including 'private' remedies such as the one cited above may have been possible since the state shared and upheld similar and sometimes more rigid patriarchal concerns. The case of Ahili, a non-Brahmana woman who was charged with having adulterous relations with another villager, is significant. The mamlatdar fined the adulterous man and imprisoned Ahili. However, the husband appealed to the Peshwa that Ahili had not been punished sufficiently. The Peshwa government under Nana Phadnis then ordered that Ahili's nose be cut off in the presence of an official sent by the government.[84] The symbolic castration of Ahili was probably meant to be a deterrent to other potential offenders.

Adulterous women could be imprisoned after conviction as, for example, in a case recorded in 1772-73. A Brahmana woman named Rukmi was charged with having committed adultery with both Brahmanas and Shudras. She also ate with the Shudras. The defaulting woman was imprisoned (probably for a considerable term) put on a food ration of two seers per day, and supplied with two saris per year.[85] The punishment meted out to the Brahmana woman suggests that she had committed a double offence; adultery was offence enough but Rukmi, by including Shudras among her partners, was committing the most reprehensible offence for a Brahmana woman, that of a *pratiloma* (hypogamous) connection.

A significant aspect of the punishment meted out to women accused of adultery was the inclusion of enslavement ordered by the state. In 1788, for example, a woman was convicted for adultery and imprisoned for three months. At the end of this period when she was to be freed it was found that there was no one to vouch for her future 'good' behaviour, i.e., there was no one available to keep her under effective surveillance. Since the authorities were apprehensive that the 'errant' woman would repeat her offence she was sold as a slave (*batik*) for Rs 50.[86] This case is significant because it regards unguarded women as a permanent hazard; handing such a woman over to a master leaves it to the master to dispose of her sexuality and her labour in whatever manner he chooses.

Punishments for adulterous women are more numerous, suggesting that adulterous men got off comparatively lightly, if punished at all. For instance a Brahmana man who committed adultery with a Brahmana woman in 1773 merely had to perform a *prayascitta* consisting of 24 *pradakshinas* (circumambulations) of Brahmagiri and Harshagiri (sacred spots in the vicinity of Poona).[87] The one category of adulterous men who faced punitive action were those who were involved in relations with women of a higher caste, particularly if the woman was a Brahmana. In 1772, a non-Brahmana named Balaram Manikram exhibited illicit love for a Brahmana woman. Balaram's property was confiscated and sold and a fine of Rs 1,000 was recovered from the sale.[88] In contrast to the comparative laxity shown towards men involved in adultery, none of whom appears to have faced imprisonment, a woman could face imprisonment or enslavement even without being adulterous. In 1799 a woman was abandoned by her husband when she made public his impotence. Interestingly, she was then convicted of leading an immoral life and fined. Since she could not pay the fine she was reduced to the status of a *kunbina* and was made to labour for others.[89] Here punishment was not for the actual violation of the strict sexual code for wives but the violation of *strimaryada* (code of conduct for women), something no good wife would do. Under the *pativrata dharma* the impotence of the husband was not regarded as being of any consequence; certainly it was a taboo subject, not to be made public, since it made the sexual needs of the wife explicit, and delinked them from reproduction.[90]

Adultery was regarded as offensive, not merely because of the problem of ensuring legitimate reproduction, but also because it represented 'excessive' sexual energy which gender codes considered deeply reprehensible in the case of women. Punishments, especially imprisonment, were structured by caste considerations but always fell unequally upon men and women. Adulterous women of the middle and upper castes (not just Brahmana women) were regarded as serious offenders in the eighteenth century because, as in the past, caste and class reproduction were jeopardised. Therefore, the Peshwa state acted vigorously against 'errant' women of all castes. It is significant that in the case of women of the lowest castes, their offence of excessive sexuality was punished by making them available to men of the higher castes through state intervention or by forcing such women to render their labour to the government. A recent view on the issue of adultery is that the Peshwai, especially in its last phase, charged lower-caste women with adultery in order to enslave them. A distinction was made between batiks and kunbinas; while kunbinas laboured in *karkhanas* (artisanal units of the state) and the field, batiks were used to provide sexual services and formed the main recruitment field for the *lavani tamashas*. Since the government itself was a major owner of female slaves, turning 'adulteresses' into slaves would provide a ready supply of female slaves in the court, kitchen, stable, granary and *natakshala*. The Peshwa state thus simultaneously upheld normative gender codes for all castes in the matter of adultery but maintained caste distinctions in practice in the way the offence itself was dealt with. Pragmatic use was made of the sexuality and labour of the 'adulterous' low-caste woman.[91] In this context we might also note Fukazawa's analysis of slavery in the Peshwai. He provides evidence of females predominant in the institution of slavery, with only six males among a total of 90 slaves enumerated in the records.[92]

The relationship between labour, caste and gender was germane to the conceptualisation of widowhood. The maximum difference, in practice, between castes in eighteenth century Maharashtra existed in the case of enforced widowhood and the remarriage of widows, with the strictest ban on remarriage reserved for the highest caste: the Brahmanas. Elsewhere I have explored the underlying patterns of enforced widowhood and enforced marriage among the high and the low castes; here the focus is on the enforcement of ascetic widowhood for certain castes, ultimately by the authority of the Peshwai, along with the practice of a secondary form of marriage called *pat* for widows of certain other castes.[93]

As we have noted earlier, the Brahmanya of the Peshwai reserved the most privileged position for the Brahmanas but also expected the strictest observance of caste norms from them. Violations were dealt with by enforcing permanent excommunication from the social community of Brahmanas. Brahmana women, in turn, were closely guarded as wives and expected to observe ascetic widowhood of the most extreme kind after the death of their husbands. The outward symbol of ascetic widowhood, the tonsure of Brahmana widows, was also strictly enforced in Maharashtra. Resistance to the custom was virtually impossible for the widow in the eighteenth century since widows, as propertyless, shelterless women, lived in the custody of kinsmen and within the larger social unit of the caste group into which they were born. But it is significant that even if the immediate kinsmen of a widow made it possible for her to remain untonsured, the ultimate authority of the Brahmanical state in the form of the Peshwai acted to uphold the Brahmanical gender codes enforced by religious authorities. There are instances of widows who remained untonsured for certain periods of time with support from their natal kinsmen, mainly fathers or brothers. However, the Brahmana community invariably secured excommunication orders from a religious head such as the Shankaracharya, as for example in the case of Malharpant of Karhad who was banned from marrying till his untonsured widowed sister was tonsured. When Malharpant defied the ban, he was excommunicated under orders from the Shankaracharya.[94] In another case a brother who had given shelter to his unshaven widowed sister was excommunicated along with his entire family. The Shankaracharya also ordered similar excommunication of a father because his widowed daughter had retained her hair.[95] We may note that there is an indication here of something of a counter-ideology to the oppressive practices for Brahmana widows, especially in the instances of very young girls and young women. The miseries of the experience of widowhood could evoke a sympathetic response from the natal family, both men and women. But since fathers and brothers had custody or guardianship over the widows in their families, only they are visible in references such as the one here. An important example was that of Bhaupant, a great figure in the Peshwa's court. Unable to bear the tragic future of his infant daughter, Bhaupant wished to resign his official position. Since he was very important to the Peshwa's administration the Peshwa sought learned opinion on the remarriage of the young widow. Learned opinion in Poona was not encouraging but the pandits of Banaras were more sympathetic. However, the whole venture was abortive since the Poona Brahmana priests convinced Bhaupant's wife that the marriage would be un-Shastric and heinous, and she refused to go through with the remarriage of her daughter.[96] In the nineteenth century, too, it was often fathers and brothers who are described in recorded sources as anguished by their widowed daughters'/sisters' condition and supporting changes in social practices.

Despite the indications of a counter-ideology it is clear that it was weak. The dominant ideology was committed to the need for tight control over widows. We have evidence that the ultimate authority of the Peshwai was fully invoked to maintain enforced widowhood including tonsure from the *Yadi Dharmasthapana*, literally memorandum of the establishment of the dharma, of 1735; six separate orders related to Brahmana widows. One of them (Order number 15) lays down that the Brahmana child widow, on attaining puberty, is to discard the hair on her head, along with ornaments and the blouse.[97] Thereafter the Brahmana widow was permitted only a single garment (*ekavastra*) in the characteristic colour of dark maroon worn by Brahmana widows in Maharashtra. Order number 37 gives details of when the tonsure of widows is to be performed: the first or the tenth day after the death of the husband.[98]

The tonsure ceremony itself was fairly elaborate as it was accompanied by religious rites such as the *homa*, prayascitta and the all-important dakshina. The relationship between material and ideological elements in enforcing the rite of the *keshwapan* (tonsure)

is evident from an account of expenditure of a widow from a
Vaidya family in the year 1798. The total expenditure of the various
ceremonies was forty-one rupees, the major beneficiaries for the
dakshina in various ways were the Brahmanas themselves since
almost three-fourths of the money spent was given to the
Brahmanas. Apart from this some money was spent on cloth, gold
and silver, which was also shared by the Brahmanas.[99]

The possibility of contesting the Brahmana dharma on the
tonsure of widows appears virtually impossible from the order of
the *Yadi Dharmasthapana* which laid down that only on the
completion of the keshwapan of the widow was the death pollution
in the house of the dead Brahmana terminated; only then was the
purification of the house and the widow completed. Until the
completion of the keshwapan of the dead man's widow, other
Brahmanas were barred from having any relationship with the
entire household, all of whom were regarded as impure.[100] The
widow thus carried the burden and the responsibility for the purity
of the entire household upon her tonsured head. In view of such
strict orders and the surveillance maintained by the community of
Brahmanas, who had much to gain from the reiteration of the belief
structures regarding tonsure (ideologically and materially), all acts
of attempted resistance were swiftly and effectively suppressed by
patriarchal structures working through the Brahmana community,
the religious authorities and the Peshwai.

The Peshwai also felt the need to reiterate in 1735 the social and
ritual distinctions through which the structural opposition between
the wife and the widow was expressed. In one of its orders it
forbade the Brahmana widow to eat along with married women; a
corresponding order banned the married woman from sitting in a
pangat (row of persons taking food) with Brahmana widows.[101] The
distinction between the wife and the widow was to be assiduously,
and at all times, maintained in the Brahmanya.

The opposition between the wife and the widow was
conceptually most apparent in the case of Brahmana and other
high-caste women: the basic opposition was between the sexually
active woman as reproducer, ideally of sons, and the sexually
inactive non-reproducer, the woman whose sexual existence had
ended with the death of the husband. The question that arises is,
why was it that the reproductive potential of a whole class of
women could be regarded as dispensable in the conceptual

framework of Brahmanical patriarchy? A possible explanation can be that the demographic structure of the Brahmana community, traditionally, and even when it was based in agriculture as among the Chitpavan Brahmanas, did not require all women to function as reproducers; the demographic structure of the Brahmana community could, without damage, afford to withdraw some women from reproduction. By and large the Brahmana community needed to reproduce a body of specialists, a literati engaged in ritual and intellectual pursuits. Over the centuries natural demographic expansion had created more specialists than were strictly necessary. Thus the practice of levirate among the relatively undifferentiated Vedic 'Aryans' living in a primarily pastoral society had become reprehensible as caste and class stratification intensified by the time Manu was writing.[102] Thereafter it became concentrated among the Shudra, peasant labouring castes such as Jats who still continue to practise it.[103] What the Brahmana household needed was a son to give the funeral oblations to his father. If the dead man did not have a son the widow was permitted to adopt a son from amongst their kin. The ideological structures of enforced widowhood, wherein the death of a husband could conveniently require the widow to cease sexual activity, were not unrelated to the material conditions obtaining among the highest castes. The ban on widow remarriage was thus transformed into a highly valued feature of high status, the hallmark of certain castes and a 'privilege' not to be shared with inferior castes.[104] Sacred, indissoluble marriage was the sign of a superior culture and the Brahmanas as the highest caste were entitled to the most sacred ritual. The eight forms of marriage described in the Shastras conform to this basic distinction between the need for proper sacred rituals for the Brahmanas and permitting the less acceptable forms of marriage for the lower castes.[105]

Thus we find that while enforcing a ban on widow remarriage among the Brahmanas there was at the same time an inferior form of marriage, locally known as *pat*, prevalent in Maharashtra among the agricultural castes such as the Kunbis.[106] Kunbi women participated directly in production as they worked in the fields. Additionally, they reproduced a class of producers. The demographic compulsions of labouring castes were quite different from those of the high castes such as the Brahmanas. Apart from the small-holding agricultural castes such as the Kunbis, low-caste women too were not debarred from remarrying or cohabiting as they too contributed to increasing the numbers of those who laboured. Both among the agricultural castes and among the landless 'low' castes, since women functioned as direct producers and as reproducers of producers, their continued sexual activity following widowhood was in consonance with the larger labour needs of the economy.

In this structure which was both open and closed at the same time, with different cultural and social norms for different castes (but held together within a larger structure where caste and gender codes were so integrated that caste, as a system of production, also shaped the hierarchy of social practices), the Peshwai introduced certain modifications. Both Gune and Kadam have suggested that the Peshwai expanded state control over the traditional judicial arrangements.[107] We have seen evidence of the state's grip over the working of the caste system and of enforcing 'traditional' occupations upon castes, as also of maintaining distances between them. The appointment of nominated members on the local *panchayats* was one means of asserting effective control over decisions. Another was the system of fines and taxes upon practices such as pat. Apart from expanding the revenue base of the state it reinforced the view that such customary practices were inferior in the eyes of a 'Brahmanical' state. The Peshwai was presenting itself as a unique kind of state, more 'moral' than earlier state forms had been.

The Peshwai thus both 'permitted' remarriage for certain castes and debarred certain upwardly mobile castes from enforcing celibate widowhood upon their women. Those castes in which widows were permitted to remarry were however required to pay a tax upon the occurrence of a pat connection.[108] There were other arrangements relating to rights over children by the earlier marriage and to jewellery etc., given by her earlier husband which had to revert to the kinsfolk of her first marriage,[109] as also any of the husband's property she may have controlled, among certain castes, as his widow.[110]

Often, fathers sought permission from the government for pat connections as there was no one to provide for their widowed daughters. In one case a father argued that there was no one to provide his daughter with food, clothes, and 'company'.[111] The government's position was however linked to the payment of *gunehgari* and *nazar* which meant that the women's remarriages were not in their own hands. Further, it was contingent upon their kinsmen's or the second husband's ability and, willingness to pay the due amounts to the government functioning as a superior authority whose sanction was required to formalise the connection. The practice of pat marriages may thus have come to figure more as a theoretical possibility under the Peshwai rather than as a widespread custom. The significant factor however is that it was permitted for some and denied to others. The marital and sexual arrangements of all women were monitored and reorganised ultimately by the eighteenth century state in Maharashtra.

Given the established relation between gender, caste, labour, the patriarchal community and the state, adultery,[112] especially by the widow, represented the most dangerous subversion of the ideological structures of Brahmanical patriarchy: the whole edifice of Brahmanya was threatened by it. The Peshwai which was committed to the upholding of the Brahmanya acted decisively to suppress such subversion. We need to remember that without the support of the state, the community of Brahmanas, could only have used social coercion by enforcing excommunication (*ghatasphot*) upon the widow.[113] It was the state that used its superior coercive power by imprisoning Brahmana widows charged with *badkarm*. There are examples of widows who were imprisoned in various forts and made to perform penal labour.[114] In one case a Brahmana widow who had been tonsured later allowed her hair to grow and also wore bangles. She lived with a Golak (a 'low' caste) and bore him a son. When the Peshwa, Madhavrao I (often regarded as the most ideal ruler among the Peshwas), came to know of the case he ordered that the widow be sent to the Purandar fort to be imprisoned, along with her eight-year-old 'illegitimate' son. The Peshwa also ordered that both mother and son be employed in the work of mixing mortar every day.[115] Even the last Peshwa, regarded as something of a debauch, a man who married eleven times, the last occasion only a few weeks before his death,[116] had no qualms about doing his duty by upholding the Brahmanya for Brahmana widows. In January 1796, he ordered the imprisonment of a Brahmana widow who had committed adultery.[117]

Summing up the relationship between women, the social community and the state, we may say that adultery remained the most important offence in eighteenth century Maharashtra. It was the non-observance or the defiance of the sexual codes that brought women into the public gaze and led to the most stringent action by the community and the state. It is significant that permanent excommunication, wherein the individual's connection with the family and community is irreversibly broken (as the offending individual is regarded as dead) in the ghatasphot was used most often in the cases of sexual misconduct of Brahmana women. In the case of Brahmana men it seems to have occurred only when a Brahmana man broke his connection with Brahmanya by conversion, as documented in a case of the conversion to Islam cited above. Men lost their Brahmanya by renouncing it, women lost their Brahmanya through sexual lapses; their Brahmanya lay in their chastity, in their pativrata dharma within marriage, and in a chaste and prayerful widowhood.

As we have seen, it was the sexuality of upper-caste women (in the case of Maharashtra, mainly Brahmana women) that was closely monitored and highly valued. It was also these women who were most carefully socialised in their specific *stridharma* — the pativrata dharma. The pativrata dharma schooled women in the ideology of their social group as embodied in the notion of wifely duties in general and of fidelity in particular, accepting the belief system of the community. And since the ideology was powerful and richly elaborate the iniquity inhering in the gender codes was invisibilised. The sources provide at least some evidence in the case of women of the upper strata who came to be complicit in the structures of gender and caste and participated in the crucial venture of social reproduction: they engaged in reproducing the material structures which privileged their social group as well as the values and ideology of the group to which they belonged.

Such an example is provided by Anandibai, the wife of Raghunathrao, a prominent member of the ruling Bhat family from the Chitpavan Brahmana sub-caste who described the rule of the Peshwas as *Brahmani daulat*,[118] meaning the rule for, by and of the Brahmanas, identifying with it even in its male values.[119] On the other hand Radhabai, the mother of Peshwa Bajirao I, both identified with and personally upheld stridharma, enforcing the moral order for women. When a woman from the Chambhar caste of leather-workers, regarded as low, was accused of adultery in 1740, she was permitted by Radhabai to perform an ordeal by fire to prove her innocence. She was honoured with a gift of a sari when she succeeded in going through the ordeal without getting burnt.[120] Radhabai was also deeply concerned about her son Bajirao I's infatuation for Mastani, his Muslim mistress. She exhorted her other son, in a letter written in 1740, to remonstrate with Bajirao I and use his influence to wean him away from the relationship.[121] Radhabai, it must be noted, was the mother of the actual founder of the Peshwai and her upholding of certain moral values would have been significant in shaping the Peshwai notion of Brahmanya.

Ramabai, the wife of Madhavrao I, who is described as immolating herself on the death of her husband in 1772, was another key figure in upholding the stridharma of Brahmana women. The proof of her *satitva* was accompanied by elaborate rituals and the distribution of massive dakshina to Brahmanas and servants: Rs 14,600 is listed as the expenditure incurred on the occasion; jewellery estimated at Rs 60,000 was also given away to various beneficiaries.[122] Brahmanya was upheld, both with regard to women and the larger community of Brahmanas.

But even as women from elite families reflected the successful internalisation of the pativrata dharma and were complicit in the material and ideological structures in which they were idealised and rewarded with great reverence for their satitva, there were great strains upon the gender codes and belief structures around them. The incidence of widowhood, including child widowhood, would be high due to both the mortality patterns and the polygamy popular in the Peshwa's family. Ascetic widowhood, tonsuring and the marginalisation of the widow without sons with its attendant hardships would create a high level of insecurity. Polygamy would also aggravate succession disputes and intrigues, a regular feature of the family politics of the elite.[123] The stridharma or the pativrata dharma could easily break down in such situations and is likely to have required constant refurbishing to sustain the existing codes of gender and caste. In a similar situation in the court of the Maratha rulers of Tanjore in the eighteenth century, we know that texts to socialise women of the royal household were commissioned by senior women in the ruling family.[124] Ideological structures had evidently to be renewed with the complicity of at least some women. Unlike the 'low' castes who desired a different status and whose attempts at higher status were ultimately suppressed by the use of state power, gender structures were such that although the coercive power of the state was required to keep it going (as we have seen with respect to adultery) many women were complicit in the structure that gave men power over them.

In concluding our analysis of eighteenth century Maharashtra in relation to caste, gender and the Peshwai, we may note that the Peshwai ensured that all castes maintained the status order with a pre-eminent position for the Brahmanas. It also reinforced the structures of Brahmanical patriarchy, because to a large extent the pre-eminent status of the Brahmanya itself depended on the undiluted purity of its women. The Brahmanya's superior ritual and moral status entitled it to rule and to consolidate itself economically through dakshina and other economic privileges cited earlier, apart from its hold over administrative positions based on the Brahmanas' reading and writing skills.

However, the Brahmanya's title to its privileged position was not always self-evident; in fact the moral and ritual superiority of the Brahmanas needed to be physically demonstrated and perceived by the other castes as marking the Brahmanas off from themselves. The Brahmanya of the Brahmanas had two major foci: one was the strict observance of the purity and pollution taboos and the other was the purity of its women. It is in this context that the proclamation of the *Yadi Dharmasthapana* assumes importance. Issued in 1735, within twenty years of the Peshwaship becoming hereditary, and almost as soon as the new government had stabilised, it represented the public image of the Peshwai. It was a statement that the Peshwai was serious in its intent to 're-establish' the dharma. Crucial to the dharma were rules and norms about Brahmana women — pre-pubertal marriages, the maintenance of distinctions between married women and widows, and the strict observance of ascetic widowhood, both visibly and actually. Only thus could the superior morality and purity of the Brahmanas be established. In the final reckoning, it was the Brahmana women who carried the major responsibility of upholding Brahmanya and provided legitimacy to their caste, enabling it to maintain its claim to the highest ritual position as well as to social and political power in a state that was represented as a dharmarajya.[125]

NOTES AND REFERENCES

1. Ravinder Kumar, *Western India in the Nineteenth Century*, London,

Routledge and Kegan Paul, 1968, pp. 39ff; Richard Cashman, *The Myth of the Lokamanya*, Berkeley, University of California Press, 1975, pp. 17–18.

2. According to Karve, Shivaji always appointed three chief officers in charge of each hill fort; the three were similar in status but of different caste, usually a Maratha, a Brahmana and a Prabhu (Irawati Karve, *Maharashtra: Land and its People, Maharashtra State Gazetteers*, General Series, Bombay, 1968, p. 136, cited in Meera Kosambi, 'Glory of Peshwa Pune', *Economic and Political Weekly*, Vol. 24, No. 5, 1969, pp. 247–49, p. 249.

3. Kumar, *Western India*, pp. 12–14.

4. In their home district a saturation point had been reached with little scope for an expanding population. Fortunately for the Chitpavans, their opportunities increased dramatically in the arena of political power with the appointment of a Chitpavan Brahmana as Peshwa. A favourable employment situation increased manifold their emigration from Ratnagiri (Maureen L.P. Patterson, 'Changing Patterns of Occupation among Chitpavan Brahmanas', *Indian Economic and Social History Review*, Vol. 7, No. 1, 1970, pp. 378–79).

5. André Wink, *Land and Sovereignty in India: Agrarian Politics in Eighteenth Century Maratha Svarajya*, Cambridge, Cambridge University Press, 1986, p. 69.

6. V.K. Chiplunkar, *Nibandhamala*, cited in Cashman, *The Myth*, p. 8.

7. M.G. Ranade, 'Introduction to the Peshwa's Diaries', in M.G. Ranade, *Rise of Maratha Power and Other Essays*, Bombay, P.C. Manektala, 1961 (reprint), p. 181.

8. The Brahmanas of the Konkan were perceived as having a great passion for land, even if they had to get it by uprooting 'heirs of ancient lineage'. Azad Bilgrami, a Mughal chronicler, writes that they wanted to be the 'proprietors of the whole world' (cited in Irfan Habib, *Agrarian System of Mughal India*, p. 349, re-cited in P.V. Ranade, 'The Feudal Content of Maharashtra Dharma', *Indian Historical Review*, Vol. 1, No. 1, 1974, p. 48).

9. Laurence W. Preston, 'Sub-regional Religious Centres in the History of Maharashtra: The Sites Sacred to Ganesh', in N.K. Wagle (ed.), *Images of Maharashtra: A Regional Profile of India*, London, Curzon Press, 1980, p. 78. Among the most important Brahmana inamdars who had risen from obscurity when the Peshwas ennobled particular individuals in order to consolidate their own position, were the Patwardhans. By the time the Peshwai ended they held the most substantial landed estates in Maharashtra. Apart from others, the Chitpavan families of the Ranades and Kurlekars came to possess

substantial *jagirs* in the Peshwai in return for loyal military service (Kumar, *Western India*, pp. 14 and 39; Patterson, 'Changing Patterns', p. 379).

10. Kumar, *Western India*, p. 44.

11. H. Fukazawa, *The Medieval Deccan: Peasants, Social Systems and States; Sixteenth to Eighteenth Centuries*, Delhi, Oxford University Press, 1991, p. 87, n. 3; P.V. Ranade, 'The Feudal Content', p. 46.

12. B.G. Gokhale, *Poona in the Eighteenth Century: An Urban History*, Delhi, Oxford University Press, 1988, pp. 106–16.

13. Meera Kosambi, 'Glory of Peshwa Pune', p. 248.

14. The institution of the dakshina was not new; it was instituted by a Maratha *sardar* but taken over by Bajirao I (Kosambi, 'Glory of Peshwa Pune', p. 249).

15. Kumar, *Western India*, p. 39.

16. Wink, *Land and Sovereignty*, p. 232.

17. *Ibid.*, pp. 233–34. The controversy erupted on the occasion of the grant of an *agrahara* village, Malkhed, to an assembly of 54 Brahmanas of the four Vedic denominations of Deshastha, Chitpavan, Karhad and Saraswat (Shenvi). A special court, convened at Poona to decide the issue, went in favour of the Saraswats. The Saraswats later became embroiled in factional struggles at various Maratha courts and backed the Sindhia against the Peshwas. Some of them were executed to clear the field of opposition. The Peshwa Bajirao II exonerated himself of his offence by 'establishing' that the Shenvis were *trikarmi* Brahmanas, not full Brahmanas at all (Wink, *Land and Sovereignty*, pp. 232–34).

18. Wink, *Land and Soveriegnity*, pp. 232–34.

19. N.K. Wagle, 'A Dispute between the Pancal Devajna Sonars and the Brahmanas of Pune Regarding Social Rank and Ritual Privileges: A Case Study of the British Administration of Jati Laws in Maharashtra, 1822–1825', in N.K. Wagle (ed.), *Images of Maharashtra: A Regional Profile of India*, London, Curzon Press, 1980, pp. 129–59, p. 129.

20. These disputes and contests would crucially affect gender relations since caste ranking was determined by gender codes and the extent of control over female sexuality in order to establish the purity of blood of the caste in question.

21. Thomas Duer Broughton, *Letters Written in a Mahratta Camp During the Year 1809*, London, John Murray, 1813, p. 76.

22. Kosambi, 'Glory of Peshwa Pune', p. 247.

23. Jayshree Gokhale-Turner, 'Region and Regionalism in the Study of Indian Politics: The Case of Maharashtra', in N.K. Wagle (ed.), *Images of Maharashtra*, pp. 88–101, p. 93.

24. Romila Thapar, *A History of India*, Vol. I, London, Penguin Books, 1966, pp. 101–02, 122.
25. H. Ludders Berlin, *A List of Brahmi Inscriptions*, Varanasi, Indological Book House, 1973 (reprint).
26. D.D. Kosambi, *Myth and Reality: Studies in the Formation of Indian Culture*, Bombay, Popular Prakashan, 1962, p. 32.
27. Gail Omvedt points out that the interpretations of Bhakti and Shivaji are among the most controversial subjects of the historiography of Maharashtra. The first writers on both subjects go back to the nineteenth century and scholars continue to hotly debate both issues even today. On Bhakti, see for example M.G. Ranade, *Rise of Maratha Power*; J. Deleury, *The Cult of Vithoba*, Poona, Deccan College Post Graduate Research Institute, 1961; Kumar, *Western India*; D.D. Kosambi, *Myth and Reality*; Gail Omvedt, *Cultural Revolt in a Colonial Society: the Non-Brahman Movement in Western India 1873–1930*, Bombay Scientific Socialist Education Trust, 1976; Eleanor Zelliot, *From Untouchable to Dalit: Essays on the Ambedkar Movement*, Delhi, Manohar, 1992.
28. Omvedt, *Non Brahman Movement*, p. 53.
29. Kosambi, *Myth*, p. 33.
30. The hostility manifested towards the Manbhavs by the Brahmanas, who were the targets of the Manbhavs' critique of caste and Brahmanic ritualism, was decisively expressed during the Peshwai in 1782. They were prohibited from preaching and were to lose their caste status since they 'destroyed' Hindu temples and idols and wore distinctive marks (cited in Fukazawa, *The Medieval Deccan*, pp. 110–11, n. 22).
31. Kosambi, *Myth*, p. 33.
32. Omvedt, *Non Brahman Movement*, p. 53. Chakradhara's radical critique of caste and a demand for a fundamental alteration of the Hindu social order was never directly addressed by the Varkari sants (Jayshree Gokhale-Turner, 'Region and Regionalism', p. 95).
33. J. Deleury, *Cult*, p. 202.
34. Kosambi, *Myth*, p. 33.
35. Omvedt points out that while the political kingdoms in the region patronised Sanskrit, the composers of devotional literature based themselves on the language of the region, part of the popular dimension of the devotional cult (*Non-Brahman Movement*, p. 53). How important the move was to the lowly is documented by Mahipati in the life and teachings of the sants of Maharashtra (J.E. Abbot, *Poet-Saints of Maharashtra*, cited in Kumar, *Western India*, p. 8).
36. Kosambi, *Myth*, p. 35.

37. Relations of power and dominance in the appropriation of cults are evident in the legends of Vitthala. One legend refers to the taking away, by force, of the image of Vitthala from Pandharpur to Hampi by a Vijayanagara king. But Vitthala, who was the god of the humble and the poor, was chastised by his Pandharpur devotees for deserting them out of lust for comfort, riches, and glory. Finally, after the appearance of a miracle, a sign of Vitthala's preference for the devotion of the poor, the Pandharpur devotees were allowed to take back the image to its original home. It is telling that this story is given no credence by scholars today and the absence of the image at Hampi is attributed to that all-devouring force: the Muslim invasion (Pierre Sylvain-Fillozat and Vasundhara Fillozat, *Hampi-Vijayanagar: the Temple of Vitthala*, New Delhi, Sitaram Bhartia Institute of Scientific Research, 1988, pp. 20–23).

38. Kosambi, *Myth*, p. 34.

39. Kosambi, *Myth*, p. 33; Zelliot, *Untouchable*, p. 4.

40. Zelliot, *Untouchable*, pp. 4–7; N.K. Behere, *The Background of Maratha Renaissance in the 17th Century*, Bangalore, The Bangalore Printing Press, 1946, p. 165.

41. Zelliot, *Untouchable*, pp. 14–27.

42. Uma Chakravarti, 'Women, Men and Beasts: The Jataka as Popular Tradition', *Studies in History*, Vol. 9, No. 1, NS (1993), pp. 43–69, p. 66.

43. One of the legends about Eknath eating in a Mahar home, described in Mahipati's *Bhaktalilamrta*, resolves this potential conflict situation in a very convenient way. It is God in the form of Eknath who eats in the Mahar house, not Eknath himself. The Brahmanas who are checking out the activities of Eknath find him eating in his own house at the same time as he was meant to eat in the house of the untouchable and therefore cannot outcaste him (Zelliot, *Untouchable*, p. 23).

44. Kosambi, *Myth*, p. 34.

45. Ruth Vanita, 'Three Women Sants of Maharashtra: Muktabai, Janabai, Bahinabai', in *Women Bhakta Poets*, special edition of *Manushi*, Nos. 50–52, January–June, 1989, pp. 45–61, and Susie Tharu and K. Lalitha (eds.), *Women Writing in India, 600 B.C. to the Present*, Vol. I, Delhi, Oxford University Press, 1991, pp. 107–15. More recently, Vidyut Bhagwat has pointed out the need to appreciate the radical potential of the Mahanubhav and the Varkari traditions, especially of the women sants, which provide a rich storehouse for any emancipatory project for women (Vidyut Bhagwat, 'Marathi Literature as a Source for Contemporary

Feminism', *Economic and Political Weekly*, Vol. 30, No. 17, April 29, 1995, pp. WS 24).

46. Kumar, *Western India*, pp. 6–10; M.G. Ranade, 'Saints and Prophets of Maharashtra', in *Rise of the Maratha Power*, pp. 5ff.

47. Omvedt, *Non Brahman Movement*, pp. 53–66; Kosambi, *Myth*, pp. 32–36, Zelliot, *Untouchable*, pp. 3–32, Jayshree Gokhale-Turner, 'Region and Regionalism', pp. 94–96.

48. Omvedt, *Non Brahman Movement*, p. 55.

49. *Ibid.*, Jayshree Gokhale-Turner, 'Region and Regionalism', p. 95.

50. Irawati Karve, 'On the Road: A Maharashtrian Pilgrimage', *Journal of Asian Studies*, Vol. 22, No. 1, November 1962, pp. 13–29.

51. Jayshree Gokhale-Turner, 'Region and Regionalism', p. 95. Associated with the idea of Bhakti as a bridge is the notion of a common Maharashtra dharma, something that united all classes of people in Maharashtra as part of a project of constructing a common 'regional' culture. But, as Gokhale-Turner argues in relation to the caste system, Maharashtra dharma was not a homogeneous ideology which commanded the allegiance of all social groups in the region; rather it had a specific meaning for each social group: Brahmana, Maratha and Dalit. While for the Brahmanas it implied a situation where the 'dharma' was upheld and the textual laws observed, and the Brahmanas occupied a place of honour and therefore the Peshwai, for the Marathas it meant not the Peshwai but the displacement of Brahmanas from positions of political power and the establishment of Shivaji's descendants. For the Dalits, on the other hand, Maharashtra dharma would evoke the ideals of equality yet to be realised in some future society (Jayshree Gokhale-Turner, 'Region and Regionalism', p. 96).

52. Zelliot, *Untouchable*, pp. 24–26.

53. Kosambi sees Bhakti as traced back 'into the Gita as a philosophy which was based, in the final analysis, upon the inability to satisfy any but the barest material needs of a large number of people' (*Myth*, p. 41).

54. Gokhale, *Poona*, pp. 176–79.

55. Despite the individual distinctions between one Peshwa and another a consistent policy of expanding Brahmana control and intensifying the reach of Brahmanic values over society is clearly discernible as the evidence cited below, covering the entire period of the Peshwai, shows. There is an underlying pattern to the ordinances and the punishments recorded in the Peshwa daftar in connection with reinforcing caste hierarchies and gender codes suggesting that although all Hindu rulers upheld Brahmanic ideologies, the Peshwai's investment in such ideologies was of a different and higher

order. This was particularly true in the region around Poona where the Peshwas were in direct control. The picture might vary in the areas under the control of non-Brahmana sardars but there is less documentation of these territories. In the territories under the Brahmana sardars such as the Patwardhans the normative and material structures of the Peshwai appear to have prevailed (Fukazawa, *The Medieval Deccan*, p. 85).

56. Hiroshi Fukazawa, 'State and Caste System (Jati) in the Eighteenth Century Maratha Kingdom', *Hitotsubashi Journal of Economics*, Vol. 9, No. 1, June 1968, p. 42.

57. Sudha V. Desai, *Social Life in Maharashtra under the Peshwas*, Bombay, Popular Prakashan, 1980, p. 39.

58. Fukazawa, 'State and Caste System', pp. 32–44.

59. *Ibid.*, p. 33.

60. G.C. Vad, *Selections from the Satara Rajas' and the Peshwas' Diaries* (abbreviated hereafter as *SSRPD*), nine vols., Poona, 1906–1911, cited in Fukazawa, 'State and Caste System', pp. 38–39. It is significant that the Peshwai recognised the relationship between the nature of the state and the power it could or did not wield in reversing or in continuing customary law, which was 'adharmic' from the point of view of textual law.

61. *SSRPD*, Vol. 7, No. 763, cited in Fukazawa, 'State and Caste System', p. 39.

62. Fukazawa, 'State and Caste System', p. 36.

63. *Ibid.*, p. 42.

64. *Ibid.*

65. *Ibid.*

66. *SSRPD*, Vol. 8, No. 1142, cited in Fukazawa, 'State and Caste System', p. 43.

67. *Ibid.*, Vol. 8, No. 1132, cited in Fukazawa, 'State and Caste System', p. 43.

68. See, for example, Arthur Steele, *Summary of the Laws and Customs of the Hindoo Castes within the Dekhun Provinces Subject to the Presidency of Bombay*, 1827, reprinted as *The Hindu Castes: Their Law, Religion and Customs*, Delhi, Mittal Publications, 1986, and N.K. Wagle, 'British Administration of Jati Laws', in N.K. Wagle (ed.), *Images of Maharashtra*, pp. 130–31.

69. Uma Chakravarti, 'Conceptualising Brahmanical Patriarchy: Gender, Caste, Class and State', *Economic and Political Weekly*, Vol. 27, No. 14, 1993, pp. 579–85. The argument on the relationship between caste and gender will be evident also in Chapter Two.

70. See, for example, G.S. Sardesai (ed.), *Selections from the Peshwa Daftar* (hereafter *SPD*), Poona, 1907, Vol. 43, No. 55 and No. 60,

cited in V.S. Kadam, 'The Institution of Marriage and the Position of Women in Eighteenth Century Maharashtra', *Indian Economic and Social History Review*, Vol. 25, No. 3, 1988, pp. 341–70, p. 347.

71. *SPD*, Vol. 45, No. 52, cited in Kadam, 'The Institution of Marriage', p. 347.

72. *Ibid.*, p. 346.

73. Prominent examples of marriage alliances to consolidate political and social power among the Peshwa family are those of Bajirao I, Balaji Bajirao, the grandson of Bajirao I, and Nana Phadnis, all of whom married daughters of prominent bankers. In turn, the daughters of the Peshwas' families were often married into the families of bankers. Seven of the most powerful families of the eighteenth century were related through matrimonial alliances and formed what has been termed the Chitpavan Brahmana caucus of Poona. These alliances were a means of more easy access to loans and the pattern was set early on by Bajirao I himself when he married Kashibai of the Joshi-Chasker family and thereby established a strong financial basis to the Peshwadom. The Peshwas required loans for military campaigns and administrative expenses. In return the banking families received benefits of various kinds, as, for example, the Joshis, who were given rights to collect octroi duties at nine ghats — trade routes that passed through the hills — and *watandaris* of some townships (Gokhale, *Poona*, pp. 120–21 and 132–33. Also see Frank Perlin, 'Of White Whale and Countrymen in the Eighteenth Century Maratha Deccan: Extended Class Relations, Rights and the Problem of Rural Autonomy under the Old Regime', *Journal of Peasant Studies*, Vol. 5, No. 2, 1977, pp. 172–232, p. 178 and p. 225, No. 22).

74. *Manu*, IX, 88, translated by George Buhler, *Sacred Books of the East* (hereafter *SBE*), Vol. XXV, Delhi, Motilal Banarsidass, 1984 (reprint), p. 343.

75. Arthur Steele, *The Hindu Castes*, pp. 356–59.

76. Nur Yalman, 'On the Purity of Women in the Castes of Ceylon and Malabar', *Journal of the Royal Anthropological Institute of Great Britain and Ireland*, 93, 1962, pp. 25–28.

77. Syed Sirajul Hasan, *The Castes and Tribes of the Nizam's Dominions*, Delhi, Asian Educational Services, 1989 (reprint, first published 1920), p. 105.

78. Kadam, 'The Institution of Marriage', pp. 346–48.

79. P.V. Kane, *History of Dharmasastra*, Poona, Bhandarkar Oriental Research Institute, 1941, Vol. II, Part I, pp. 444–45.

80. Kadam, 'The Institution of Marriage', p. 350.

81. *Ibid.*
82. Evidence used in this section is somewhat circumscribed in the original. It is based mostly on the *nivadapatras* or the decisions taken in certain cases which embodied the award of punishment with the seal of royal authority. What is most significant is that more than half the cases cited as social, religious or moral cases by Gune for the period 1734–1790 are of adultery (V.T. Gune, *The Judicial System of the Marathas*, Poona, Deccan College Post Graduate and Research Institute, 1953, pp. 85, 259).
83. *SPD*, Vol. 43, No. 63, cited in Kadam, 'Institution of Marriage', pp. 364–65.
84. Kadam, 'Institution of Marriage', p. 364.
85. *Ibid.*, p. 363.
86. Gokhale, *Poona*, p. 166.
87. Kadam, 'Institution of Marriage', p. 361.
88. Gokhale, *Poona*, p. 167.
89. *Ibid.*, p. 166.
90. In the Brahmanical *dharmashastras*, the normative text for most Brahmanas, a woman's sexuality was recognised as legitimate only insofar as it was the instrument for reproducing progeny for the husband.
91. Sharmila Rege, 'State and Sexuality: The Case of the Erotic Lavanee and Tamasha in Maharashtra', in Patricia Uberoi (ed.), *Social Reform, Sexuality and the State*, Delhi, Sage Publications 1996, pp. 23–38.
92. Fukazawa, *The Medieval Deccan*, pp. 116, 123–24.
93. Arthur Steele, *The Hindu Castes*, p. 169.
94. Kadam, 'Institution of Marriage', p. 356.
95. *Ibid.*
96. C.Y. Chintamani (ed.), *Indian Social Reform*, Madras, Minerva Press, 1901, p. 291.
97. V.S. Bendre (ed.), *Maharashtretihasachi Sadhane*, Vol. 2, No. 402, cited in Kadam, 'Institution of Marriage', p. 355.
98. *Ibid.*
99. Kadam, 'Institution of Marriage', p. 356.
100. *Ibid.*, pp. 356–57.
101. *Ibid.*, p. 355.
102. *Manu*, V, 157–62, *SBE*, pp. 196–97.
103. Prem Chowdhry, 'Customs in a Peasant Economy: Women in Colonial Haryana', in Kumkum Sangari and Sudesh Vaid (eds.), *Recasting Women: Essays in Colonial History*, New Delhi, Kali for Women, 1989, pp. 302–36, pp. 312ff.
104. Nevertheless, since the model of womanhood developed by

Brahmanical patriarchy was linked to the caste system, it meant that castes with a high self-image attempting to move up in the hierarchy would seek to emulate gender codes of the high castes to establish the case for their own high status.

105. *Baudhayana Dharma Sutra* 1.11.13–16, trans. by George Buhler, *Sacred Books of the East*, Vol. XIV, Part II, Delhi, Motilal Banarsidass, 1975 (reprint) p. 207; *Manu* III.20–24, trans. by George Buhler, *SBE*, pp. 79–81.

106. Arthur Steele, *Hindu Castes*, pp. 26, 168.

107. V.T. Gune, *The Judicial System*, pp. 85, 133; Kadam, 'Institution of Marriage', pp. 341–43. According to Gune there was a triple process of punishment: *Raj danda, Jati danda*, and *Brahma danda*, punishment by royal authority, by the caste, and by the Brahmana assembly (Gune, p. 109).

108. Kadam, 'Institution of Marriage', p. 351.

109. *Ibid.*, pp. 352–53.

110. Steele, *Hindu Castes*, p. 176. A widow's performance of *pat* was considered superior to a woman marrying a second time after leaving her first husband. In such cases the remarriage expenses of the first husband would have to be borne by the woman's second husband. Kadam cites a series of cases where the judicial authorities were approached for permission to form *pat* connections. Permission was given following the levy of *gunehgari* (Kadam, 'Institution of Marriage', pp. 351–53). It is significant that a number of the cases cited related to missing husbands, a consequence of the Maratha army's forays over long distances and for extensive periods of time, leaving many wives virtually in a state of widowhood. The second marriages or *pat* connections were complicated because sometimes the first husband would turn up. The second husband was required to give an undertaking to settle any complications arising from such situations (Kadam, 'Institution of Marriage', pp. 353–54).

111. R.V. Oturkar (ed.), *Peshwekalin Samajik va Arthik Patravyavahar, 1772–1854*, Poona, 1950, No. 138, cited in Kadam, 'Institution of Marriage', p. 352.

112. It is something of a contradiction to speak of adultery in the case of a widow. However, in castes where the widow is not permitted remarriage she is regarded as still married to her dead husband (see Chapter Three) and is therefore committing adultery. In the lower castes, especially in north India, the widow may be regarded as the sexual property of her male affines and therefore committing adultery if she has relations with any other partner (Pauline Kolenda, 'Widowhood among "Untouchable Chuhras"', in Pauline

Kolenda, *Regional Differences in Family Structures in India*, Jaipur, Rawat Press, 1987, pp. 289–354).

113. Ghatasphot in the case of a widow committing adultery meant that she was turned out of the house and abandoned. It represented the permanent and irreversible excommunication of a woman. A semblance of her funeral obsequies was then performed by burning her effigy, composed of grass, along with other ceremonies associated with the death of a wife (Steele, *Hindu Castes*, p. 32).

114. Kadam, 'Institution of Marriage', p. 363.

115. *Ibid.*, Gokhale, *Poona*, p. 167.

116. Gokhale, *Poona*, p. 58.

117. Kadam, 'Institution of Marriage', p. 364.

118. D.B. Parasnis (ed.), 'Itihas Sangrah', *Aitihasik Tippane*, Vol. 1, No. 19, 2 September 1778, cited in Kadam, 'Institution of Marriage', p. 342.

119. Anandibai, 'a woman of extraordinary force', came to be perceived as the most notorious woman in the Peshwa family for engineering the murder of her nephew (by marriage) who was then Peshwa. Anandibai is reputed to have used her skills as a literate woman to substitute an alphabetic character in a letter, thereby changing its meaning to ultimately effectuate the murder of Narayanrao. Her notoriety was recalled throughout the nineteenth century by men resisting the education of women. The playwright Khadilkar used the memory of Anandibai to great effect in painting a picture of the debauched end of the glorious Peshwai (personal communication from Sudhanwa Deshpande). Her son finally became the last Peshwa, Bajirao II, in 1796 but she herself had died in 1794 with her last years spent in frustration and humiliation (Gokhale, *Poona*, pp. 9, 48, 51, 55). Anandibai's notoriety points to a recognition by Brahmana men that the Peshwai was threatened from *within* while it was trying to enforce normative codes for its subjects and that a major agent of the contradiction was the Brahmana woman. It must be noted, however, that Brahmanya had been threatened by a woman who was nevertheless investing in the larger Brahmana 'daulat': the privileges of the group as a whole.

120. Gokhale, *Poona*, p. 186. The case is an interesting example of the general disapproval of adultery among the lower castes too. The accused woman's desire to prove her innocence in the presence of Radhabai, the embodiment of stridharma, is also notable. Stridharma was something of a model to be emulated even by the lower castes. But there are other aspects of this case which are notable. First, trial by ordeal was a recognised form of evidence in the Peshwai (V.T. Gune, *Judicial System*, pp. 90ff). What is most

---

Caste Contestati
Nationalis

The British takeover of Poona
structure of relations establishe
intervention in western India
social relations which need to
standpoint of gender, caste,
particularly relevant. How fai
Brahmanical patriarchy break
control of the Brahmanas upo
way? How did other social
situation and in what way wa
some of these new social force

Immediately after their take
the British were keen not t
disruption in the social life of i
merely cautious of but almost
class which, in the Peshwa
Brahmanas.[3] In the Deccan
introducing drastic changes ba
initiated by Cornwallis in Beng
for wanting to develop a syste
ways'.[4] On the whole, Elphins
institutions and ways of goverr

In particular the new admi
the Brahmanas as a class. The n
a section of the Brahmanas
government, the bulk of th
Brahmanas had held the leadin

significant is the Ch:
presence of a femal
charge of adultery. T
from enslavement (s
now honoured for
associated with high-

121. Gokhale, *Poona*, p. 4
122. *Ibid.*, p. 74.
123. Kumkum Sangari,
     Incitement', *Econom*
     1, 1993, pp. 867–82
124. Julia Leslie, *The Perfe*
     to the Stridharmapa
     University Press, 198
125. Gune's evidence for
     mostly Brahmana
     importance in this cc
     of upholding the Br
     that led Brahmana w
     and marked them ou
     themselves in the 'dh

they had derived substantial benefits from it in a variety of ways. Thus, however 'neutral' the new government professed to be in matters of religion, the Brahmanas would notice and dislike the changed situation especially since the supposed 'neutrality' would not satisfy their material needs. There was also a recognition that the Brahmanas had considerable influence over public opinion. It was therefore necessary to placate them.

One important way in which this was done was by continuing the custom of giving grants to temples and the annual dakshina festival, distributing money to individual Brahmanas, although in a more modest and altered way. A special attempt was made to ensure the satisfaction of the more important and learned shastris selected from among those on whom Bajirao used to lavish large sums. There was also a recognition that if the most learned men were brought to look up to the government for support they would willingly render any service the government should wish, such as revising the laws of the Shastras, or settling their doubtful and disputed meaning.[5] Other important members of the ruling class, such as holders of *jagirs* and *inams*, also retained their privileges. After negotiation, protracted in some cases, all the great *jagirdars* were allowed 'practical independence' within their jagirs. This was in accordance with the fundamental principle of the settlement that their position should not be worse than it had been under the former government.[6] The British administration had thus acknowledged the importance of preserving the privileges of chiefs with a view to having some portion of the old nobility 'flourishing and contented'.[7] Since many of the great jagirdars and inamdars were Brahmanas, their power, both religious and secular, was not radically altered by the early working of the colonial state in the Poona region.[8] Given the British anxiety to prevent disaffection, moderate the impact of the colonial takeover, and conciliate those anxious about their new status, especially the Brahmanas, it is not surprising that a non-Brahmana raiyat told Elphinstone, the governor of Bombay, in 1823 that the 'power of the Brahmanas is doubled since they lost the country'.[9]

The same anxiety led the colonial state to steer a path away from the Christian missionaries who saw in the British takeover of the Poona region an opportunity for expanding their own activities. When a missionary suggested the establishment of mission schools in the Deccan in 1818, Elphinstone, who recognised that professed neutrality in religious matters would not, in itself, allay the fears of the Brahmanas, replied that the government would not want them to be alarmed by fears of conversion.[10] It was therefore Elphinstone's policy to exclude the missionaries from the Deccan in the early stages of colonial rule.

The problem of the relationship of the colonial state to Christianity and to certain practices within Hinduism, as British rule was consolidated, was more complex. While practical considerations demanded caution and flexibility in handling customs such as the dakshina grants to temples, they nevertheless created certain dilemmas. In 1842 the British withdrew a particular cash allowance to the Dev of Cincvad on grounds of its 'official connection' with idolatry. How much this position owed to the colonial state being wedged between its own rationalist or even Christian ideology and the aggressiveness of the Christian missionaries is difficult to say without close examination. What is apparent, however, is the shifting position of the British, first in terminating and then in renewing the allowance to the Dev[11] as they floundered for a policy that would safeguard them from all sides.

Early British attitudes to gender fell into a familiar pattern. It was necessary to establish control over the subjects of the new colonial state and without ruffling the feelings of the Brahmanas and other important groups, take over existing norms while making a point about their own notions of social order. The handling of gender was therefore complex and cannot be seen only in issues like *sati* but in the everyday actions of the executive.

One such action occurred soon after the British takeover of Poona when Robertson, the new British collector, proceeded to act with vigour against 'immorality'. In Robertson's view, the greatest evil was 'infidelity in the marriage bed'. Reforms in this sphere would be of political value in his opinion especially since a check to practices 'sanctioned' by the Peshwai would make for a comparison highly favourable to the British government. An opportunity arose when the police arrested a Brahmana for having committed adultery with a widow of the same caste and had attempted to settle the matter with a bribe to the police. The latter had initially demanded Rs 15, which was scaled down to Rs 6, whereupon the Brahmana offender was freed. Robertson deftly combined the old and the new in his handling of the issue. The

Brahmana offender and the widow were sent round the town: the widow's face was blackened, her garments were tied to those of the adulterer while the public crier proclaimed their offence. This was a traditional punishment but Robertson's proclamation was so framed as to simultaneously show the even-handedness of British justice: the offending Brahmana was awarded Rs 20 to compensate for his ill-treatment at the hands of the police.[12]

The upholding of traditional norms was the dominant motif in the handling of gender in the early years of colonial rule in Maharashtra. This is evident from the decision of the Elphinstone government (Regulation II of 1827) to uphold the authority of panchayats in certain classes of disputes. The Bombay government felt that the introduction of a court system based on western norms into many matters of a civil nature would swamp the courts with work and cause a stagnation of business.[13] Further, the panchayat system was 'popular' with the people who referred to the *panches* as Panch Parmeshwar.[14] The Bombay government felt that the system rested on popular initiative and was an integral part of society. Thus, Regulation II of 1827 (Section 27) held that civil courts had no jurisdiction to deal with caste questions.[15] Matters of caste custom (like marriage norms and practices) remained with the existing system of panchayats. Caste custom could also be regarded as an aspect of the 'religion' of a caste as we shall see below. From the standpoint of this study it may be noted that since the purity of caste and normative marriage arrangements were contingent upon the monitoring of female sexuality, its violation subjected women to the authority of the panchayat which, as we have seen earlier, could result in loss of caste, kin and community. Women whose major 'lapses' or crimes related in the main to marriage rules, thus continued to be governed by traditional laws executed through the panchayats and were not immediately, and in all matters, provided with the 'protection' of the British courts.

That women were entirely dispensible to the agenda of the British during their early rule in western India, was starkly brought out in the case of the murder of a young girl of 15 or 16 by Appa Desai, the great Jagirdar of Nipani, in 1825. Since the offender was a prominent member of the ruling elite and close to the deposed Peshwa, the British found it expedient not to intervene in any way — the murder was regarded as a 'minor irregularity'; it was also argued that since, under the Peshwas, the great jagirdars had powers of life and death over their subjects, there was no justification for the government to intervene except in cases where there were 'flagrant instances of abuse of power'.[16] The murder of a young girl clearly did not count especially as the murderer had the capacity to create dissatisfaction if subjected to British disciplinary authority.

The attitude to gender was also clearly tailored by caste and class considerations. Accepting the notion of private space in the case of women from upper caste and class backgrounds, the law was to respect 'traditional' norms in relation to them. Bhil women however, were treated exactly like their menfolk in a 'war of extermination' unleashed against them by the British. One of the lieutenants employed in a punitive campaign burnt 35 dwellings in a Bhil settlement, killed six persons including two women and took 13 women prisoner. The episode excited the ardour of the lieutenant and he hoped to have the pleasure of 'spilling more blood'. While the administrative authorities chastised the lieutenant for using intemperate language in an official despatch, and there was some correspondence on the tactics to be adopted in further campaigns, no doubts seem to have been raised on how Bhil women were treated by the British authorities.[17]

The handling of sati during the years up to 1830 epitomises the contradictory pulls experienced by the early colonial state in western India in relation to gender, law and tradition. Various positions were adopted and experiments initiated in an attempt to reconcile these. Again the key concern appears to have been to create the least disaffection and carry the endorsement of the Brahmanas as far as possible. The many policies adopted included the attempt to define, regulate and persuade rather than to consider abolition.[18] Significant aspects of 'persuasion' were recommendations at different times of offering pensions to widows (a practice associated with the Peshwai) who had been dissuaded from self-immolation, maintenance to male kinsfolk to provide for the widow's support, the offer of a government job to male kinsfolk who agreed to support the widow, and the termination of government jobs of those men in whose families women had been immolated. None of these policies was sustained for any length of time because it was feared that the government's gesture of granting maintenance or a gift would be misused.[19] Throughout, there was an attempt to find a 'native' solution to terminating the practice and a recognition that Maharashtra was different from Bengal. After the abolition of sati in Bengal, Malcolm, the new Governor of Bombay Presidency, was still recalling the spectre of Brahmana discontent.[20] In western India what clinched the adoption of a position on issues of gender was the potential for sedition by the Brahmanas who had lost the powers they had under the Peshwai and therefore had to be 'conciliated'.

II

While the British were keen to act cautiously with respect to 'tradition' and 'religion' and keep Brahmanical discontent within containable levels, the end of the Peshwai implied the emergence of a new political configuration. That power was not now directly in the hands of the Brahmanas was quickly grasped by various castes and the British takeover was thus perceived as an occasion which opened up the possibilities of contestation and an altered socio-political order. It was clearly a moment to be seized by castes excluded from the privileged place occupied by the Brahmanas.

The Peshwai had also been a period of contestation between various castes with the Chitpavan Brahmana figuring as one of the disputants in all contests. These were not always resolved but in the cases where they were, the resolution invariably had to do with who had more access to state power among the disputants. Other disputes which remained unresolved or had been temporarily resolved could be re-opened when the balance of political forces was altered. One of the first caste disputes to come up was among the Panchal Devajna Sonars and the various Brahmana *jatis* of Poona. It had remained unsettled, at least as far as the Sonars were concerned, throughout the Peshwai for about a century. When it resurfaced in 1822, it immediately became a test case for the British position on caste disputes. Briefly, the details of the case[21] were as follows:

The Konkane Sonars (Sonars from Konkan) calling themselves the Panchal Devajna Rathakaras had claimed the right to observe 16 major *samskaras* according to the Vedic instruction (*Vedokta*) and the performance of the *munja* (investiture of the sacred thread) for their boys. In 1822, a dispute between the Devajnas and Brahmanas was triggered off with the performance of a munja ceremony at the house of a Sonar. The ceremony was performed by a Brahmana but another Brahmana faction of that city led by

Malhar Mule took serious objection to the proceedings, contacted the Poona Brahmanas and secured an award from their elders censuring the Brahmana who had performed the investiture. The 'erring' Brahmana was threatened with physical punishment if he did not undergo penance and he, in turn, appealed to Pottinger, the collector of Ahmednagar, for protection. Pottinger took immediate action and ordered the flogging of the leader of the censuring party, much to the dismay of the Governor-in-Council in Bombay who considered that non-interference in caste disputes was so obviously expedient that the collector ought to have known that without specific instruction.

The case was forwarded to Poona for a trial by the panchayat. The applicants (those who objected to the performance of Vedic rites) also demanded that the Sonar be punished for infringing the dignity of the Brahmanas, and further that the Sonars should be disallowed the Vedic rites through a government decree. A panchayat of five Brahmanas was appointed with a sixth as *sarpanch* or 'referee' by the Brahmanas. The Poona Brahmanas were the plaintiffs and the erring Nagar Brahmanas were the defendants.

The final verdict of the panchayat was, predictably, a refusal to accept any of the documentary evidence provided on behalf of the Sonars as authentic; they ruled that the Sonars should 'maintain the distance' between Brahmanas and lower castes through appropriate behaviour, wear their *dhotis* as prescribed for lower castes and not in Brahmana fashion, use images of copper and avoid the use of namaskar as a form of greeting, besides other things.

Most significantly, the Brahmana award concluded also that its execution rested with the government, which was required to summon, fine and admonish the Sonars not to offend again. At the same time, the offending Brahmanas of Nagar who had actually conducted the Vedic rites for the Sonars, were sentenced to perform expiatory rites. The government responded by permitting the disciplining of the fellow-caste men but not the Sonars. Finally, the Sonars dismissed their erstwhile Brahmana priests and carried on practising the Vedokta.

The dispute between the Devajna Sonars and the Brahmanas is notable in a number of ways. To begin with, because it was the first jati dispute to come up before the British after the collapse of the Peshwai, it is representative of the issue of contestations between castes. It is also important because it marks a recognition by castes seeking high status, and others already established as high, who resisted such moves, and was a crucial moment in the history of rank-ordering which could reverse or reinforce the power of the Brahmanas. Although the controversy between the Brahmanas and Sonars was located in Ahmednagar, it was the Poona Brahmanas, particularly the Chitpavans among them, who took the lead in chastising their own caste-fellows and in disciplining the Sonars. For the Konkanastha Chitpavan Brahmanas, as those who had virtually controlled state power during the Peshwai and consequently the caste most adversely affected by its collapse, the situation was most volatile. It is not surprising that in opposing the claims of the Sonars the Poona Brahmanas led by the Chitpavans under Nilkantha Shastri stated that their 'dignity' had been infringed.[22]

Caste contestations occurred outside western India as well, for example in the territories of the British in south India where too the British courts were expected to decide such contests. The contestations did not always run the same course in the different arenas. However, the decisions in one area were used as evidence in others.[23] Further, simmering disputes could be reopened depending upon particular resolutions. The dispute between Chitpavans and Kayastha Prabhus of Pune and Satara going back to the Peshwai, culminated in Baroda in favour of the Prabhus. It was reopened when the Chitpavans, following the Bombay government's permission to impose sanctions on recalcitrant members of the their own caste, appealed to the Bombay government to force the Baroda state to implement sanctions against the recalcitrant Brahmanas there.[24] Occasions of reverses for the Brahmanas came up when non-Brahmana ruling elites enabled other non-Brahmana castes to assert their claims to high status as part of their own ongoing contests against the Brahmanas.[25]

Caste contests were also occasions when castes mobilised their caste-fellows across regions. Devajna Sonars in the Deccan drew upon the support of influential business community of Sonar *shetias* from Bombay. One of the most important shetias of Bombay, Jagannath Shankarseth, a Sonar, made an effective intervention when it appeared that the British were siding with the Brahmanas. The Governor-in-Council in Bombay quickly reassured Jagannath that the Pune decision would not be applied in Bombay.[26]

The Sonar-Brahmana dispute in the Deccan was clearly a test

case for formulating policy guidelines by the new colonial state for jati laws. It caught the British in a bind since they did not want to take a public stand against the Brahmanas in Poona. While they were certain of the need to maintain neutrality on religious matters, they were in a difficult position when both parties in the dispute complained that 'their' religion was being 'infringed and interfered with'. The situation was aggravated because both sides cited textual evidence which the British were convinced had been tailored to suit the occasion.[27]

Faced with the trap of administering such a situation among contending castes, the British floundered: the colonial state was not unified in its response. The Commissioner for the Deccan stationed at Poona favoured the Brahmanas and used the argument of Shastric penalty for Shudras violating the ban on reading the Vedas which he believed the British were pledged to continue. The Commissioner's pro-Brahmana stand was consistent: its rationale was dual. The first part was the familiar argument about not ruffling the feathers of the erstwhile ruling class. But most pragmatically he also argued that maintaining the hierarchical order would keep the 'subjects' disunited and unable to combine against the British. An equalising policy would ultimately reduce British stability in his view.[28]

The Governor-in-Council in Bombay, however, ruled against the Commissioner and argued that the different castes should be left to sort out their own rules. Thus, while the Brahmanas could 'enforce' discipline upon fellow Brahmanas, it was not for the British or for the Brahmanas to enforce discipline against the actions of the Sonars.[29]

The crux of the matter in the Sonar-Brahmana dispute had been the Brahmana demand that the British ensure the compliance of other castes with Brahmana superiority and punish defiance when it occurred. The new colonial state was unwilling to accept a role in which it had to impose legal strictures upon the defiers. The 'neutrality' of the British in relation to disputes about rank order was the space into which the non-Brahmana castes inserted themselves. Using this space, the Sonars carried the day; emboldened by the neutrality, they dismissed the Brahmana priests who were refusing to perform certain rites for them and raised a new controversy. The Brahmanas wanted to remain the priests of the Sonars and receive the ritual fee without conceding the Vedokta to the Sonars. However, they had no means of enforcing such an arrangement in the new political situation where the alliance between them and the state had been disrupted. A number of castes could now seek upward social mobility, defy the disapproval of Brahmanas who were unable to chastise them and finally use the Census to establish their claim to high status.

The British could see that they had opened up a Pandora's box. The Sonar-Brahmana dispute and its complexities led the Bombay government to launch an all-India consultation on the status of the Sonars. In 1824 the British tried to elicit information on how previous governments had dealt with other such 'false' claims.[30] They also needed to know what customs operated in different parts of the country. To this end information from 75 castes in Poona was sought on a list of questions which were used in formulating the Code of Regulations or the Panchayat Law of 1827.[31]

Significantly, gender was a crucial component of disputes about caste status. Apart from practices relating to samskaras, investiture, and the recitation of Vedic mantras it was the purity of the women that established a caste's claim to high status. In claiming the right to Vedokta and *upabrahmana* status, the Devajna Sonars contended that on the death of their husbands, their women underwent a tonsure, did not marry a second time, observed enforced widowhood, and that some even practised self-immolation.[32] Since there were many sub-groups among the Sonars, who claimed the right to Vedokta and the upabrahmana status, the distinction between the Devajna Sonars and ordinary Sonars needed to be established; here too the different practices of enforced widowhood and the practice of pat were a critical determinant of their varying statuses. When Steele's survey of castes was conducted in the Poona region, only one other sub-group among the Sonars, the Kanade Sonars, listed enforced widowhood as a prevalent custom. The rest accepted the practice of pat marriages among their sub-groups and did not press any claims to the Vedokta or upabrahmana status.[33] From this we may deduce that not all sub-castes among the Sonars were equally socially mobile.

In resisting the Vedokta claims of the Devajna Sonars the Poona Brahmanas were deeply conscious of the place of enforced widowhood in determining high status. Thus, at the height of the controversy they admonished the Sonars and ruled that a widow was allowed to remarry in the Sonar jati and if she was so inclined the Sonars should not be allowed to prevent it: if they did they should be fined.[34] The intimate relationship between caste status and gender codes had a long history in pre-colonial India and that link was not likely to weaken suddenly in the new socio-political situation.

In 1830, another caste contestation erupted between the Marathas and the Brahmanas which highlighted the nature of the moment represented by the British capture of state power. It is important here to note the double moves made by the Maratha caste in defining itself, the place of gender in such a contest, and ideological parameters within which such caste contestations occurred and the manner in which they fed into the non-Brahmana movement.

The first volley in the Maratha-Brahmana contest was fired by Pratapsinh Bhosale, a nominal descendant of Shivaji. He had been installed as Chhatrapati in Satara by the British in the hope that this would remove a possible source of disaffection, and more importantly, establish a figure for western India who was not a Brahmana. In theory this might have helped to undercut the claims to social leadership of the Chitpavan Brahmana Peshwa and his supporters. However, Pratapsinh's position was one of symbolic importance rather than of real power as far as the British were concerned. His tenure in office from 1818 to 1839 was important for moves of upward social mobility within the Maratha-Kunbi cluster of castes, for the employment of *varna* divisions in the conduct of political rivalries, and for changes in the significance of the category of Maratha. The main feature of the period was a bitter, long-drawn-out dispute between elite Maratha families, led by Pratapsinh, and the Chitpavan Brahmanas of western Maharashtra. The issue was whether the elite families were entitled to call themselves Kshatriyas, which the Brahmanas now hotly contested. The struggle over the right to Vedokta by the Marathas was actually a struggle for political power and authority between Pratapsinh and the Chitpavans. Significantly, both the Brahmanas and the Marathas showed a sharp awareness that a fundamental change had occurred in the nature of their relationship with the assumption of power by the British. For the Marathas it was a moment when they might recover some of their lost position; for the Chitpavans it was a test case for staking their continued right to maintain and enforce the traditional religious hierarchies in matters of dispute over ritual and caste relations.[35]

Between 1820 and 1828 the Brahmana party led by the Chitpavans, among whom the main protagonists were Balajipant Natu, Chintamanrao Patwardhan and Nilkantha Shastri Thatte (the main actors in the Sonar dispute as well), campaigned to limit the Vedokta to the Brahmanas since in the Kaliyuga the true Kshatriya had disappeared. There were now only two castes, the Brahmana and the Shudra, according to the Brahmana party. The offensive of the Brahmanas can be attributed to their growing awareness that the East India Company, unlike the Peshwas, was not prepared to take on the role of executors of the Brahmana religious authority. The Chitpavans, thus, feared that castes of all kinds would press claims to higher status that had been denied them under Peshwa rule, and their fears were being confirmed.[36] At this point it was necessary for Brahmana orthodoxy to assume an aggressive stance in retaining caste supremacy and to close ranks against others. The position of the Brahmanas against the Marathas, if it succeeded, would act as a deterrent and effectively scuttle similar moves by other, not so elite, castes and therefore the controversy was particularly virulent.

The Brahmana argument was based on two major positions: the first struck a mortal blow to Maratha sense of pride by questioning the validity of the rituals performed by Shivaji and his descendants. Second, the Brahmanas emphasised the complete administrative dependence of the Marathas, as Shudras, upon their Brahmana ministers; they had, in the Brahmana view, never wielded authority although they might have had de-facto power which is all that, as Shudras, they could wield.[37]

The whole dispute reached a climax in 1830 when it was decided to hold a public debate to resolve the issue. Each side appointed a team of pandits. The atmosphere was so tense over the days of the debate that Pratapsinh feared for the safety of the pandits and it was ironic that he came wearing a sword to protect them. The verdict of the debate confirmed Pratapsinh Bhosale's title to the Vedokta rites.

In seeking to have the Kshatriya status of the Bhosales (and therefore their right to the Vedokta) recognised Pratapsinh had to contend with the ambivalences in the category of Maratha. Defining the Marathas as a varna and identifying the varna with

Kshatriya status, with rulership and mastery over land and military powers, meant confining the Kshatriya status to a small social elite distinct from the general category of the Kunbis. In establishing this distinctive identity, the claim to certain qualities, customs and practices went alongside a distancing from the humble Kunbis. For example the *assal* or 'true' Maratha families, claimed a genealogical link with the old kingly Rajput families of north India.[38]

Such a distinction was based upon the notion of *marathamola* or the ways and practices of the genuine Marathas which included a strict code for their women who would not appear before strangers. The supposed lack of purity of the women was something the Brahmanas had raised to reject the Maratha claim to Kshatriya status, saying that all pure Kshatriyas had been wiped out by Parashurama and that their women had then resorted to the Brahmanas to beget children and had thus lost caste.[39] This was hotly contested by the Marathas in the 1830 debate. The Marathas claimed also that their womenfolk practised sacred widowhood and were barred from remarriage. It is significant that the charge of violating endogamy and thus causing the breakdown of caste was one of the main allegations against the Marathas. What is even more interesting is that the Kshatriya women who survived the massacre of their menfolk were alleged to have had relations with Brahmana men. Caste purity had to be maintained only by women.

An acceptance of the gender codes of the upper castes was the critical index in seeking the caste status of one of the three higher varnas, that is in the Brahmana, Kshatriya or Vaishya models whose lifestyle determined the status being claimed. In the case of the Marathas it was the lifestyle of the ruling class, the kingly model, which was a central element in distinguishing and distancing themselves from the Kunbi cluster of castes. Pratapsinh recorded his anxiety and irritation at the efforts of the ordinary Kunbi families to connect themselves to the assal families.[40] The conflict between the Marathas and the Brahmanas reflects the limitations of a contest between elite groups; in essence it sought to reverse the situation which obtained under the Peshwas when the Brahmanas had become the dominant caste. There was no questioning of the hierarchy of the caste system. In varying degrees similar strategies were followed by non-elite groups such as the Kunbis in their attempt to change their status to a higher one. By the time the censuses of 1891 and 1901 were recorded, many Kunbis in certain districts were returning themselves as Marathas. At the same time other caste disputes such as those of the Sonars were following the same tactics in which gender codes played a crucial role in staking their claim to the Vedokta. The right to the Vedokta might be conceded only if it was established that a caste had traditionally practised celibate widowhood and sacred indissoluble marriage. Every move of Sankritisation by a caste whether following the Brahmana, Kshatriya or Vaishya model, was predicated upon establishing the purity of its women.

The above disputes showed the emergence of a number of issues: the earlier dominance of the Brahmanas in the state as well as in civil society underwent certain changes. The British control of the state eroded the power of the Brahmanas in the state and to a certain extent this weakened Brahmana power even in civil society. In the nineteenth century, the weakened hold of the Brahmanas on state power opened up the contestations of non-Brahmana castes who pressed their claims for a recognition of a higher status and brought on the resistance by the Brahmanas to the granting of such claims. The establishment of British power thus widened the arena of caste contestations.

However, these caste contestations were expressed in the traditional idiom, that is, by claiming the Vedokta and seeking the status of the Brahmanas or Kshatriyas and staking the claim itself on the purity of the caste and on established practice, or on the adoption by the caste of the highest gender codes. Ironically, the British presence, while opening up spaces for caste contestations indirectly, and unintentionally, provided for a renewal of those cultural values that reiterated traditional high-caste gender norms. At the same time, since the British were cautious about the possibilities of Brahmana disaffection and also left the jagirdars in possession of their lands they did not disrupt the local power structures. Traditional structures of dominance did not therefore undergo major changes in the first few decades of colonial authority in Maharashtra.

In concluding this discussion of early caste contests in nineteenth century Maharashtra it might be useful to note that the ideological parameters within which such contests occurred are being reconceptualised. Caste contests have conventionally been viewed as attempts at sankritisation wherein lower castes accept the ideological principles of the caste system and aspire to the status of higher castes by giving up certain customs and practices and accepting the values of the Brahmanical order. Such moves do not critique the caste system or question its ideological moorings but simply create a new hierarchy. An analysis of the ideological underpinning of sanskritisation can be sharpened by arguing that hegemonic ideology works to limit the cultural imagination of the lower orders[41] and makes it difficult to radically reconceptualise society. Thus the acceptance of upper-caste/class norms is mandatory for a group seeking upward mobility — it is built into the way caste ideology works and it is this process that we see more evidence of in the history of the caste system. It is only when an onslaught is made on the cultural hegemony of the Brahmanas, and on the ideology of the caste system as conceptualised by the Brahmanas, rather than on the place occupied by them that a real critique of the caste system can be made.

III

The long-term and more durable consequences of the establishment of British power through its policies took a while to unfold but by the middle of the nineteenth century they were being felt. The creation of a new system of administration, particularly a bureaucracy and a legal system based upon a distinctive system of recruitment to fill its lower rungs, opened up opportunities to particular segments of Maharashtrian society, leading to the emergence of a professional class. This section formed the backbone of the 'middle' class. Entry into these professions was through an English education. Access to education and to the new professions were twin factors in the process of class formation. Economic changes and urbanisation also provided opportunities to certain sections in the formation of new classes. These processes were simultaneously 'open' and closed: while technically open to all castes, making possible mobility and opportunity, they were unequally accessible to different castes and, not infrequently, virtually closed to the lowest among them.

It thus became clear that the breakup of pre-colonial society was not automatically going to work in favour of all sections. This resulted in sharp contests for control over new opportunities. The upper castes, particularly the Brahmanas, attempted to retain their pre-eminent position in society, and middle and lower castes attempted to prise open the structure and alter the balance of social forces in their own favour.

In this, Maharashtra was different from Bengal. In Bengal the process of class formation appears broadly to have been an extension of pre-colonial elite groups (which had been more heterogeneous than in Maharashtra) without marked conflict; in Maharashtra the formation of class was accompanied by more obvious tension. The upper castes, particularly the Brahmanas, did ultimately feed into the professional middle class and maintain an unbroken hold on education and government service but this did not occur without opposition. Further, caste contestations came to shape the nature of nationalism: the Brahmanas' attempts to retain their hold over material resources and social pre-eminence required also their hegemonic control over society and over the reshaping of the future. Throughout the nineteenth century the Brahmanas' virtual monopoly over education (especially in the Poona region) and the professions continued and a firm grip on the national movement during the last quarter of the nineteenth century was one way in which the lower-caste critique of Brahmana power was diffused.

British policies on education in Maharashtra can be traced back to Elphinstone's decision to continue the dakshina to Brahmanas in a modified form after their takeover of the Peshwa territories in the Deccan. Although this was a move to 'conciliate the upper classes'[42] it was also hoped that the Brahmanas could ultimately be led away from a study of religious texts to more 'useful' branches of learning such as law and mathematics and via these to western values. In pursuance of these hopes the Bombay government set up the Hindu College in Poona in 1821.

The new form of dakshina was, however, resented by orthodox Brahmanas and a confrontation between them and the British was building up over their educational policy. When the British decided to freeze the dakshina in 1836 the reaction from orthodox Brahmanas was sharp. A petition signed by 800 shastris and pandits protested against the 'undermining of the moral foundations of Hindu society'.[43]

The government of Bombay, however, hoped to counter the protests of the signatories with a new generation of Brahmanas going through the Poona English School who were expected to support the political and social objectives of the British government. They were not disappointed. A group of Poona Brahmanas sent in a series of representations in 1850, indicating a division in the ranks of the Brahmanas, and showing that many Brahmanas were anxious to exploit the opportunities British rule was opening up to them.[44] The linking of educational policies with the handling of Brahmanas and Brahmanical learning was a central element of the various moves made by the British between the 1820s and 1860s in Maharashtra. While the British-Indian government wished to transform the nature of learning for the Brahmanas it was not uncomfortable with a special place for them, and more generally the upper castes, in the educational institutions. For example, Wood, in directing the establishment of universities, stated that the government was to 'place the benefits of education plainly and practically before the higher classes in India'.[45]

Of two reasons justifying the limited reach of education the first was the shortage of funds which required maximum effect with minimal investment.[46] A second and more important justification was the anxiety of the British to not upturn the 'social practices of Hinduism where learning was traditionally confined to the higher castes'. As early as 1825 Elphinstone had argued that if the new system of education first took root among the lowest castes it would never spread any further. In his view it was also inconsistent with the British attempt to found the new government on a 'more extended basis'. The 'lowest castes' were the most despised but they were also the 'least numerous of the great divisions of society'.[47] The English school that taught the popular branches of the sciences was envisaged as a school for the children of the upper classes. To prevent a 'mixture of ranks as might prevent the higher order of natives from using the school' no boy was to be admitted until he was approved of by a committee.[48] Thus, apart from the content of learning the question of *who* it was intended for and who was to be left out were a critical component of educational policies.

From the very outset thus the educational policy of the British was the subject of a variety of contestatory positions.[49] Some missionaries were sharply critical of the government's pro-Brahmana policies of material support to Brahmanical knowledge. They supported a more diffused spread of learning to break the monopoly of knowledge in the hands of the Brahmanas, and as a means to break the hold of the Brahmanas upon the rest of society in order to pave the way for the Christianisation of the population. Some missionaries had also found the lowest castes to be the best pupils. But since the British administrators were keen to placate the Brahmanas the early facilities of education remained highly restricted. On no account were the British to appear to *prefer* the lower castes. As Elphinstone put it, while education for the lower castes might put the British at the head of a new class 'superior to the rest in useful knowledge' since they were a minority, despite their new attainments, the British would not be able to 'prefer' them, because this would lead to the upper castes hating and despising the British.[50]

It must, however, be noted that though the onset of British rule did not usher in a sudden golden age of lower-caste education, indirectly it did bring in some signs of widening educational opportunities through the burgeoning of educational establishments in the hands of Protestant missionaries. Seeing a fertile ground for proselytisation among the lower castes, the missionaries did their utmost to point out that Hinduism had deprived them of their rights in matters of education and religion.[51] Although government schools remained restricted the onset of company rule appeared to the lower castes to bring in new opportunities for their advancement. Thus, while the upper castes availed themselves of British government facilities, the lower castes attempted to gain access to similar education through the schools of the missionaries[52] as Phule did.

The early imbalance in educational opportunities continued throughout the nineteenth century. In 1884, out of 109 students in the Deccan College Poona, 107 were Brahmanas even though the caste constituted only 4 per cent of the population in the region.[53] Even in Bombay, whose educational and service profile was very different from Poona, there was an overwhelming representation of the upper castes in the college, with Brahmanas comprising more than 50 per cent of the students in 1884.[54] Here, however, the monopoly of the Brahmanas had clearly been mediated by other upper castes such as the Vanis and Prabhus, especially the latter. The Prabhus had a long association with Bombay and with learning skills. They had served both the Portuguese in Bombay and the Peshwas in Poona. As clerks under the East India Company they prospered in Bombay in the 17th and eighteenth centuries.[55] Their monopoly of clerkships in Bombay was so great that their caste name became a synonym for an English 'writer'.[56] When English education was introduced in Bombay the

Prabhus appear to have grasped the importance of the formal training and they maintained a steady position as a leading community in the Elphinstone College and were better represented than the Brahmanas. However, what is striking is the steady inroads made into this position by the Brahmanas. By the middle of the 1860s the positions had been completely reversed and the Brahmanas now dominated the institution among its Hindu students.[57] This pattern in Bombay reflects the manner in which the Brahmanas recovered their social position following the apparent reversal of their fortunes with the collapse of the Peshwai.

Brahmana domination of the institutions of education enabled them to make up their loss of direct political control by continuing to exercise a grip on the administration and they consequently remained the most influential social group in Maharashtra. They thus occupied professional positions in the British administration at all levels far in excess of their proportion in the population as a whole, in India and more specifically in western India.

The concentration of educational opportunities and entry to the civil services among the Brahmanas as well as the dominance this gave them was an important element in the social processes and class formation of nineteenth century Maharashtra. A broad congruence between caste and class was sustained, with the foremost pre-colonial elite group of the Brahmanas feeding directly into the new professional class. The Prabhus too, who had at one time had a virtual monopoly over certain positions in Bombay, continued to be fairly well represented in the professions. A few other castes of Maharashtra also became more visible: the Sutars through entry into company service as clerks, especially in Bombay city, as well as the Sonars. The Sonars became significant not through entry into education and the professions but because of their wealth. Despite their controversial caste status, because of their wealth, a section of them rose to established positions in Bombay society.[58] Some individuals among the non-Brahmanas also used the new opportunities in road-building and urbanisation as contractors, as Phule did, to establish themselves economically.[59]

Over the decades this burgeoning class, with its social composition drawn essentially from the upper castes, also reproduced itself, with the largest proportion of students at the college level being the children of government employees and professional men, who, in turn, had been drawn from families where it was traditional to serve the government even in pre-colonial times.[60]

The broad congruence between caste and class was a consequence also of the manner in which British policies (which were themselves Janus-faced, both breaking into and able to work with traditional social hierarchies) were devised, set in motion and affected different strata of Indian society. Thus, even as it broke the intellectual 'monopoly' of the Brahmanas by opening doors to 'all classes', it created an educated class comprising various castes, and set off occupational and social mobility, as contended by Misra.[61] Because the 'opportunities' provided by the British were both open and closed, these new economic and social processes were generated without a radical alteration of the relationship between caste and class, especially because the relationship between these and property was not altered by the colonial state. The social power of the Brahmanas was therefore considerable.

In order to understand the social and economic place of the Brahmanas as the dominant elite group in the second half of the nineteenth century we need to outline the relationship of the different components of the community to class, one as a professional middle class and the other as a group in property relations.[62] The two are of course interrelated and the caste contestations as well as the reassembling of power were contingent upon the interpenetrative nature of the two working together. However, because the Brahmanas, in their capacity as the professional middle class, shaped public opinion visibly during the second half of the nineteenth century in the Deccan it is useful to focus on them.

The economic profile of the Brahmanas in the Bombay presidency including the Poona Deccan indicates a close connection with land as rent receivers and cultivators (but never as agricultural labourers). According to the 1911 census, in the three major subdivisions among the Brahmanas, Chitpavans, Deshasthas and Gauda Saraswat Brahmanas, 20.5 per cent, 20.8 per cent and 21.0 per cent respectively were rent receivers.[63] In the Deccan area a substantial section of the inamdars were Brahmanas who held these inam rights due to their position as village accountants or priests or because they had been military feudatories under the Peshwas.

Not surprisingly, they dominated the Deccan Sardars' and the Inamdars' associations.[64] The 1911 census further indicates that 25.6 per cent, 23.1 per cent and 17.1 per cent of the Chitpavan, Deshastha and Gauda Saraswat Brahmanas were cultivators.[65] In the case of the Chitpavan Brahmanas whose history during the nineteenth century has been well documented, the traditional association with land did not diminish through entry into the professions but appears to have intensified. The Bombay Gazetteer reported that the professional classes had a marked fondness for land investment and that lawyers and government servants were among those buying lands.[66] Further, this fondness for land had undoubtedly increased under British rule. This buying spree would have added to the rentier aspect of Brahmana association with land.[67] The 1920s anti-landlord movement was synonymous with an anti-Brahmana movement in Ratnagiri, the home of the Chitpavan Brahmanas who held most of the lucrative tenures.[68] Most importantly, the Brahmanas' penetration into administration, especially revenue administration, enabled them to work the new land revenue laws to their advantage.

The Brahmanas also found profit in moneylending. The absence of an indigenous trading caste in Maharashtra had led to some of these activities being taken over by the Brahmanas along with Gujarati Vanis and Marwaris who had come in from outside. In the case of the Chitpavan Brahmanas 7.4 per cent were listed as dependent on trade in 1911. The Satara Gazetteer lists Brahmanas among the most important sections of the moneylenders but adds that few lived solely through moneylending.[69] Omvedt counts Brahmanas as a prominent element in the commercial bourgeoisie.[70] However, this prominence was confined to the Deccan — in Bombay it was Parsis, Gujaratis and Marwaris who dominated trade and moneylending.

It was in the professions that the Brahmanas were most visible in the nineteenth century. In the first decade of the twentieth century 13.6 per cent of the Chitpavans were dependent upon incomes from professions.[71] Significantly, opportunities provided by education and the use of English education were grasped by the less prosperous sections of the Brahmanas.[72] Thus, while the Brahmanas were not homogeneous as a community, stratification within the caste was being transformed through upward social mobility via entry into the professions. This, in turn, consolidated the position of the community as a whole in relation to the rest of society. The family histories of the Chitpavan Brahmanas indicate that as the century progressed the earlier antagonism of the community to the British gave way and by the end of the century government service was the favoured occupation.[73]

The material position of the Brahmanas in land, trade and government service was enhanced by their dominance in certain key professions such as law, teaching and particularly in journalism.[74] Brahmanas accounted for about two-thirds of all editors listed between 1901 and 1921. The newspapers edited by the Chitpavans accounted for half the circulation of Marathi newspapers throughout this period. As the print media expanded, Brahmanical control over communication was a crucial means of moulding public opinion, in advancing their point of view and marginalising the voices of other sections. Together with the spreading-out of Brahmanas, through their growing numbers in the professions which took them across a wide area, they gained enormous influence over the countryside. The power they wielded was different from the kind they had exercised during the Peshwai when they had constituted the state; now in the nineteenth century in a new situation, it was a great deal more indirect, but it remained impressive as they continued to dominate public life.

IV

The continuation of a broad *varna-varga* congruence (even as social relations in nineteenth century Maharashtra changed) was the basis for a powerful non-Brahmana movement, the earliest of its kind in colonial India. The attempts at altering the status of castes culminated in desperate moves by various non-Brahmana castes to be recorded as Kshatriya or Vaishya during the censuses of 1891 and 1901.[75] But the real edge to caste contestations came not with individual castes seeking upward mobility but with a coherent and cogent critique of the caste system itself. This too was not entirely unknown. What was new were the arguments in the critique and the emergence of a political movement against pre-colonial social relations, perceived as surviving fairly unaltered even under colonial rule, in the work of Phule and his associates in the second half of the nineteenth century. The two processes were linked to each other — sometimes castes were involved in both. There were ideas which were shared in the two processes and a mutual feeding into each other but there were some crucial distinctions that need to be noted. These differences made for vastly differing gender ideologies and political consequences. In Phule's[76] conceptualisation of caste a definitive turning-point in the history of caste contestations was reached. Phule's rejection of the process of sanskritisation, broke through the ritual idiom of caste movements which had worked within the parameters of Brahmanic ideology. This rejection was not confined to the religious sphere, as had largely been the case with earlier critiques of the caste system (such as those expressed by the Bhakti sants), but was more emphatically based on exploiting existing social and economic relations. Using a conflict approach to an analysis of society which pitted the Brahmanas, as upholders of an unequal social system, against those who were oppressed, humiliated and exploited, Phule represents a unique moment in the nineteenth century analysis of the caste system. He saw caste unambiguously as an unacceptable system for the lower castes; in this his analysis was in sharp contrast to the writing of upper-caste intellectuals whose analysis of caste, in the main, was marked by a false and forced consensus.

Phule focused in particular on caste as a cultural hegemonic system which he elaborated with considerable skill. Further, because he successfully broke the hold of Brahmanic ideology upon the explanatory structure of social relations he was unique too in his approach to gender. He alone, among nineteenth century social reformers, was able to stand outside Brahmanical patriarchy and, although gender was not a central factor in his analysis of caste and the reproduction of inequality, his rejection of the caste system and of Brahmanic Hinduism enabled him to adopt a more radical approach to gender inequality than any of his contemporaries.

It may be useful at this point to outline some of the elements that made Phule's innovative approach to caste and gender possible. Omvedt has pointed out that the new challenge from below represented by Phule and the non-Brahmana cultural movement in the nineteenth century was distinctive. That is, though themes from the past were used, unlike the leaders of the cultural revolts of earlier times Phule's handling of the past refused to be absorbed into the usual processes of Brahmanic Hinduism. The context of colonialism, both in terms of its impact on social and economic relations, the emergence of new social and professional classes, and its relation to caste as well as in terms of new ideologies, was the determining factor in the critique of caste in nineteenth century Maharashtra.[77]

The repertoire of arguments made available at this time through missionary polemics, against the inequalities of Hinduism, was probably an important input into Phule's formulation of caste. A more significant input came from the criticism of religion in the French enlightenment and the political thought of France and England in the post-revolution decades. Thomas Paine, in particular, with his emphasis on the natural rights of individuals and the need to subject traditional institutions to free discussion and criticism, contributed to developing the critical arguments of Phule and his colleagues. The ideas of Paine were useful in staving off the 'attractions' of Christianity. Following the arguments in the 'Age of Reason' Phule and his friends rejected conversion to Christianity advocated by some of his contemporaries.[78]

Phule's critique of Hindu society, like that of some other Hindu radicals, cannot thus be directly attributed to Christian missionaries or to European radicals but to a simultaneous reinforcement and counterbalancing of one with the other. Phule drew from many sources but did so selectively and this enabled him to resist seeking religious tradition or authority of any kind. However, the most critical input into the critique was derived from Phule's personal experience (and his awareness of others) of the routine humiliation heaped by the Brahmanas upon the lower castes. This is more than evident from his biography and his writings. These are replete with examples of such experiences which form the basis of his critique of the material and ideological power of the Brahmanas over the lower castes.[79]

The reconceptualisation of the caste system from a lower-caste point of view, shifting the attention from social mobility within the caste system to a rejection of the system itself was clearly the work of Phule and his colleagues in the non-Brahmana movement. The earliest published work in Marathi written from this standpoint was Tukaram Tatya Padaval's *Jatibhed Vivekasar (A Critique of Caste Divisions)* (1861). Padaval was a Bhandari, a caste of toddy-tappers in Maharashtra. Phule was closely connected with the publication of this work which argues the arbitrary nature of the caste system. The whole edifice of caste and notions of caste purity are regarded as based on a delusion, consciously promoted by the Brahmanas, and the misplaced caste pride of other high-ranking groups which are thus complicitous in the Brahmanic ideology.[80]

The most interesting aspect of Padaval's argument is his account of the attempts at upward mobility by a range of social groups using the Kshatriya and Vaishya models of sanskritisation and the strong Brahmana resistance to these attempts. Padaval notes further that the decline or rise in status was directly related to the fluctuations in the political power of various elite groups such as the Marathas. He also points to the pragmatism of the Brahmanas on the grant of status to an aspirant caste group; in emulation of Shivaji, they granted Kshatriya status to the Marathas who had been regarded as Shudras earlier.[81] The awareness of the long-standing disputes over the issue of caste status reflected in Padaval's work suggests that these caste tensions fed directly into the non-Brahmana movement.

Arguments such as Padaval's were carried forward in Phule's view of caste; he strongly distanced himself from the attempts of the Kunbis to identify with Kshatriyas by wearing the sacred thread and as Marathas by seeking the right to Vedokta rituals.[82] He argued that such moves obscured the realisation that all social divisions were part of the 'same engine of social oppression'.[83] He was particularly critical of the double moves such strategies for higher status entailed since identifying with the higher castes (and accepting the premises of the caste system) implied a distancing from other castes regarded as low in the hierarchy. Phule regarded these moves as falling into the trap of Brahmanism and as a result ensuring the continuation of the division of the oppressed among themselves[84]

It was Phule's attempt to make the lower castes conscious of the injustice and inequality of the caste system as a whole. For this reason, unlike other leaders of the non-Brahmana movement who used the argument of Kshatriya identity and Maratha status as a conscious strategy in recruiting support among rural audiences, Phule was extremely cautious in his handling of the term 'Maratha', and questions of the 'true' identity of the Marathas. Instead, he posited a basic contradiction between the Brahmana elite and the mass of cultivating and labouring castes, and in this way he pointed to the existence of a 'fused community of oppressed' which transcended the fragmentation of the labouring groups into cultivating Kunbis and untouchable Mangs and Mahars. This community, the *Bahujan Samaj*, was held together also by their recognition and rejection of both the social categories of conventional Hindu beliefs and the religious authority of its guardians.[85]

Phule's understanding of caste, as inextricably linked with Brahmanic Hinduism, underpins the entire body of his work from the 1850s through to the 1880s. He skilfully drew up an analysis locating the nature and sources of Brahmanic power especially with regard to the Brahmanas' monopoly over knowledge and the control this gave them over the rest of society. The monopoly of knowledge systems, available only to the Brahmanas in traditional society, was being extended, in Phule's understanding, through the appropriation of educational facilities even in colonial times. The power these prerogatives had given the Brahmanas in the administration both in the Peshwai and in the colonial state was also crucial in their continued hold over society. And although he did not devote the same energy to the material contradiction between Brahmanas and non-Brahmanas, cultivators and labour (between those who labour and those who do not), between the Bhatji-Shetji and the Bahujan Samaj, Phule is one of the first to outline the link between ideological power and its material basis.

Phule's criticism is sharp since he regards the social and political values of Brahmanism as fundamentally distorted. He and other radical non-Brahmanas of his time perceived the sacred texts of Hinduism, which legitimised the social practices of Hindu society, as the critical source of control in the hands of the Brahmanas.[86] Throughout his work entitled *Gulamgiri* Phule stressed that the practices of Hindu religion were indefensible because they violated human rights. Further, he attempted to conceptualise a case of natural human rights for all societies and perceived a basic affinity between all oppressed people of the world, whether as blacks in America or low castes in India.[87]

A notable dimension of his attack on the social practices of Hinduism was his conviction that the Hindu religion was specifically the world-view of the Brahmanas. This world-view served their interests not only in matters of religious authority but also in establishing their secular power and cultural hegemony over others. Further, as the lower castes lived and worked within the political, social and ritual relationships laid down by the Brahmanas, they unwittingly succumbed to the interests of the Brahmanas themselves. In one of his early works, the *Traitya Ratna* or *Third Eye*, Phule put forth the view that the Hindu religion represented both an ideological imposition upon the lower castes and, through the insistence on numerous rituals and ceremonies advantageous to the Brahmanas, a cause of their material impoverishment.[88] Phule's distinctive analysis of caste marked him off from the understanding of even the most radical of the liberal Brahmana social reformers. He was furthest from their understanding in the explanation he provided for the origins of the caste system and in his generally unorthodox handling of the past.

Phule's exploration of the past to explain an inegalitarian present in which the lower-caste toiling masses were subjected to the power of the non-labouring upper castes, particularly the Brahmanas, was focused upon two moments: the first dealt with the origins of a system of inequality in the ancient past and the second with the more recent history of Maharashtra. Phule's handling of these moments was so unorthodox that it was violently contested by orthodox Brahmana writers, accustomed as they were to a monopoly of writing history.[89]

For Phule, unlike contemporary reformers who traced the first colonial encounter in India to the British (and sometimes to the Muslims), the most significant colonial encounter in Indian history was the one that occurred in the pre-historic past — that of the Aryans. He thus turned the colonial question around by depicting the contemporary Brahmanas as the real 'aliens' who had conquered the indigenous peoples and subordinated them by usurping the rightful power and property of the original inhabitants.[90] The conquerors then imposed their religion as an instrument of social control in order to keep the subordinated peoples in a state of permanent subjugation. The invention of the caste system was thus a critical instrument by which the Brahmanas concealed their original act of usurpation and ensured the perpetuation of their own privileged position.[91]

An aspect of Phule's analysis of Aryan conquest and of the origin of the caste system that marked him off from other nineteenth century reformers coming to terms with their troubled past, needs to be stressed: his rejection of the term Aryan as 'noble', as representing a superior period, a veritable golden age. The idea of a golden age was a pervasive viewpoint shared by conservative scholars and reformers alike outlined in the next section.[92] For Phule, however, the 'golden age' of the upper-caste nineteenth

century writer was instead the moment of great betrayal since it was
the occasion for the usurpation of the lands of the original
inhabitants. The real golden age had been the pre-Aryan realm of
the Kshatriyas under the benign rule of King Bali.[93] The figure of
Bali was identified in nineteenth century popular culture through
proverbs and other symbols with the tillers of soil as also with a
'golden age', a happier idyllic society now lost. Using the radical
one of the two interpretations of Bali in which some celebrated his
defeat at the hands of Vamana and Brahmanas, and others,
especially Shudras, prayed for the restoration of his kingdom
because he had taken their part against Vamana and the Brahmanas,
Phule 'carefully organised an account of the hidden history of low
castes for them'.[94]

Shivaji, too, was a key figure in the contest over the past. Phule
centre-staged him before Brahmana writers did with his publication
of a *pavada*, a ballad-like form that traditionally described the
exploits of heroes. Using an existing tradition, understood in a
language familiar to rural audiences, Phule's pavada presented
Shivaji as the leader of Maharashtra's lower castes whose
achievements were attributable to the strength of his Shudra and
ati-Shudra armies rather than to the intellectual skills of his
Brahmana ministers. Rejecting the attempts to project Ramdas as
the actual hero of Shivaji's exploits, and as *go-Brahmana pratipalak*,
he warned the lower castes about the attempts of Brahmana teachers
to appropriate Shivaji to their cause, as freeing the country from
the foreign unbelievers, and filling them with false religious
patriotism.[95]

Phule linked the figure of Shivaji with that of King Bali whose
mantle Shivaji inherited; thus ancient history was connected to a
more recent one with both Bali and Shivaji struggling to protect
the land from foreign conquest and Shivaji was assimilated to a
much older tradition of non-Brahmana rulers as protectors of the
common man. The Shivaji ballad was addressed to a humble
audience in order to be of use to Kunbis, Malis, Mangs and Mahars
as the ruined Kshatriyas of yore. Phule's version appropriated the
central episode in Maharashtra's recent history to the history of
those who laboured and those who protected the land. As
O'Hanlon argues, through this alternative to Brahmana-centred
interpretations, Phule hoped to provide an ideology for the lower
castes with its own tradition of social leadership.[96]

In reinterpreting the past, Phule was deeply conscious of the need to counter the Brahmanical version of the past as a means to prise the control of knowledge from the hands of the Brahmanas who had been responsible for erasing the history of their usurpation and subjection, and for legitimising the iniquitous social system. This desire to manipulate knowledge was behind the Brahmanas' attempt to appropriate Shivaji's real project to their own ends. For these reasons the contest over history was fierce as history was 'knowledge' about why contemporary society was organised the way it was.[97]

Phule's version of history was, not unexpectedly, received with outrage by the predominantly Brahmana press. The *Vividhadnyan Vistaar*, for example, reacted with a mixture of hysteria, scorn and contempt for the 'unknown' author who dared to arrogate to himself the skill of a historian. The reviewer of the Shivaji ballad spoke on behalf of all 'Hindus' and stated that to accept it would bring sheer disgrace upon the courageous Shivaji and upon all Hindu people. Another review of *Gulamgiri* in the same paper was even more eloquently patronising as it suggested that Phule should consult the Royal Asiatic Society about his derivation of the terms Mahar and Kshatriya.[98] The formation of an accepted canon in history loaded the weights unevenly for an alternative to the canonised version, especially if it came from the likes of Phule. Many years later Ambedkar recalled the main features of the contested history of Maharashtra and pointed out that the work of non-Brahmana writers would be met with a conspiracy of silence, either by taking no notice of it or by dubbing it useless.[99]

Phule's interpretation of the past was one aspect of the attempt to break the cycle of inequality, Brahmanic ideology and the reproduction of the structure. A more lasting and vital way to do so, in Phule's opinion, was through education since it was the Brahmana's claim to knowledge that enabled him to wield power over others in traditional society. Phule believed that the presence of the British made it possible to overturn the lower-caste exclusion from learning. He was aware of the need to open up educational avenues for them. The urgency to grasp the limited opportunities lay in the realisation that the Brahmanical monopoly over education had continued even during British rule which, in turn, had led to the rise of an administrative elite which had reconsolidated

Brahmana power. This was an unmitigated disaster for the lower castes and implied the defusing of their revolutionary potential.

Given the centrality of education in Phule's attempt to empower the lower castes and to end the Brahmanic monopoly of learning it is not surprising that his first piece of writing, *Traitya Ratna*, the *Third Eye*, was on education; he hoped that it would enable the lower castes to 'see' by providing them with new modes of social perception. Phule was most critical of British policies on education because these had enabled the Brahmanas to retain their monopoly of this vital resource.[100]

The unfulfilled aspirations of the Kunbis and the castes below them became a central feature of the non-Brahmana contestation of the social processes in nineteenth century Maharashtra. Appearing before the Hunter Commission in 1884, Phule, who was spearheading the non-Brahmana movement, argued that it was the ignorance of the British government that had led it to support policies which strengthened the hold of the Brahmanas over the rest of society. Access to civil service and the liberal professions such as law, the two avenues to progress open to 'all' people, was through schools and colleges set up by the British under the diffusionist theory of education which had actually never worked as 'diffusion' because of the selfishness of the Brahmanas. According to Phule, instead of disseminating the education they had acquired among the lower castes the Brahmanas had exploited their positions to *monopolise* the civil service and liberal professions. Phule demanded the introduction of compulsory primary education in the villages and special incentives to lower castes in the institutions of higher learning.[101] He further argued that since the bulk of its revenues were from a tax paid by the peasants, the government was morally obliged to focus its attention upon the Kunbis rather than upon the Brahmanas who only constituted a 'minority'.

Phule's critique was supported by an analysis of the situation as it obtained not only in Maharashtra but also elsewhere, where the Brahmanas were defending their monopoly over education and ensuring the exclusion of the lowest castes such as Mangs and Mahars from it.[102] Where, and when, schools were thrown open to the lower castes the higher castes fiercely 'defended' their privileges. The 1901 census reported that in South India, high castes would not allow children of low-caste origin to sit within the same building. When efforts at equality were enforced, schools remained closed for years and there were frequent disturbances of the peace. The contests over educational privileges even led to the high castes burning the crops of the lower castes who dared to send their children to school.[103] Given these conflicts, it is not surprising that even as late as 1931 only 2.9 per cent of the Mahars, 2 per cent of the Chambhars, and 1.6 per cent of the Mangs were literate.[104]

Clearly these contests and social tensions were not confined to educational opportunities, or the violation of spaces which the upper castes regarded as their prerogative, but to the eventual openings that education implied in terms of positions in the administration. Faced with an insensitive government and a hostile society Phule spent a great deal of energy in the early years of his public career in setting up schools for Mangs, Mahars and women, becoming the leading crusader for democratisation of opportunities in Poona.

Phule's belief in the power of education to liberate the subordinated and introduce them to new modes of social perception could have been the starting-point for his interest in reforms for women. He was only 21 when he opened his first school in Poona in 1848: significantly, it was for low-caste untouchable girls.[105] By initiating his own educational institutions with a school for girls, Phule was making a statement on the lowest among the low in Hindu society: the low-caste woman. In setting it up in Poona, still the centre of conservative Brahmanas, Phule was also throwing an open challenge to them and their views (on banning learning for the low castes and women) which had restricted knowledge and made it an instrument of power.

The importance of the project of education was evident in the arguments Phule and his colleagues advanced for it: the failure to educate women was the prime cause of the impoverishment of contemporary Indian society.[106] The link between the decline of education and the decline of a people was not unique to Phule but was a common argument of nineteenth century reformers. What was distinctive however was the rationale for female education. While for the upper caste or middle class social reformer it was to provide fitting 'helpmeets' for the new class of men, for Phule education was the third eye — the instrument of a new mode of understanding social relations. Further, this was as essential for low-caste women as it was for low-caste men. Phule pinpointed this in a speech while castigating traditional attitudes:

In their opinion, women should forever be kept in obedience, should not be given any knowledge, should not be well educated, should not know about religion (and) should not mix with men...[107]

The potential explosiveness of education for low-caste girls was evident in an essay written by Muktabai, a fourteen-year-old Mang girl in Phule's school. She had been a student of this school for about three years when she wrote the essay, 'About the Griefs of the Mangs and the Mahars' ('*Mang Maharachya Dukha Visaiyi*'),[108] describing the humiliating conditions under which the Mangs and Mahars existed. It is clear from Muktabai's essay that it is mainly her experience as a Mang, rather than as a Mang girl in particular, that informs her understanding of dominance and power. What is also evident is that Muktabai represents the best example of Phule's belief that a special vision, a *traitya ratna*, would be the outcome of education and would have the means to strip the falsity of Brahmanic ideology. It enabled her to proclaim, 'Let that religion where only one person is privileged and the rest deprived, perish from the earth, and let it never enter our minds to be proud of such a religion.'[109]

Muktabai's brief essay dwells on themes which, in varying degrees, inform nineteenth century non-Brahmana writing: the first is an acute awareness of the Peshwai as a period of extraordinarily arbitrary power for the Brahmanas and thus an unmediated time of oppression for the low castes. Their hold over the administration, especially the revenue administration (a gift of the Peshwai), had given the Brahmanas a unique control over the labouring peoples. Second, the prohibition of knowledge for the low castes was the work of the Brahmanas. Third, she dwells on the theme of dispossessing the ancestors of the lower castes of their lands and the distribution of material assets and power between the Brahmanas and others — the Brahmanas as revenue officers and the other castes in degrading occupations such as the barber 'who has to go about shaving the heads of widows'. Fourth, Muktabai is extremely insightful about the way Brahmanic ideology works to create a complex structure of hierarchy where the low castes themselves are graded into less polluting and more polluting, with the former having power over the latter. The fragmentation of the underprivileged was an important theme of Phule's writing but Muktabai's inclusion of relations between Mangs and Mahars in her short essay indicates an awareness of the multiple processes involved in the humiliation of untouchables — processes which had survived despite the formal cessation of Brahmanic power with the end of the Peshwai.

It is only when Muktabai describes the inhuman consequences of untouchability that her insights into the experiences of low-caste women are evident. Beginning with an attack on the psychological and material dimensions of untouchability and the grief and poverty it entails, Muktabai addresses the Brahmanas:

> Oh learned pandits wind up the selfish
> prattle of your hollow wisdom and
> listen to what I have to say, when
> Our women give birth to babies they
> do not even have a roof over their
> heads. How they suffer rain and
> cold! Try to think about it from your
> own experience. Suppose the women
> suffered from puerperal disease,
> from where could they have found
> money for the doctor or medicine?
> Was there ever any doctor among
> you who was human enough to treat
> people free of charge?[110]

Another vulnerable group like low-caste women were low-caste children whose humiliation began in early childhood itself:

> The Mang and Mahar children never
> lodge a complaint even if the Brahmin
> children throw stones at them
> and injure them seriously....[111]

Muktabai's essay ends abruptly, 'Oh God! What agony is this! I will burst into tears if I write more about this injustice.'[112] Even so, the anguished Muktabai understood and rejected the existing social order and provided a scathing critique of Brahmanical power in nineteenth century Maharashtra. The newly acquired skills of literacy for this untouchable woman had made it possible to question, in print, the most 'sacred' person in the social hierarchy, and reject unequivocally his 'knowledge' and his authority.

The theme of knowledge, its closely-guarded nature in caste society, and its potential for reversing the low status of the lower castes is evident also in Savitribai Phule's letter to her husband Jyotiba, written in 1856, in which she describes a conversation with her brother. Away at her parental home to recover from an illness, Savitribai spiritedly defended her activities in Poona where she taught Mangs and Mahars. 'The lack of learning is nothing but gross bestiality', she told her brother. 'It was the possession of knowledge that gave the Brahmanas their superior status. Learning has a great value. One who masters it loses his lowly status and achieves the higher one',[113] she added, rebutting her brother's plea that she and Jyotiba should follow the customs of their caste and the dictates of the Brahmanas rather than take on different social roles from those allotted to them.

Muktabai's and Savitribai's writings represent one aspect of Phule's reformist intervention in relation to women: the focus on the education of low-caste women and their empowerment through it; the other arena of intervention was the humiliation imposed upon Brahmana widows.[114] While Phule did not dwell noticeably upon upper-caste women within their own families, the widow's place at the receiving end of Brahmanical patriarchy (which was beginning to feature in reformist discourse as we shall see in the next section) became the centre of some characteristically dramatic moves by him. The structural relationship between the low castes, subjected to the power of the Brahmanas, and the Brahmana widow, subjected to the power of Brahmanical patriarchy, was implicitly recognised in Phule's reformist work. The material and sexual consequences of enforced widowhood were responsible for a large number of such young women becoming pregnant and having to hide their condition for fear of excommunication. Phule and Savitribai provided them support by setting up an orphanage for the children born to Brahmana widows. In his forthright manner Phule published handbills proclaiming the setting-up of an orphanage to prevent infanticide, thus picking on one of the most vulnerable spots in Brahmanism, the linchpin of upper-caste gender codes, enforced widowhood and its consequences. With this, Phule forced into the open a problem that the Brahmanas would rather have dealt with in the customary manner — by pretending that it did not exist — or through punitive measures such as ghatasphot, a symbolic death ritual for those who were outcasted, leading to the complete social boycott of the widow. More routinely, the humiliation of widows was compounded by enforced tonsure. Phule is popularly credited with spearheading a barbers' strike where they refused to perform the customary tonsure of widows.[115]

While Phule devoted considerable attention to enforced widowhood among upper-caste women he was conscious of the differences among women based on caste and their place in the system of production. In the *Shetkaryaca Asud*, for example, he described the hardships experienced by labouring women when he contrasted this with the relative ease of the lives of Brahmana women.[116] Brahmana women laboured at home, and were subject only to the power of Brahmana men; women of the lower castes laboured at home as well as in the fields. They were subject to a double control, from upper-caste men and from men of their families. In the last decade of his life Phule's understanding of women's oppression changed somewhat: he argued that they were conditioned by a structure of relations that we might recognise as akin to patriarchy. This understanding was expressed when Phule publicly defended both Ramabai and Tarabai Shinde; in Ramabai's case he mounted an attack on Brahmanism, in which much of the high-caste woman's oppression was located. In Tarabai's case he went further, as he was critical of his own compatriots in the non-Brahmana movement with regard to recognising women's subordination.

Phule's defence of Tarabai is most significant. As a non-Brahmana woman she had taken a public stand in her work, *Stri-Purusha Tulana* (1882),[117] against women's subordination and had shocked some of the non-Brahmana activists because of her indictment of forms of patriarchy among Kunbis and other non-Brahmana castes. Phule's intervention was thus extremely important. It was a recognition that the non-Brahmana movement had neglected the need for an analysis of gender. Phule's reaction to Bhalekar's criticism of Tarabai was as fierce as his critique of Brahmanism.[118] The traditional Indian family system was based on a double standard of morality. There was an urgent need to break down the authoritarian structure within the family and build a new and egalitarian relationship between men and women, leading to social equality.

Some of these heightened concerns are evident in Phule's last work, *Sarvajanik Satyadharma*, where he replaced the term *manus* (man) with *sarva ekander stri purush* (every woman and man) and in the marriage promises of the Satyashodhak weddings where the groom admitted that he could never experience women's suffering, but vowed to give his bride full rights.[119]

Phule's vision of a radical democratic society was his answer to traditional social relations where the suppression of the lower castes existed along with that of women. Finally, even though his concern for gender equality did not receive the same focused attention as caste, in Phule's conceptualisation the future of democratic society was to be based on a new set of relations linking equality, labour and education together for both exploited men of the lower castes and oppressed women of all castes.

V

From the preceding discussion, it is evident that the history of the nineteenth century in this region is the history of the challenge to Brahmana dominance, the reconstruction of this dominance and the tensions generated by this challenge. At this point it is important also to take account of the development of differences among Brahmanas. Although capable of acting unitedly in support of their material position the Bramanas were not homogeneous. This is evident from their response to the social changes engendered by the documented history of the second half of the nineteenth century in the Maharashtra Deccan. Under considerable stress throughout the century, the community was split into an articulate minority advocating certain limited social and cultural changes, and an orthodox majority acting militantly in defence of an unaltered tradition. This internal stress within the community lasted in different forms throughout the century and into the next, forming 'class' segments who shared a similar material relationship but responding in contradictory ways to social and cultural changes then under way. Among the two main class segments, the one pushing the reform agenda attempted to become culturally and politically the dominant force in society;[120] equally the larger and more strident segment which resisted reform also resisted the attempt of the former to shape the identity of the class as a whole. It is striking that, throughout, gender played a crucial role in the internal struggles within the community and in other communities similarly facing internal stresses. These struggles coalesced around the larger cross-community upper caste elites of Bombay and the Deccan forming the region's 'middle class' which was itself split into two major segments. Within the larger body of the Brahmanas a section with access to English education and with membership of the emerging professional class, sometimes characterised as the 'new Brahmanas',[121] represented the winds of change in the community; they were the first evidence of the cultural and social crisis being experienced by the community. Their first move was to seek a shift in the deployment of the dakshina funds from Sanskrit learning to useful, modern western studies.[122] The group advocating this position came to be called Young Poona. The new Brahmanas spearheaded a fairly modest critique of Hinduism in the 1830s, 40s and 50s, very different from the full-scale attack mounted by Phule during the 1870s and 80s. Representative of this trend were Gopal Hari Deshmukh, Bal Shastri Jambhekar and Krishna Shastri Chiplunkar.

Bal Shastri Jambhekar was among the first Hindus to generate a debate through the press on the momentous social changes by setting up, in 1832, the Anglo-Marathi newspaper *Darpan* in Bombay. The failures of Hindu society to meet the challenges thrown up by British rule was one of the central themes of the debates in the newspapers, where the need for an expansion of India's intellectual horizons and for a revaluation of her traditional beliefs was advocated.[123] Gopal Hari Deshmukh, who wrote under the assumed name of Lokahitawadi, used the *Prabhakar* to make it the main mouthpiece of early reformist opinion in western India. The newpaper mounted a critique of ascriptive values in Hinduism, the privileges of Brahmanas, and the devaluation of women and the lower castes. There have been attempts to characterise these ideas as derivative of Christian missionary propaganda[124] but it is important to note that what the reformers were doing was to detach certain ideas from specific Christian beliefs and apply these to the issues they took up.[125] As we shall see, they were defenders of a reformed Hinduism and were strongly opposed to conversions.

One of the lesser known but significant representatives of its reformist attitude was Krishna Shastri Chiplunkar, son of a temple priest who had been a student in the Sanskrit college. Appointed a professor of Marathi at the same college, he risked outcasting along with two other pandits by supporting the entry of non-Brahmana students being suggested by the government although almost no non-Brahmana was interested in Sanskrit studies.[126] It was Krishna

Shastri Chiplunkar's view that old tradition could only preserve itself by adapting to changes in a new environment.

The criticism of Brahmanical ritual practices featuring in the early debates of the reformers and the challenge to the orthodoxy's purity principles culminated in a brief and disastrous early experiment of setting up something like a secret society. Hindu reformers in Bombay, led by students and ex-students of the Elphinstone College (roughly at this time the institution was headed by a rationalist English principal who was the bane of Christian missionaries), set up the Paramahansa Mandali. The Mandali believed that caste divisions, idol-worship and enforced widowhood were wrong. This organisation broke caste taboos by eating food prepared by low-castes Hindus. Knowing how 'provocative' this act would be, the Mandali decided to keep its activities secret till its membership grew to 500 when it would be strong enough to withstand a counter-attack. The attempt at secrecy was unsuccessful; reports of its rumoured activities circulated in the press and in 1860 when the secret membership list was made public in the press the group was abruptly terminated. The collapsed Mandali members made a climbdown and acknowledged that they had been as 'excessive' as the orthodoxy they had sought to challenge.[127]

The ignominious end of the Mandali was a lesson to the 'radicals' among the Brahmanas since its experience had not been particularly cushioned, even in cosmopolitan Bombay where the Brahmanas were important but did not dominate, as they did in Poona. In Poona the orthodoxy was much more firmly entrenched. Poona was also more homogeneous and attacks on the caste system never really took off. Nevertheless, for a brief period the liberals among the Brahmanas and early non-Brahmana reformers managed to work together. This collaboration was focused essentially around education, with a number of schools being set up in Poona. During the latter years of the 1850s the collaboration began to collapse as Phule rejected the paternalism of the Brahmanas, and the latter began to turn more inward with an increasing anxiety about the threat to their identity from Christian missionary activities.[128]

The complex location of the 'liberal' reformist Brahmanas wedged between orthodox Brahmanas, Christian missionaries and their own unformed ideas was evident in the case of Narayan Seshadri, a Deshashta Brahmana who converted to Christianity in

1843. Apart from anger at the conversion, controversy surrounded the issue of Narayan Seshadri's 12-year-old younger brother who had stayed with Narayan at a mission in Bombay and had therefore been polluted. The question of his pollution triggered off a debate — while the reformers argued that the boy could be readmitted to caste following the prescribed rituals, the orthodox section in the city comprising Brahmanas, their priests and the sanskritising Prabhus under their Shetia leader argued that this was unacceptable. While the matter was sent up to the Shankaracharya for arbitration, the reformist Brahmanas, Jambhekar and his supporters, had to perform purificatory rites before being accepted back into caste. Significantly, controversies such as this and those relating to widow remarriage tended to reinforce caste identities on both sides.[129] The potential threat to caste and religious identity tightened social and religious bonds and reaffirmed the encapsulated identities of castes against the integrative urban pressures, even in Bombay.

The early contradictions among the Brahmanas over issues of culture and caste norms in the face of social challenges between those who advocated reform and those who resisted it (and those who were confused) coalesced in the issue of the widow remarriage campaign of the 1860s.[130] Concern over the problems of enforced widowhood in the case of very young girls went back to the Peshwai, as the reformer C.Y. Chintamani noted in his reconstruction of the issue at the turn of the nineteenth century. The cause remained alive in a desultory way through its championing by individuals such as Subbaji Bapu Sastri, a Telugu Brahmana who published a pamphlet in 1837, and an anonymous 'learned Brahmin of Nagpore'. The latter was encouraged by the former to stand forth as a 'champion of the females of his caste' and to point out the evils and degradation caused by the unnatural law prohibiting remarriage of widows.[131] Two marriages of widows took place in 1853 and 1854 respectively.[132] This was before Vidyasagar championed the Widow Remarriage Bill in 1856 and published the famous pamphlets that provided textual sanction for remarriage which sparked off a stormy debate as the issue was taken up seriously by the educated in western India.

VI

Throughout the nineteenth century the low status of women as exemplified by the plight of the child widow, condemned to a life of enforced celibacy, became the subject of a highly visible and widespread discussion. In the first half of the century attention was concentrated on the custom of sati, but with its abolition in 1829 attention shifted to coerced celibacy of upper-caste Hindu widows, for while Act XXVII of 1829 saved women from a 'compulsive death, it did not grant them the right to a fruitful entrance into life'.[133] In Bengal the issue generated a major debate, conducted through the print medium, which made for a veritable 'battle of the books'. Learned scholars in the fray were accompanied by more popular writers of essays and derisive verse who responded to arguments put forward by Vidyasagar to support the case for Shastric approval for widow remarriage. The passage of the enabling law in 1856 making it 'possible' for widows to marry did not, by any means, exhaust the debate which carried on through the rest of the nineteenth and early twentieth centuries in different centres. This debate and the various stages in the movement for widow marriage have been fairly well documented, including a detailed analysis of the debate in western India.[134] For our purposes what is important is to dwell on the issues that were highlighted regarding widowhood and the manner in which some of the issues tied in with the earlier conceptualisation of widowhood even as they contested enforced celibacy for widows.[135]

An early and rare outlining of the relationship between the miseries of widowhood and the propertylessness of the widow had been made by Rammohan Roy in his tract on sati. Roy pointed out that the propertyless widow had three options — to slave for others, walk the paths of unrighteousness, or die on the funeral pyre of her husband.[136] With the abolition of sati the discussion on widowhood quite naturally moved on to other aspects, but what is interesting to note is how limited this discussion was and how little it focused on the material dimensions of widowhood among the high castes. What is striking also is to see the difference in the writing and analysis of the men, reformers and traditionalists — even men in authority in the colonial government — on the one hand, and on the other, the women, especially the widows themselves, when they began to write in the late nineteenth century. While the men tended to outline the dangerous consequences of enforced widowhood, dealing at length with the repressed sexuality of widows and its disastrous effects upon society, the women showed considerable concern for the existential conditions of widowhood. Enforced celibacy, the distortion caused by it as perceived by the reformers, or the dead husband's continued claim over his wife's sexuality as supported by the traditionalists, remained the central focus of men's concerns. These concerns were extensions of the issue of the sexual and social death of the widow in the Brahmanic conceptualisation of widowhood, reflected in its symbolic structure. Rituals included the tonsure of the widow, which may be read as a renunciation of sexuality or even as castration, marking the cessation of her sexual existence.[137] The undertone to the widow remarriage movement was the anxiety about the unchannelled sexuality of the widow. This went along with the humanitarian rhetoric of the need to alleviate the miseries of the child widow.

The management of female sexuality after the death of the husband had figured centrally in the discussion on sati and it extended into the debate on widow remarriage, but, significantly, was used by opposing groups; in the first case it was used by conservatives to support sati and in the second by reformers to support widow remarriage. The conservatives had quoted the Shastric position on the widow's sexuality using the commentary of Hareet and argued, 'As long as a woman shall not burn herself after her husband's death she will be subject to transmigration in the female form (and) she will fall into vice. This way the husband can rest assured that she will remain virtuous'.[138]

In overt contrast to this position and as early as 1841 (well before the formal move to legislate for widow remarriage) an anonymous 'learned Brahmana of Nagpore' in outlining the case for the second marriages of 'infant' widows, used a mixture of arguments, but began by turning the Shastric position on its head by evoking a different Shastric norm for women. He argued that the prohibition against the second marriage of widows was highly unwise because first, it disappointed the 'palpable purpose of the Creator' in having sent women into the world, i.e., to bear children; second, because inevitably it led to great moral depravity and vice on the part of the widow; third, because it inevitably caused a 'frightful amount of infanticide and abortion'; fourth, because the maintenance of these widows in an 'honourable and virtuous course of life' caused a 'ceaseless' though 'fruitless' anxiety to their parents and parents-in-law; and fifth, because these widows inevitably 'rendered corrupt and vicious themselves by the hard and unnatural laws operating against them cannot be prevented from corrupting and destroying the honour and virtue of all other women with whom they associate'.[139] For all these reasons the second marriage of widows was not just advisable but necessary.

The petition to legalise widow marriage submitted to the government from a section of the people in Bengal was likewise motivated by concerns about the problem of sustaining the virtue of the widow. Sympathetic to the widow's position because of the 'unnatural quality of celibacy', it warned of its harmful consequences to society. Enforced celibacy, 'cruel and unnatural in itself', was further 'highly prejudicial to the interests of morality' and was otherwise 'fraught with the most mischievous consequences to society' according to the petitioners.[140] In arguing for widow marriage reformers also often pointed to the relationship between widowhood and prostitution. The reformers suggested that as the young child widows grew up into full womanhood they created a social problem of some magnitude because of their propensity to fall into 'illicit relationships' and thereafter into prostitution.[141]

Such views were evident also in the government position. In moving the bill to present the rationale for widow marriage, J.P. Grant laid the greatest stress upon the immorality which enforced widowhood produced upon society. This was likely to evoke a more positive response from all quarters than his sympathy for the horrors of *brahmacharya* upon little girls which J.P. Grant stated that he was committed to changing.[142]

The anxiety about the widows' propensity to fall prey to their passions and their inability to live up to the enforced *brahmacharya* was linked to a widespread belief among nineteenth century men that female nature could subvert even the most stringent surveillance. A nineteenth century writer cautioned that, however a mother may guard the virtue of her widowed daughter and however forcibly she may inculcate the purity of life and manners it proves but a feeble barrier against the irresistible impulse of passion. Further, the 'repressed' widow was an immense attraction to male relatives.[143] The excessive sexuality of women, a view deeply entrenched in the Brahmanical texts and didactic literature,[144] was apparent in all the discussions about women in the nineteenth century but was most intensively seen in the age-of-consent debate.

It indicates the pervasive continuation of male constructs of female sexuality into the nineteenth century debates on gender issues.

It is interesting to note that while Indian men seemed to worry only about the sensuality 'natural' to women, and the consequences of the nubile widow's repressed sexuality upon society, the British, by and large, perceived the problem of widowhood in the context of the lack of moral control of both men and women, i.e., of Indian society as a whole. Widow remarriage was one solution advocated by them to prevent the widows from getting into trouble in a generally depraved situation. For the British the lax morals of the community would inevitably lead to further lapses on the part of the widows. Justifying the act to legalise widow marriage, a report filed by the India based correspondent of *The Times*, London, stated, 'In this country, between the tropical climate and a code of manners lax beyond anything Europe can conceive such widows are likely to go wrong. Hindu fathers are well aware of the dangers and heavy dowries will be given to overcome lingering prejudices and secure the family permanently from disgrace'.[145]

The anxiety displayed by the British for the moral lapses consequent to the enforced celibacy among upper-caste widows was enhanced by their concern for the effects that such depravity would have upon other women within the home, and through their corruption, the ensuing degeneration of all Hindus. As the education and training of children was consigned to the care of mothers, sisters and aunts, themselves corrupted through contact with widows, the depravity of all Hindus was inevitable according to this view. Tracts were in circulation, sometimes penned by practitioners of medicine, who as specialists had an 'insider's' knowledge of what went on within the cloisters of high-caste Hindu homes. One such account published in 1841 documented a number of cases of liaisons involving widows all taking place within the family. Abortions were common but, if the matter became public, taking recourse to drastic solutions like murdering the widow to uphold family honour was frequent. Those who were involved in the maintenance of family honour were usually the fathers and brothers of the late husbands of the widows.[146]

That there was social sanction for the killing of 'fallen' widows was also evident in accounts like that of Wilkinson, a medical practitioner located in central India. Wilkinson was horrified at such drastic examples of the continued control by the heads of households on female kin in relation to sexual behaviour.[147] Despite the questionable motives of tracts like the one cited above, which was typical of imperialist discourse, the fate of widows within the affinal households was subject to the total control of male kin. That many widows were seduced by male kin and became dispensable victims of the power hierarchy within the home is evident even though the writing itself tends to attribute these lapses to the laxity of morals of a whole people rather than to power relations within the home.[148]

It is also important to recognise that although the sexuality of the widow remained the focal point of much of male discourse, the aberrations that the repression of widows led to also drew the sympathy of men, especially the natal kinsmen of the widows. In Bengal some fathers had even appealed to the shastris to re-explore the Shastric position on widow marriage. For example, as far back as the middle of the eighteenth century Raja Rajballav of Vikrampur (Dacca), unable to accept the permanent widowhood of his teenaged daughter, enlisted the support of scholars on the question of widow marriage.[149] Similarly, moved by the miseries of widowhood experienced by his young daughter, Shyamacharan Das of Calcutta sought permission from the pandits to arrange a second marriage for her.[150] Vidyasagar himself was moved by a mixture of sympathy for the young widow and repugnance for the double standards which permitted even old men to continue remarrying right till the end of their lives. Since all girls were married before puberty such old men invariably married young girls. Thus at the time of their own death the widow left behind was often a child.[151]

In Maharashtra it was often fathers and brothers of the widows who took an interest in the widow marriage movement and organised second marriages for 'virgin' widows in their families. While in part the motivation for such marriages may have been pragmatic, as widows often lived in their natal households in Maharashtra, it was also because it was difficult to watch daughters and sisters suddenly being transformed into non-persons, regarded as inauspicious, and excluded from normal communal activities, often while still in their childhood.[152] A moving description, written by a widow herself, of how the family priest banished a child widow in the midst of festivities in the household, whilst the helpless father stood by unable to intervene, indicates the guilt and anguish suffered by fathers.[153] Helpless and ineffective in such situations, it was the 'tyranny of cruel custom' which held men in their grip that was regarded as responsible for the fate suffered by their loved daughters and sisters.

What is notable about men writing about widowhood in the nineteenth century is the paucity of analysis on the structural arrangements in which high-caste Hindu widows were located, or the lack of control widows had over their own lives because of their economic dependence upon male kin. Even the most liberal and sympathetic male reaction to widowhood, and the solution to it, revolved around enforced celibacy and the denial of motherhood to the child widow. Thus the movement for their marriage came to be supported on grounds of the 'unnaturalness' of enforced celibacy upon child widows. In the main it was the repressed sexuality of the widow, the compulsions of a moral society, or the needs of the child widow for a home and children which were the issues that dominated the discussions of men who argued the case for reform. The humanist impulse was an important aspect of those advocating a change in the status of the widow and was born out of a sense of male guilt at the double standards prevalent in society.

The reformers' rationale for advocating widow remarriage captures many contradictory elements as will be evident in the course of this work. As a group they were to display considerable ambivalence towards both issues of gender and of caste. They had moderate notions of change with a desire to alleviate some of the worst expressions of the inequalities in both institutions rather than any drastic altering of existing practices. However, what was noticeably consistent was a genuine concern for the plight of the child widow forced into a state of social death. These emotions are best captured by Gopal Hari Deshmukh, a champion of the widow reform movement. In a piece published in the *Shatapatre* he wrote:

I think the misery of women is so great that when I remember it my hair stands on end. These Brahmins instead of killing their daughters put them into greater misery... And still there are some who speak against widow remarriage... Doesn't the heart stir when the throats of girls of twelve, fifteen, twenty, and thirty years are being cut ... You yourselves unprotestingly become the butchers of your own daughters. There is no comparison on earth to a nation like yours ...[154]

Further, an improvement in the status of the widow was also intimately tied to a new self-image of the educated upper castes.

Certain minimal notions of an individual's (including women's) rights and of a new identity for the community to which the reformers belonged as befitting its position of social leadership in a new environment were other elements in the 'liberal' position. Nevertheless the reformist discourse was often limited to rhetorical concern as many of the reformers were unable to act effectively on behalf of the widows even in their own families.

The concern expressed by the reformers was countered by the mobilisation of the traditionalists against them. Resistance to the arguments of the reformers though strong was however articulated more in action during the 1870s with few of their published accounts surviving. In the 1880s however oblique arguments were often expressed about widowhood when Malabari sought opinion[155] on the problems of infant wives. A frequent statement represented a convenient male response which was that there was no *enforced* widowhood in India,[156] rather that it was widows themselves who did not want to be remarried. According to this view, 'the majority of widows will not listen but actually shun the company, nay detest those sympathising philanthropists who volunteer advice to remarry, for the sin of remarriage is deeply engraven at present on their minds'.[157]

Men resisting widow remarriage also pointed out that as the practice was associated with lower-caste cultural norms, even castes which had taken to such practices under trying circumstances felt that they were degraded by it. Its degrading characteristic was such that the common prostitute would regard herself as one step above a widow who remarried.[158] Others pointed to the wide social consensus against remarriage and emphasised that mothers and fathers of widows would 'rather commit suicide' than accept the remarriage of their daughters.[159] Even tonsure was represented as a voluntary act which widows 'adopted' of their own free will. This was a reflection of the widow's desire for a religious life.[160] One reaction was that widows were like 'Italian nuns'.[161] In any case human nature was marvellously plastic and a state of life which many women deliberately adopt and which extrinsic circumstances imposed on others in all civilised lands could not be without compensating consolations.[162]

Widowhood was also naturalised; it was a misfortune which could strike anyone. It had nothing to do with particular institutions among particular communities which applied only to women. Mandlik, a prominent specialist in Hindu law, wrote: 'To become a widow is a misfortune. There is no balm to a soul so wounded except the one obtained by entering into a higher kind of life. . .'[163] He also propounded ascetic widowhood as a naturalised state for women: 'The Savitri *upakhyana* shows that the second marriage of a woman is opposed to Hindu religious convictions. The Savitri days are the holiest festivals for females in India'.[164]

To exonerate themselves of their own complicity in the oppression of widows men sometimes argued that they actually enjoyed high status and were not oppressed at all. In fact they were the final authority on all matters of the household. As they had more 'leisure' than married women it was the widows who directed the house.[165] The most effective erasure of upper-caste male complicity in enforced widowhood may be seen in the argument that it was a 'wise economy of Providence' that among every civilised people, some men [where were they?] and women should remain single (either through widowhood or by choosing not to marry, as in the West) so as to remain disentangled from the anxieties and trials of matrimony for ministering to those in sorrow and suffering. Widows were necessary to act as ministering angels.[166]

Because of the virulence of the resistance to widow remarriage, which in a way reflected the inability of the upper castes to make changes in the family codes and caste norms on one issue without threatening the entire structure, the reformers too were careful in isolating the child 'virgin' widow as the object of their concern. In no way did they critique the entire structure of Brahmanical patriarchy, the caste practices or the property structures in which they were embedded. Perhaps this will explain why the reformers spearheading widow remarriage throughout the controversy presented their position as no radical innovation but merely an attempt at restoring 'the days of our past history'.[167]

In order to propagate their limited agenda of remarriage in the case of the child widow and using the argument that it was consonant with past practices, the reformers set up the Vidhava Vivahottejak Mandal (Hindu Widow Marriage Association) in 1866. They directed their attention at the high castes and announced their intention to consider 'the best means of re-introducing the practice of remarriage of females of the high caste community who have, or may, become widows and to advocate the cause *on the authority of the Hindu Dharma Shastra'* (emphasis added).[168] Appropriately the composition of the mandal, though dominated by Brahmanas, did have prominent members drawn from other castes such as Moroba Kanoba, a Pathare Prabhu, and the Maratha chief Ramachandra Rao Appasaheb. Thus while the battle for widow remarriage had to be fought within each caste, the association and the issue cut across the upper castes and by the end of the decade it became an issue also for the Kapol Banias and Pathare Prabhus. It was an issue which brought together the educated class, especially in Bombay where the first such wedding was performed.[169]

Two lines of communication were used in mobilising opinion in support of widow remarriage. The first was the reformist newspaper *Indu Prakash*, which carried contributions to the debate, and the second was the newly-available mofussil network of graduates who had by now spread out effectively over a wide area. Vishnu Shastri, a key actor in the controversy, carried the debate in person through a tour of the principal towns lecturing on the widow remarriage question. It was the first attempt to test whether 'public opinion could influence the application of Dharmashastra' by appealing to the literate public of Maharashtra, comprising largely Brahmanas.[170]

As the debate intensified the orthodox defenders of the status quo prepared themselves to move from opposition to the government for passing the act to combating their own caste-fellows by setting up their own organisation for the protection of the Hindu Dharma called the *Hindu Dharma Vyavasthapak Mandal* recalling the events of the sati controversy in Bengal in the 1820s.[171] Matters were precipitated when the issues moved from questions of interpretation to concrete action in the form of the remarriage of a widow performed with reformist support in Bombay in June 1869.[172]

The wedding was performed in the relatively more cosmopolitan Bombay in the house of the Pathare Prabhu, Moroba Kanoba. It was sponsored by seven reformist Brahmanas and attended by a large body of the elite from various towns of western India. The bride, Venubai, was a widow aged 17 who had been widowed within eight months of her earlier marriage at the age of nine. Both her parents were dead. Her father died at the age of eighty-five, only three months before her remarriage to a bachelor, Pandurang Vinayak Karmakar, aged 25, educated in Marathi and English, and an assistant school master in an Anglo-vernacular school in the Khandesh collectorate. The marriage was performed by the eldest of her three brothers. A few days later the young couple gave a reception to a group of persons comprising Pathare Prabhus, Shenvis, Sonars and Brahmanas. According to the report of the event the wedding was performed by Vishnu Shastri Pandit following the usual ritual practices of the Brahmanas.[173]

The wedding had been public in every sense, beginning with an advertisement for a groom in the pages of the *Indu Prakash* to threats of burning the house in which it was performed and of assaults upon the bride, arrangements to prevent a riot and finally to the use of excommunication by the infuriated opposition (proclaimed at a public meeting held at Thakurdwar in Bombay).[174] The problem posed before the Brahmanas was whether all those who had attended the wedding should be excommunicated (these would include a motley group, other castes, apart from Brahmanas and some Englishmen). Finally, it was decided to excommunicate the immediate offenders, the couple, Venubai's brother and the seven signatories who had organised the wedding.[175]

The conflict had now clearly gone beyond the limits of working out a consensus within the community. The reformers and their opponents settled for having a full fledged *shastrartha* to debate the Shastric points and the reformers brought in the Shankaracharya to preside over the public debate.[176] It was reported that the Shankaracharya had been secretly agreeable to negotiating a compromise permitting remarriage of child widows if the reformers dropped their campaign to include widows whose marriages had been consummated. The reformers, believing that they could carry their point of view, reportedly rejected the compromise.[177]

The debate itself was marked by controversy about the application of pressure leading to floor-crossing and other allegations of unethical actions by the orthodox to achieve a majority in their favour. They had earlier refused to permit the liberal historian and Sanskritist R.G. Bhandarkar, who supported the campaign for widow remarriage, to take an official part in the debate because he was a Saraswat Brahmana.[178] Among the arguments used was one advanced by the reformers that widow remarriage was permissible in the Kaliyuga and the orthodox arguing that it was not yet the Kaliyuga! The conclusion of the debate was so bitter that it led to prosecutions over defamation. The issue of widow remarriage had been so surcharged for the orthodox that they considered it permissible to lie in the 'service' of religion.[179]

Their violent defence of enforced widowhood was, for the orthodox, the culmination of a long period of disquiet beginning with the British refusal to support Brahmana disciplinary power over other castes, as well as their notions about the loss of respect they had suffered in society, the loss of their income and an anxiety about conversion and the cultural uniqueness of their caste. Giving up the cherished ideal of sacred marriage for women, the strict control over female sexuality generally and the enforcement of the non-sexuality of the widow was tantamount to the loss of the identity of the Brahmanas. What had distinguished the Brahmanas from other castes traditionally was their exclusive right to certain ritual practices, their monopoly over learning (now theoretically and also to some extent in real terms eroded) and the strictest of sexual codes for their women, and of course, enforced widowhood.

The key to the strength of the resistance to widow remarriage (and thereafter to other gender issues in the nineteenth century) lay in the fact that it represented a feature of lower-caste morality and sexual practices; the adoption of a lower-caste model was now being advocated for the highest caste. While the lower castes' adoption of the practices of upper castes was well-established as a measure of upward social mobility, the reverse was unheard of and unthinkable within the framework of Brahmanic ideology. Until recently, the Brahmanas had fiercely resisted attempts at Sanskritisation (as we have outlined, earlier) by the lower castes; now the very same 'pre-eminent' caste was to adopt a practice which would bring them down to the level of those they despised. Further, caste contestations had intensified throughout the century; consequently far from declining in incidence, enforced widowhood was growing as it was adopted by every upwardly mobile caste in western India.[180] Such a situation of social flux exacerbated tensions with which the widow remarriage issue got entangled and this accounts for the passions it aroused; gender and caste were inextricably linked in the orthodox Brahmana position on widow remarriage.

Perhaps it was the failure of the reformers to address the interpenetrative nature of gender, caste, property structures and hierarchised cultural norms for different castes that, when finally the history of the widow remarriage controversy is examined, what stands out is the meagreness of the results.[181'] For all the energy that was thrown into it by the reformers, till the end of the century only about 38 widows had been remarried.[182] Clearly the passion on both sides was out of all proportion to its consequences. However, while little was achieved in concrete terms on widow remarriages, necessitating a renewal of attention in the 1880s, the bitterness and polarisation resulting from it led to contradictory consequences. First, the limits of the 'liberal' position were very evident and so was the continuation of a very real power, the power to excommunicate, in the hands of the Brahmanas. The two were of course related because the sobering of the reformers was achieved through the power of excommunication.[183] All the significant participants were ostracised and sometimes had to recant their positions through the application of larger social pressures even if they had earlier managed to stand their ground, as for example in the case of Gopal Hari Deshmukh. When his married daughter's mother-in-law threatened to dissolve the marriage, Deshmukh succumbed and performed prayaschitta. He also made a public statement in the columns of the *Indu Prakash* on why he had done so.[184] Despite his prayaschitta he endured such severe ostracism that he declined to accept the Bombay government's invitation to testify before the Finance Commission in London the following year for fear of orthodox reprisals against his crossing the ocean.[185] Ranade stood his ground initially but caved in in 1873, to the horror of all reformists, when he succumbed to family pressures against marrying a widow after his first wife died.[186] In Bombay too the reformers found that they could fund a scholar to travel abroad but not eat with the scholar on his return, or they could encourage widow remarriage but not have social relations with the couple thereafter.

The Brahmana and upper-caste reformers were subject to such ambiguities since they could not stand outside the coercive power of the community and were not willing to break with their kin and caste-fellows.[187] Their location within their caste, their larger social position and their attempt to reinterpret tradition and remain within it provided the parameters within which they struggled to manoeuvre, somewhat ineffectively. It is not surprising that Vidyasagar himself died a disillusioned man. Before his death he shared his disappointment with a visitor from Maharashtra to whom he said that he was now finally convinced that the Hindus, as Hindus, would never accept social reform.[188] The recourse to coercive social action by the orthodox Brahmanas against the reformers was considered 'natural' but the conclusion of the widow remarriage debate which ended in unintended court cases was seen by many Brahmanas, not merely the orthodox among them, as allowing the conflict to escalate beyond the purview of the Brahmana authorities. In this the reformers were regarded as overstepping themselves and in the polarisation that followed the reformers were a beleaguered minority.[189] Gender was to remain the most divisive issue for the different caste/class groups till political strategies and nationalism replaced it as the basis of internal splits among the upper castes during the closing years of the nineteenth century.

For the rest of the decade the reformers dropped gender as an issue and thereafter Brahmana reformers never, of their own accord, centre-staged it as a cause to support although they took sides when others initiated a debate. Rather, the reverse happened as we shall see. Since the remarriage conflict had split the Hindu elite, they tried to breach the split and moved to 'political' and economic issues outside religion and culture on which there was less disagreement in the 1870s among the Brahmanas. The establishment of the Vedashastrottejaka Sabha in 1873 drew all shastris, old and new, to promote Sanskrit studies with Bhandarkar and Ranade playing a leading part in it. The Prarthana Sabha with which they were associated also consciously steered a moderate path, unlike the more radical Paramahansa Mandal's stand earlier on, and tried to remain close to the Brahmana mainstream. And finally, when the reformist Brahmanas moved to set up the Poona Sarvajanik Sabha, an alliance of professional and landholding elites dominated by Brahmanas, the founding statement provided that the body would deal only with 'political' issues (where one could unite as a class) and avoid divisive social and religious issues which would fragment them.[190]

VII

The founding of the Poona Sarvajanik Sabha was the first formal attempt by the Brahmanas and other upper-caste elites to solidify their paternalistic leadership of society. Comprising the pre-colonial elites who had been the social leaders but who were now threatened with both internal and external strains, the Sabha was a means of reconstructing, along new lines, their social leadership in Western India. In the sixties and seventies the increasing opportunities for the elites to partake of civic and political action in Poona convinced the Brahmana reformers that to be effective, and have an impact on British opinion, such action must be based on a coalition of all social and economic elites. They thus made unity of the upper castes, who still remained the elite, their highest priority.[191]

The aim of the Sarvajanik Sabha was to press for wider Indian participation in the administration, to place their own interests before the rulers and to interpret the conditions and needs of their society.[192] The early activities of the Sabha had begun characteristically with an issue regarding the management of the Parvati temple, possibly as a means of taking up a cause with a wide appeal among the Brahmanas, but as the decade progressed, with the considerable economic distress in the Deccan, the Sabha reached out to the countryside and mobilised opinion against the revised land revenue assessments.[193] The active work of the Sabha on the revenue question was decisive evidence of its claim to social leadership; the extremely widespread rural opposition was consistent also with Brahmana interest given the intimate connection with the land for a large number of them.

The outbreak of the Deccan Riots in 1875 during which attacks were made on the Marwari and Gujarati money-lenders (and where the Brahmana money-lenders often supported the attacks on the 'outsiders') led the Bombay government to suspect the hand of the Sabha activists in the disturbances. The work of the Sabha in collecting evidence during the famine and the outbreak of dacoities led by the Chitpavan Vasudeo Balwant Phadke, who wished to restore Maratha rule, in early 1879, led to increased suspicion about the Brahmana-dominated Sabha connections. The Brahmana position on the riots had actually been ambivalent. Some of their money-lenders were also frightened by the militancy of the peasant action. Phadke had found little support among the Brahmanas for his activities and was forced to fall back on the Ramoshis and other low castes.[194] Nevertheless the British transferred Ranade from Poona to Nasik,[195] a move which marked the beginning of the Bombay government's Brahmanophobia which increased phenomenally during the rest of the decade. Ironically, Ranade, regarded as a British collaborator by the Brahmana orthodoxy, became suspect by the British themselves — at least during the heyday of the Sabha's activities.

As the Sabha's consolidated its claims to social leadership of society as a whole during the 70s, the non-Brahmana movement, now officially launched with the setting up of the Satyashodhak Samaj, contested the paternalism of the Sabha. Initially, although Phule had been contemptuous of the organisation, dismissing it as a 'Bhatt sabha',[196] he had remained associated with it selectively. Since the Sabha was preponderantly Brahmana in composition with Chitpavans outnumbering others, the non-Brahmana leaders came to regard it as an ideological rival and were sharply aware of its power. They were conscious that the Sabha embodied a particular view of Indian society and regarded itself as the proper social leadership which would mould future Indian political institutions. The non-Brahmana leaders were equally conscious that the viewpoint of the Sabha was different from their own.[197] If the Sabha was a means of uniting the elites after its internal conflicts over gender, its success in doing so generated a new arena of contestation between the elites and others.

The Sarvajanik Sabha was one of the regional bodies that fed into the provincial and then the Indian National Congress.[198] Its narrow social composition continued to be reproduced even in the Congress and the non-Brahmana alternative to it in the form of the Satyashodhak Samaj indicates that the Sabha's claim to speak for the whole of society was contested by those who saw themselves as excluded from that class but subsumed under it. The critique of the limited social base of an organisation subsuming others and speaking for them was to be replayed with the Congress both in the late nineteenth and early twentieth centuries.

During the last two decades of the nineteenth century, Brahmana power was seriously under pressure for a second time. The attitude of the colonial state towards the community fluctuated according to the understanding or predilections of the current set of administrators. The growing Brahmanophobia was sometimes expressed as applying to the entire body of Brahmanas but more often it was focused specifically on the Chitpavans.[199] Colonial strategy was to veer around playing one sub-caste off against another; for example the Saraswats against the Chitpavans. Individual administrators considered the reformers more reliable than the more conservative sections among the Brahmanas and equally it was suggested that other non-Brahmana castes such as Prabhus or Marathas, or even the Muslims, could be encouraged in order to break the Brahmana monopoly.[200] The Brahmanas were aware of the hostility towards them and were bewildered by it. Their sense of anxiety and alienation led the bulk of them to search for a more cohesive sense of identity as well as to fiercely prevent an erosion of their power which was being seriously challenged by the castes below them.

Certain economic and demographic pressures working upon the Brahmanas increased the sense of crisis and beleaguerment. The number of educated, predominantly Brahmanas in the Poona Deccan, had swelled in the post-1870s. Since the British policy had always been to recruit Indians only at the lower administrative level, the growing numbers of the educated found if difficult to get employment and were also excluded from the higher rungs. The Director of Public Instruction noted in the 1870s that the public service was clogged with a surfeit of graduates. By the 1880s the education bulge was being fully felt. Further, the crunch was aggravated in the case of the Deccan elite since the occupational biases of the Brahmanas fitted them for little else than public service.[201] The excess of graduates in a situation of British policy vacillations towards them, and the criticisms of the non-Brahmana leaders about Brahmana monopoly over education and the public services, led them to feel that the days of their privileged position might be numbered.

Changes in the system of land tenure coincidentally also occurred in roughly the same period. The Deccan Riots of 1875 were followed by remedial land legislation and considerable experimentation was under way in the Konkan around *khoti* whereby the government attempted to regularise the system of land tenure and the relationship of the Khot to his underholders. Many of the khoti tenures dated from Peshwa times when the rulers had appointed officials to collect revenue. The extent of khoti rights was the subject of disputes through the nineteenth century with the government viewing the Khot as a revenue farmer and denying him full proprietary rights. Many of the Khots, including Tilak's family, were involved in expensive and long-drawn-out legal disputes around the tenures. Significantly, one of Tilak's first public acts was to petition the Bombay government against the 1879 bill (which nevertheless became an act in 1880) to amend the khoti settlement.[202] It is likely to have adversely affected the Chitpavans (who were concentrated in the Konkan) in particular. Further, as pressure on the land increased through policy changes and demographic expansion, the migration into Poona for education and recruitment into public service also became greater.[203] The sense of dislocation would be deepened, with the economic crisis and educational crisis feeding on each other. Thus, by the end of the nineteenth century social and economic forces had produced a kind of cumulative effect which pressed heavily on the elite. Non-Brahmana criticism of Brahmana monopoly over education and the public services had, as we have seen, been a central theme in Phule's writing, especially in the post-1870s. At the turn of the century the Maratha rulers of states, especially Kolhapur, were actively encouraging a policy of increasing the recruitment of non-Brahmanas into the public services, which directly affected Brahmanas who had dominated the services in them.[204] The expansion itself was declared in a public statement to reserve 50 per cent of the positions for backward communities following Brahmana resistance to conceding the Kolhapur Maharaja the right to the Vedokta ceremonies. Combined with this was the Bombay government's growing awareness of the need to 'secure a due admixture of the various races and castes', to ensure 'fairplay by all classes' in the administration and, as a first move, to implement ways of increasing non-Brahmana participation in education. Since the Brahmanas predominantly availed themselves of free studentships in high schools, in 1885 reserving half the free scholarships for Muslims and 'backward' Hindu castes was proposed to rectify the situation.[205]

Despite the pressures on the Brahmanas, their position during the 1890s and even into the first decade of the twentieth century continued, objectively, to be one of strength rather than weakness: they were both consolidating their position in the services and institutions of the presidency and at the same time effectively warding off those who were challenging and wanting to curtail Brahmana hegemony. It has been suggested that the very strength of the Brahmana position, which they were consequently eager to defend, made them sensitive to any change and willing to contest any effort to diminish their authority.[206] But given the challenges and contestations, *subjectively* the Brahmanas were experiencing a prolonged period of stress, all of which fed into a crisis of identity that was articulated in a series of attempts at resolving it. Under these circumstances, in the 80s and 90s of the nineteenth century the Brahmana elites were simultaneously engaged in three tussles: among themselves in differing caste/class segments in an attempt to resolve ideological differences around gender, community, nation and politics; then, as a composite elite against the non-Brahmana contestation of their claim to elite status; and finally, flowing from the two arenas, a tussle to control the provincial wing of the Indian National Congress and thereby shape the future as well as maintain a grip on it.

Following roughly after the widow remarriage controversy, sections of the educated Brahmana elite gave expression, with steadily growing intensity, to the cultural crisis by rooting themselves in tradition as it existed rather than reinterpreting tradition as the 'reformers' had done during the widow remarriage controversy. Typical of this trend was V.N. Mandlik, an eminent jurist whose career resembled Ranade's, but who never made it to the Bombay High Court as Ranade did. These were the two main protagonists on the reform question during the 1880s holding opposing views on the relationship between legislation and social change, revealing how politicised the question of social reform had become. In 1869 Mandlik had published two articles in his newspaper, *Native Opinion*, where he took a conservative stance on widow remarriage. He drew the attention of the reformers to what he called the 'moral worth'[207] of the measure rather than trying to build a case solely on religious sanction. He was among the first to argue against social legislation and for a gradual transformation from within,[208] a position to be used forcefully by Tilak later on. Elsewhere he argued that it was necessary to understand that the simultaneous existence of 'perfect conservatism in regard to some institution (mainly gender, we should add) and a wide departure from old grooves in others' (such as taking to English education and service under the British) was possible and existed among the Brahmanas.[209]

Mandlik's views were influential not merely because of his command over the law but because he was a member of the Bombay Legislative Council for a number of years during the period 1874 to 1884. He was thus strategically placed to articulate fears of 'alien encroachment' upon tradition. As an authority on the Hindu law of inheritance (the foundation of the Hindu joint family and therefore of women's lives), he led the opposition to bills proposing greater inheritance rights for women. During debates in the Legislative Council he argued that the legislature must be 'supremely cautious, and avoid all interference with the social and religious fabric of the Hindu communities' on some assumed standard of public good to which 'we Hindus do not subscribe'.[210] He also argued that the untouchables were not ready for education.[211]

The principal issue of contention through the 1870s and 1880s was the degree to which Brahmanas should transform their basic traditional institutions of caste, gender codes and religion. What is significant is that western education was no guarantee of the acceptance of major changes in the social and cultural practices of the Brahmanas. It is notable that many of the new graduates became fierce proponents of traditional Brahmanical practices while sections of the earlier generation had been vocally advocating a certain set of moderate changes.

The best example of the new western-educated Brahmana proponent of 'tradition' was Vishnu Shastri Chiplunkar, son of the well known 'liberal' shastri Krishna Shastri Chiplunkar, who had advocated the introduction of non-Brahmana students to the Sanskrit College, been associated with Phule in some of his early ventures at schooling for the lower castes, and had been penalised for dining with an Englishman in 1870.[212] Vishnu Shastri levelled fierce criticisms at his father Krishna Shastri in the *Nibandhamala,* a paper run by him, for advocating reforms including widow remarriage on the ground that his father's generation had been overwhelmed by the new learning, and had thoughtlessly abandoned traditional values which were far 'superior' to the modern. Among those who came in for criticism was Lokahitwadi V.H. Deshmukh, Phule, the Prarthana Samaj, and the missionaries for belittling Hindu traditions.[213] The anti-reformist position of Mandlik and Vishnu Shastri Chiplunkar was carried forward with dramatic effect by Tilak, who used every possible occasion to build opinion against the *'Sudharaks'* and establish a decisive control over Brahmana opinion, always represented as Hindu opinion.

Until the mid-80s when the polarisation between the two caste segments of the Brahmanas resurfaced over a gender issue, the issue of child marriage and enforced widowhood (again a sign for 'cultural' and 'religious' values), and the identity of the nation, the Brahmanas' debates about tradition did not exclude their ability to function as an interest group when their material position was seemingly or actually threatened. Indeed, even after the violent nature of the polarisation in the late 80s and early 90s the Brahmana attitude to the non-Brahmana movement's push for increased representation in the public services and in educational institutions was unified (although the manner in which it was expressed could be aggressive or subtle according to the specific caste segment in which one was located). The Poona Sarvajanik Sabha argued that the Bombay government's reserving of studentships for non-Brahmanas was anti-Brahmana and tantamount to 'singling out the Brahmanas and setting them up against other classes'. Further, it was a departure from the policy of strict religious neutrality.[214] Later, when the Maharaja of Kolhapur reserved positions in the state's public services, the newspaper *Mahratta*, speaking for all Brahmanas, complained that it was aimed at weakening the Brahmana community and was designed to facilitate the 'hot-house growth of one caste'.[215]

The reformers and traditionalists demonstrated unity of purpose effectively again in 1901 when the Bombay government was contemplating legislation on the issue of land alienation on the lines of the Punjab Act. The proposal sparked off a 'fierce' and hysterical clamour unprecedented in the presidency with protest meetings taking place in every major town. Both rural and urban elites were involved in the protest and in sending off a barrage of petitions against the bill. The protesters included Ranade (before he died), Gokhale, to whom his mantle had passed, and of course the Tilakites, many of whom had links with the money-lending class amongst Brahmanas. Earlier, in 1891, Tilak had opposed the Agriculturalists Relief Act which was designed to prevent the raiyat from falling into the clutches of the money-lender.[216] Reformers and traditionalists among Hindus and other businessmen in Bombay all came together in 1901 to oppose the proposed move partly through support to laissez-faire ideas, partly through their own land interests and partly through direct links with the moneylending class. They were vocally supported by the middle-class press.

Internal unity among the Brahmana elite on issues of direct

material interest however was insufficient to hold them together on issues of culture, religious belief and practice, including gender, and especially politics, but even here we must note many of the shared assumptions of most Brahmanas. The shared assumptions were an outcome of a common upper-caste legacy, a largely Brahmanic Hindu worldview where the differences lay in the emphasis on particular aspects of the legacy rather than in the structure as a whole as will be outlined below. This was particularly true during the post-widow remarriage debate period when Bhandarkar and Ranade, both active members of the Prarthana Samaj, were typical of the 'Sudharaks' and Mandlik, Chiplunkar and Tilak of the 'conservatives'. The Sudharaks were by now chastened, much more desirous of remaining within the Brahmana mainstream (especially Ranade) and they strove hard to express their positions on issues such as caste, religion and even gender, in moderate terms. Their differences, ideologically, were with the non-Brahmanas, especially with Phule, over his focus on the exploitative nature of Brahmanism, over what Shivaji symbolised and what value to attribute to the term 'Aryan' — generally on Phule's understanding of the past as an explanation of the present. All Brahmanas shared a view of the Aryans as dynamic, vigorous and noble. Brahmanism was for Ranade the Aryan faith which had served to unite north and south in ancient India.[217] The Aryan theory was a convenient device among many Brahmana intellectuals to mark off the 'foreign' hordes with a Semitic or Turkic-Mongoloid background who poured into India and to whom was attributed the introduction of many ills in Indian society, most important of which was the degeneration of women's status. Further, for Ranade, the Aryans were the chosen race and he lamented that their chivalrous civilisation was suppressed in certain ways by the 'lower races and tribes'.[218] Significantly, he also advocated the 'Aryanisation' of those castes traditionally excluded from the scriptures. And finally, in a characteristic slide, he linked these views to the present and to his politics by suggesting that Providence had sent the English to India to provide a living example of 'pure Aryan customs' with regard to the treatment of women. With English support the Hindus could free themselves from the patriarchal Muslim tradition and could restore their old healthy practices.[219]

On the other side of the supposed divide between reformers and conservatives Tilak's emphasis was, again characteristically, on the powers of conquest of the Aryans which he lauded. This he linked to the high degree of civilisation they had attained in their original home close to the North Pole, giving them the capacity to 'exterminate or assimilate all the non-Aryan races with whom they came in contact in their migration in search of new lands'.[220] Differences were clearly only in regarding conquest as a civilising 'force' or in unambiguously approving it as an indication of physical prowess.

Similarly, both Ranade and later Tilak regarded Shivaji as a 'national' hero. Ranade wrote powerfully about the exploits of Shivaji who was the focal point of his influential book published in 1891, *The Rise of the Maratha Power*. Building around a Kshatriya tradition and within the framework of a composite Maharashtrian identity Ranade makes Shivaji emerge as a hero burning with 'national spirit'. However, Ranade attributed the 'national spirit' itself to the composite regional tradition of the Maratha Bhakti poets. The legacy of Shivaji in his view was not exclusively a Brahmana or even a Hindu tradition. It tried to put Shivaji above caste and religion and link him with tolerance and moderation.[221] But in all of this Ranade was also among the first to turn to history to enhance the position of the Poona elite. It was particularly significant in countering Phule's version of Shivaji as a Shudra hero, and in attempting to demonstrate the essential 'compatibility' of the interests of various castes and classes. The Shivaji tradition helped to establish the legitimacy of the Poona Brahmanas of the Sarvajanik Sabha to lead their society. Tilak only extended all these elements when he introduced the Shivaji festival as a means of mobilising the elites *and* the masses against the British. He also took great care to identify his endeavour with the catholic tradition of Ranade's version of Shivaji[222] and thereby received the support of the reformists' paper *Sudharak*. But it is in interpreting the figure of Ramdas as the spiritual mentor of Shivaji that the difference between Ranade and Tilak emerges. This difference marked their distinctive approaches to history. While Ranade emphasised the synthesis and 'protestant' dimensions of Hinduism embodied in Bhakti, the conservative historians privileged the Brahmanic element, in particular in Hinduism. The real hero of medieval Maharashtra (before political use was made of Shivaji) for the Tilakites was Ramdas, for whom Maharashtra dharma was a call to an ancient theocratic state. Ramdas was cast as a militant saint, a *brahmachari* who was a Hanuman-worshipper — a figure of masculine strength. Ramdas, in this version, set up *akharas* for physical training along with *mathas* all over Maharashtra to prepare the populace for the impending struggle with the Muslims. This view of Ramdas was a construction of a section of Brahmana historiography, especially of the Rajwade School which acted as a counter to Phule's interpretation of Shivaji as the Shudra hero of medieval Maharashtra.[223] It Brahmanised Shivaji and it worked to almost make Tilak a direct inheritor of the Ramdas legacy.

The crux of the difference between the Sudharaks and the Tilakites thus was not in the recourse to tradition, which both shared, but with a distinctive highlighting of certain phases and elements in it. While the Sudharaks, especially Ranade and Bhandarkar, concentrated a good deal on the early 'progressive' and glorious civilisation of ancient India, those who were anti-reform tended to concentrate much more upon the more recent glories of Maharashtra, especially on the Chitpavan combination of Kshatriya-Brahmana values in the same person as articulated in the Peshwai. Brahmana role reversal under the Peshwai was applauded by Vishnu Shastri Chiplunkar, and Bajirao I was depicted as a romantic, brave, and religious ruler.[224] Working together, both the Sudharak view of history and that of the opponents of the reformers were to dominate the Brahmana mind and marginalise Phule's view which had cast the Brahmanas as usurpers and exploiters.

The difficulties of manoeuvring a 'rational' position on caste while retaining their social base among the upper-caste, primarily Brahmana, elite in the Poona Deccan were evident in the reformers' handling of this sensitive subject. At the level of ideas it was possible to argue against it, which the reformers did, while at the same time rationalising its historic role. Ranade also stressed its flexibility, arguing that in the past the system was dynamic and open, enabling the lower orders to rise to higher status. History in India thus proved that it had changed and could change, but by slow absorption — assimilation rather than 'convulsion'.[225] But in practice, caste norms including the coercive power of the Brahmanas, determined the limits of how far one could go on personal conviction. None of the reformers, especially not Ranade, managed to throw off Brahmanism in their personal lives. Increasingly, as the crisis built up, even their paternalistic support for non-Brahmana activities had to be curbed for fear of social disapproval from their elite constituency.

The anti-reformers on the other hand had no such dilemmas to resolve. They could reveal their Brahmanism quite openly; Mandlik had argued that the untouchables were not yet ready for education. Tilak could say at various times that the caste system was like the medieval European guild, untouchability was degrading but it was a fact of Indian life, that artisans should stick to their craft and leave politics to Brahmanas, that the so-called 'Kshatriyas' should not demand the Vedokta,[226] and that the real problem to confront was that all Indians were slaves and Shudras in relation to the British.[227] It seems the anti-reformers could take a more open stand on caste after the reformist Brahmanas drew away from Phule. Tilak refused to sign a pledge against untouchability[228] and the *Kesari* made a special target of Phule for being irreligious (when Phule was mobilising non-Brahmanas against using Brahmana priests at their ceremonies). The Tilakites were also particularly gleeful at the conservative reaction to Phule among the non-Brahmanas who were critical of his radicalism.[229]

Despite the shared ground on many positions on tradition and history, ultimately because of the larger cultural crisis the more moderate and syncretic position of the reformers could not satisfy the majority of the Brahmanas politically; they responded more enthusiastically to the orthodox views of Tilak because it was more openly based on a reiteration not just of tradition, but of the traditional power of the Brahmanas. This was evident in the critical sphere of gender issues and the way these issues were used to outmanoeuvre the reformers as a political force, and thereafter to establish leadership over the elites as well as the community over which they presided. Internal conflict within the Brahmana community in western India resurfaced once more in the 1880s around a series of social and political issues and culminated in the bitter polarisation over the Age of Consent Bill. Through these internal conflicts, some expressed as personal rivalries and others as social differences, Tilak consolidated first the position of the anti-reformers and then established his group as the 'popular' social leaders of western India.[230] It is significant that through these years, personal rivalries for leadership within the Brahmana community came to be recast as political and ideological differences. The transition was achieved through a mobilisation of conservative popular opinion on the emotive gender issues of child marriage, enforced widowhood and the proper age for the consummation of a marriage. Tilak displayed considerable skill in effecting the shift of focus from factional struggles for control over institutions, and therefore over leadership, to the polarisation around gender. It is in the larger context of caste contestation, class formation and the emergence of nationalism, processes that we have tried to outline in this chapter, that we can explore the structural changes experienced by women of the new 'middle classes' in nineteenth century Maharashtra.

NOTES AND REFERENCES

1. Although there are a number of monographs and analyses which explore agrarian changes, social changes and the emergence of nationalism in the nineteenth century in western India, there is no existing work that incorporates gender into its analysis especially in its relationship to caste contestation and class formation during the same period.

2. Kenneth Ballhatchet, *Social Policy and Social Change in Western India, 1817–1830*, London, Oxford University Press, 1957, p. 30.

3. For example, to compensate for some of the excesses perpetrated during the takeover by European and Indian soldiers, it was necessary to have the plunderers, the Europeans in particular, punished in the streets of the town. The Brahmanas who had fled were recalled to perform purificatory ceremonies and placated with gifts of money. As Elphinstone wrote, 'Never scruple to give large sums when temples of note are really polluted. It shows our anxiety to respect the religion of the country' (Ballhatchet, *Social Policy*, p. 28).

4. Ballhatchet, *Social Policy*, p. 31; R. Kumar, *Western India*, p. 75.

5. Ballhatchet, *Social Policy*, pp. 86–87.

6. *Ibid.*, p. 73.

7. *Ibid.*, p. 75. In relation to British rule and the inamdars it has been argued that the British conquest was essentially a change in opportunities, and hence the strategies of the inamdars, rather than a decisive break in their wielding of power. The main themes in the relations between the state, Maratha or British, and its privileged subjects did not substantially change. According to this view there has been an overemphasis on the political fact of conquest and the disjunctions were less in many areas than they have been made out

to be. The relations between the inamdars and the state were disrupted not by the British but after Independence in 1952. As the revenue minister said, the rights of the inamdars granted by the British 'were nothing short of a bribe paid for acquiescing in foreign domination and refraining from a mutiny'. The cards were well played and in general the inamdars continued to be loyal servants of the British (Laurence W. Preston, 'The authority of the state in Western India, 1818–1857', in D.W. Atwood, M. Israel and N.K. Wagle, *City, Countryside and Society in Maharashtra*, Toronto, University of Toronto Press, 1988, pp. 77–95, p. 79).

8. Ballhatchet, *Social Policy*, pp. 144–46.
9. *Ibid.*, p. 153.
10. Elphinstone wrote in a letter to J.D. Suares dated 3.11.1818, 'The Brahmanas are the greatest sufferers by the change. From their temporal power and influence they possess the means of creating alarm and disturbance to a degree that renders the utmost prudence and vigilance necessary on our part. No engine could be put into the hands of this discontented priesthood so powerful as an opinion that we entertained even the remotest design of converting the people,' Ballhatchet, *Social Policy*, pp. 83–84.
11. Preston, 'The Authority of the State', p. 85.
12. R.D. Choksey, *The Last Phase: Selections From the Deccan Commissioner's Files (Peshwa Daftar), 1815–1818. With an Introductory Note on the British Diplomacy at the Court of the Peshwa*, Bombay, Phoenix Publishers, 1948, pp. 223ff.
13. Judicial Department, Vol. 48 of 1882, cited in Kumar, *Western India*, p. 81.
14. Kumar, *Western India*, p. 79.
15. Sripati Roy, *Customs and Customary Law in British India*, Delhi, Mittal Publications, 1986, [Reprint of 1910 edition]. The new government however assumed criminal jurisdiction and also created a structure of courts above the Panchayats. These were to draw heavily or exclusively upon western principles of law (Kumar, *Western India*, p. 80).
16. Ballhatchet, *Social Policy*, p. 210.
17. *Ibid.*, pp. 223–224.
18. In 1823, for example, Robertson made strategic use of the annual dakshina ceremony where gifts were given to Brahmanas in order to debate the issue of sati. Five hundred learned pandits participated in the discussion with Robertson himself functioning like a learned pandit as he took part in the deliberations. Robertson's position that the legality of sati rested on the exercise of 'free will' was forcefully argued by Vitthal Upadhyaya (Ballhatchet, *Social Policy*, pp. 284–5).

19. Ballhatchet, *Social Policy*, pp. 287–90.
20. *Ibid.*, p. 302.
21. My argument on this issue is based on a meticulous marshalling of the facts of this case as described and analysed by Wagle in N.K. Wagle, 'A Dispute Between the Pancal Devajna Sonars and the Brahmanas of Pune Regarding Social Rank and Ritual Privileges: A Case Study of the British Administration of Jati Laws in Maharashtra, 1822–25' in N.K. Wagle (ed.), *Images of Maharashtra: A Regional Profile*, London, Curzon Press, 1980, pp. 129–159.
22. *Ibid.*, p. 132.
23. *Ibid.*, p. 133.
24. *Ibid.*, p. 145.
25. *Ibid.*, p. 130.
26. *Ibid.*, p. 136. Jagannath had earnest hopes that he and his fellow castemen would be admitted to the Brahmana caste (see A. Crawford, *Our Troubles in Poona and the Deccan*, Westminister, Constable and Company, 1897, p. 210).
27. Such tailoring was occurring both for the ends of the British Administration and caste interests. The Commissioner for the Deccan took a dim view of Trivengadacharya's championing of the Sonars and the *Rathakara Samskara Kalpadruma*, the text he cited. The text itself was only compiled the previous year by Trivengadacharya (Wagle, 'British Administration of Jati Laws,' pp. 132, 153).
28. Wagle, 'British Administration of Jati Laws', p. 140.
29. *Ibid.*, p. 141.
30. *Ibid.*, p. 137.
31. Arthur Steele, *The Hindu Castes*, pp. vi-xix; Ballhatchet, *Social Policy*, p. 200.
32. Wagle, 'British Administration of Jati Laws' p. 131.
33. *Ibid.*
34. *Ibid.*, p. 134.
35. Rosalind O'Hanlon, *Caste, Conflict, and Ideology*, Cambridge, Cambridge University Press, 1985, p. 24.
36. *Ibid.*, pp. 24–26.
37. *Ibid.*, p. 27. The summary of the details of the Maratha-Brahmana caste dispute is based on pp. 27–41 of O'Hanlon's discussion of the political conflict around the varna status of the ruling family of Satara.
38. Only 96 'pure' Maratha families could trace their lineages to the traditional Rajput *vanshas*. These 'genuine' Kshatriya families claimed the right as Kshatriyas to domestic rituals, chiefly at the time of marriage and death, based on sacred texts drawn from the

Vedas. The others were entitled only to words drawn from the less sacred Puranas (O'Hanlon, *Caste*, p. 17).

39. *Ibid.*, p. 34.

40. *Ibid.*, p. 38. Pratapsinh wrote in his diary, 'If this goes on dharma itself will not remain. Each man should stick to his own caste but in spite of this these men are trying to spread money around in our caste. But make no mistake, all Kshatriyas will look to protect their caste in this matter' (G.S. Sardesai (ed.), *Selections from the Peshwa Daftar: Papers Referring to Pratapsinh, Raja of Satara*, pp. 85–86, cited in O'Hanlon, *Caste*, p. 38).

41. Sekhar Bandhopadhyaya, 'Caste, Class and Culture in Colonial India', *Indian History Congress Symposia Papers: 1*, Delhi, 1992, p. 10.

42. Ballhatchet, *Social Policy*, p. 255.

43. Kumar, *Western India*, pp. 50–55, 265, 268.

44. *Ibid.*, pp. 268–69. The experience of the controversy over the *dakshina* indicates that even a minority of Brahmanas could successfully push through their point of view if it was allied to the government's position.

45. B.B. Misra, *The Indian Middle Classes: Their Growth in Modern Times*, London, Oxford University Press, 1961, p. 161.

46. As Trevelyan argued, 'The poor man is not less the object of the committee's solicitude than the rich'; but while the means at their disposal were extremely limited, here were millions of all classes to be educated. It was absolutely necessary to make a selection, and they therefore selected the upper and middle classes as the first object of their attention, because by educating them first they would 'soonest be able to extend the same advantages to the rest of the people' (*Ibid.*, pp. 151–52).

47. Mountstuart Elphinstone, minute 13.12.1825, cited in Ballhatchet, *Social Policy*, p. 258.

48. Ballhatchet, *Social Policy*, p. 262.

49. There were broadly four sets of contestations: two between the British and the Brahmanas and between the orthodox Brahmanas and 'new' Brahmanas over the content of education, and two between the colonial government and the missionaries and between the Brahmanas and non-Brahmanas over the inclusion of the lower castes in the educational agenda.

50. Ballhatchet, *Social Policy*, p. 258.

51. O'Hanlon, *Caste*, pp. 5–6.

52. Richard Tucker, 'The Early Setting of the non-Brahmin Movement in Maharashtra', *The Indian Historical Review*, Vol. 7, Nos. 1–2, 1981,

pp. 138–39. In the Ahmednagar mission school Mahars constituted the largest number of students.

53. Kumar, *Western India*, p. 283. Also see Dr. Gadgil, *Poona: A Socio-Economic Survey*, Part II, Poona, Gokhale Institute of Politics and Economics, 1952, pp. 286–87. Gadgil provides substantial evidence for the domination of Poona Brahmanas in educational institutions right into the 1930s.

54. Kumar, *Western India*, p. 283.

55. R.E. Enthoven, *Tribes and Castes of Bombay*, Vol. III, Delhi, Cosmo, 1975 (reprint) pp. 249–51.

56. Christine Dobbin, *Urban Leadership in Western India: Politics and Communities in Bombay City, 1840–1885*, London, Oxford University Press, 1972, p. 6.

57. *Ibid.*, p. 265.

58. Dobbin, *Urban Leadership*, p. 6.

59. Richard Tucker, 'Early Setting of the Non-Brahmin Movement', p. 155; Arthur Crawford, *Our Troubles*, p. 153.

60. Dobbin, *Urban Leadership*, pp. 35–38.

61. Misra, *The Middle Classes*, p. 338.

62. While such an analysis for all castes is needed to obtain a comprehensive picture of the process of class formation and the relationship between caste and class, I focus here on the Brahmanas. It is easier to focus on them because this is one caste for which documentation exists. However, the focus may also be justified because the Brahmanas, as a caste, dominated the shaping of gender issues and were at the centre of caste contestations.

63. Omvedt, *Cultural Revolt*, p. 94.

64. *Ibid.*, p. 82.

65. *Ibid.*, p. 94.

66. *Gazetteer of the Bombay Presidency*, Vol IX, p. 180, cited in Gordon Johnson, 'Chitpavan Brahmins and Politics in Western India', in Edmund Leach and S.N. Mukherjee (eds.), *Elites in South Asia*, Cambridge, Cambridge University Press, 1990; Frank Conlon, *Caste in a Changing World: The Chitrapur Sarawat Brahmans, 1870–1934*, Delhi, Thomson Press, 1977 p. 104.

67. Conlon also reports that Saraswat Brahmanas in the south Konkan had their lands cultivated through tenants. Frank Conlon, *Caste in a Changing World*, p. 33.

68. *Indian Statutory Commission*, Vol VI, p. 229, cited in Johnson, 'Chitpavan Brahmins', p. 104.

69. Michael Metelits, 'Social and Economic Forces Operating on Local Bodies of Nineteenth Century Deccan Municipalities,' cited in Omvedt, *Cultural Revolt*, p. 75.

70. Chitpavan Brahmanas dominated in the towns and Deshasthas in the villages (*Ibid.*).
71. *Census of India*, 1911, Vol. VII, p. 338, cited in Johnson, 'Chitpavan Brahmins', p. 104.
72. *Ibid.*, p. 102; also see D.K. Karve 'My Life Story', in D.D.Karve (ed.), *The New Brahmans: Five Maharashtrian Families*, Berkeley, University of California Press, 1963, pp. 17ff, for a personal account.
73. *Gazetteer of the Bombay Presidency*, Vol. X, p. 113.
74. Johnson, 'Chitpavan Brahmins', pp. 106–07.
75. M.N. Srinivas, *Social Change in Modern India*, Bombay, Orient Longman, 1972, pp. 96–100.
76. This section relies heavily on two excellent and comprehensive studies on the non-Brahmana movement and Phule by Gail Omvedt (*Cultural Revolt in a Colonial Society*) and Rosalind O'Hanlon (*Caste, Conflict and Ideology*). I have merely tried to synthesise certain questions relating the contestations and tensions flowing from them with their bearing on gender.
77. Omvedt, *Cultural Revolt*, p. 66.
78. Phule was introduced to Paine's work by 'an anti-British Brahmana' who wished to unite all castes to win back political control from the British. Phule used the work for a radicalism of a very different kind (O'Hanlon, *Caste*, pp. 111–14).
79. For example, Phule's biographer describes an incident in which Phule was invited to a marriage party of a Brahmana friend but was insulted by other Brahmanas present on the occasion. Later when he and his wife Savitribai were engaged in running a school for low-caste girls they faced severe abuse and harassment from the orthodox sections of the Poona Brahmanas (Dhananjay Keer, *Mahatma Jotirao Phooley: Father of the Indian Social Revolution*, Bombay, Popular Prakashan, 1974, pp. 17, 25–26).
80. Padaval's book formed an important part of the repertoire of arguments of the non-Brahmana movement; it was being distributed in 1874 in the villages along with Phule's books on Shivaji and on Brahmana social power (O'Hanlon, *Caste*, pp. 226, 233).
81. O'Hanlon, *Caste*, p. 226.
82. Phule gives an interesting account of the hollowness of the claim to 'Maratha' status by people who regarded themselves as the old aristocracy. As the conversation proceeds Phule corners one such claimant into admitting his Kunbi connections (Appendix to Phule's *Shetkaryaca Asud* cited in Omvedt, *Cultural Revolt*, p. 110).
83. O'Hanlon, *Caste*, p. 265.
84. *Ibid.*

85. *Ibid.*, p. 131.
86. *Ibid.*, p. 80.
87. *Gulamgiri* is dedicated to the 'good people of the United States' for their abolition of black slavery and expresses the hope that the people of India may take it as an example and emancipate the lower castes from 'Brahmin thraldom' (*Gulamgiri*, trans. Ved Kumar Vadalankar, Bombay, Sadhana Prakashan Samiti, 1974, p. 5).
88. O'Hanlon, *Caste*, pp. 122, 200–01.
89. *Vividhadnyan Vistar*, July 1869, cited in O'Hanlon, *Caste*, p. 175.
90. Phule's explanation of inequalities as stemming from the ancient act of appropriation played a pivotal role in group identity formation (O'Hanlon, *Caste*, p. 151). The lower castes could see themselves as searching for a lost wholeness represented by the land in the unconquered state which was contrasted to the hierarchies introduced following the conquest. For a people denied an understanding of their past this explanation would be extremely enabling.
91. O'Hanlon, *Caste*, pp. 141–42.
92. Joan Leopold, 'The Aryan Theory of Race', *Indian Economic and Social History Review*, Vol. 7, No. 2, June 1970, pp. 271–97; Uma Chakravarti, 'Whatever Happened to the Vedic Dasi: Orientalism, Nationalism, and a Script for the Past,' in Kumkum Sangari and Sudesh Vaid, *Recasting Women: Essays in Colonial History*, Delhi, Kali for Women, 1988, pp. 27–87, pp. 38ff.
93. O'Hanlon, *Caste*, pp. 170–71.
94. *Ibid.*, p. 175.
95. *Ibid.*, pp. 169–71.
96. *Ibid.*, p. 186.
97. In this context Phule's gesture of sending some of his early writing to the Dakshina Prize Fund assumes significance. The Dakshina Committee had turned down Phule's version of Shivaji and rewarded Eknath Annaji Joshi's conventional Brahmanical version of Shivaji instead. Earlier they had turned down Phule's first piece of writing, the *Traitya Ratna*, which remained unpublished during Phule's lifetime (O'Hanlon, *Caste*, pp.123, 179).
98. *Ibid.*, p. 218. Another example of a vitriolic attack came from the pen of the famous Vishnu Shastri Chiplunkar who wrote dismissively about Phule whose name he always prefaced with 'Shudra' — Shudra Religious Teacher, Shudra World Teacher (Keer, *Mahatma Jotirao*, p. 146).
99. Omvedt, *Cultural Revolt*, p. 63.
100. Phule's disenchantment with the British was evident in the *Traitya Ratna* where the peasant household's travails at the hands of the

Brahmana priest become explicable to them through a reconceptualisation of God provided by a missionary. Finally the peasant couple resolve to educate themselves at Phule's night school since the key to a true understanding of their own society lay in education (O'Hanlon, *Caste*, p. 129).

101. Jyotiba Phule's evidence to Education Commission, *Report of the Education Commission*, Bombay, Vol II, Calcutta, 1884, cited in Kumar, *Western India*, pp. 307–308.

102. Tucker, 'Early Setting of the Non-Brahmin Movement', p. 139.

103. B.B. Misra, *The Middle Classes*, p. 307.

104. *Census of India*, 1931, Vol. VII, Part I, Bombay Report, cited in Omvedt, *Cultural Revolt*, p. 77.

105. Phule's biographers detail the difficulties he faced in keeping the institution going, of the outraged reaction of the orthodox and the pressure exerted upon his family which caved under it. Phule and his wife Savitribai had to leave home because of social pressure upon his father. In the face of difficulties in finding teachers Savitribai herself took on the task of teaching the girls and was subjected to much abuse and humiliation by the orthodox who were furious at the temerity of a low-caste woman in empowering herself and then empowering others like her (Keer, *Mahatma Jotirao*, pp. 23ff).

106. O'Hanlon, *Caste*, p. 119.

107. *Dnyanodaya*, 1 April 1853.

108. Muktabai, 'Mang Maharachya Dukhavisayi' (1855) reprinted in *Dnyanodaya* centenary volumes (ed.), B.P. Hivale, 1942, cited in Susie Tharu and K. Lalitha (eds.), *Women Writing in India*, Delhi, Oxford University Press, Vol. I, pp. 215–16.

109. *Ibid.*

110. *Ibid.*

111. *Ibid.*

112. *Ibid.*

113. *Ibid.*, pp. 213–14.

114. Keer, *Mahatma Jotirao*, pp. 86–87; Gail Omvedt, 'Jotiba Phule, the Bahujan Samaj and Women', unpublished typescript.

115. Marathi film on Jyotiba Phule, shown on Doordarshan in 1990.

116. O'Hanlon, *Caste*, p. 262.

117. Tarabai Shinde, *Stri-Purusha Tulana*, Poona, 1882, tr. by Rosalind O'Hanlon, *A Comparison Between Women and Men: Tarabai Shinde and the Critique of Gender Relations in Colonial India*, Madras, Oxford University Press, 1994.

118. Jyotiba Phule, *Satsar* (*The Essence of Truth*) September and October 1885, in Y.D. Phadke, *Collected Works of Jotiba Phule*, Bombay, Maharashtra Rajya Sahitya ani Sanskriti Mandal, 1991, pp. 345–83.

119. Omvedt, *Cultural Revolt*, pp.111–12.
120. Himani Banerji, 'Mothers and Daughters: Gender and Class in Educational Proposals for Women and by Women in Colonial Bengal', *Journal of Historical Sociology*, Vol. 5, No. 1, March 1992, pp. 1–30.
121. See for example D.D. Karve, *The New Brahmans*; Kumar, *Western India*, p. 278.
122. Kumar, *Western India*, p. 270.
123. O'Hanlon, *Caste*, p. 91.
124. Tucker, 'Early Setting of the Non-Brahmin Movement', p. 144.
125. O'Hanlon, *Caste*, p. 93.
126. Tucker, 'Early Setting of the Non-Brahmin Movement', p. 144.
127. *Ibid.*; O'Hanlon, *Caste*, p. 99.
128. Tucker, 'Early Setting of the Non-Brahmin Movement', pp. 154–55.
129. J.C. Masselos, *Towards Nationalism: Group Affiliations and the Politics of Public Associations in Nineteenth Century Western India*, Bombay, Popular Prakashan, 1974, pp. 35–36.
130. The widow remarriage controversy was to rage in many castes with similar splits in each caste. However, the focus here is only on one, i.e., the Brahmanas, although for purposes of analysis we may draw on others.
131. Anon., *An Essay on the Second Marriages of Widows by a Learned Brahmin of Nagpore*, with an introduction by Lancelot Wilkinson, no publisher, 1841, Manuscript in National Library, Calcutta.
132. W.M. Kolhatkar, 'Widow Remarriage in India', in C.Y. Chintamani (ed.), *Indian Social Reform*, Madras, Minerva Press, 1901, p. 294.
133. Ishwarchandra Vidyasagar, *Marriage of Hindu Widows* (with an introduction by Arabinda Poddar), Calcutta, K.P. Bagchi and Company, 1976, p. vi.
134. See for example C.Y. Chintamani, *Indian Social Reform*; Charles Heimsath, *Indian Nationalism and Hindu Social Reform*, Princeton, Princeton University Press, 1964, and S. Natarajan, *A Century of Social Reform in India*, Bombay, Asia Publishing House, 1959.
135. In order to develop a proper focus on the male viewpoint on widowhood I have summarised the main trends in the positions throughout the nineteenth century rather than confine it to the 60s and 70s when the widow reform movement was in its most controversial stage.
136. J.C. Ghose (ed.), *The English Works of Rammohun Roy*, Calcutta, Bhowanipore Oriental Press, 1885, pp. 364–65.
137. Uma Chakravarti, 'Gender, Caste and Labour: The Ideological and

Material Structures of Widowhood', in Marty Chen (ed.), *Widowhood in India*, Delhi, Sage, forthcoming.

138. *Ibid.*
139. *An Essay on the Second Marriages of Widows*, p. 8.
140. *Marriage of Hindu Widows*, p. x.
141. *Calcutta Review*, Vol. 25, pp. 351–58, reprinted in *Marriage of Hindu Widows*, p. 139.
142. *Government of India, Legislative Council Proceedings from January to December, 1856*, Vol. II, p. 438, cited in Heimsath, *Indian Nationalism*, pp. 83–84.
143. D.C. Sen in *Prabhasi*, cited in Dagmar Engels, *Changing Role of Women in Bengal, c. 1890–1930, With Special Reference to British and Bengali Discourse*, unpublished Ph.D. thesis, School of Oriental and African Studies, London, 1987, p. 69.
144. Uma Chakravarti, 'Conceptualising Brahmanical Patriarchy in Early India: Gender, Caste, Class and State', *Economic and Political Weekly*, Vol. 28, No. 14, April 3, 1993, pp. 579–585.
145. *The Times*, August 15, 1856.
146. Lancelot Wilkinson, 'Introduction' to Anon., *Essay on the Second Marriages of Hindu Widows*, pp. 8–9.
147. *Ibid.*, pp. 9–11.
148. A comparison between the 'colonial' and 'indigenous' perception of widowhood and 'illicit' sexual activity indicates that there are vital differences between the two. The upper-caste literate male was not, in our view, functioning as an authoritative spokesman of 'colonialism's gendered idioms' as O'Hanlon suggests. More often than not he was deploying the gendered idioms of Brahmanical texts as this exonerated him of participating in acts attributed to the consequences of a widow's repressed sexuality. In this I differ from O'Hanlon (Rosalind O'Hanlon, 'Issues of Widowhood in Colonial Western India,' in Douglas Haynes and Gyan Prakash, *Resistance and Everyday Social Relations in South Asia*, Delhi, Oxford University Press, 1991, p. 102).
149. Scholars from Nabadwip were also consulted but the position taken was that although there was nothing in the Shastras to prohibit widow marriage it was against the time-honoured customs of the people (Ishwarchandra Vidyasagar, *Marriage of Hindu Widows*, p. vii).
150. Initially the pandits stated that the custom of widow marriage was approved for Shudras but later withdrew sanction for all, when the movement for widow marriage was launched, since the movement was intended for widows of all castes (Vidyasagar, *Marriage of Hindu Widows*, pp. vii, 115).

151. Two events were crucial in Vidyasagar's life: one, the remarriage of one of his teachers to a young girl who was left a widow soon after the consummation of the marriage; and two, the visit of a young widowed girl to his family home. From the emotional outburst of Vidyasagar's mother after she had talked to the young widow in the inner quarter of the house, it appears that the widow was a victim of her circumstances and may have been seduced. Vidyasagar's mother was obviously moved by the girl's plight, as she came out with tears in her eyes and said to her son, 'You have read enough of the Shastras; have you found no sanction of the Shastras for the remarriage of the miserable infant widow?' Vidyasagar's own sympathy for the child widow was more than strongly endorsed by his mother's (Vidyasagar, *Marriage of Hindu Widows*, p. 113). The bodily mortification and fasting prescribed for widows in Bengal were extremely harsh. Even water was forbidden during the *Ekadashi* fast. There are accounts of widows licking the moist earth to quench their thirst during this fast in the hot season (personal communication from Tanika Sarkar). That even sons experienced trauma watching their mothers transformed from *sumangalis* to shaven-headed, defeminised beings is documented in biographical accounts of the nineteenth century(see D.D. Karve (ed.), *New Brahmans*, p. 196).

152. See Radhabai Inamdar et. al., *Position of Widows*, Essays compiled by the Director of Ethnography for India titled, *Experiences of Widows and Other Girls*, Collection addressed to Sir Herbert Risley, 1911, Eur. MS. Division 356, India Office Library, p. 8.

153. Such were the emotions expressed by Anandibai Karve's father at the sight of her first-born son, following her controversial remarriage to Professor Karve, opposed not only by the community but also by her mother. When the father was excommunicated by his caste-fellows he explained his position to his children, including two other widows, in these words: 'All my daughters and sons have experienced and known the joys and sorrows of married life. But Baya (Anandibai) has not fully experienced married life. She has committed no sin in remarrying nor we in consenting to the marriage.' Sometime later when he saw Anandibai's first child he took the baby on his lap; while tears of joy flowed from his eyes he cried, 'It is by His (God's) grace that Baya has this beautiful jewel of a boy. It is a wicked custom to prevent child-widow remarriage, thereby depriving our country of those who might become pillars of strength to her' (Parvatibai Athavale, *Hindu Widow: An Autobiography*, tr. by Rev. Justin E. Abbot, Delhi, Reliance Publishing House, 1986 [Reprint], pp. 18–19).

154. Gopal Hari Deshmukh, *Shatapatre* no. 99, cited in Stanley Wolpert, *Tilak and Gokhale* (Ph.D dissertation, re-cited in Heimsath, *Indian Nationalism*, p. 102).
155. Dayaram Gidumal, *The Status of Women in India or a Handbook for Hindu Social Reformers*, Bombay, Fort Publishers, 1889.
156. *Ibid.*, p. i.
157. *Ibid.*, p. ii.
158. Lancelot Wilkinson, 'Introduction', p. 4.
159. Gidumal, *The Status of Women*, p. ii.
160. *Ibid.*, p. lxxv.
161. *Ibid.*, p. lxxvii.
162. *Ibid.*
163. *Ibid.*, p. lxxvi.
164. *Ibid.*
165. *Ibid.*, p. lxxiv.
166. *Ibid.*, p. lxxv.
167. M.G. Ranade, cited in S. Natarajan, *Social Reform*, p. 5.
168. *The Times of India Calendar and Directory* for 1869, p. 304.
169. *Marriage of Hindu Widows Advocated by the Pathare Reform Association of Bombay*, Appendix L, *Social and Political Revolution: Hindu Marriage a Fact*, Extracts from Newspapers pp. xiv ff. (Manuscript, National Library Calcutta); Masselos, *Towards Nationalism*, pp. 88–90.
170. Richard Tucker, 'From Dharamashastra to Politics', *Indian Economic and Social History Review*, Vol. 7 No. 1, 1970, p. 333.
171. Masselos, *Towards Nationalism*, p. 89.
172. *Social and Political Revolution*, pp. xliv ff.
173. *Ibid.*
174. Masselos, *Towards Nationalism*, pp. 90–91.
175. Wamanrao Kolhatkar, 'Marriage of Widows', in C.Y. Chintamani (ed.), *Indian Social Reform*, p. 300.
176. Parvati Athavale, Anandibai Karve's sister, records that it was the discussions at the *shastrartha* that influenced her father to accept that widow remarriage was permissible. Clearly the debate thus had a cathartic character (Parvati Athavale, *Hindu Widow*, 1986, p. 17).
177. *Ibid.*, p. 301.
178. Tucker, 'From Dharmashastra', p. 335.
179. Kolhatkar, 'Marriage of Widows', p. 305.
180. Tarabai Shinde, *Stri Purusha Tulana*, p. 75.
181. A striking aspect of the entire widow remarriage controversy during this early phase was that no women featured in the debate. Even the reformers had no women in their ranks; thus, in an issue that crucially affected their lives no women spoke at least in any audible

way. It appears that upper-caste women, the objects of the reform, were tied up in larger social forces over which they had no control and which they could not shape.

182. Y.D. Phadke, *Social Reform Movements in Maharashtra*, Delhi, Maharashtra Information Centre, 1989, p. 20.
183. Gidumal, *The Status of Women*, p. lxxxxviii.
184. C.Y.Chintamani, *Indian Social Reform*, p. 306.
185. *Native Opinion*, 11 January 1871 (cited in Tucker, 'Dharmashastra', p. 338).
186. Ramabai Ranade, *Amchya Ayushatil Kahi Athavani* (tr.) by Kusumvati Deshpande, *Ranade: His Wife's Reminiscences*, Delhi, Publications Division, 1963, pp. 33–34.
187. B.N. Motivala, *Karsondas Mulji: A Biographical Study*, Bombay, Karsondas Mulji Centenary Celebration Committee, 1935, pp. 215 ff., S. Natarajan, *Social Reform in India*, pp. 60–62.
188. Chintamani, *Indian Social Reform*, p. 187.
189. Tucker, 'Dharmashastra', p. 337.
190. Masselos, *Towards Nationalism*, pp. 96ff.
191. Tucker, 'Early Setting of the Non-Brahmin Movement', p. 147.
192. Richard Cashman, *The Myth*, pp. 27–28.
193. David Hardiman (ed.), *Peasant Resistance in India, 1858–1914*, Delhi, Oxford University Press, 1992, p. 29.
194. R.C. Majumdar (ed.), *British Paramountcy and Indian Renaissance*, Bombay, Bharatiya Vidya Bhavan, 1963, p. 909; also see Johnson, 'Chitpavan Brahmins', p. 109.
195. Ramabai Ranade, *Reminiscences*, pp. 51–52.
196. Tucker, 'Early Setting of the Non-Brahmin Movement', p. 154.
197. O'Hanlon, *Caste*, pp. 190–92, 258.
198. *Quarterly Journal of the Poona Sarvajanik Sabha*, Vol. 5 for 1879–97, cited in Johnson, 'Chitpavan Brahmins', pp. 109–10.
199. For an extreme articulation of Brahmanophobia see Arthur Crawford, *Our Troubles in Poona and the Deccan*, pp. 77ff., 85, 115.
200. *Ibid.*, pp. 136ff.
201. *Report of the Director of Public Instruction in the Bombay Presidency for the Year 1877–78*, Appendix D, p. 81 cited in Cashman, *The Myth*, p. 41.
202. Cashman, *The Myth*, p. 218.
203. Professor D.K. Karve's memoirs describe the way poor Brahmanas struggled to educate their sons so that they could find jobs in the administration (D.D. Karve, *New Brahmans*, pp. 19–22, 112, 115).
204. Omvedt, *Cultural Revolt*, pp. 125–27.
205. Cashman, *The Myth*, pp. 37–38.
206. *Ibid.*, p. 39.

207. *Native Opinion*, 11 July 1869, and 8 August 1869.
208. Natarajan, *Social Reform*, p. 63.
209. V.N. Mandlik, 'Introduction', *The Vyavahara Mayukha*, Bombay, 1880, p. ii, cited in Tucker, 'Dharmashastra', p. 339.
210. *Writings and Speeches of the Late Honourable Rao Saheb Vishwanath Narayan Mandlik*, Bombay, 1896, pp. 129–30, cited in Tucker, 'Dharmashastra', p. 339.
211. *Native Opinion*, 19 March 1865, cited in Tucker, 'Early Setting of the Non-Brahmin Movement', p. 154, n. 4.
212. Tucker, 'Early Setting of the Non-Brahmin Movement', p. 144.
213. Cashman, *The Myth*, p. 40.
214. *Ibid.*, p. 38.
215. *Mahratta*, 1 February 1885.
216. Cashman, *The Myth*, pp. 148–50.
217. Joan Leopold, 'The Aryan Theory of Race', *Indian Economic and Social History Review*, Vol. 7 No. 2, June 1970, pp. 271–97, p. 278.
218. *Ibid.*, p. 281.
219. M.G. Ranade, in M.B. Kolasker (ed.), *Religious and Social Reform*, quoted in J. Leopold, 'The Aryan Theory', pp. 279–81.
220. B.G. Tilak, *The Orion*, or *Researches in the Antiquity of the Veda*, Poona, Tilak Brothers, 1893, p. 464.
221. M.G. Ranade, *The Rise of Maratha Power*, pp. 5–6, cited in Cashman, *The Myth*, p. 103.
222. Cashman, *The Myth*, pp. 105–06.
223. *Ibid.*, pp. 14–16.
224. V.K. Chiplunkar, *Nibandhamala*, Poona, 1926, p. 992, cited in Cashman, *The Myth*, p. 8.
225. M.G. Ranade, *Miscellaneous Writings of Mr. Justice M.G. Ranade*, Bombay, Manektala and Company, 1915, p. 126.
226. Cashman, *The Myth*, pp. 200–02. It is significant that even at the time when Tilak was making political use of Shivaji the question of conceding Kshatriya status to him as a Maratha was resisted by the conservative Brahmanas including Tilak. While Shivaji was a 'brave' man, all his bravery, it was argued, did not give him right to a status that very *'nearly approached that of a Brahmin'* (emphasis added). Further, the fact that Shivaji worshipped the Brahmanas in no way altered social relations, 'since it was as Shudra that he did it — as a Shudra the servant, if not the slave, of the Brahmin' (Gordon Johnson, 'Chitpavan Brahmins', p. 114).
227. Cashman, *The Myth*, p. 185.
228. *Ibid.*, p. 201.
229. Omvedt, *Cultural Revolt*, p. 170.
230. Cashman, *The Myth*, pp. 168–170.

PART TWO

The establishment and consolidation of the colonial state, its repercussions on traditional elites and the social processes it generated affecting castes, the process of class formation, and the construction of history and of nation, were the backdrop for major changes in gender relations in the nineteenth century. Part Two is focused centrally on gender. Among the issues addressed here are: in what way did the colonial state's new structures, transform and reorganise gender; what was the new agenda being set for women by paternalistic reformers of the nineteenth century; was this agenda common to all women or aimed only at particular categories among them? How was it received by women; how and in what way was their 'consent' produced; to what extent did women share in the new agenda and act as willing reproducers of class and gender norms; and, finally, to what extent did women withhold consent to the dominant model of patriarchy emerging in the late nineteenth century.

3

Law, Colonial State and Gender

I

A crucial area that requires analysis is the relationship between the colonial state, law, family, caste panchayats and gender in the nineteenth century. Unfortunately, there has so far been no work that has focused on this. Our exploration of these themes therefore cannot answer questions so much as raise them. To begin with we need to ask: in what way did the new laws of the colonial state affect women and how was this similar or different for men? Did the colonial state regard women as its direct subjects or as mediated through the family? How far did women remain under the authority of the family and the caste? What was the relationship between the caste panchayat and the larger legal culture of the second half of the nineteenth century? What was the relationship between 'Hindu' law,[1] customary law, and statutory law? How did these affect women? And finally was the new legal culture enabling for women or was it more repressive than textual or customary law? Many of the questions that need asking will remain only partially raised in my preliminary analysis of three legal issues of gender in nineteenth century Maharashtra: the law on widow remarriage, on conjugality, and on the age of consent, but the questions around them will, I hope, be pursued by others in the full-length study they deserve.

The Hindu Widows Remarriage Act of 1856 was the second intervention by the colonial state in a matter pertaining to 'custom' with the sanction of religion. Unlike the act on sati which banned a practice, the Widows Remarriage Act was meant to remove a ban and enable widows to remarry where they were not permitted to do so. Lucy Carroll[2] has provided an exhaustive and illuminating account of the consequences of this act; here we will concentrate on drawing attention to certain issues which emerged from its interpretation.

First, it is important to note that the act, possibly unintentionally, effectively reversed the principle of distinctiveness and discreteness of customs of different castes. Since the prevalence or otherwise of certain customs such as enforced widowhood had been in many ways the *basis* of the hierarchy of castes, as argued earlier, the new act was bound to have certain repercussions on gender and on culture. However, as Carroll points out, the British appear to have believed that they were legislating in a situation of *tabula rasa*, creating a practice where none had existed.[3] This innocence may be attributable to the fact that, by and large, only the high castes were visible to the British and to the middle-class reformers; thus, when legislation was introduced it tended to extend the biases and the ideology of textual Hindu law to apply to those who had been either outside or on the margins of such customs earlier. (This process of incorporating more and more people from the margins was not new; it can be traced as far back as Manu who, while conceding the need to respect custom and usage of families and particular communities, also stated that the people should learn their several usages from 'a Brahmana born in that country'. Thus, customary rules were altered constantly in spirit, and sometimes in tenor, greatly through Brahmanical expositors.)[4]

The ambiguities and contradictions inherent in attempting to mesh textual Hindu law and statutory law, the issue of its applicability, especially in the matter of widow remarriage, led to virtually three-quarters of a century of 'dramatic judicial controversy'.[5] The controversy focused on the penalty clauses included in the Act whereby the widow forfeited her claim to the property of the dead husband when she remarried, whereas in many castes which had permitted widow remarriage it was not necessary to do so. The new law regarded her *as if she had died* for purposes of claiming an interest in her deceased husband's property. An early judgement had laid down that remarriage was equivalent to the 'civil death of the widow'.[6] Thus, as the new law was interpreted in the High Courts of Calcutta, Madras and Bombay, the customary law on the relationship between widowhood and property among certain castes was displaced and in its stead Brahmanical values which held widow remarriage in disrepute came to impose the penalty of forfeiture for violating the norm of the 'chaste, ascetic, prayerful widow'.

In the decades during which the British Indian courts attempted to resolve the issue of a widow's remarriage and her relationship to the property of her first husband within 'Hindu' law, as defined in the new statutes, both British and Indian judges treated Hindu law as complete and fixed, whereas it was extremely fluid even at the time when its fixation was sought. This was largely because what comprised Hindu law was debatable and was variously understood as Brahmanical textual law, or customary law, or a mixture of both. Further, the relationship between the two was itself unclear. Changing notions of what constituted Hindu law, particularly when it applied to gender codes, were best captured by the contradictory interpretations of the Widows Remarriage Act. Since the Act had inscribed forfeiture into the clauses, judges had a trying time explaining its merits and its consistency with the conceptions of 'Hindu' law. This led to a spate of opinions and differing judgements.

First, it became necessary to define the nature of wifehood in Hindu law and thereafter to define the nature of the widow's relationship to her dead husband as well as his property, and further to locate the purpose for which she was given the right to enjoy it. The difficulties of ascertaining many of the tricky questions the Hindu law on remarriage entailed were recognised by Justice Wilson who pointed out that second marriage was a 'thing' the textual authorities had not contemplated. Nevertheless, the position was taken that the widow enjoyed her dead husband's property based on Brihaspati's text which stated, 'Of him whose wife is not deceased half the body survives. How then should another take his property while half his person is alive?' Thus in her capacity as half the body of her deceased husband the widow is capable of conferring spiritual benefit upon him by her positive acts; she inherits as she continues to be his *patni*.[7] But precisely because she is half the body of her deceased husband, and enjoys his property in that capacity, she could not also be half the body of another person following remarriage; she must cease to be half the body of one before she could become half the body of another. Forfeiture of the property of the first husband was clearly necessary and it was in accordance with the principles of Hindu law because the 'fiction' upon which the right of the widow had been based now ceased with her remarriage.[8] The fact that the judges could argue that forfeiture was in accordance with Hindu law when the remarriage itself for the uppermost castes had not been in accordance with it, was an anomaly which appears as a running thread in the contradictory positions taken by the judges, as we shall see, but for the moment the judges chose to bypass it as they had enough contradictions on their hands in the 'half the body' metaphor.

The other major problem confronting the judges was the nature of wifehood among the lower castes or Shudras where customary law had permitted remarriage and further where, among many castes, the remarrying widow did not forfeit her interest in the deceased husband's property. Justice Mukherji perceived a basic difference in the nature of wifehood among the lower castes: in his perception they clearly did not believe in the doctrine that the wife is one-half of the body of the husband and that, on his death, his widow survives as one-half of his body;[9] thus, wifehood was qualitatively different among the lower castes than among the high castes. The privilege of Shastric law was intended by the law-givers to be applicable only to the Brahmanas, Kshatriyas and Vaishyas and not to the Shudras. Since the Shudras practised non-sacred marriage it was considered perfectly consonant with their customs that the widow need not forfeit property on remarriage. Indeed it would be 'inappropriate to apply reasoning based on the general principles of Hindu law, intended only for the upper castes, to decree forfeiture for the low-caste widow', according to the judge. Forfeiture should be applicable only in the castes which regarded wifehood as sacred and widowhood as a spiritual state. Implicit in this interpretation was the argument that the statutory law of 1856 on widow remarriage was neither wholly drawn from Hindu textual law nor from customary law. It is evident from the judgements that judges of the Bombay and Calcutta High Courts were attempting to collapse the difference between the two, whereas judges of the Allahabad High Court were implicitly arguing for a continuance of a caste-differentiated law.[10] Clearly there were major contradictions in any attempt to legislate for all 'Hindu' women.

An allied problem of the difference between Hindu law and customary law, between wifehood among the upper and lower castes, was the question of who exactly the Shudras were and whether a particular caste was Shudra or not. This in turn would determine the applicability of the Hindu law. This was particularly difficult in a situation where many low castes were sanskritising and adopting customs of the higher castes. The courts took contradictory positions on whether Hindu law applied to the lower castes, sometimes dismissing and at other times accepting claims of the parties appealing to the court. The 'inability' of many of the lower castes to testify about law and custom in their families, or to distinguish between one system and the other, was mocked at, whereas the different judgements reveal that the judges were themselves divided and confused about which customs were traditional and applicable in a given situation. This led them to hold different positions at different times for the Rajbansis, a 'low' caste in the Bengal region. In the process the judges often applied not only the law of the parties concerned but of a different people.[11] It has been suggested that the courts found it easier to decide the caste status of the twice-born because they had a list of diagnostic customs regarding ideal conduct for them based on the Shastric texts. The customs of the Shudras, or defining who the Shudras were, remained a problem because there was no such ready reference for them. However, once the courts took a decision about a caste they became a source of authoritative decisions[12] in caste-ranking, in regulating the ceremonial privileges of a caste, or the customs that were valid for a caste, including those that would apply to women.

Through the various twists and turns taken by the British Indian courts the theme of the inherent conflict between Hindu law and statutory law is evident as also the serious inconsistencies created by regarding the statutory law as reconcilable with traditional Hindu law. Justice Mukherji of the Allahabad High Court conceded that the orthodox would not recognise the marriage (of a widow) as valid in castes where the strict rules of Hindu law applied even though the British Indian courts may do so.[13] Even more offensive to many persons, including the judges, was the view taken by the Privy Council that an 'unchaste' widow did not forfeit the right to her husband's property after she had succeeded to the estate.[14] Justice Mukherji as a 'Hindu' judge refused to accept this view. He was emphatic that such a decision could never be regarded as Hindu law as the Hindu law could not be interpreted apart from the dictates of conscience and reason. Hindu law could never reconcile within its conception a situation in which the widow forfeited the property of her deceased husband in case she lived 'with a single man' but could enjoy it while indulging in the 'grossest immorality'[15] of an adulterous relationship outside of marriage. Arguing that such an interpretation, based on the case law, would cause shock to 'one's moral conscience', Justice Suleman, also of the Allahabad High Court, decided against the widow forfeiting her husband's property on remarriage.[16] This was clearly the more moral interpretation of the new statutory law as it enabled the lower-caste widow to keep her property and be chaste in her second marriage.

The varying interpretations of the British Indian courts were clearly throwing up grave contradictions. It is evident that while the colonial state, either on its own, or in conjunction with a section of the reformist middle class elite, was initiating legislation affecting women, neither it nor the reformist elite was willing to transform the entire set of relationships relating to the remarriage of widows, family structures, conjugality, and property. The state was therefore not consistent in its handling of these questions. The position taken by the Justices of the Allahabad High Court is an example of this ambivalence and different perspectives were adopted by the courts in different regions according to certain interests of the colonial state in handling customary law. In Punjab and Haryana the question of the widow forfeiting her deceased husband's property was not the central issue — rather it was the insistence that the widow's remarriage must be restricted within the custom of the *karewa*, which was remarriage to the deceased husband's brother, thereby ensuring that the property remained within the affinal male kin control circle. This was upheld by the British administration since the colonial economy and its military recruitment hinged upon upholding 'peasant' customs where a woman's productive and reproductive capacities were fully utilised by the affinal kinsmen but were also exclusively under their control.[17]

The reaction of the courts to the interpretation of statutory laws regarding gender codes may also be related to the nature of class formation in different regions. The appearance of a professional middle class, as in the presidency areas of Calcutta, Bombay, and Madras, and an educated elite, could act as a push towards homogenisation and a greater reliance towards 'reformed' Hindu law, which is what the statutory law was attempting to provide.

The interpretation of the law on widow remarriage and forfeiture in western India, especially in Maharashtra where Brahmanic influences were significant but caste contestations and upward mobility moves were also frequent, appears to have been shaped by some of these forces. The push towards universalising came partly from the cultural nationalism of the upper castes and partly from British preference for textual law, which they had made the basis of building up case law in various presidency areas and which overrode their preference for customary law in the Punjab. The 'universal' applicability of the law, a position taken by a combination of British and Indian judges, was a decisive move in the direction of a uniform 'Hindu' law which did not recognise differences according to caste. Consequently, the judges took the view that there was no question of a contradiction between Hindu law and customary law for purposes of applying the new statutory law to Hindus. It was the judiciary's balancing act, or rather its act of masking what it was doing in applying one set of laws but having to pass them off as 'Hindu law'; this led Nelson to write that the British might bind the people by new laws but they were required to pretend carefully that they were maintaining the existing laws and customs of the country.[18] However, not everyone was taken in by this careful pretence and at least one person who called himself a 'Hindu lawyer' warned others about the need to keep a watchful eye on the courts, especially the High Courts which were in his view invidiously tampering with Hindu law.[19]

From the point of view of this work, it is significant that the Bombay High Court had initially taken the position, which the Allahabad High Court sustained, that where caste usage permitted the widow to retain property inherited from her deceased husband the forfeiture clause of the 1856 Act would not be applicable. Accordingly in *Parekh Ranochor v. Bai Vakhat* (1886) the widow retained the property.[20] But in 1896, at the turn of the century, a full bench of the Bombay High Court overruled the earlier decision which had denied the validity of the forfeiture clause for widows belonging to those castes where remarriage was conventionally permitted.[21] Justices Farran, Parsons, and Ranade took their stand neither on customary law nor on Hindu law but on the statutory law, taking a very literal view of the wording of Act XV of 1856. Homogenising all castes and the differences between them, Farran held that the Act applied to *all* Hindu widows. Arguing that the law must be read as having universal applicability, he found nothing in its clauses that suggested that it was intended to apply the rule of forfeiture only to those widows who were for the first time permitted to contract valid civil marriages under the act. Thus, Farran was emphatic about the universal applicability of the clauses to 'all Hindus alike, whatever their caste or the interpretation of Hindu law authorised by their caste may be'.[22] He argued further that the position taken by the Allahabad High Court undermined the express provisions of the Act based on 'an assumption'. His own assumption instead was that the legislature 'intended' to 'assimilate' Hindu law in particular to apply to all castes and to thereby make the law, as administered, 'accord with the *true* principles of Hindu law' (emphasis added).[23] Thus, the true principles of Hindu law on widowhood, violated by customary law according to Farran, were to penalise the widow for failing to observe sacred widowhood; all castes were now to conform to the ideals of 'Hindu' womanhood and the courts were a means of ensuring this position.

Justice Ranade took a slightly different view from the Chief Justice's while concurring with him on the decision of forfeiture. Elaborating on the intent and provisions of Act XV of 1856, Ranade held that some of the assumptions of the act, particularly that the ban on the remarriage of widows was almost universal with only some exceptions, had been mistaken. Ranade was a Chitpavan Brahmana and an active historian and social reformer. He would, thus, have been conscious of the ban on widow remarriage being a 'privilege' held on to by the Brahmanas and the highest castes against the attempts by upwardly mobile low castes seeking to adopt it in order to claim high status for themselves throughout the eighteenth and nineteenth centuries. The practice of enforced widowhood was thus the exception, confined only to about 20 per cent of the population, whereas the statutory law had presumed that it was lifting the ban for the bulk of the population. Further, Ranade had also recognised that the statutes had presumed the need for prescribing remarriage rituals to conform to the rituals of the first marriage whereas in the castes where widows remarried, the rituals for a remarriage, called pat, were distinct from the first marriage called *lagna*.

However, Ranade considered these assumptions to be immaterial to the intent and correctness of the statutory law of forfeiture which he regarded as conforming to the 'original' practice even among the castes that conventionally permitted the remarriage of widows: the statutes had only *declared what was universal practice*.[24] He thus believed that the legislature had validly adopted the principles of universal applicability on the basis of Arthur Steele's *Law and Custom*, ignoring, as Lucy Carroll notes, the fact that Steele's study had been confined to the Brahmana-dominated Poona region where Brahmanising influences were at work long before the British takeover. He also chose to ignore the evidence before the subordinate judge that in the particular case under appeal the practices of the caste of the widow *did not* entail forfeiture on remarriage.[25]

Ranade's position amounted to the Shastric position that a man's property was to be enjoyed only by the 'chaste' widow who lived up to the sacramental notion of 'Hindu marriage'. The disparate practices among various castes had been recognised as the customary laws of various communities and the Brahmanical lawgivers had tried to provide acceptance for them in the texts. Though disparate, the customary laws had a coherence and were explicable within the larger ideology of textual Hindu law, which not only *provided* for distinctive laws for different castes but *privileged* them as these were the basis of the hierarchical ordering of castes. In Ranade's view, however, the relationship between customary law and textual law was not as contradictory as the Allahabad High Court was making it out to be by emphasising different norms for the upper castes and for the Shudras respectively. Justice Mukherji of the Allahabad High Court had attempted to reconcile Manu's norms for the twice-born with the new statute law by continuing the distinction between the customs of the lower castes and the uppermost castes.[26] He resisted homogenisation which would *erase* the distinctions between castes implicit in the new statutory law. Forfeiture should, according to him, apply only to the high-caste widows who had traditionally been 'privileged' by having exclusive access to sacred marriage. Similarly, Justice King argued that strict 'Hindu law could not be applied to castes which had always permitted remarriage'.[27] In contrast Ranade, as a 'nationalist' Hindu, was arguing the point of view that it was not only possible to reconcile customary law and textual law within 'Hindu' law as in the past but also desirable to do so in the present and in the future where all Hindus *should* have the same law. This the statutory law had now achieved in the case of widows, remarriage, and their relationship to property by insisting that all widows, whatever previous custom, *must* forfeit property on remarriage.

It is significant that the framers of the clauses of the statute and Ranade took the position that they were outlining the 'true' situation as it had obtained in the ancient past. The preamble to the statute on the Hindu Widows Remarriage Act stated that the legal incapacity of Hindu widows to contract a valid marriage was not a 'true' interpretation in consonance with the precepts of their own religion.[28] Ranade argued, however, that the forfeiture by the widow was the 'universal' practice even among the lower castes that had, according to custom, permitted widow remarriage.[29] This was the 'true' position which was consistent with the position of the widow reform movement — to permit remarriage but along with the corollary of forfeiture. This was a necessity for the upper-caste propertied classes in order that the male affinal kin retain the control of property through cutting off links with the widow once she remarried. If the property of the deceased had been a means to maintain the widow and ensure that she performed the necessary acts for his spiritual merit, she was now to be maintained by her second husband, for whom, and with whom, she was now to perform ritual acts. The position of the reformers, Ranade included, was to make the child virgin widow a real wife, to relieve her of her 'unnatural' state, but not to give her control, even limited in nature, over two sets of property. The forfeiture clause was thus imperative in countering the possible opposition of the upper castes, who strongly resisted the remarriage of upper-caste widows.

From the above discussion it is evident that despite the different positions taken and arguments offered by various courts in interpreting the Widows Remarriage Act a certain thread is discernible whereby changes regarding gender codes appear to be moving in the direction of conformity with the tenets of textual Brahmanic Hinduism. In this process the British and the high-caste Hindus, who were sometimes the judges and often the lawyers in the cases, acted in conjunction. Further, judges of both races had little or no sympathy for the practices common among the lower orders, who in any case were regarded as 'ignorant' and 'unfamiliar' with the laws. The preference for textual law, and thence for statutory law, was evident in the desire for one set of laws from the point of view of ease and convenience.[30] In sum, one can also discern an essentially conservative agenda (despite the humanist rhetoric) of the British administrators and sections of the upper-caste Indians who took the position that it was best to give women some rights but also to limit them. Most importantly, even though the lifting of the ban on the remarriage of widows for women of the upper castes implied the adoption of a lower-caste practice, the incorporation of such practices was to be minimal. The adoption of the full range of practices prevalent among the lower castes, such as non-sacramental marriage (where the wife was not regarded as half the body of her husband), which had enabled her to hold the property of her deceased husband even after remarriage, was unacceptable. Thus, even as the castes were homogenised into a larger Hindu legal structure, and even as there was an apparent de-sanskritising move in lifting the ban on widow remarriage, British administrators and their Indian counterparts ensured the maintenance of Brahmanic ideology and Brahmanised patriarchy and at the same time made these the basis of the norms for everybody else. In effect, this meant that the lower-caste woman was required to conform to the norms for the upper-caste woman. Although there was some approval for these changes there was a degree of resistance from the upper-caste middle class, especially from those who could see what the implications of these changes were. The reactions of one such 'eyewitness' to the changes are typical not only of the somewhat contradictory nature of the processes but also of the contradictory nature of the reactions of men of this class, as will be evident from the passage below:

...I think what requires reconsideration and revision the most is that part of Hindu law, or rather Hindu law as interpreted by our judges, which bears upon women's rights — I mean her concrete not her abstract rights. I hate for instance the new ruling that a wife refusing conjugal society to her husband can be sent to prison for her refusal. I hate all the customs which are not sanctioned even by the fourth abridgement of Manu which we now have but which are nevertheless enforced by the courts, although they are opposed to the spirit of all our institutions.... Our institutes lay down that an unchaste widow be deprived of her inheritance from her husband but our High Courts say she should not be, because (and there lies the sting of the ruling) by adopting the old rule 'not only will a fruitful cause of domestic discord be largely extended but a motive will be afforded, to say the least of it, for publishing and bringing into the court the most deplorable scandals'. How complimentary to us. A decision based mainly on this reason is not supposed to shock native opinion but a decision that a remarried widow by her remarriage is not to lose her inheritance is supposed to be one that would 'certainly be a shock to native opinion'. In other words we prefer unchastity to remarriage and that is what is called administering the Hindu law.... Our loving High Courts have [also] chosen to extend the rule [of mutual fidelity which has become so one-sided that a husband can default during his wife's lifetime but she may not even on his death] to even those among whom the caste would dissolve marriages for valid reasons, for the fiat has gone through that even a Sudra wife, allowed by her caste to remarry must prove a divorce by her husband or go to jail for bigamy and adultery. On the one hand we have customs enforced among the highest castes which are utterly repugnant to their 'best traditions' and on the other we have customs thrust upon the lower castes which are utterly unsuited to their constitution and to their institutions, and in either case it is a woman who suffers most.... My dear friends, the very foundations of Hindu law have been corrupted, and I say to all practical Hindus to take up the reform of Hindu law. First of all, keep a sharp eye on the High Courts...[31]

From this long and impassioned account, only one thing is clear — there were all manner of changes occurring with respect to the laws affecting women. For the rest the 'Hindu lawyer' (as he called himself) was deeply uncomfortable with the British administration of Hindu law which enforced repugnant customs upon the high castes and ignored the need for a different set of laws for the low castes, thereby erasing the distinctions between the 'constitutions' of the two. The 'Hindu' lawyer was a contrast to Ranade, just as the British administration of Hindu law in the High Court of Allahabad on the forfeiture clause for the remarrying widow was a contrast to the High Courts of Bombay and Calcutta. The entangled relationship between law, custom, caste, property, and gender was not so easy to disentangle on the question of widow remarriage as we have seen but also with respect to conjugality as we shall see in the next section.

In the second half of the nineteenth century women were being gradually drawn into the ambit of a new legal structure administered by the British Indian courts. As the quantum of legislation increased and the authority of caste panchayats became dysfunctional, or redundant in certain cases, women became subject to dual authority structures. Their everyday lives and many of their so-called 'lapses' continued to be governed by the social power of the community, exercised through the caste panchayats where customary law was applied, but at the same time the new statutory laws also began to govern their lives, especially on certain issues relating to property, thus making them subjects of the state in extraordinary situations. Both upheld the authority of the patriarchal family and property structures even though the two systems were apparently dissimilar and at times in conflict with each other. The overlap between the systems and their relationship to that new entity, then being constituted, called 'Hindu law' also remained problematic and unresolved throughout the second half of the nineteenth century.

The contradictions in the existence of and overlap between different sets of practices and their validity in law, especially with respect to gender, became evident gradually from the mid-nineteenth century onwards. The legislature had ensured the continuance of custom by Section 26 of the Bombay Regulation IV of 1827. Judicial officers were instructed to give effect to the 'ancient customs and usages' of the people.[32] The panchayats were also empowered by the same laws to decide civil cases. In 1868 the Privy Council had further laid down that under the system of Hindu law, clear proof of usage would outweigh the written text.[33] This was merely an extension of the position of the Dharmashastra texts where the king was to settle the issues according to the 'peculiar' law of each caste and the recognition that custom was powerful and could even overrule the sacred law.[34] Hindu law was merely an aggregate of the different usages of castes.

The structure of institutions with overlapping jurisdictions and the application of law according to caste usages, however, did not function with any neat fit. Many cases were not conclusively resolved by the caste panchayat and went up to the courts for adjudication. A body of case law then built up on various issues. These require an independent and in-depth analysis but among the significant problems that emerge in the cases cited here are the particular instances where caste autonomy was regarded as inviolable and, in contrast, where larger questions of morality may have been cited by the court to strike down the decision of the caste; characteristically many issues of 'morality' were actually issues of gender. For example, in a case where the plaintiff sought recognition by the court of his right to be head of the caste and the privileges and precedence accruing therefrom, the court held that the question at issue was a caste question and to hold otherwise would be to interfere with the 'autonomy of the caste'.[35] A similar principle was followed in several other cases; in one the court held that, if a caste was regarded in any sense as a self-governing body, as contemplated by Regulation II Section 21 of 1827, it should be left to decide issues according to its customary mode of procedure.[36] Even when a Brahmana who married a widow according to the Hindu Shastric rituals was obstructed from entering the inner shrine of a temple to present an offering, the court held that the right claimed by the Brahmana to enter the temple was of a civil nature; it was not a question of legal status but of caste status and did not therefore interfere with 'custom'.[37]

However, the authority of the caste to decide certain issues and maintain its autonomy in such cases was often struck down by the courts. The provision for this overruling came from the argument that the customs prevalent could be upheld by the courts only if they were not repugnant to public interest or abhorrent to public morality.[38] An anxiety about public morality led the courts to repeatedly overrule usages of caste when it came to women remarrying during the life of their husbands and in other matrimonial matters generally. For example, a woman of the Teli caste whose husband contracted leprosy remarried during his lifetime. She did so with the consent of the caste. She was charged with bigamy and the charge was upheld.[39] In another case a husband claimed the restoration of his first wife who pleaded that according to the custom of the Aheer caste whenever a husband married a second wife, the first wife was at liberty to take a second husband. In this case the first husband had done so and was therefore not entitled to a decree for a restoration to him of his first wife. The court sought the opinion of the Hindu law officer who found no authority in the Shastras to support the wife's contention and the court declined to uphold the wife's argument. What is notable is that the compiler of caste usages and the working of customary law in British India laid down that even if caste custom did permit such an arrangement as the one cited by the wife the court would have struck it down as being immoral.[40]

In a case that came up to the Bombay High Court in 1864 involving a custom prevalent among the Talapoda Koli caste of Surat which permitted a woman to leave her first husband and to contract a second marriage during his lifetime, and without his consent, the court did not recognise the wife's plea that her second marriage was valid. The court went on to lay down that even if such a caste custom existed it was invalid as being '*entirely opposed to the spirit of Hindu law*', implying that a caste custom which did not conform to 'Hindu law' was not valid.[41] In a similar case among Sompura Brahmanas the judge held that even if the husband had consented to his wife's remarriage during his lifetime, the marriage would have been held to be invalid.[42] In a number of other cases too that dealt with the question of caste customs enabling a woman to leave her husband and marry another man of her free will, or with the consent of the caste, the court held that the customs were not valid. According to the court the practices were immoral and sought to 'legalise adultery'.[43] Thus, while in general the court recognised that the panchayat or head of caste could determine marriage and grant divorce, in certain cases the courts declined to recognise the authority of the panchayat to grant divorce. For the section of the Hindu intelligentsia which wished to uphold the power of the panchayats this was a negative feature of the new judicial structures. A respondent exhorted the public to keep a watchful eye on the courts. In his opinion the people sometimes found their own solutions to cases and particular problems. The High Courts, instead of upholding these caste decrees, were interfering with the remedies on the grounds of morality, he alleged.[44]

The general principle that the courts would accept the decisions of properly constituted panchayats did not preclude them from enquiring into the decisions and even reversing them. This depended on the understanding of the judges about whether certain customs actually were practised in certain castes; even when established, some were struck down as violative of morality. Bonds and agreements between marriage partners could also be struck down. This happened in a case where a married woman sought a divorce from her husband on the strength of a bond executed by him before marriage; in this he had agreed to consider the marriage void if he ever left the village in which his wife and her friends resided, or in case of cruelty, or in the event of his ever marrying another woman. The High Court held that such a contract was opposed to 'public policy' and therefore did not render the marriage void.[45] The relationship between caste custom, arbitration by caste panchayats, marriage practices of particular castes, and their acceptance by the British Indian judicial system was not quite resolved and was subject to interpretation and reinterpretation as can be seen in the cases cited above. For this reason whether an issue went to the caste panchayat at all would be contingent on the nature of the dispute, the issues it threw up and the perception of the parties about the ability of the caste panchayat to effectively 'settle' a dispute. Certain points of dispute may also have been unresolvable through simple recourse to caste customs as they could arise from new situations, part of the economic and social changes occurring in the nineteenth century.

II

One of the most famous cases to throw up these and other issues was that of *Dadaji vs. Rakhmabai*.[46] Revolving around the links between property, conjugality, law and the state in the context of the middle-class service gentry in an urban location, the case captured the attention of the press not just in Bombay and Poona, and in the other presidency towns Calcutta and Madras, but even in Banaras and Lahore. There were reverberations of the case in England with letters to the *Times* from concerned citizens. Apart from the issues that arose in the case itself as framed by the parties concerned, their lawyers and the judges, the newly constituted middle class across the country framed its own issues at a more popular level on women, marriage and the consequences of education for women.

Briefly, the outlines of the case were as follows.[47] Rakhmabai was the daughter of Jayantibai and Janardhan Pandurang. Jayantibai was widowed at the age of 19 when her daughter was two. Since Jayantibai's caste of Sutars (carpenters), a caste with multiple referents such as Somavanshi or Panchakalshi Kshatriya, customarily permitted widow remarriage, her father, Harish Chandra Jadoji, arranged a second marriage for her to Dr Sakharam Arjun, a leading surgeon and social reformer of Bombay, four years after she was widowed. In 1875 when Rakhmabai was 11 or 13 (the parties at dispute gave different ages) she was married to Dadaji Bhikaji, a distant relative of the family, who was then 19 or 20. According to Rakhmabai's family's version of the events, for some time Dadaji lived and underwent attempts at education in the household of his cousin/father-in-law. This arrangement broke down at some point and thereafter Dadaji went to stay with his mother's brother Narayan Dharamji.

During the period of Dadaji's stay in his father-in-law's household his marriage to Rakhmabai was not consummated, a fact which was not contested by him. In 1884 after trying unsuccessfully to get Rakhmabai to come and live with him in his uncle's household, Dadaji moved the courts against her, filing a suit for restitution of conjugal rights. Suits for restitution of conjugal rights were new, hardly ten years old, but significantly, in 1882, just two years before Dadaji tried to make Rakhmabai come to live with him at 'his residence', a denial of conjugal rights was made punishable by imprisonment. Dadaji was probably encouraged to file a suit following this new clause since few women would be able to stand up to the ultimate possibility of imprisonment. During the years following the introduction of suits for restitution of conjugal rights there had been a series of other cases between parties who were Parsi, Muslim and even Hindu, but this one immediately took Bombay, and later India, by storm for reasons which will become partly evident in the discussion below. The case came up before Justice Pinhey who decided on 21 September 1885 in favour of Rakhmabai and awarded her costs for the trial. He did not call for the counsel for defence to present arguments, taking a decision on the written submission which clearly indicated Rakhmabai's unwillingness to go and live as Dadaji's wife.

An analytical summary of the arguments that came up on both sides as well as from the court is presented below:

Dadaji, who is described as a Hindu of the Sutar or carpenter caste in the court records, was careful about the details he provided of his marriage, residence and the processes adopted by him to get Rakhmabai to come and live with him. His suit stated that he had married Rakhmabai 'according to an approved form'.[48] (There is a suggestion here that the rites may have been appropriate for the caste, not necessarily Vedic rites, but that they completed the marriage form.) Subsequently Rakhmabai continued to live with her stepfather Dr Sakharam Arjun. During the first year she occasionally visited Dadaji's house but not thereafter. Dadaji however was a 'constant visitor to the house of Sakharam Arjun'. The suit recorded that the marriage had never been consummated although Rakhmabai 'had long since attained puberty' as Dr Arjun was 'averse to early consumption thereof'.[49] It is significant that Dadaji drew the attention of the court to the fact that it was his residence which was meant to be the conjugal household to which Rakhmabai had come from time to time in the first year. At the same time he was also careful to state that he only visited the house of Sakharam Arjun but did not reside there on any long-term or permanent basis. Dadaji also highlighted the fact that the marriage was not consummated at the *instance* of Dr Sakharam, a decision from which he excluded himself.

The plaint went on to state that when Dadaji wrote to Dr Arjun requesting that Rakhmabai be sent to Dadaji's house Dr Arjun's reply had acknowledged that Rakhmabai's continued stay in her natal house had been with the 'consent of relations on both sides' because of the 'unfortunate circumstances' of the plaintiff. According to Dadaji when his uncle and brother went to fetch Rakhmabai she refused to go with them. Thereafter the solicitor's letter to her, with the undertaking that Dadaji would give her 'suitable maintenance and lodging according to his rank and position', also met with a written refusal from Rakhmabai to go and live with him. Dadaji then filed a suit in which he sought the intervention of the court for (a) the institution or restitution of conjugal rights from Rakhmabai, (b) suitable action so that the defendant Rakhmabai may be restrained by injunction from continuing to live in the house of Dr Arjun, and that Rakhmabai be 'ordered to take up her residence' with the plaintiff.[50]

Rakhmabai's written submission admitted the marriage, but stated that she was only eleven at the time and had not arrived at the 'years of discretion'. She alleged that Dadaji used to visit her stepfather's house for medical treatment and that he filed the suit at the instigation of 'certain evil-minded persons' who had done so for their own interest.

Rakhmabai gave the following grounds for her refusal to live with Dadaji: '(1) The entire inability of the plaintiff to provide for the proper residence and maintenance of himself and the wife, the defendant (2) the state of the plaintiff's health, as he suffered frequently from asthma and other symptoms of consumption and (3) the character of the person under whose protection the plaintiff was living and to which he was calling the defendant to join him'.[51] It is evident from the above that Rakhmabai, did not challenge the point that the husband's house should necessarily be the residence of the wife but declined to go there because of the nature of the household where she was required to live. Dadaji's counsel's response to the allegations was to raise the additional issue of whether the allegations, if correct, amounted to sufficient justification under Hindu law for the defendant to refuse conjugal rights to the plaintiff.[52]

The defence for Rakhmabai's refusal to go to live with Dadaji hinged upon the question of her having given no personal consent to her marriage. The counsels for Dadaji then argued that marriage among Hindus was not a contract but a religious duty. Citing Mayne's *Hindu Law*, they also argued that the absence of personal consent through infancy was immaterial. The suit was valid both with regard to institution and restitution of conjugal rights; with regard to consummation the suit was for institution of conjugal rights since this marriage, like most Hindu marriages, was solemnised before puberty. But on the other hand, the fact that Dadaji had consented to 'allow his wife' to stay with her stepfather after she had attained maturity made the suit simultaneously one for the restitution of conjugal rights. Dadaji's counsel further pointed out that his claim for the restitution of his conjugal rights had never been disputed until a month before the suit. Then, clinching his argument, Dadaji's counsel pointed out that from the *moment of marriage* a Hindu husband is a wife's legal guardian, even though she might be an infant, a statement that was meant to repudiate any suggestion that the natal kinsfolk of an infant wife could continue to be her legal guardians even if she stayed on at their residence. And further, because a Hindu husband is his wife's guardian, it was argued that he has an immediate right to require her to live with him in the same house as soon as she has attained puberty: her home must necessarily be her husband's house.

The problem with this set of arguments in the Rakhmabai case, however, was that she had stayed on at her stepfather's residence even after she attained puberty. To counter any suggestion that this could mean that conjugality had never been instituted, as Rakhmabai's counsel could and did argue, Dadaji's counsel advanced the view that in this specific case 'Dr Sakharam's, where Dadaji *frequently* visited her (thus establishing conjugality) *was constructively* the husband's place of abode or, at least, it was a place appointed by him for the purposes of her residence' (emphasis added). Dadaji's counsel, again citing Mayne, also argued that suits for the restitution of conjugal rights did lie among Hindus (the argument that such a suit did not lie was being put forward by Rakhmabai's counsel) and that the 'poverty of the husband' cited as reason for Rakhmabai's refusal to go and live with Dadaji did not constitute a matrimonial offence, or operate as a legal bar to the husband's right to his 'wife's society and assistance'.[53]

Justice Pinhey, who was hearing the case, dismissed the counsel's reliance on Mayne who had, according to him, too broadly expanded the decisions of the courts. He was therefore of the view that Dadaji must prove his case for the validity of the laws on the restitution of conjugal rights. Dadaji's counsels produced witnesses who testified on various issues including the material position of Dadaji, the 'respectability' of Dadaji's uncle's household where Rakhmabai was called upon to live, and Dadaji's health. The property of Rakhmabai's father Janardhan Pandurang was also dwelt upon as well as the information provided that the marriage expenses on both sides had been defrayed by the executor of Janardhan Pandurang's will.[54]

Pinhey did not call upon Rakhmabai's counsel to argue their defence any further or to produce witnesses. He had strong views on the case which he articulated forcefully. He was clearly exercised about the implications of the case which he stated 'had been on his mind all through the week' before he gave his verdict, during which time he had looked into the authorities. Drawing upon his long experience in the judiciary (he retired soon after the verdict in this case) he concluded that it was a 'misnomer' to call this a suit for the 'restitution' of conjugal rights. He conceded that according to the practice in England, when a married couple *after* cohabitation separated and lived apart, either party could bring a suit against the other for restitution of conjugal rights. Later on the courts in India had also introduced this right into legal practice. But, he pointed out, the Rakhmabai case was not of that character as the parties had been through a religious ceremony eleven years earlier, when Rakhmabai herself was only eleven. The parties had *never* cohabited. The issue now was that the court was required to use its judicial power to *compel* Rakhmabai to go to the plaintiff's house so that he might 'complete the contract with her by consummating the marriage'. Rakhmabai, however, now that she was of 'full age', objected to going to live with him, objected also to allowing him to consummate the marriage, and objected too, according to

Pinhey, to ratifying and completing the contract entered into on her behalf by her guardians while she was of 'tender age'. Therefore, it seemed to him that it would be a barbarous, a cruel, a revolting thing to do to compel a young lady, under such circumstances, 'to go to a man whom she dislikes in order that he might cohabit with her *against her will*.'[55]

Pinhey dismissed the suit on the ground that there was not 'one case either in England or in India' in which a court had compelled a woman who had gone through the religious ceremony of marriage to a man to allow that man to consummate the marriage against her will. In Pinhey's view the courts could not be a party to a forced consummation. He bemoaned the fact that such a possibility had arisen at all through a transplantation of a law which originated in England under 'peculiar circumstances', i.e., under circumstances peculiar to England, where marriage was concluded between 'consenting adults'. Pinhey was convinced that the practice of allowing such suits had no foundation in Hindu law. He recalled that for many years after he came to India such suits were not allowed. It was the 'amalgamation of the old supreme Sadar Courts in the High Court bringing English lawyers into the mofussil that had led to such suits being filed in the Indian courts'. (The right to restitution of conjugality was thus the work of English lawyers.) Pinhey held that since, under Hindu law, the suit would not be cognisable under the civil courts he would not carry the practice any further than supported by English authorities especially since the relief demanded by Dadaji (which in Pinhey's view was not merely a shift of residence but a forced consummation of a marriage) was revolting not only to civilised persons but to all persons. The suits for restitution of conjugal rights were being discredited in England and should 'never have been introduced into India'. In so far as they had been introduced Pinhey would have followed the authorities. But since even in India there was no case like that of Rakhmabai (all of the earlier had been cases of restitution, and not institution, of conjugal rights) Pinhey was not going to create a precedent, or in any way *extend* the practice of the court. On a personal note, Pinhey also made a reference to the cultivated and enlightened atmosphere of the well-known citizen Dr Sakharam Arjun's house in which Rakhmabai had been brought up.[56] He was glad therefore that he was not obliged to grant the relief Dadaji asked for. But, significantly, Pinhey was also obliged to conclude with the observations that he did not endorse the contention that Dadaji was not entitled to claim the society of his wife because he was poor, since a poor man had as much right to claim his wife as a rich man had. He did not therefore concede the ground of incompatibility, or even wish to entertain it.[57] It was forced cohabitation and his understanding of conjugal rights in English law and its inapplicability in Hindu law, especially in using force to institute such rights, that had led him to dismiss the suit. Throughout his statements the issue never explicitly addressed, but implied in almost everything Pinhey said, was the question of rape within marriage. It was to emerge once more in the Age of Consent debate.

Dadaji was unwilling to give up and was advised by his supporters to appeal, which he did; the case now came up for admission before Justices Sargent and Bayley.[58] (Pinhey had retired in the meanwhile to the delight of many outraged by his positive decision for Rakhmabai.) Dadaji's appeal was argued by Macpherson, Vicaji and Mankar. They reiterated the view that the defendants had admitted the marriage which was *complete* when the marriage ceremony was performed. Thereafter the wife became a member of her husband's family and *ought* to reside with him. Consummation in their view was not necessary to effectuate the marriage, and the husband had a right to the 'society' of his wife, and the courts were bound to enforce that right. The law they quoted was Section 260 of the Civil Procedure Code (XIV of 1882) which recognised such a right and provided the means of enforcing it. They conceded that while the means of enforcing the right had been abolished in England it remained valid in India under the above-mentioned law. They also cited the courts having granted the right in a number of cases and argued, 'If the right and the incidents be the same among Christians, Mohammedans and Parsis, why should the remedy be denied to the Hindus?'[59] In effect Dadaji's counsels at the appellate stage were using two sets of arguments. The obligation of conjugality following the completion of the sacramental aspect of the marriage performed according to an 'approved form' was drawn from Hindu law; the *enforcement* of the conjugal obligation was however drawn from English law. The transfer of residence of the wife was the object of this instrumental use of law. Since both sets of laws were in operation Dadaji claimed relief under both.

The argument of the defendant presented by Latham and Telang rested primarily on an extension of Pinhey's view that a suit for the restitution of conjugal rights did not lie in Hindu law and that in any case such a right had not yet been enjoyed and therefore could not be enforced. They considered consummation of material importance, pointing out that even the title of the English law showed that such rights lay only where the wife had already granted conjugal rights. Citing the provisions of Section 8 of Act XXI of 1886, they argued that it showed that the Indian legislature was strongly of the view that there was no English authority for enforcing the *commencement* of cohabitation. They also argued that even if the right of restitution of conjugality existed between Hindus such a position was as recent as 10 years; further, the lower courts in these cases had mistakenly based their position on two cases decided by the Privy Council but where the parties were Parsi in one case and Muslim in another. The courts had not considered carefully what the Hindu law was upon the subject.[60]

Expanding on their argument, Latham and Telang outlined the origin of the restitution of conjugal rights from the ecclesiastical courts and not from English common law or English equity law; the ecclesiastical courts could only enforce by excommunication. In any case the Privy Council had declared in one of its judgements that ecclesiastical law had no application in India, and that (here) only the 'law and usages of the country mattered'. Clinching their argument, they declared that even if it was accepted that ecclesiastical law could be applied it would be necessary to prove that the marriage had been based on 'free consent', which the plaintiff must necessarily fail to do. Finally it was argued that suits for restitution of conjugal rights were repulsive to civilised nations and that they should not be extended to Hindus unless they could be shown to be known to Hindu law. In their view the courts had discretionary powers and were not *bound* to make a decree under an alien law.[61]

The defence thus pivoted around the fact that the restitution of conjugal rights was not in accordance with Hindu law and that merely because it was upheld for Mohammedans it did not mean that it could apply to Hindus; this position stressed the uniqueness of Hindu law which was distinct from English law but also from Mohammedan law. The implications of this view were that each community was distinct and the laws of each community, especially on matters such as marriage, should conform to the usages of that community.

As the defence proceeded, C.J. Sargent asked Rakhmabai's counsel to indicate the circumstances which should influence the court in declining to give the relief demanded by Dadaji. Rakhmabai's counsel outlined these as the occurrence of the marriage at a time when the wife was incapable of giving a reasonable consent and the poverty and 'poor social position' of the husband. Pinhey's decisiveness about the case was not shared by Sargent who noted that since the points raised by the defence about Dadaji's position were not investigated the court did not have evidence on these points.[62] This was conceded by Rakhmabai's counsel but he also added that the court had a certain discretion which it could exercise while granting a decree as the trial court had done. Telang added further that while the Hindu law books prescribed the duties of a husband and wife they said little about how to enforce the performance of such duties. Since the duties were religious they were enforceable only by religious machinery; further, according to the Vyavahara Mayukha which mentioned the duties of a man and his wife the only mode of enforcing those duties was by the imposition of a fine by the king. Most pertinently the only case contemplated by the Hindu law was that of a husband abandoning his wife which resulted in a fine payable to the king. He rounded off his argument by pointing out that there was no provision (in the texts) at all for the case of a wife separating from her husband, and, in the absence of such provision, the court could reasonably assume that the same remedy or punishment would be applied, i.e., by paying a fine.[63] Implicit in this argument was the recognition that traditional Shastric law had never envisaged a situation where a wife might decline to go to her husband if he wanted her with him. What is evident from this argument is that there were now elements which made it possible for a woman of property, located in an urban situation, to decline a marriage obligation and pursue an alternative existence outside marriage. The new class situation provided a propertied and educated woman certain options which had not been available to women before.

Telang then brought in an issue which was not being addressed directly by the courts or the appellants — the existence of the caste authority and its crucial place in the working of the amorphous/flexible Hindu law.[64] He argued that the case could be brought before the caste authorities for their decision but not to the civil courts and he used an intricate argument to support his position:

No doubt [the] caste council might always have ordered the wife to go to her husband but the caste may do that still. The caste can enforce social duties. The civil courts may not. The civil courts now exercise the authority which belonged to the king when the Hindu law books were written; the functions of the civil court are to be ascertained by references to what are laid down as the duties of the king.[65]

In short Telang was arguing that while the British Indian courts had inherited the powers of the king they had not inherited the powers of the caste council which, presumably, the latter continued to hold intact even in the 1880s — or in Telang's view they ought to have done so. The position of the defence thus rested quite self-consciously and unambiguously on the inapplicability of such a case within Hindu law and, further, that the courts were bound to apply the *particular law* of the contracting parties upon them, which were the 'customs and usages of the caste'.[66]

In response to Telang, Macpherson, the counsel for the appellant, now had to take Hindu law directly into his argument whereas originally the position had been based mainly on statutory law and case law of the British Indian courts. He had little difficulty in reconciling statutory law, English law, and Hindu law on the issue of the husband's right to his wife's conjugality. He admitted that while there may be no direct authority for the suit in Hindu law he denied that it was in any way inconsistent with Hindu law since there was nothing in that law which forbade it. In his view the principle laid down by the British Indian courts in *Munshee Buzloor Raheem vs. Shamsoom Begum was* applicable to Hindus.[67] Macpherson was making a double move: while reconciling Hindu law with statutory law he was arguing for the principle of universal applicability and against the uniqueness of Hindu law. At the same time he was cautious about suggesting that statutory law could, or should, supersede Hindu law if they were inconsistent with each other.

In arriving at a decision the court took up the central issue of whether a suit for the institution or restitution of conjugal rights would lie in the present case. The judges Sargent and Bayley were of the view that there was a series of suits on the restitution of conjugal rights which had been entertained by the civil courts in the case of 'natives', both Hindu and Mohammedan. The examples the court cited included two cases where Hindu wives had sought restitution of conjugal rights although the better known cases were those where the husbands were the plaintiffs. Sargent therefore took the view that since it was clear that there was such a jurisdiction 'as long as it was not taken away by legislation' the courts could not exercise the kind of discretion urged by Telang, nor could they go into the root of the jurisdiction: i.e., since there was already a body of case law the original validity could not be reopened. In response to Telang's argument that Hindu law did not recognise the compulsory discharge of marital duties, but only treated them as duties of imperfect obligation to be enforced by religious sanction, the court argued that although no text of Hindu law provided for a king ordering a husband or a wife to return, no text was cited which forbade compulsion. Further, since Telang had conceded that the duties between husbands and wives had always been the subject of caste discipline, with the establishment of a systematic administration of justice in Sargent's opinion the civil courts must necessarily assume jurisdiction over conjugal rights as determined by Hindu law and enforce them according to their own modes of procedure.[68] Sargent, in taking this view, even as he referred to caste discipline 'ignored' the structure of caste authority, or even of possible differences in caste customs in the context of marriage practices and treated them under the 'hold-all' term 'Hindu law'. The court was not going to look at the validity of the issues raised in the case according to the caste law of the Sutars, by which term the parties had earlier been described, but as Hindus to whom Hindu law would be applied by the new structure of the courts which had inherited the authority of both the caste council and the Hindu king.

The court also took note of the defendant's argument about the relationship between consummation and institution of conjugal rights but argued that such a position was a misapplication of the ecclesiastical law. Further, the court argued that since the defendant had not contended that consummation was necessary in Hindu law to make the marriage valid, the position of the defence was not tenable[69] — it was irrelevant whether conjugal rights were being denied before or after consummation because it was the duty of married persons to live together. Most importantly, consummation was not necessary to effectuate a marriage any more in Hindu law than it was in English law. Consummation was not thus the essence of conjugality or of marriage. Therefore the judge held that there had been a violation of conjugal duty on the part of Rakhmabai which entitled Dadaji to the remedy he sought which was 'the society of his wife', at the husband's residence.

The problem of 'infant' marriage was also confronted by Sargent as it had featured implicitly in defining consent and the court applied its mind to custom. Conceding that it was customary for the 'infant wife' to return to her own house after the marriage celebration until she reached puberty, it could be argued that the court should not order the wife to join her husband until she was of mature age (implying thereby that the institution of conjugal rights could only take place at the time of puberty). However, since Rakhmabai was long past the age of puberty[70] such a reasoning also would not hold. The argument of the defence that since the defendant had had no voice in her marriage with the plaintiff, to join him against her will for the purpose of consummation would be more than 'ordinarily revolting to delicate feelings', as Pinhey had put it, was more difficult for the court to tackle. Also, the court had to confront the possibility that if the defendant continued to deny conjugal rights, imprisonment would have to be decreed since it remained enforceable in India whereas it had been dropped in England by ordering alimony for the 'deprived' husband instead.

On the question of the defendant having no voice in the choice of husband the court extricated itself by placing the responsibility of such a situation squarely upon Hindu law — if it accepted the defence it would be tantamount to upholding the view that all marriages in India among Hindus were invalid because the parties were children. The court argued that nowhere was it suggested that the 'marriages of Hindu children are not perfectly valid without the exercise of volition on their part'.[71] This as we shall soon see was the crux of the bind the court was in; if they denied conjugal rights to the husband on the ground that the wife was not a consenting party to it, no Hindu marriage would stand. This the court just could not decree.

The position of the defence was regarded by the court as virtually being asked to 'disregard the precepts of Hindu law' which treated the marriage of daughters as a religious duty imposed on parents and guardians, and instead to view the matter purely from the

English point of view which 'sees in marriage nothing but a contract to which the husband and wife must be consenting parties'.[72] Turning Telang's argument of invalidity of restitution of conjugality in Hindu law completely around, the court pointed out the 'true' nature of Hindu law, which required the ratification of infant marriages by the parties and by the courts because of the religious obligation to marry off daughters by fathers according to prevailing norms. The courts thus could not exercise discretion in favour of Rakhmabai as urged by the defence.

The court concluded its view on the validity of Dadaji's claim by rejecting the position that the court should draw fine distinctions between a woman 'who had never lived with her husband and is averse to joining him and one who had lived with him and perhaps acquired a moral loathing for him and therefore objected to returning to him'.[73] The court found its hands tied even though it recognised that it may have been advisable not to adopt stringent measures to compel the performance of conjugal duties. But because as long as the law remained, the civil courts were bound to uphold it on the ground of 'consistency and uniformity of practice',[74] Sargent and Bayley admitted the appeal on 18 March 1886 and remanded the case for decision on merits to be judged by that new mixture of 'Hindu' law, statutory law and case law on conjugality. The case came up for decision before Mr Justice Farran. By this time Rakhmabai's counsel considered it necessary to tell the court that Rakhmabai had determined not to live with the plaintiff as his wife. This indicated that in the event of a decree against her she would rather face the consequences and court imprisonment than join him against her will. It is significant that Rakhmabai sought non-performance of marital obligations as defence both during the case and even later, rather than divorce or dissolution of the marriage, which may not have been available to her under 'Hindu law' or British Indian law as applied to Hindus. At no point was caste custom brought in, either over non-performance of marital obligation, or in seeking a dissolution of the marriage. The identity she sought for herself was that of a 'Hindu' lady, and subject to oppression in that capacity, when she wrote to *The Times of India* (26 June and 19 September 1885) under a pseudonym during the trial. In the meanwhile there was a raging battle in the press over the Rakhmabai case with both parties finding support from contending factions of the middle classes in western India. Farran delivered his judgement on 3 March 1887, ordering Rakhmabai to 'return' to her husband's house (to which she had never been for any length of time) within a month or face imprisonment for 6 months,[75] the maximum penalty possible under the clauses operable in the restitution of conjugal rights.

All the parties tried to buy time rather than have Rakhmabai go to jail; obviously this was not exactly what Dadaji had intended. Rakhmabai did not appeal against the judgement since her counsel did not advise taking the matter to the Privy Council.[76] Simultaneously, compromise moves were afoot and these materialised in July 1888 whereby Dadaji agreed to give up his claim on Rakhmabai in return for a sum of Rs 2,000,[77] reputedly to cover his legal costs but in any case a substantial figure in those days. The implications and reverberations of the case for Rakhmabai personally, for women in general (102 women had signed a petition against Rakhmabai's impending imprisonment) and the middle class in particular did not, however, end so neatly. Among the reactions was an official one from the government on the advisability of dropping the clause of imprisonment from the statute on restitution of conjugal rights.[78]

III

The Rakhmabai case encapsulates the interaction between caste mobility, class formation, fluid legal structures, appropriate gender codes and new notions of a 'community' within the larger framework of colonialism and nationalism. The feeding of particular castes, some clearly attempting to move up in the social hierarchy, into the larger process of class formation and the creation of a new urban professional elite are best typified in Rakhmabai's social location and the 'moment' in which the case came up. The unresolved tensions inherent in such a cross-cutting moment are also discernible in the arguments and counter-arguments put forward in the court and in the larger court of public opinion captured fairly effectively by the press.

Rakhmabai was described in the suit instituted by Dadaji as a Sutar,[79] traditionally a caste of carpenters classified broadly among the intermediate castes of Maharashtra. However, the Imperial Gazetteer describes their origins as Panchakalshi, a caste regarded as related to the Pathare Prabhus, who were traditionally associated with clerkships.[80] Although they had originally been a prosperous caste they became depressed to the level of Sutars by the loss of their lands to the Portuguese. Thereafter, they had also become clerks with the Company and later in private firms and had joined government schools and entered professions. With their rise in social status they adopted the name of Somavanshi Kshatriyas and began to carry out a number of reforms in their marriages and other ceremonies. This process had been noticed by Tukaram Tatya Padval in his book *Jatibhed Vivekasar* published in 1861. The Sutars, like certain other castes, had also taken to wearing the sacred thread, according to Molesworth, on the ground that they were Kshatriyas.[81] In 1884 (the year Dadaji moved the court for restitution of conjugal rights) the community founded the 'Kshatriya' Union Club, for the promotion and education of their poor. The internal stratification within the caste was of fundamental importance in the Rakhmabai case since it surfaced within the marital relationship and the arrangements of the household. Rakhmabai came from the educated prosperous part of the caste, Dadaji from its poorer labouring section. It is significant that the internal stratification within the caste was specifically linked to the Rakhmabai case by an editorial in the *Mahratta*. This pointed out that the origin of the case could be traced to the present transitional period wherein a father having risen to a position *had* to give his daughter in marriage to a member of his caste who was less advanced than himself.[82]

These moves at organising as a caste, creating a particular identity for themselves and helping the less privileged members of their caste were not unique to the Sutars/Somavanshi Kshatriyas/Panchakalshis. Other castes in Bombay such as Sonars, Pathare Prabhus, and even the Chandraseniya Kayastha Prabhus, along with many more, followed similar trajectories not only in the Bombay region but across many parts of India.[83] The trends seem to have had a close bearing on the simultaneous process of the formation of a cross-caste elite group with the attendant creation of a larger identity. These multiple identities appear in the references to Rakhmabai even in the pages of the newspapers and judicial records where she is variously described as Sutar, Panchakalshi and Hindu. The multiple referents of Rakhmabai's caste suggest that upwardly mobile sections of a caste, sought to appropriate a range of statuses in a fluid economic and social situation. These may also have been methods of seeking to establish congruence between caste status and class position.

Rakhmabai's location within a newly-forming class which comprised various castes, is evident also in the specifics of her family history. A significant point about her circumstances was the connection with substantial property inherited from her father, Janardhan Pandurang Save.[84] Her mother's remarriage, permitted by her caste of Sutar, was however unusual for the upper-class elite, which, at that time, rarely witnessed the remarriage of an 'adult' widow, particularly one who already had a child.

A significant aspect of the different referents to Rakhmabai's caste as Pathare and Panchakalshi, apart from Sutar, is the contradictions thrown up by them from the point of view of customs prevalent among them, especially in the context of occupation, divorce, pat connections and women's access to property following remarriage. According to Steele, Sutars practised widow remarriage as a widow was entitled to make a pat connection.[85] Enthoven describes the Sutars of Bombay as allowing widow remarriage in some places and not in others. Only widows attended the remarriage of a widow. (Sutars ranked above the Marathas and below the Vanis. The men dressed like Deshastha Brahmanas or the Maratha Kunbis, the women like those of Maratha Kunbi caste.) Traditionally they were carpenters who made and mended ploughs and other agricultural implements. The town carpenters built houses and shops and pieces of furniture. They claimed descent from the divine architect Tvasta and in the nineteenth century there was a movement among them to claim rank as Brahmanas.[86]

The Panchakalshis, according to Enthoven, were also known as Somavanshi Kshatriya Pathare, or as Sutars or Vadvals. Vadvals were managers of orchards, while Sutars were carpenters. The Panchakalshis traced their descent from Bhim Raja, also the ancestor of the Pathare Prabhus of Bombay, and hence their claim to Kshatriya status. (One can see from the above that different referents of the caste were seeking different affiliations simultaneously: as Sutars to Brahmanas, as Panchakalshis to Kshatriyas.) [The caste believed that originally they were warriors, but later took to agriculture and day labour. Under the Portuguese they became skilled mechanics and carpenters, particularly house- and boat-builders. Most of the Panchakalshis in Bombay were clerks and mechanics and some were in the learned professions.] They permitted widow remarriage, but it was not as common among them as among the backward classes. In most cases where a widow had a child she did not 'care to remarry' but there were exceptions. She then gave up all connections with her dead husband's family and they in turn kept aloof from her and her second husband on all public occasions. The remarried widow is described as giving up all ornaments from the family of the deceased husband, and this would imply that she gave up all forms of property, especially immovable property. Custody of children followed no particular rule and could vary according to the circumstances of the case.[87]

Pathares are described by Enthoven as found chiefly in the island of Bombay; their name signifies a fallen status believed to be fallen from warriors to 'writers'. They claimed Kshatriya status. In their role as writers they played a conspicuous part in the early settlement and development of Bombay and came to occupy positions of trust and responsibility under the British government. [Their monopoly of clerkships was so general that their caste name became a synonym for 'English writer'. By the late nineteenth and early twentieth centuries they were becoming successful lawyers, doctors and engineers.[88]] No specific details are mentioned about remarriage of widows, or their relationship to the property of the dead husband following remarriage.

The description of the social and professional location of the four major men around Rakhmabai captures the various occupations of the Sutars, Panchakalshis, and Pathares enumerated above. Rakhmabai's maternal grandfather, Harish Chandra Jadav, was a *karkoon*, a clerk in the Bombay government. He was born in 1825 in Bassein and brought at the age of six by his father to Bombay where he began his education in Marathi. He later went on to the Elphinstone School where he studied English. Rakhmabai's biography (written by her grand-niece) which stresses the Somavanshi Kshatriya and Pathare aspects of Rakhmabai's caste, also tells us that the Pathares were known for karkoonships. When he was educated sufficiently Harish Chandra was appointed a clerk in the Bombay Presidency. He was reputed to have had beautiful handwriting and was appreciated for his general skills by the English who appointed him a Justice of the Peace. He was also proclaimed a Rai Bahadur at the Delhi Durbar because of his knowledge of English. He had access to Englishmen and his house was a centre for the 'progressive' men of his time.[89] Harish Chandra taught his daughter, Jayantibai, to read and write. She was married to a young enterprising boy, Janardhan Pandurang, who was a contractor engaged in house-building. Bombay's rapid expansion clearly provided many opportunities and Janardhan Pandurang was a wealthy man when he died at an early age, leaving his wife widowed at nineteen. Rakhmabai was then only an infant. Jayantibai is described as feeling 'orphaned' by the loss of her husband and so returned to her father Harish Chandra's house. At Janardhan's death Jayantibai 'inherited' substantial assets including movable and immovable property comprising three houses, a garden, household furniture, ornaments and other articles.[90]

While it appears that Jayantibai received the property through a will it is not absolutely clear how she retained it and whether her possession of it was challenged by Janardhan's distant male kin following her remarriage, because there do not appear to have been any close male kin.[91] The rules of the caste are explicitly cited, both in the information on caste customs collected by the Bombay Government[92] and in Rakhmabai's biography, on the custom of widow remarriage. However on the question of retention of the property following remarriage either there is silence or a certain amount of implicit information, as in the case of the Panchakalshis, just cited above, about forfeiture.[93] Since the caste of Panchakalshis/Pathares were clearly upwardly mobile and the Bombay courts generally applied the rule of forfeiture to the remarrying widow, Jayantibai's possession of the property could have been contested successfully if there had been male kin who tried to do so. However, the Bombay Government had even in 1886 allowed a widow to retain property from her deceased husband because of the existence of previous caste custom. They finally upturned this judgement in 1896 when all widows, regardless of caste custom, were required to forfeit.[94] There is thus evidence for a somewhat fluid situation both with respect to custom and the decisions of the courts. Since the evidence is not conclusive in Jayantibai's case it is only possible to suggest that it was to avoid the contradictions in the fluid legal situation with respect to widowhood, remarriage and property from the deceased husband that Janardhan may have used new legal channels such as an outright gift or a legacy under a testament to enable Jayantibai to hold the property even after remarriage, either for herself, or for Rakhmabai until she could inherit in her own right. Dadaji however alleged that on her remarriage Jayantibai, who had been made sole heiress to the property on the death of her husband, was disinherited by her second marriage and thereafter 'his wife' Rakhmabai had become the sole heiress.[95] Rakhmabai's biography states that Harish Chandra Jadoji was made the executor of the will and this is corroborated by Dadaji in his 'exposition'. The biography contests the view that Jayantibai was disinherited on her remarriage and specifically states that later it was Jayantibai who, of her own volition, gave the property to Rakhmabai, suggesting that Jayantibai continued to be the legal inheritor even after she remarried.[96]

Jayantibai's remarriage itself suggests a mix of caste custom and new norms for widow remarriage. Caste custom could permit pat unions for a man who had already been married before, as Sakharam Arjun had been. He was a widower with no children. But the new union was not merely customary. Jayantibai was acquainted with Sakharam and had corresponded with him about her views on the widow remarriage movement, then beginning to make its impact on the educated elite. Her honesty and frankness are said to have impressed Sakharam who chose her to be his *sahadharmini*, a very different connotation from the pat unions sanctioned by the caste.[97] Sakharam Arjun represents another of the multiple trajectories of the Panchakalshi/Pathare/Sutar group of castes. Born into a poor family in 1839, he was educated at home till the age of eleven. Education however was clearly the key to his fortunes opening up. He proceeded to Elphinstone School and thereafter to the Grant Medical College where he received the LMP degree. He became a Professor of Botany, a teacher of Surgery and an author of many books, some of which were prescribed as texts. Rakhmabai's biography describes him as the first Indian to receive such honours in his field, making him a well-known figure in the public eye at the time the Rakhmabai case hit the headlines. He too was appointed a Justice of the Peace, as well as Chief Surgeon to the Viceroy. He took a keen interest in women's issues, both writing and speaking about them among other social issues addressed by him in his capacity as a *sudharak* or reformer. Rakhmabai and her younger half-sister attended some of these lectures. Just as Jayantibai had shown initiative in corresponding with Sakharam, Sakharam is described as manifesting his social concerns by refusing to marry a young virgin when he was widowed. Among the books he authored was one describing the ideal wife in a work entitled *Grihini Kantha Bhushan*, meaning the ornament that is the housewife. Rakhmabai is also described as growing up in his care and under his guidance.[98]

From the above account it is evident that the initial handicap of Sakharam's poverty had been surmounted by education, initiative and the new opportunities opening up to the urban professional middle class. Rakhmabai was educated according to the norms of this burgeoning class and her education included English. But since English education and middle-class location had to meld with 'Hindu' values (specifically named as such by Jayantibai) and the ever-present requirement of the class to broadly conform to caste custom, especially an endogamous marriage, an early marriage (at eleven) was arranged for Rakhmabai to Dadaji, a distant relation of the family.[99] In pursuance of the self-image of this new class however the family wanted an educated partner for Rakhmabai. It is not easy to discern whether such partners were available within the endogamous marriage circle in a caste which was sharply stratified from within into a tiny, prosperous, and professional segment and a large labouring and humble segment. Rakhmabai's appeal to the British Government to legislate on the issue of child marriage published in *The New Review* in 1890 refers explicitly to the difficulties of finding suitable partners since the caste system strictly prohibited intermarriage. In this context, it is significant that Rakhmabai's biography specifically points out that Dadaji belonged to its *shramjivi* section.[100] This is consistent with the social profile of the caste as we saw in the case of Sakharam Arjun. (Sakharam had however succeeded in transcending his background through education, professional opportunity and 'talent'.) Given the difficulties it is possible that the family considered that a boy, though poor, could be 'groomed' to be a suitable partner and in order to facilitate such grooming appears to have tried a variation of an established custom of the *ghar jawai* (resident son-in-law). This custom is specifically mentioned as one of the practices among the caste of Sutars by Steele.[101] Rakhmabai's family probably secured a verbal contract with the family of Dadaji whereby the latter would be provided for by his in-laws, reside with them, pursue an education,[102] and thereby be transformed into a fitting partner for Rakhmabai. The arrangement suggests that the wife's residence was intended to be the conjugal residence for the young couple as it was here that the grooming could most effectively be carried out. One of the basic issues in the case in the court had been that the wife becomes a member of her husband's family on marriage and *ought* to reside with him as the husband has a right to her society.

Events, however, did not unfold according to plan for Dadaji. Both parties to the dispute conceded that Dadaji had lived in Rakhmabai's house. From the evidence it appears that Dadaji was not educated enough to find professional employment but whether this was due to lack of enthusiasm or incapacity is not clear. Rakhmabai's family alleged that Dadaji was under the influence of an uncle who did not conduct himself with propriety, and that he kept unsavoury company and developed 'bad' habits when he returned to live with his relatives. The non-consummation of the marriage, even after Rakhmabai reached puberty, was also conceded by both sides and is one of the most significant aspects of the case. The forcible consummation of the marriage, implicit in the demand for the restitution of conjugal rights, became *the* central issue even though there were numerous other aspects to the case.

During the years that Rakhmabai stayed on in her natal family she pursued a pattern of existence that became popular in her class. As a daughter of a social reformer, Rakhmabai joined the Arya Mahila Sabha in the early 1880s and became its secretary. Founded by Pandita Ramabai, it included the women of families such as those of Ranade and Bhandarkar.[103] The formation of a cross-caste class circle for women was a major change in inter-caste relations, given the restricted nature of inter-caste interaction for most people, and particularly for women. That such interaction was unusual even at the turn of the century is evident from the memoirs of the Brahmana playwright G.C. Kolhatkar. The playwright makes a special mention of the 'egalitarian' nature of his own childhood interactions which included Guravs, Sutars, and Marathas among his companions.[104] Part of the clash between the two parties in the Rakhmabai case — of which there are many complex strands — may be located in the changing self-image of a class, including its distinctive but hazy gender codes, as yet not properly formulated but clearly in a state of tension with older gender codes.

Some of the features outlined above are discernible in the

arguments used by Rakhmabai in the court as well as in the correspondence attributed to her. There were three grounds given for Rakhmabai's unwillingness to go to Dadaji's residence and cohabit with him (all of which were unconventional in traditional 'Hindu' marriage). The first suggests notions of a class status that Rakhmabai was used to and considered herself 'entitled' to. The second suggests that the husband was to be a 'fitting' partner (in a reversal of the requirement normally laid down by a new class of men for their wives but also naturalised in their case, because all men had a right to a suitable wife who could be 'groomed' into her role in her affinal household where her in-laws had the authority and sanction to execute this task). The third suggests that there were certain essential elements to what made up a 'respectable' family. Caste similarity was thus not enough any longer — class socialisation and education needed to be similar for compatibility and a 'true' marriage.[105] Such a position outraged most people among the very elite that Rakhmabai belonged to, as is evident from a public lecture on the Rakhmabai case which was given by a surgeon called Kirtikar and which was published in the *Mahratta*. Kirtikar proclaimed himself a friend of the family and therefore in a position to provide inside information on Rakhmabai's personality and educational training. He was very sceptical of her education and strongly objected to her lawyers having described Dadaji as a coolie, which suggested that Dadaji lived off manual labour whereas he was 'merely working honestly'. Kirtikar ended his lecture by advising Dadaji to dump Rakhmabai, who was anyway unattractive even if she was rich, so that she could be 'left to study philosophy while he got on with being a coolie'.[106] There would be much public sympathy for Dadaji following Kirtikar's 'public' lecture, both as a deserted husband and as a poor man whose only fault was that he had married a rich woman. Nevertheless, at least one sympathetic letter in the press recognised that had Rakhmabai been more 'fortunately wedded (and in the proper maturity of years) she would have been, with her accomplishments and her talents, the centre of a prosperous and happy family'.[107]

As in the cases of widow remarriage, in the Rakhmabai case, too, there was evidence of an uneasy relation of Hindu law to statutory law. But while in the widow remarriage issue a conscious move had been made to legislate in order to enable the remarriage of widows of the upper castes, in the case of restitution of conjugal rights there was no such clear move on the part of the British Indian administration. Instead the right had grown through a body of cases and consequently contradictions between Hindu law and statutory law were much sharper. The question of what constituted Hindu law remained as problematic in the Rakhmabai case as in the widow remarriage issue. Unlike the widow remarriage cases where caste custom was a crucial question in arguing the issue of the widows' forfeiture, the argument of the specificities of caste custom never became a central issue in the Rakhmabai case. However, the authority of the caste council was invoked by the defence, making it an implicit issue. The question of caste authority then became another strand in the unresolved tangle of legal questions relating to gender in the Rakhmabai case.

In analysing the issues which surfaced in this particular case, one that compels attention is the question of why Dadaji went to court to get Rakhmabai to come to live with him as his wife, and why he used English law to pursue this objective. Why did he not bring up the matter of Rakhmabai's refusal to move to his residence to live with him as his wife before the caste council of the Panchakalshis/Sutars? Does his appeal to the court, based on principles of English law, indicate that he considered the caste council either ineffective or unsuitable? Does Dadaji's action imply that by the 1880s the panchayats had no ability to *execute* their decisions, only retaining a power to excommunicate? Although effective at one level, this would be ineffective in *making* people act in certain ways. Or did the action imply that if anyone was ready to take on the consequences of the excommunication, the highest act of coercion the caste council was capable of, then they could do as they desired? Were the caste panchayats functioning in an urban setting at all? Was the power of the caste, especially among the non-Brahmanas, to enforce caste 'norms' on its richer members declining? More pertinently, could the caste council be effective without the coercive backing of the state which it may have had during the Peshwai but could no longer avail itself of? (This is suggested by Malabari and may have been the reason why Telang invoked the authority of the caste as the appropriate body to deal with Dadaji's complaint. He was aware that the caste could excommunicate, and even fine, but not 'punish'.) Further, how effective could the caste authorities be against established wealthy members? Would the upwardly mobile Sutars/Panchakalshis, keen on building up the position of the entire caste, be willing to take up a problem like Rakhmabai's and thereby divide the caste within itself?[108]

All these factors, and others, are possible reasons why Dadaji preferred the British Indian courts rather than appealing to the caste council. Most pertinent however, is the possibility that Dadaji recognised that the caste panchayat would only 'dissolve' the marriage but not be able to force Rakhmabai to perform her duties under the law of conjugality. Dadaji's appeal to English law is most likely to be an indication that only under it would the new relationship between conjugality, residence, and property, which appears to have been crucial in the Rakhmabai case, enable Dadaji to make Rakhmabai shift residence gain 'independent' control of her own property, and thereby bring it under Dadaji's control.

In this context it is useful to explore the allegations Dadaji made against Rakhmabai's family. In a pamphlet published on 14 April 1887, when the contest over Rakhmabai's person was at its height, Dadaji stated that the root cause of the dispute between him and Rakhmabai was the refusal of his selfish in-laws, to part with property worth Rs 25,000 which had been left to Rakhmabai by her father and which 'ought' to have been his. The contest over her person and where she resided was as much about property rights (especially because immovable property was involved) as about matrimonial rights, with the two being inextricably linked in this case. Dadaji, who otherwise earned Rs 30-40 a month when he found work, and lived with and was dependent on his uncle, staked himself as the legal owner of Rakhmabai's property. He had been careful however not to formulate this claim in the suit instituted by him, where the issues were framed as the right of a husband to his wife's 'society'. However, the 'exposition of the facts' in the pamphlet suggests that property was the central issue of the case. Dadaji even went on to make clear that such a contest over property could happen in any family and had no connection with the family being Hindu or non-Hindu. (The public however saw this as a contest over the nature of Hindu marriage and the Hindu wife's obligations, not over property in a 'Hindu' family.) Rakhmabai's response to Dadaji's pamphlet also deals at length with the issue of property, its actual worth, and the nature of the arrangements by which she received income as she defended the charges against her mother's selfishness. On her death almost sixty years later, Rakhmabai's will provided for a detailed distribution of her property among her natal kin and others with whom she had developed a close attachment during her years as a doctor.[109]

The crucial question that had been posed by the Rakhmabai case thus was: who is the 'custodian' or controller of a married woman's property when she inherits from her father? It appears that Dadaji regarded such a question as resolvable only within the framework of English law. Under English law, as applied in India, Dadaji's move to seek restitution of conjugal rights could have given him custody of his wife's person, and therefore of her property. Even if she failed to be 'restored' to him through her refusal, the changed law in England had introduced the payment of alimony rather than imprisonment.[110] If the courts had provided this remedy, which Dadaji may have hoped for rather than imprisonment, he would have gained access to some part of her income.

Given the entangled nature of the issues raised in the Rakhmabai case one of the anomalies of the proceedings thus came to be that those wanting the wife to perform her duties appealed to the British Indian courts and argued also that the English law of restitution should be applied not just to Mohammedans and Parsis but also to Hindus,[111] whereas those holding the relatively 'liberal' position of Rakhmabai's right to refusal used the argument (even though somewhat ambiguously) of the inapplicability of the law on conjugal rights to Hindus. Of course we must bear in mind that what constituted 'Hindu' law or 'Hindu' custom remained open to interpretation. Was it textual law for the upper castes and customary law for the lower castes as suggested by the disputes over the widow remarriage cases? In this context, a notable feature of the Rakhmabai case is that the question of Hindu law as used by all the parties, lawyers, judges and those who used the press, appears as a homogenised entity rather than disparate, or unique according to caste. As we have seen, caste custom was the central feature of the cases relating to widow remarriage and forfeiture. Why was Hindu law treated as a unified entity in the case of Rakhmabai but not so in the widow remarriage cases? Was the question of a wife's refusal of the husband's right to cohabitation a cross-caste, cross-class issue and therefore having the widest applicability?

But if we recall the history of caste contestations and the fierceness with which the Brahmanas resisted the homogenising of gender codes against the traditionally discrete cultural and ideological arrangements dictating caste behaviour, the problem that arises is: was the homogenising of all existing codes into a unified Hindu law an uncontested process? Further, how did the Brahmanical elite reacting to legal changes, especially to unified notions of family which traditionally had been organised around a set of distinctive norms and rules as a means of maintaining hierarchy and difference? These differences were being steam-rollered through codification and notions of one set of laws for all Hindus. Or do we understand that the process of class formation and an embryonic 'national' identity created the conditions for the emergence, within a largely Brahmanical model, of unified gender codes which obscured the contradictoriness of earlier codes for women based on class and caste? That something of this kind had begun is evident from the critique of the process from the anonymous Hindu lawyer we cited earlier.[112]

Some of the characteristics outlined above may be discerned in Telang's arguments in favour of Rakhmabai's refusal to go to Dadaji, organised around the dual position of a unified Hindu law on the one hand and a recourse to caste authority on the other. However, what Telang left unsaid when he asked Dadaji to go to the caste council is the precise custom or text under which the caste authorities might decide the case. The unresolved relationship between caste law, Hindu law, and statutory law remained even in the arguments put forward by those arguing the case. In contrast, Mandlik's position, which was firmly supportive of Dadaji's claim over Rakhmabai, was that caste usage had become subsumed under Hindu law. The multiplicity of the local and customary usages were swept aside and Mandlik created in its stead a unified 'Hindu' law under which Rakhmabai must perform her conjugal obligations.

A central feature of the Rakhmabai case was that all the persons involved in framing the issues, the lawyers on both sides and the judges who gave differing judgements, based themselves either on Hindu law or on consistency of the English law with Hindu law but then went on to interpret it differently, sometimes in diametrically opposite ways. Using force to make a woman live with her husband was thus both the essence of the Hindu family structure according to Mandlik and antithetical to the norms of Hindu law according to Telang. Further, for Mandlik, the force husbands could apply to their wives was almost naturalised with respect to the 'traditional' system. In his view 'caste heads had always received complaints from Hindu husbands and these authorities had always compelled wives to go and live with their husbands.'[113]

The specific features of Hindu law were also sharply contested in the larger court of public opinion in which Rakhmabai was being tried. The differences in the positions in terms of issues with legal implications were the question of 'Hindu' marriage as sacrament, the necessity for consent, the point at which a Hindu marriage became binding — whether at the time of the marriage rituals or at the time of the consummation — the indissolubility of the tie, and finally whether the laws themselves were immutable or changeable, and if changeable, who had the power to change them.

As we have seen in the discussion on widow remarriages the sacramental nature of marriage for women had been conceded in the case of high-caste women but equally its non-sacramental nature was broadly endorsed in the case of lower-caste women by accepting its dissolubility at different points of time for different low-caste groups. In Rakhmabai's case, interestingly, a direct position on the non-sacramental nature of marriages amongst the Sutars (which had enabled Rakhmabai's mother to remarry according to custom) was not highlighted. On the contrary it was always 'Hindu' law, in its liberal reformist interpretation, which was invoked. Implicitly, the defence for Rakhmabai was working with notions of a marriage as something closer to a contract (recalling the dissolution of marriage amongst non-Brahmana castes), and at the same time reformulating the sacramental aspect of a Hindu marriage as based on consent *and* the act of consummation. In a sense the central question here became: could Hindu law *endorse* a consummation against the will of the wife — that is, could one sanction what would amount to the rape of a wife to uphold a sacred marriage? This in particular seemed to be unthinkable for Telang, Malabari and Raghunath Rao. *The Indian Spectator*, Malabari's paper, argued that Hindu marriage was a *sanskara* only when women gave *intelligent* assent to it.[114] Raghunath Rao argued that no marriage amongst Hindus was complete without consent. Vamanji Modak endorsed the right to personal liberty and the centrality of consent in marriage, which he lamented had been lost sight of in 'our country'.[115] (According to Kane [citing Brahmanical texts], a woman who refused her husband sexual access could be defamed in the community and turned out of her house but this was not a delinquency for which she could be imprisoned.)[116]

The view that the Hindu marriage *was* a sacrament but in order to become a sacrament it must be consented to by the husband and the wife led inevitably to the position that infant marriages were an anomaly in Hindu law. This was the view of one section of the reformists in nineteenth century western India. From this followed the archetypal fears of Hindu society, generated by the Rakhmabai case. The *Times of India* had, for example, hailed the judgement of Pinhey as 'a shrewd blow at the whole system of infant marriages, a blow that coming from so authoritative a quarter, could not fail to have a most wholesome influence in the direction of reform'.[117] No wonder the *Native Opinion*, Mandlik's paper, regarded that Pinhey's judgement had struck at the root of the marital tie and that it was entirely subversive of the 'principles that have governed society for ages'.[118] Fully conscious of the strength of opinion which supported Mandlik rather than the *Times of India*, the judges Sargent, Bayley and Farran were apprised of the pitfalls of assuming a position that a marriage without consent, i.e., an 'infant' marriage, was not obligatory upon the parties. If they took such a position the entire edifice of Hindu marriages would collapse as pre-pubertal marriage for girls was regarded as the essential characteristic of the normative marriage structure among the Hindus. It was impossible to argue that marriages of children among Hindus were not perfectly valid merely because the wife had no voice in the choice of the husband. The judges Sargent and Bayley had therefore stated emphatically that the marriages of Hindu children were perfectly valid without the exercise of volition on their part. Basing themselves on the 'religious' nature of Hindu marriage (since the precepts of Hindu law treated the marriage of daughters as a religious obligation imposed upon parents and guardians), they rejected the purely English point of view which saw in marriage nothing but a contract to which the husband and wife had to be consenting parties.[119]

The fears that the Rakhmabai case aroused and which reverberated in the Age of Consent issue during the next few years were the implied devaluation and disavowal of the non-consensual marriage. Consent and pre-pubertal marriages for girls were mutually contradictory and the law of the land, it was emphasised, *did not* require the girl (in whose case the taking of consent was an impertinence) to be a *party to the contract*. She was the *subject* of a contract into which her parent or guardian entered. The validity of the non-consensual infant marriage thus inevitably became the focal point of the legal and social implications of the Rakhmabai case. Malabari recognised this when he summed up the issue before the court — acceptance or refusal to sanction the validity of unconsummated infant marriages.[120] Since Rakhmabai's marriage was unconsummated the anxiety about the court's upholding of Rakhmabai's refusal to cohabit with Dadaji was doubly threatening. This was because in the 1860s William Muir had suggested that the courts should refuse to recognise unconsummated marriages.[121] If the courts had upheld Rakhmabai's refusal every unconsummated marriage could be struck down as null and void. It was this possibility that made Rakhmabai's case so controversial. Other restitution cases initiated by the husband had come up before the courts, one going all the way up to the Privy Council, but these had hardly caused a ripple. It was because Rakhmabai's case involved the issue of unconsummated, infant marriage, and came at a time when public opinion of Hindu nationalism was consolidating, which in turn was so closely tied to gender identity, that it caused such a storm.

The absence of consent and the right to repudiate an early marriage when it came to consummation and formal cohabitation also destroyed the idea of the marriage as a sacrament. The eminently rational but conservative *Mahratta* captured the anxieties of 'Hindu' society but also the trap that most reformers themselves were in over the question of 'infant' marriages. Consent, intelligent consent, would mean pushing up the age of marriage for girls to 15 or 16, which no reformer was at that point willing to advocate openly. The reformist elite was thus pushed into a corner over the question of consent, marriage as sacrament, and the almost universal practice of early marriage. When Farran ultimately ruled against Rakhmabai he partially set at rest the fears that Rakhmabai had unleashed in Hindu society. Tilak's paper summed up virtually all the anxieties arising from the Rakhmabai case when a reader pointed out that over the years the courts had left little powers to the castes and religious organisations by assuming jurisdiction over social matters such as the enforcement of caste discipline.[122] If the courts were now swayed by 'personal considerations' there would be no law left at all. The question before the court was not to change the law to provide relief for a particular individual but to ascertain the law of the land. The court had to decide whether Hindu marriage was a sacrament or a contract. Dadaji's 'Exposition' appearing in the *Mahratta* held that 'from the days of the *rishis* onwards' marriage was regarded as a sacrament in Hindu law and the *saptapadi* made it binding on both sides.[123] Consummation was a distinct and separate ceremony after that of the marriage and had nothing to do with its validity or otherwise. The sacredness of the marriage tie would have been in danger if Rakhmabai had succeeded. Farran's judgement prevented this.

The Rakhmabai case was the first of its kind wherein a married woman publicly refused to discharge her marital duties and it was therefore bound to be dramatic. This was not strictly true. In a sense Rakhmabai's guardians were perhaps the ones who had retracted the conjugality implied in the marriage on specific grounds and may have either supported her decision or even decided for Rakhmabai. However, to the public that was avidly following the case it was perceived as a case of a wife's refusal since that was how the issues were framed and how the court itself treated Rakhmabai — as a woman with a will of her own. The anxiety aroused by Rakhmabai's refusal to cohabit with her husband thus was one that arose not merely from the British Indian courts via Pinhey declining to uphold the sacramental and indissoluble nature of the Hindu marriage but from a young wife disavowing the marital obligation. The anxiety was heightened by Rakhmabai's arguments for the disavowal, the incompatibility and unworthiness of the husband. The fact that Rakhmabai was 'English'-educated and a woman of substance clinched the fears of the upper-caste middle class. Every Hindu bride from this class could do what Rakhmabai did, drop the facade of 'willing' surrender and refuse to conform to the ideological and material arrangements of nineteenth century Brahmanical Hindu patriarchy. As one anxious male put it, 'Was the peace and happiness of the whole of the Hindu society to be disturbed by one single individual?'[124] Aware of this anxiety, Dadaji invoked the need for Hindus to do all that lay in their power to render a union between a Hindu man and a Hindu woman happy. He also warned that 'wilful, disobedient persons' (meaning wives) would follow the Rakhmabai example and thus all marriages would be affected. He alleged that non-Hindus would not understand 'this matter' but the 'true Hindu would suffer martyrdom for it'. Those who were his 'true co-religionists' would understand Dadaji's feelings and the danger represented by Rakhmabai's stance.[125] Another letter in the *Mahratta* by a man assuming the pseudonym of 'Sobriety' charged Rakhmabai with 'wanton opposition to the law of the land'. The writer was convinced that Rakhmabai had very few supporters among 'Hindus proper', implying that neither Rakhmabai nor her supporters were real 'Hindus'. The man also declared that while he was generally 'conservative' about government action, in this particular case he would support it because it was necessary to apply coercion to recalcitrant women.[126]

For Tilak and his newspaper, the *Mahratta*, a conservative position on Hindu womanhood was central to the agenda of garnering support from the upper-caste elites for a militant Hindu nationalism and Tilak's first public foray to consolidate opinion was over Rakhmabai. Ably served by the contradictions in the personal lives and the ideologies of the reformers, Tilak found the Rakhmabai case a good launching-pad for his attack on the reformers' position on women in which education would have been the least controversial plank. Tilak's newspaper readers were however opposed even to this, and Rakhmabai's education and her unwillingness to accept an uneducated husband, bandied about in the press but never made a part of the legal argument, came in very handy in the onslaught on education. 'It is said that education expands and purifies the mind. But what is the case now? The thing is that God has so made the females that they are quite unworthy of either liberty or enlightenment,'[127] wrote an anxious reader who ended by arguing that supporting education would be a foolish thing to do in light of Rakhmabai's behaviour. Another newspaper also located Rakhmabai's rebellion against her lawfully wedded husband in her western education. She had consequently become a 'foolish ill-advised and imperious young woman' who was inspired with 'fine' notions of independence and freedom which western education had instilled into her.[128] A letter to the *Mahratta* also outlined the alternative to a system of training which alienated a woman from her own religion and people. This could only be ensured through a thorough training in Hindu ways. The Shastras were a means to avoid the pitfalls of Rakhmabai's training and the Shastras had clearly said that 'all she has to do to [is] to worship her husband and thus she will become famous in heaven'.[129]

The traditional model of womanhood, discarded by Rakhmabai, was recommended to her at various points but particularly when Farran decided on imprisonment if she continued to withhold conjugal rights from her husband. It was suggested that the remedy lay in Rakhmabai's own hands as she could still go to her husband. In this way she would 'immortalise' her name.[130] Recalling Manu, it was pointed out that as a woman Rakhmabai was not her own master and never could be so at any point of her existence. Marriage was a sacrament among Hindus and *no law* could untie the marriage knot, not even the legislature. The sacred bond of marriage, a central feature of Hindu tradition and therefore of Hindu law, was too elevated to be contested by recourse to such concepts as 'justice, equity and good conscience'. Hindu wifehood was above such notions.[131]

Throughout the attack on Rakhmabai as a spoilt western-educated woman, parodied as flying to her piano, and reading Milton rather than nursing her ailing husband,[132] (someone who had disavowed her marital obligations but also the unique sacred traditions of Hindu womanhood), there was a play on the figure of Savitri and of Rakhmabai having turned her back on this powerful image. Since Rakhmabai's husband was alleged to be suffering from a lung disease, the Savitri example was particularly evocative. Savitri had known that her husband was bound to die and yet had *chosen* to marry him. Thereafter she had managed to snatch her husband back from the jaws of death by her wifely devotion; in contrast the new woman, exemplified by Rakhmabai, was refusing the chance to be immortal and a modern-day Savitri by even attempting to be a ministering angel to him. According to the newspaper, this would have provided a model which would be imitated all over India.[133]

From the failure of western-educated women to hold on to the eternal values of Hindu culture embodied in Savitri it was natural to move to that favourite terrain of Hindu nationalists, the east versus west, non-consensual 'sacred' marriage versus consensual/contractual marriage. Rejecting the model of consensual marriages which was tantamount to a 'civil', desacralised arrangement for sexual fulfilment in contrast to the sacramental nature of Hindu marriage, the occurrence of 'social' scandals was highlighted. This brought into disrepute the system of consensual marriages which was not capable of ensuring domestic and social happiness.[134] The argument of the superiority of Hindu family structures and the examples of Hindu womanhood, especially that of Savitri, permitted most men to deflect the central legal, social and moral questions raised by the Rakhmabai case: should she be forced to consummate her marriage to Dadaji *against her will?*

Using force to uphold conjugality where consummation had not yet occurred became the focal point of embarrassment for the British Indian administration, the Anglo-Indian press supporting Rakhmabai, and even the 'rational' conservatives, especially when Rakhmabai forced the court to decide her fate after stating her own position in no ambiguous terms: she *would not go*, not even if the court upheld the right of restitution of 'conjugality' to Dadaji, preferring the severe punishment of imprisonment still in existence in the rule books. Once the court ruled imprisonment for 'recusancy' the question of a false and forced consent as inhering in the law on conjugality became apparent. Neither the Anglo-Indian press, representing broadly the English point of view, nor the Hindu middle class would concede that it was right to use coercion to *enforce* conjugality upon a wife and sought to shift the onus away from their own positions on how to deal with an unwilling wife.

The British Indian administration, in particular, was in a fix. The judgement had been a natural consequence of its legal structures with its multiple laws, ambiguity about what the law in each case was,[135] overlapping legal jurisdictions and institutions, its political concerns which determined how far it could go against a subject people, and its own investment in patriarchal institutions. But because the judgement on imprisonment created new alignments and revealed contradictions in its own position as well as in the positions of those who had wanted conjugality to be imposed upon Rakhmabai, it was necessary to find scapegoats. The issue then became: was imprisonment a consequence of English law or Hindu law? The Anglo-Indian press which had supported Rakhmabai on her disavowal of non-consensual marriage and was loyal to the British Indian administration, openly expressed its disapproval of the judgement and generally argued that the judiciary was forced into the unhappy situation since it was under oath to administer Hindu law; it was under Hindu law that coercion was applied on Rakhmabai and it was under Hindu law that she would go to prison. It was used also to exonerate the British administration of charges of despotism and to demonstrate the unfitness of Indians to rule themselves, and provided another opportunity to make derogatory remarks about Hindu society generally.[136]

On the other side, it was equally imperative for those who had been arguing that Rakhmabai *must* perform her conjugal duties and that Hindu marriage was immutable, to distinguish between the legal arguments, the judgement on the validity of the marriage (even in the case of an unconsummated infant marriage) and the 'enforcement' taking the specific shape of imprisonment.[137] This distinction, which even the opponents of Rakhmabai *had* to make, is what she finally achieved through the tortuous legal battle during which she consistently refused to accept the authority of the husband, 'Hindu' society, or even the state, to *force* her to cohabit with Dadaji. She probably knew that even Dadaji's 'party' did not want imprisonment because it was useless and it would not 'effectuate' the marriage; Tilak for example preferred the attachment of her property or alimony. This was more in keeping with Dadaji's interest. There was no point in pursuing a perverse woman like Rakhmabai in Tilak's opinion. Instead she should be punished by the court for disobeying its order by attachment of property or by the imposition of a fine.[138]

The judgement on imprisonment thus had to be disowned. The responsibility for it was put squarely on English law. The *Hindu Patriot*, which sustained a conservative opinion on gender, captured the essence of the dual position on the final judgement in the Rakhmabai case. It approved of Justices Sargent, Bayley and Farran daring 'to enforce the Hindu law of marriage' but condemned the judgement on imprisonment as derived from English civilisation and law. Hindu law, in its view, looked upon the use of force on a woman with the 'greatest abhorrence', in contrast to the monster created by the British Indian law which had extended English civilisation to India. It was English civilisation that declared that the 'custody of a wife's *person* belongs, as a right, to her husband'.[139] The paper did not object to the bringing in of the restitution of conjugal rights but denounced the effrontery of attaching its faults to Hindu law. How the Hindu law of marriage could be enforced without handing over custody of a wife to her husband, even when she refused her consent to such an arrangement, was not the concern of the paper. It was, however, imperative to absolve the Hindu law of marriage of the taint of coercion, especially coercion applied directly by the state to a Hindu woman even if she was being recalcitrant and characteristically un-'Hindu' about her duties as a wife.

It must be noted though that not everyone was embarrassed about sending a woman to jail under Hindu law. As one satisfied male put it, the High Court's decision on Rakhmabai had been 'received with approval from one end of India to the other by the Hindu press because it was in consonance with Hindu law and tradition'. He wondered how the 'High Court could be charged with showing undue zeal with any approach to truth' as the *Bombay Gazette* had done. According to him much capital was being made out of the fact that there was no text in the Hindu law books providing for the restitution of conjugal rights. This apparent omission was explicable in his view because the idea of the Hindu wife refusing to go to live with her husband was 'utterly absent in the minds of ancient text writers and commentators'. But he added:

This circumstance however does not make it very difficult to conjecture what their opinion would have been had a Rakhmabai arisen in their times. The religious writers who make it obligatory upon the wife to follow certain duties in order to promote the spiritual welfare of the husband even after his death would necessarily have provided a severe punishment for a contingency that would have become possible in this century.[140]

Crucial to the view of the writer of this letter were the principles underlying the basic structure of Hindu law. It was necessary to use coercion if the norms of Hindu law were to be upheld and the law would have to adapt itself to the contingencies made possible in a different time from that envisaged by the writers of traditional texts.

Another letter to the editor written about a fortnight later took on the argument that the 'old Hindu law did not recognise suits for the enforcement of marital rights and that there was no procedure to enforce the decree of the court'. The letter pointed to assurance provided by a 'friend from a first class Maratha state' that

long before British influence was felt in the native courts, based on custom, the wife was taken hold of bodily and given in possession of her husband. In case this was not possible she was sentenced to imprisonment which, in that state, was far worse than rigorous imprisonment here.

The letter concluded that whether one looked at the evidence of

Manu, Yagnavalkya, or the 'custom of our castes' or the procedure
followed by the native courts in the native states, there was a means
of enforcing marital rights and obligations through the courts of
the land.[141]

The *Bombay Gazette's* position that it was absurd to ask the
courts to enforce sacramental obligations, of which marriage was
the most important, was unacceptable to most men in the
nineteenth century not only because marital rights were at stake but
also because other rights were involved. An editorial in the
Mahratta summed up the position on the non-enforceability of
sacramental obligation taken by the *Bombay Gazette* even as it
suggested that Dadaji should accept a settlement out of court:

Enforcement of obligations [is] legal in Hindu law. Manu [VIII 335 and
371] and Yagnavalkya [II 237] both the highest authorities empower a
king to punish the defaulting wife... The authority of the castes now vests
in the courts and it is natural that they should now have the same power
of enforcing their decrees which the castes and the king had under Hindu
law... We have no objection to a special sanction made by a competent
authority in the case of Rakhmabai, but there can be no law without
sanction... If the Bombay Gazette position is accepted the whole property
law of the Hindus based as it is on rights arising out of sacraments such
as marriage, adoption etc. must cease to be enforced henceforth.[142]

Here was a recognition that marriages were not merely about
sacramental obligations that wives must render to husbands but also
about property. This was amply evident in the Rakhmabai case
which went far beyond the Hindu law on marriage and conjugal
rights as it inevitably threw up issues of the relationship between
marriage, conjugality and property even as the debate in the press
tended to sweep property under the carpet.

The contradictions and shifts in the position of both sides in the
Rakhmabai case were built into the entangled understanding of the
law, whether English or Hindu, especially the latter, and the
complicity of both in upholding patriarchal structures. Only for
someone like Malabari were the limitations of and contradictions
between existing Hindu customs (accepted as Hindu *law* by others
but not by him) and statutory law, drawn often from English law,
evident in their working out through the Rakhmabai case. At one
stage he recognised the limited possibilities of a judgement
upholding Rakhmabai's position when he said that although she

had an able and supportive attorney like Telang, it was hard to see what could be done *unless* the final court of appeal refused to recognise the validity of 'unconsummated' infant marriages. While Malabari recognised the coercion exercised by contemporary Hindu society where the 'caste' of the girl insisted upon pre-pubertal marriages, it was the 'cobbling process' of the British Indian legal system that had further created a severe anomaly by introducing the concept of the 'restitution' of conjugal rights drawn from English law; such a law, a barbaric relic of ecclesiastical law, even in England, could never envisage a situation where it might be applied to the Hindu custom of infant marriages. It was completely contradictory to introduce what Malabari considered the 'unmanly' idea of the restitution of conjugal rights without importing the system of adult marriages. Although the root of Rakhmabai's problems lay in the existing Hindu custom of non-consensual marriages, the way an unwilling wife like Rakhmabai was being legally 'hunted down' was English. He strongly denounced the way the judges were upholding a marriage into which a Hindu girl was being forced by caste (custom), a marriage to which she was 'as much a party as any of the judges of the court'. Instead of striking such a marriage down the judges had actually offered to serve as 'constable and jailor' and had completed the outrage by conveniently shifting the onus of the outrage upon the law of the Hindus.[143] Malabari was acutely conscious of the fact that in the late nineteenth century though the caste council had the liberty to deal with a recalcitrant member it had to stop short of resorting to physical violence, the right to which was vested solely in the British government. The British government in India alone had the power to execute action against Rakhmabai (or 'release' her from her conjugal duty) and it was choosing to use its coercive power over her by threatening her with imprisonment. In Malabari's anguished writing we can see the interlocking dimensions of different patriarchies working together to uphold marital rights and obligations drawn from overtly dissimilar cultures and legal codes but performing similar functions. While the numerous questions raised by the case are only beginning to emerge in outline and are impossible to resolve in this work, a tentative analysis of the case suggests that the interlocking of an indigenous patriarchy with new forms of patriarchy brought in by the colonial state produced a situation where apparently spaces opened up for women but were simultaneously restricted. The choice available to Rakhmabai of resisting a forced consummation had become possible partly because of her specific circumstances, a natal family that regretted the marriage they had contracted for her, the caste to which she belonged, and her relatively secure position in a certain class and urban domicile which possibly put her outside the power of traditional caste authority and social disapproval — all of this was being now denied by another structure of authority. Both structures upheld patriarchal ideologies and institutions and could therefore co-exist with each other. Ultimately, when Rakhmabai 'bought' her freedom under the compromise, it was not dissimilar to compensation, which could have been worked out in the caste panchayat, for husbands whose wives left them among many non-Brahmana castes. Through a circumlocutory process, the issue ended where it could have begun. However, the issue of non-consensual marriages and the rights of husbands within them, although severely tested, remained more or less where it was: upheld by a cross-cutting alliance between 'Hindu' society and the colonial state.[144]

IV

The problems inherent in a non-consensual marriage which had been at the heart of the Rakhmabai case surfaced once more in the Age of Consent controversy. The central issues, as they were portrayed by the defenders of Brahmanical customs, revolved around the religious practices of the 'Hindus' in pursuance of their religious goals, and the colonial government's lack of authority to legislate in matters of religious observance. For the reformers and the colonial government the question was of 'protecting' the child wife from being subjected to a premature and often forced consummation. The debate was conducted in a highly charged atmosphere with the anxieties of the Hindu middle class about their place in society, and their unique identity, overlapping with a new and aggressive stage in nationalist politics; together they coalesced to produce the cry of 'religion in danger'.[145] Characteristically, the feverish passions unleashed were about religious observances affecting the most private arena: the marital rights of Hindu men over their wives.

The roots of the Age of Consent Bill are traceable to the

continuing problem of the nineteenth century: the 'status' of women, especially widows, whose condition was attributed to the practice of early marriage. Malabari's collection of his tracts and lectures linking widowhood with early marriage was published in 1884[146] and became the starting-point of a push towards statutorily raising the age of marriage for girls. Malabari's radical views on consequences of early marriages were not, however, shared by all reformers and even the government was reluctant to support the series of measures he recommended to discourage the practice of early marriage. The government expressed its reservation by arguing that the legislature should not enact new laws and place itself in direct antagonism to social opinion.[147] As a compensation to the reformers, who too had to be placated, it even went so far as to suggest that the government would consider introducing legislation to amend the 1856 Widow Remarriage Act to allow the remarried widow to keep property inherited from her first husband, which was not a proposition that the reformers supported[148] (see Ranade's position on this discussed earlier on p. 132)

An alternative suggestion put forward by the reformers was to leave the question of regulating the age of marriage and, instead, augment the law on the age of consent for legitimate sexual intercourse with girls, fixed at 10 in the Indian Penal Code in 1860, by raising it to 12.[149] This was regarded as a way out of the impasse by the reformers as it would merely extend an existing law rather than introduce a new one.

The shift in focus from early marriage to premature consummation, however, created an unexpected legal problem by separating the ritual of marriage from the consequent sexual cohabitation between husband and wife. Further, the Age of Consent Bill, by laying down when a man could have sexual access to his wife legally, also deemed premature access to her rape. This legal position was unprecedented in English law, which did not recognise rape within marriage as a possibility, presumably because marriages in England were regarded as consensual. In England the opinion of Lord Hale stood: it was considered that the husband cannot be guilty of rape committed by himself upon his lawful wife, for 'by their mutual matrimonial contract the wife hath given herself up in this kind unto her husband'.[150] Thus in one stroke marriage practices were doubly devalued in India and public attention to the issue was therefore enormous.

All the contradictions inhering in the changed relationship between family, community and the state, as reflected in the laws on marriage, now came to the fore.[151] Significantly, although the Age of Consent controversy was conducted in somewhat abstract terms and as applicable to all women rather than on substantive issues arising from an actual case, it followed the shocking death of 10-year-old Phulmoni through forcible intercourse by her 35-year-old husband.[152] The judge, though sympathetic, found his hands tied and ruled that the charge of rape was inapplicable because Phulmoni was 10 and intercourse was legal according to the 1860 law. Justice Wilson had admitted the brutality involved but pointed out that neither 'Judge nor Juries have any right to do for themselves what the law has not done'.[153] The government used this case and the wave of moral revulsion in some quarters to hastily introduce legislation raising the age of 'consent' to 12 in the case of women.

The issues arising from the proposed Bill were therefore debated against the backdrop of Phulmoni, and Harmaiti,[154] the husband who had caused her death, became synonymous with male brutality. The guilt that some of the male reformers had felt about women's oppression was heightened by this dramatic uncovering of the bestiality of men. Dayaram Gidumal had referred with disgust to the dark side of male nature where men 'brutalised women by their sensuality', and 'imposed their wills upon their wives in sexual matters placing no restraints upon themselves'[155] even before Phulmoni's death. And after her death it was Bhandarkar (who had found nothing reprehensible in early marriage) who captured most effectively the anguish of reformers faced with the plight of the Phulmonis:

Often the marriage of a girl, under certain circumstances, proves her death warrant. This matter has within the last few years forced itself powerfully upon my observation. A young man of 30 or 35 loses his first wife. Straightaway he proceeds to marry another who is a girl of 10 or 12. That girl dies by the time she reaches 20; another takes her place immediately thereafter. She too dies similarly thereafter... A great many of such cases have occurred within the last few years. The medical men whom I have consulted say that the results are due to the marriages being ill assorted, that is, to the great inequality between the age of the girl and of the strong vigorous man. I do not know how to characterise these cases except as cases of human sacrifice.[156]

Such anguished feelings of guilt and disgust aroused by the death of Phulmoni had to be aggressively countered by the supporters of traditional Brahmanical patriarchal practices. Further, since Phulmoni, unlike Rakhmabai, could not be attacked, nor could Harmaiti be publicly defended,[157] the issues raised were those of religion and 'nation', and the authority of an alien state to legislate on the nature of Hindu marriage.

Those opposing the Bill built their arguments essentially on its being violative of the religious practices of the Hindus. Using a text of Raghunandan which was regarded as prescriptive in Bengal it was argued that it was incumbent upon the Hindu husband to have intercourse with the wife immediately following the first menstruation to complete the garbhadhanam, thereby ensuring the purity of the womb and of the future offspring. Since the onset of puberty could vary but was likely to occur before 12, the proposed legislation would violate the 'dharma' of the Hindu. The second argument used was that since the ceremony of the garbhadhanam was a religious practice and the Queen's proclamation of 1858 had guaranteed non-interference in religious matters, the government had no authority to legislate on such an issue. These arguments were first raised in Bengal where the erstwhile 'reformer' R.C. Mitter opposed the Bill,[158] but they soon gained currency elsewhere including Maharashtra, where Tilak used them to great effect in his battle for his own political constituency against the Brahmana reformers.[159]

The arguments of the opponents of the Bill were most effectively countered by Telang, an eminent jurist of Hindu law. Telang advocated the view that the sovereign owed it to her/his subjects to 'protect them from harm', and that far from being 'meddlesome interference' this was the paramount duty of the state which was constituted primarily to 'secure life'. Using the testimony of the Phulmoni case as evidence he pointed out that 'harm, unjust harm — most fatal harm' was done to Hindu child wives by their husbands 'prematurely claiming to exercise their so-called marital rights' upon their persons.[160] Did the opponents of the Bill, queried Telang, consider that the 'Queen had pledged directly or indirectly not to interfere to either prevent or punish such harms?' Further, did the opposition believe that all enjoyed the equal protection of the law when a girl could be ravished by her husband with impunity even before she became 'apta viri'?[161]

On the question of the 'Hindu' custom of garbhadhanam, whose validity he questioned and interpreted very differently, he shifted the focus from rights to duties. Telang's position was that there was nothing like 'unrestricted rights of husbands' and that the duties of the husband had to be consonant with the wife's well-being. Further, the sin of killing foetuses by not giving unrestricted rights of the husband to the wife was a 'legal fiction'. In any case the alleged sin, even if it was so regarded, could easily be expiated by doing a few breathing exercises (*pranayamas*) or spending a few annas.[162] (This was not appreciated by Tilak.[163]) There was thus no major dilemma in his view for the 'orthodox' Hindu husband as suggested by R.C.Mitter.[164]

Tilak's position that Hindu husbands should not be compelled by British law to flout the law of the Shastras was rebutted on the ground that even if it were to actually have such an effect, 'Marathas', as he put it, should not object to the breach of such rules in order to save Hindu women from 'inhuman' cruelty.[165] Telang was in any case convinced that the Shastric argument was an afterthought of the opponents of the Bill. He decisively advocated the view that it was the 'bounden duty of the Legislature to do what it was doing in the interests of humanity even if it meant disregarding the Shastras'.[166] No proclamation could override that duty especially if the Shastras and customs meant torture and death to individual women — or rather minor girls.[167] Equally decisively Telang was rejecting the implicit argument that governmental authority could not go into certain sacred spaces — the marital bed — which the opponents of the Bill were representing as central to the 'religious' observance of the Hindus.

Telang's celebrated step-by-step and exhaustive rebuttal of the traditional defenders of the 'Shastric' position on grounds of a rational interpretation of law, custom and Shastras, and of women's entitlement to the protection of the state, was rarely matched by other participants in the debate. However, a number of issues arose in the course of the public debate on the Age of Consent Bill which we will briefly outline here.

The first point to note is that the Age of Consent debate was the most publicly conducted discussion on female sexuality that India has witnessed in a long time; consequently the woman's body was subjected to unprecedented attention. The central issue on both sides, those arguing for the age of 12 and those arguing for the status quo, i.e., the age of 10, was to pinpoint the age when women menstruated and were therefore fit to have their marriages consummated. Medical evidence was confined to those arguing for raising the age to 12. A variety of arguments linked together by Dr Mahendra Lal Sircar regarding menstruation, pubescence, and the age at which a girl achieved the capacity for child-bearing are summarised below:[168]

Early marriage is the greatest evil of our country. I am inclined to date the fall and degeneracy of my country from the day Angiras uttered the fatal words which became law (i.e., that the learned should give their daughters in marriage whenever they reach the age of 10). This custom has had a disastrous effect on the deterioration of the race. The generations being born at the moment in the eyes of modern medicine, or of our own ancient Ayurveda, are no better than abortions or premature birth. This view of the state of things imperatively demands that for the sake of our daughters and sisters who are to become mothers, and for the sake of generations yet to be born but upon whose proper development and healthy growth the future well being of the country depends, the earliest marriageable age of our females should be fixed at a higher point. The commencement of menstruation is an index to the commencement of puberty but it would be a grave mistake to suppose that the female who has just begun to menstruate is capable of giving birth to healthy children... When we see a girl beginning to have the monthly flow we should not only watch anxiously its course and regularity but should also watch the other collateral developments of womanhood to be able to determine the better time when she can become a mother, safely to herself and her offspring...[169]

It is clear that for Mahendra Lal Sircar, and many others who thought like him, there were two major foci of concern: one was the woman's body and the irreparable damage that could be done to it. But the other cause for concern was what the pernicious custom was doing to the 'national' body — thus, the woman's body was also the nation's body and irreparable damage was being done to both. To attack existing customs, responsible for such damage, Sircar marshalled the support of two systems of medicine — the ancient indigenous system and modern western medicine. Armed with the premises of both systems Sircar privileged what he regarded as the 'intention' of nature over the dictates of religion and topped his argument with a definition of 'true' patriotism which is concern over the pernicious custom of child marriage.

Sircar also took up more squarely certain reprehensible social practices affecting women's bodies, which subjected them first to artificial methods to hasten the process of pubescence. But more offensive were the practices which subjected child wives to sexual relations by 'brutal' husbands supposedly sanctified by religion.[170] There was thus a category of girl wives who required the paternalistic protection of enlightened men and the state. Unfortunately, since men were unwilling to raise the age of marriage there was no alternative to the amendment proposed by the state. It was the 'obstinacy' of men that led to an amendment introducing the offence of rape into the institution of marriage:

The IPC has (already) made provision, however slight against outrages by brutal husbands by constituting sexual intercourse by a husband with a wife under 10 years of age as rape in the eyes of the law. Protection to girls under 10 is not really required as intercourse with a girl below 10 is not really usual. But little ones between 10 and 12 do need protection as they are regarded as fit for becoming mothers...

Deeming intercourse between husband and wife as rape under any circumstances looks like an absurdity and anomaly, subversive of the *very sacred character of marriage itself* (emphasis added) and jars upon common sense and aesthetics. Better then to raise the marriage age. But since that is impossible at present there is no alternative to the present amendment. It is a matter of extreme regret that (such a question) has to be settled by legislative interference and not by the 'good sense of the community' to which I had appealed twenty years ago.[171]

Sircar was strongly condemnatory of his countrymen for forcing the kind of situation upon society that it was faced with by 'bolstering up rotten texts', and conveying to the world that the Hindus had for centuries 'in the exercise of marital rights and under the sanction of religion been committing the gravest and most brutal outrages on immature female children.' He was particularly aggrieved that the opposition was using the argument that their way to heaven was being obstructed and their religion was in danger if the garbhadhanam was not performed the moment a girl menstruated. This he regarded as a silly, suicidal, shameless argument:

It is a shameless argument because even assuming the commencement of normal menstruation [which he doubted] it is impossible for reasons better imagined in the majority of cases to enforce Shastric injunction without actual force, i.e., without rape in the literal sense of the term.[172]

Here was a situation when men were having to speak about the unspeakable, confront anomalies in marriage, think about brutal husbands ravishing their young wives, and recognise that there could be rape within the 'sacred' institution of marriage. No wonder Sircar was anguished by the arguments of the opposition: it created an impossible dilemma for those who actually wanted the age of marriage to be raised. Sircar himself suggested the age of 16 for women. For him this would have automatically excluded the possibility of rape within marriage. Even within the ambit of the proposed law Sircar gave expression to the dilemma he was in by suggesting a softening of the punitive clauses. He concluded his impassioned arguments thus:

This much I am bound to say that except for the peculiar circumstances of the country, the enactment which constitutes [sexual] intercourse between husband and wife as rape *is an anomaly*. The punishment, unless the intercourse is attended with personal injuries, should be much lighter than in the case of ordinary rape; it should, in my humble opinion, in no case be imprisonment. In other words it should be so provided that the punishment should *never be such as to be calculated to embitter the future relationship of the married couple*.[173] (emphasis added)

Sircar's last lines capture the contradiction for all Hindu men: marriage was a sacred institution; it was indissoluble. How could one 'protect' the girl-wife legally without jeopardising the marriage itself, especially when the entire community was complicit in upholding the existing practice? The opponents of the Bill shared few of the dilemmas of the reformers. While they were unable to marshal in any substantial sense their own medical evidence on the age of menstruation, they rejected the conclusions of the doctors collected by the supporters of the Bill. As Dagmar Engels shows, they tore to pieces the evidence of the Calcutta doctors: how had the gynaecologists amongst them surveyed the age at which girls menstruate without access to the zenana? How did they know the ages of the girls whose births were not registered? The views of the doctors, they concluded, were thus based on dubious scientific procedures.[174] They rejected the opinion of the indigenous system of medicine too, arguing that its evidence was for girls of other regions. Charaka's evidence was particularly 'unreliable' since he had had the audacity to recommend beef broth for a certain ailment. Clearly he could not have been a Hindu.[175] In support of the opponents of the Bill a few 'native' doctors gave evidence to the Select Committee appointed for the purpose of gathering opinion on the issue. Among them the view was that puberty in India could often occur before 12, and that they had never seen an injury to a child wife from premature cohabitation. Since premature cohabitation was 'rare' there was no need for the Bill. In any case religious and pragmatic reasons were more important than imagined fears about girl wives in the hands of brutal husbands. It was the duty of every woman to give birth to pure sons; without the garbhadhanam the womb would be polluted and the impure sons would not be able to offer the *pindas* (ritual offerings to dead ancestors) to the ancestors.[176]

Further, pragmatic reasons required a recognition of the enormous power of female sexuality which was a 'fact of life' and it was prudish not to recognise it and make allowances for it. While the *Bangabasi*, the Bengali language newspaper with the highest circulation, painted a lurid picture of females scurrying from house to house begging males to gratify their lust if the Bill was passed,[177] R.C. Mitter's concern was focused on the need for sympathy towards the young boy who lived alone with his child wife.[178] A number of eminent respondents to Malabari's enquiries had drawn attention to the particular needs of young men; their healthy development required normal sexual gratification, lack of which would lead to frustration and loss of concentration for those pursuing their studies with earnestness. Healthy male bodies and minds thus required early marriage; therefore girl wives were a necessity. The headmaster of the Anglo-Vernacular School in Raja Deulgaon summed up this viewpoint thus:

It will be admitted that native boys feel a desire for sensual enjoyment at the age of 17. When a boy exceeds this age without means of enjoying carnal pleasures he is drawn to practise unnatural ways of satisfying his desire for sexual congress. The means adopted by the boys are most detrimental to their health.[179]

A tehsildar echoed the same sentiment when he argued for early consumption. Consummation according to him took place 'not a day too early'. 'It tends to make the husband more steady, more tractable and even more studying [studious] than he would be without it,'[180] he concluded. On the messy question of rape within marriage, which the reformers were struggling to deal with, the opponents of the Bill had no dilemma at all. They rejected outright the idea that there could be rape within marriage. Rape was not a physical matter but a matter of honour and how could the husband's actions cause dishonour to a wife? It was loss of honour rather than physical pain or psychic damage which was considered to be the main aspect of rape. Thus it was impossible to rape one's own, even immature, wife since she could never lose her reputation, said the *Samachar*.[181] There was of course the sticky problem of physical injuries, even death. This too was rationalised as a negligible price to pay, if necessary, in order to protect the sacred character of Hindu marriage.[182]

It should be evident from the preceding discussion that not everyone shared the normal revulsion experienced by a section of men regarding the vulnerability of girl-wives subjected to the brutality of men. While it is indisputable that the Age of Consent legislation was ill-conceived and messy[183] in its application, what was at the centre of the controversy was the problem created by the non-consensual Hindu marriage which hung like a millstone round the necks of men and women of the late nineteenth century. Into this institution a restricted and statutorily defined notion of 'consent' was now being introduced. But the question we need to ask is: where exactly was this consent being located? Did the wife, either in the past or now under the British dispensation, have the right to refuse the husband access to her once she was married? The arguments of Dadaji, Hindu men who closed ranks in support of Dadaji, and even the British courts, held that the wife had no such right. Further, the arguments that came up in the Rakhmabai case and in the debate on the Age of Consent Bill show that neither the state nor the community (whether resisting or approving the Bill) actually considered 'consent' as residing in the woman's decision to permit her husband sexual access to herself. Instead, as the legislation on the Age of Consent makes evident, it was the state that consented to provide the husband with sexual access to his wife at a particular moment regardless of when the marriage was solemnised. This notion had no precedent in the past. The public hysteria, the argument of religion and culture in danger, or even the position that Tilak and other militants took that an alien government had no right to legislate on such matters had deeper implications than appear on the surface.

I have argued earlier here and elsewhere that female sexuality was closely guarded and subject to stringent control in the pre-colonial period. Brahmanical texts are explicit about the fact that female sexuality (or even male sexuality, but with less emphasis) is never a matter of choice or an individual's will but rather is subject to the collectivity of the caste or kin group. Lapses were swiftly and sternly punished. The state was closely concerned with female sexuality, which was monitored through the community.[184] However, both in the Brahmanical texts and during the Peshwai the state aided and supported the authority of the husband over his wife and reiterated the community's control over female sexuality through the caste panchayats. At no point had the state assumed authority over the wife directly, superseding the authority of the husband and his kinsfolk. Through this legislation the colonial state had for the first time assumed authority, defined as protection, over the child wife, superceding the authority and the rights of the husband. The fundamental point about the Tilakian resistance to the Bill was as much a statement that female sexuality must remain a subject of caste and community control (but not of course of the women concerned) which the state, especially the alien state, must keep away from and not erode.

The colonial state's positions on 'consent' in the Rakhmabai case and in the Age of Consent Bill, though apparently dissimilar, may also be reconciled. In the Rakhmabai case it had insisted on the performance of duty: its understanding of Hindu law was that a wife could not withhold consent to the husband's access to her body; it had thus interlocked with an indigenous formation of patriarchy which certainly upheld the marital obligations of the wife to her husband and did not recognise the notion of consent. Now the colonial state had shifted ground somewhat to come into conflict with traditional patriarchal norms but it did not concede to the wife her right to actually express consent; upholding at all times the superior morality of the colonial authority, the colonial state had, even so, merely *regulated* a man's right to his wife and thus protected its 'weakest' subject, the child wife. The shift was not inconsistent within its larger agenda of upholding patriarchal institutions and keeping track of problems arising from unregulated female sexuality. (The Bill while being introduced had stated twin objectives — to prevent early prostitution and premature intercourse for the great body of female children.)[185]

It was the reformers who were caught on the horns of a dilemma.

They veered between various positions in their public and personal stances, but they too were not able to locate consent in the wife: R.G. Bhandarkar had defended 'infant' marriage[186] (especially in the face of judicial interference) and Telang had argued in 1887 while defending Rakhmabai that no change in the marriage law was required. While he did not want Rakhmabai imprisoned he objected to the Rakhmabai Defence Committee's position that marriage should not be enforced since the parties were children when it was solemnised. He wanted the marriage to be recognised and binding but held that it should be enforced only in certain ways and that should not include imprisonment.[187] Telang performed the marriages of his daughters at the ages of 9 and 11[188] (even after the passing of the Age of Consent Act which he had argued for) and Ranade had himself married an 11-year-old girl. All three 'reformers' were merely envisaging a separation of the wife from the husband for a period of time before actual cohabitation began. Only one response to Malabari's queries on infant marriages came close to recognising women's agency, and proposed that the wife could give her actual consent to the consummation of the marriage when she reached maturity. Bapat, who was a tehsildar, came up also with an 'indigenous' solution in which the wife could indicate her consent to a neutral body — the panchas of the village.[189] Significantly, it was Bapat who had also recommended early consummation in order to provide stability to young men.[190]

V

It has been implied that in the pre-colonial period there were a multiplicity of caste laws so that technically there was nothing like a 'fixed' Hindu law. However, it has been my endeavour to suggest that even the discrete caste laws functioned within an overarching conceptualisation, binding them together quite firmly and 'rationally', with the Peshwai acting as the highest authority to enforce such a structure. But social processes in the nineteenth century led to the weakening, or the disuse, of the caste panchayats through other alternatives provided by the British Indian administration, especially in urban areas. This can be said to have brought women to a certain extent into the ambit of the colonial state and its laws. This is evident in the Rakhmabai case; from other cases of the restitution of conjugality we can see that this was a classic instance where women's relationship to husbands and property brought them directly in as subjects of the colonial law. Significantly, the emerging structure gave men a choice regarding which legal system to use to make women 'governable'. The state too provided dual forums by which patriarchal power could be reinforced even while it was engaged in establishing that its authority was superior to that of its male subjects.

Women were also being brought under the colonial state through criminal cases instituted against them for offences arising from 'illegal' sexual activity; widows in particular found that the colonial state was able to mount as effective a surveillance of them and be as repressive as the Peshwai, displaying similar patriarchal anxieties and upholding the community's as well as its own norms. The Brahmana widow Vijayalakshmi found that an employee of the state first discovered her pregnant condition, kept watch on her and then followed it up by tracing the crime of infanticide back to her.[191] In Bengal, Guha has documented the case of the sister and mother of the widow Chandra being charged with complicity in her death by arranging an abortion for her.[192] They were simultaneously acting against the 'crime' of abortion which the widow had taken recourse to and bringing those women who were attempting to help the widow into the legal net by charging them with complicity. The colonial state was effectively able to pursue these cases because the community's norms coincided with theirs: both were interested in bringing defaulting women to book.

But the colonial state found that it was less effective in dealing with 'insider' crimes, when men within the family dealt with sexual lapses on their own, or when they were themselves involved as offenders.[193] Thus, the state found itself unable to penetrate into the family, even to 'protect' women, when the community's surveillance was not available to aid it. When the norms of the community conflicted with those of the colonial state we can discern a clash of patriarchal ideologies; at other times the community, family, and state all collaborated in monitoring female sexuality. Vijayalakshmi, the widow charged with infanticide, for example, found only one woman, Tarabai Shinde, to defend her publicly.[194]

We find, however, that women were also utilising the courts and the new laws to claim their rights. A young widow fought a lone battle to claim maintenance from her in-laws and lived independently without having to succumb to their power when she won the suit.[195] Many other widows went to court in matters of adoption[196] and rights to property in their in-laws' estates or even for rights in the parents' property,[197] utilising a period of moderate liberalisation after the mid-1870s.[198] But the laws remained patriarchal and the structural constraints could not be surmounted easily. The famous Ranade for example would not rule a share for a widowed daughter in her father's estate in a case that could have paralleled his own. Fathers and brothers had a moral responsibility to their married daughters/sisters but such women did not have a legally enforceable right under 'Hindu' law.[199]

Another significant point about the law in relation to gender is that by the second half of the nineteenth century cultural nationalism was unifying 'Hindus' and creating trends whereby all 'Hindus' would have one set of laws. This was particularly true of areas where cultural nationalism was an expression of a Brahmanical worldview. Thus, for example, in the Bombay Presidency, where Brahmanical patriarchy was strong, women were being unified under a 'Hindu' law whether on a widow's right to her deceased husband's property following remarriage or on conjugality where the law did not recognise customary law. Further, the 'nationalists' had one notion of womanhood for all Hindu women and were willing to import Hindu practices from other regions in constructing the notion of a sacred marriage. Not only was the discreteness of caste being steam-rollered out, but regional differences were also being collapsed in the interests of the construction of a 'Hindu wife' and a Hindu marriage, making for a more stringent model of wifehood applicable to all who aspired for a 'Hindu' identity.

NOTES AND REFERENCES

1. The term Hindu law most often stood for textual law based on the Shastras; in the context of property, marriage and adoption it was based particularly on the Dayabhaga and Mitakshara schools of law. Whether it included customary law or not remained ambiguous as the discussion will amplify. A contemporary nineteenth century pamphlet on the remarriage of widows published by the Pathare Prabhus in 1869 regards the 'sacred lore' of the 'nation' as the source

of 'national' belief. This pamphlet treats textual law as having 'national' applicability (*Marriage of Hindu Widows Advocated by the Pathare Reform Association*, Bombay, Indu Prakash Press, 1869, Appendix L, being Extracts from Newspapers).

2. Lucy Carroll, 'Law, Custom and Statutory Social Reform: The Hindu Widows Remarriage Act of 1856' in J. Krishnamurti (ed.), *Women in Colonial India: Essays on Survival, Work and the State*, Delhi, Oxford University Press, 1989, pp. 1–26.

3. *Ibid.*, p. 5.

4. Sripati Roy, *Customs and Customary Law in British India*, Delhi, Mittal Publishers, 1986 (Reprint, first published 1910) pp. 15–16.

5. Lucy Carroll, 'Law, Custom and Statutory Social Reform', p. 4.

6. Sripati Roy, *Customs and Customary Law*, p. 298.

7. *Matungini Gupta v. Ram Rutton Roy, Indian Law Report* (hereafter *ILR*) 19, Calcutta 289, p. 291.

8. *Ibid.*, p. 292. Also *Murugayi v. Vikramkali* 1877 cited in Roy, *Customs and Customary Law*, p. 116.

9. *Bhola Umar v. Kausilla, ILR* 55, Allahabad 24, pp. 36–38.

10. In other cases relating to marriage the courts were recognising that lower-caste customs *were* different. However, some customs among these castes were unacceptable to the courts and it was argued by some judges that when customary law, as upheld by the panchayat, was in conflict with the court law, i.e., the British Indian law, the latter overruled the former. Others continued to insist that lower-caste customs were very different and Brahmanical law could not operate among these castes. By implication British Indian law was to be flexibly applied to them (Roy, *Customs and Customary Law*, pp. 306–07).

11. Lucy Carroll, 'Law, Custom and Statutory Social Reform', pp. 18–22.

12. William C. McCormack, 'Caste and the British Administration of Hindu Law', *Journal of Asian and African Studies*, Vol. 1, Part I, 1966, pp. 27–34, p. 32.

13. *Bhola Umar v. Kausilla, ILR* 55, Allahabad 24, p. 41.

14. *Moniram Kolita v. Keri Kolitani, ILR* 5, Calcutta, 776 (Privy Council).

15. *Bhola Umar v. Kausilla, ILR* 55, Allahabad 24, p. 42.

16. *Ibid.*, pp. 46–48.

17. Prem Chowdhry, 'Customs in a Peasant Economy: Women in Colonial Haryana', in Kumkum Sangari and Sudesh Vaid (ed.), *Recasting Women: Essays in Colonial History*, Delhi, Kali for Women, 1989, pp. 302–36.

18. J.H. Nelson, *A Prospectus for the Scientific Study of the Hindu Law*, London, 1881, p. 149.
19. Dayaram Gidumal, *The Status of Women in India or a Hand-book for Hindu Social Reformers*, Bombay, Fort Publishers, 1889, p. lxv.
20. *Parekh Ranochor v. Bai Vakhat, ILR* 11, Bombay 119.
21. *Vithu v. Govinda, ILR* 22, Bombay 321.
22. *Ibid.*, pp. 326–27.
23. *Ibid.*, p. 327.
24. *Ibid.*, p. 331.
25. Carroll, 'Law, Custom and Statutory Social Reform', p. 12.
26. *Bhola Umar v. Kausilla, ILR* 55, Allahabad 24, p. 38.
27. *Ibid.*, pp. 56–57.
28. *The Hindu Widows Remarriage Act (Act XV of 1856), Preamble*, cited in Carroll, 'Law, Custom and Statutory Social Reform', p. 3.
29. *Vithu v. Govinda, ILR* 22, Bombay 321, p. 331.
30. Carroll, 'Law, Custom and Statutory Social Reform', p. 331.
31. Dayaram Gidumal, *The Status of Women in India*, pp. lx-lxv.
32. Vide *Bombay Regulation IV of 1827*, Section 26.
33. *Collector of Madura v. Moottoo Ramalinga Sathupathy* 1868, cited in Sripati Roy, *Customs and Customary Law*, p. 23.
34. *Narada*, 1.40, cited in Roy, *Customs and Customary Law*, p. 17.
35. *Reg. v. Sambhu Raghu*, ILR, Bombay 347 (1876), cited in Roy, *Customs and Customary Law*, pp. 107–8.
36. Roy, *Customs and Customary Law*, p. 109.
37. *Ibid.*, p.111. Caste usages were considered upholdable even when they were 'tyrannical', particularly after the British Government legislated (*Act XXI of 1850*) that an outcasted individual did not forfeit his property.
38. *Ibid.*, p. 24.
39. *Ibid.*, p. 108.
40. *Musst. Dureeba v. Juggernath* (1855), cited in Roy, *Customs and Customary Law*, pp. 116–17.
41. Roy, *Customs and Customary Law*, p. 291.
42. *Ibid.*, p. 292.
43. *Ibid.*, p. 306.
44. Dayaram Gidumal, *Status of Women*, p. lxxx.
45. *Sitaram alias Keera Heerah v. Musst. Aharee Heerahee* (1873) cited in Roy, *Customs and Customary Law*, p. 312.
46. *Dadaji v. Rakhmabai*, Suit no. 139 of 1884, *Indian Law Reports*, Bombay Series, Vol. IX, pp. 529–35.
47. Letter from Max Muller to B.M. Malabari, 27 October 1887, *Life and Letters of Rt. Hon. Friedrich Max Muller, Edited by his wife*, London, Longman's Green, 1902, Vol. II, pp. 217–18.

48. This summary is based on the account of the case contained in *Indian Law Reports*, Bombay Series, Vol. IX, pp. 529–35 and Vol. X, pp. 301–13, and Rakhmabai's biography in Marathi (Mohini Varde, *Rakhmabai Ek Aart*, Bombay, Popular Prakashan, 1982).
49. *ILR* IX, p. 529.
50. *Ibid.*
51. *Ibid.*
52. *Ibid.*, p. 531.
53. *Ibid.*
54. *Ibid.*, p. 532.
55. *Ibid.*, p. 533.
56. *Ibid.*, pp. 533–34.
57. *Ibid.*, p. 535.
58. *Ibid.*
59. *Indian Law Reports*, Bombay Series, Vol. X, pp. 301–13.
60. *Ibid.*, p. 304.
61. *Ibid.*, p. 306.
62. *Ibid.*, p. 307.
63. *Ibid.*
64. *Ibid.*
65. Telang was a consistent champion of caste authority and its validity even in the late nineteenth century; See Dayaram Gidumal, *Status of Women*, p. lxxix.
66. Telang's argument here is seeking to reiterate Section 26 of *The Bombay Regulation IV, 1827* where the caste council was left with the power to deal with certain matters (described as 'social duties'). The King, in this case the civil courts, above the council merely had the 'higher' authority of levying fines. Real power to determine the rights of husbands and wives was to remain in the hands of the caste council.
67. *ILR, X*, p. 308.
68. *Ibid.*, p. 310.
69. *Ibid.*, pp. 310–11.
70. *Ibid.*, p. 311.
71. *Ibid.*, p. 312.
72. *Ibid.*
73. *Ibid.*, p. 313.
74. *Ibid.*
75. *Times of India*, 5 March 1887.
76. As a nationalist and a cautious social reformer (see discussion on pp. 145 of this work), Telang was averse to bringing English public opinion into the case in order to get relief for Rakhmabai. His distinctive position was consistent with his arguments during the

case where he had demanded a decision by the caste council. For many reasons he also did not agree with the tactics and arguments of the Rakhmabai Defence Committee (*Times of India*, 26 May 1887).

77. Mohini Varde, *Rakhmabai*, pp. 110–16.
78. *Ibid.*, pp. 210–12.
79. *ILR*, IX, p. 530.
80. *Gazetteer of Bombay City and Island*, pp. 236–39.
81. O'Hanlon, *Caste*, pp. 43, 45.
82. *Mahratta*, 3 April 1887. The editorial also suggested that such cases arising from the contradictions of a transitional period were best settled by a compromise.
83. Dobbin, *Urban Leadership*, pp. 225–27.
84. Varde, *Rakhmabai*, p. 75.
85. Steele, *The Hindu Castes*, p. 361.
86. R.E. Enthoven, *Tribes and Castes of Bombay*, Bombay, Government Central Press, 1922, Vol. III, pp. 356–58.
87. *Ibid.*, pp. 159–68.
88. *Ibid.*, pp. 249–51.
89. Varde, *Rakhmabai*, pp. 3ff.
90. Selection from 'Exposition of Facts', *Mahratta*, 24 April 1887.
91. Varde, *Rakhmabai*, p. 220.
92. See Enthoven, *Tribes and Castes*, pp. 159–68; 249–51; 356–58; Steele, *Hindu Castes*, pp. 361–65.
93. Steele, *Hindu Castes*, pp. 422–24.
94. See pp. 129 of this Chapter.
95. Selection from 'Exposition of Facts', *Mahratta*, 11 May 1887.
96. Varde, *Rakhmabai*, p. 80; *ILR* IX p. 533.
97. The biography consistently invokes Jayantibai's identity as a 'Hindu' widow, then associates her with the reformist strand among Hindus. Following her marriage to Sakharam, Jayantibai is said to have performed the roles of *grihini*, *sakhi*, and a *priyashishya*-cum-*patni* (Varde, *Rakhmabai*, pp. 20–22).
98. *Ibid.*, pp. 6–28.
99. *Ibid.*, p. 22; Steele, *Hindu Castes*, p. 348. According to Steele's information a girl who arrived at puberty before she was married was excluded from her caste and had to remain unmarried.
100. Rakhmabai, *The New Review*, no. 16, September 1890, pp. 263–69, p. 264 (I am grateful to Antoinette Burton for this reference); Varde, *Rakhmabai*, p. 22.
101. Steele, *Hindu Castes*, p. 358. Steele states that it was customary to give a daughter in marriage on condition of service to the father on the part of a *ghar jawai*, either for a fixed or for an indefinite period.

102. This is suggested in the 'Exposition of Facts' published by Dadaji on 14 April 1887 where he states that Jayantibai wanted to 'adopt' some good boy into the family to perform the funeral rites (Varde, *Rakhmabai*, p. 78; *Mahratta*, 24 April 1887).

103. Sudhir Chandra, 'The Problem of Social Reform in Modern India: The study of a case' in S.C. Malik (ed.), *Dissent, Protest and Reform in Indian Civilisation*, Simla, Indian Institute of Advanced Study, 1977, pp. 250–62, p. 251.

104. D.D. Karve, *New Brahmans*, p. 138; Pathare Prabhus, Brahmanas, Sonars and Shenvis are the new reformist elite according to the evidence provided by a Pathare Prabhu pamphlet *Marriage of Hindu Widows*, 1869, Appendix L.

105. The issue of difference in wealth, socialisation and education between Dadaji and Rakhmabai was a running theme both in the court case as well as in the larger controversy conducted through the press and the publication of pamphlets. A section of the caste which had become wealthy and educated was distinguished from the rest in their 'lifestyle, clothing and thinking'. Consequently, the rest of the caste, poorer and less educated, was overwhelmed and felt dominated by their caste-fellows. Dadaji's account of differences between him and Rakhmabai's family makes allusions to the rich 'insulting the poor', and of Rakhmabai's shallowness in not being able to love and share a life with a poor man. He appealed to the public in his pamphlet to see his side of the case as a 'wronged' husband, being married and yet having no wife. At the same time Dadaji also pointed out that though Rakhmabai was married she was yet a virgin because of the 'machinations' of a selfish mother. He defended himself in the pamphlet about his supposedly not being educated, and claimed that he was as educated as Rakhmabai. He represented himself as a victim of calumny especially by the press, which in trying to portray Rakhmabai as a heroine had calculatedly portrayed him as a 'fool'. (Varde, *Rakhmabai*, pp. 76–78; *Mahratta*, 24 April 1887).

106. *Mahratta*, 17 April 1887.

107. *Bengalee*, 19 March 1887.

108. The caste-fellows of Dadaji and Rakhmabai were probably both embarrassed and divided on the dispute between the two parties. In his allegation against Rakhmabai in the 'Exposition of Facts' he charged her with shaming him within the caste. She in turn charged him with bringing dishonour upon her by dragging her to court. This, said Rakhmabai, was unprecedented for any woman in her caste (Varde, *Rakhmabai*, p. 82).

109. *Mahratta*, April 24, 1887; Varde, *Rakhmabai*, pp. 75–81.

110. *ILR*, X, pp. 312.

111. *Native Opinion*, 27 September 1885.

112. Dayaram Gidumal, *Status of Women*, pp. lx-lxv. In far-off Calcutta the 'low'-caste origins of Rakhmabai evoked contradictory responses. While one reaction was to dismiss its importance since she was a 'low-caste' woman (Amiya Sen, 'Age of Consent Bill Agitation in Bengal', *Indian Historical Review*, Vol. VII, Nos. 1 and 2, July 1980–January 1981, pp. 160–84, p. 166), another reaction was to uphold Brahmanical norms as applicable to everyone. All other castes were expected to conduct themselves on the model of the Brahmanas. One opinion was that the Government should therefore settle the uncertain marriage customs of the people (Tanika Sarkar, 'Rhetoric Against Age of Consent: Resisting Colonial Reason and Death of a Child Wife', *Economic and Political Weekly*, Vol. 28, No. 36, September 4, pp. 1869–78, p. 1873).

113. *Native Opinion*, 27 September 1885. The information about Jayantibai's disentitlement to the property 'inherited' from Janardhan following her remarriage is alluded to indirectly by Dadaji in his 'Exposition'. He states that on Jayantibai's remarriage Rakhmabai got the property of her father (Varde, *Rakhmabai*, p. 76).

114. *Indian Spectator*, 20 March 1887.

115. *Indian Spectator*, 1 November 1885, and letter to *Bombay Gazette*, cited in *Indian Spectator*, 27 March 1887.

116. P.V. Kane, *History of Dharmashastra*, p. 571.

117. *Times of India*, 22 September 1885.

118. *Native Opinion*, 27 September 1885.

119. *ILR* X, p. 312.

120. *Indian Spectator*, 18 March 1887.

121. Sir William Muir, Lieutenant-Governor of Bengal, had suggested that the 'law might stipulate that the "betrothals" made in tender years by third parties should not be enforced as contracts demanding specific performance unless there was a ratification of the betrothal by the principal contracting parties after they had arrived at maturer years' (Dayaram Gidumal, *Status of Women*, p. 96).

122. *Mahratta*, 10 April 1887.

123. *Ibid.*, 24 April 1887.

124. *Ibid.*, 10 April 1887.

125. *Ibid.*, 24 April 1887.

126. *Ibid.*, 10 April 1887.

127. *Ibid.*

128. *Karnataka Prakashika*, 4 April 1887, cited in Sudhir Chandra, 'Problem of Social Reform', p. 255 n. 28.

129. *Mahratta*, 10 April 1887.

130. *Din Bandhu*, 27 March 1887.

131. *People's Friend*, 26 March 1887, quoted in *Indian Spectator*, 17 April 1887.

132. *Mahratta*, 17 April 1887.

133. *Liberal* and *Din Bandhu*, quoted in *Indian Spectator*, 17 April 1887.

134. *Ibid.*

135. The ambiguity about what exactly 'Hindu law', constantly being invoked by all parties to the dispute, incorporated within itself made the reformist position extremely difficult as Sakharam Arjun pointed out. Responding to Malabari's attempt to seek opinion on infant marriages Sakharam Arjun had written, 'The Government have complicated matters by not yet making carefully a proper distinction between Hindu law, religion and custom. If Hindu law is to be disassociated from Hindu religion, as it properly should be, a great many difficulties which now stifle the growth of reform might have been easily removed.' (Dayaram Gidumal, *Status of Women*, p. 96).

136. *Civil and Military Gazette*, 19, 23, 25 April 1887, cited in Sudhir Chandra, 'Whose Laws: Notes on a Legitimising Myth of a Colonial Indian State', *Studies in History*, Vol. 8, No. 2, New Series, 1992, pp. 189–211, p. 198.

137. *Hindu Patriot*, 4 April 1887.

138. It remains unclear why exactly the British Indian courts decided on imprisonment rather than attachment of property or alimony, unless they considered these actions reserved for defaulting husbands. For a woman who refused conjugal rights to her husband the only remedy was imprisonment. Following Rakhmabai's stand the imprisonment clause was dropped but the decree continued to be enforceable by attachment and sale of property in case a wife owned any. Traditionally a wife could refuse to join her husband if he had a loathsome disease or brought a concubine into the house, or was guilty of cruelty (P.V. Kane, *History of Dharmashastras*, p. 570).

139. *Hindu Patriot*, 4 April 1887. A few persons especially in Bengal did actually endorse imprisonment. Maharaja Jatindra Mohan Tagore was strongly of the view that a husband was a wife's legal guardian. If she resisted going to him she must be imprisoned. This view was echoed by Raja Peary Mohan Mukherjee (Dagmar Engels, *The Changing Role of Women in Bengal; c. 1890–c. 1930 with Special Reference to British and Bengali Discourse on Gender*, unpublished Ph.D. thesis, School of Oriental and African Studies, University of London, 1987, p. 295).

140. *Mahratta*, 3 April 1887.

141. *Mahratta*, 24 April 1887.

142. *Mahratta*, 3 April 1887.
143. *Indian Spectator*, 6, 20 and 27 March, 1887; Sudhir Chandra, 'Whose Laws', pp. 202–03.
144. For a recognition of the interlocking of patriarchies and a pungent critique of the manner in which men made compacts with each other to rule over women see Pandita Ramabai Saraswati, *The High Caste Hindu Woman*, Philadelphia, published by Ramabai Dongre Medhavi, 1888, pp. 65–68.
145. *The Times*, 28 February 1891. Reporting a meeting in Calcutta on 25 February, the correspondent described a huge congregation of persons. Among the slogans raised was one that said 'Mercy oh Queen, our religion is threatened.' Also see V.T. Naik (ed.), *Select Writings and Speeches of K.T. Telang*, Bombay, Gaud Saraswat Mitra Mandal, 1916, Vol. II, p. 453.
146. Reproduced in *Government of India, Home Department, Selections from Records*, No. CCXXIII, No. 3, Calcutta, 1886.
147. Heimsath, *Indian Nationalism*, pp. 155–58.
148. *Ibid.*, p. 158.
149. *The Times*, 7 January, 1891.
150. Cited by Manmohan Ghose, Appendix V, 6 February 1891, *India Legislative Proceedings* No. 1–73, *Act X of 1891 and Connected Papers*, No. 38. See also Mrinalini Sinha, 'Colonial Politics and the Ideal of Masculinity: The Example of the Age of Consent Act of 1891 in Bengal', in *Proceedings of the Third National Conference on Women's Studies*, Indian Association of Women's Studies, Chandigarh, 1986, Vol. II, Sub-theme 6, p. 7.
151. Considerable attention has been focused on the Age of Consent controversy, beginning with Charles H. Heimsath's 'The Origin and Enactment of the Indian Age of Consent Bill, 1891', *Journal of Asian Studies*, Vol. 1, No. 4, August 1962, pp. 491–504; Mrinalini Sinha (see note 150 above); Dagmar Engels, 'The Age of Consent Act: Colonial Ideology in Bengal' *South Asia Research* Vol. 3, No. 2, November 1983, pp.107–34; Amiya Sen, 'Hindu Revivalism in Action — The Age of Consent Bill Agitation in Bengal', *Indian Historical Review*, Vol. VII, Nos. 1–2, July 1980–January 1981, pp. 160–84; and Tanika Sarkar, 'Rhetoric Against Age of Consent: Resisting Colonial Reason and Death of a Child Wife', *Economic and Political Weekly*, Vol. 28, No. 36, September 4, 1993, pp. 1869–78. My own analysis of the issue is focused around the relationship between law, gender, the colonial state and the upper castes with special reference to Maharashtra.
152. For details of Phulmoni's case, see Sarkar, 'Rhetoric Against Age of Consent', pp. 1873–74.

153. A. Scoble's speech, *Speeches on the Age of Consent Bill*, Calcutta 1891, cited in Sen, 'The Age of Consent Bill Agitation', p. 171.

154. The incident gave rise to the term 'Harmaitism' which was bandied about in the press and stood for the brutal sexual conduct of men (*The Times*, 29 January 1891).

155. Dayaram Gidumal, 'The Hindu Woman: Our Sins Against Her', C.Y. Chintamani (ed.), *Indian Social Reform*, p. 104.

156. R.G. Bhandarkar, 'Presidential Address to the Ninth Social Conference', 1895, C.Y. Chintamani, *Indian Social Reform*, p. 180.

157. Tilak however did privately defend Harmaiti in an insensitive and typically male letter he wrote. He was of the view that Harmaiti could not be held responsible for the death of his child wife. He was after all merely exercising his marital rights (Stanley Wolpert, *Tilak and Gokhale: Revolution and Reform in the Making of Modern India*, Berkeley, University of California, 1962, pp. 52–54).

158. *The Times*, 12 January 1891.

159. Cashman, *The Myth*, pp. 56–58.

160. V.T. Naik, *Speeches and Writings*, p. 450.

161. *Ibid.*, pp. 456–57. Telang seems to have implicitly been arguing for the old structure of Hindu law as an aggregate of customs which he may have believed had provided certain spaces which could be utilised to advantage by those wishing to. In the Rakhmabai case he privileged caste panchayats over 'English' law and in the Age of Consent controversy he strongly resisted the importation of Bengali customary practices into Maharashtra.

162. V.T. Naik, *Speeches and Writings*, pp. 460–61.

163. *Ibid.*, p. 467.

164. *Ibid.*, pp. 461–64.

165. *Ibid.*, pp. 468–71.

166. *Ibid.*, pp. 471–72.

167. *Ibid.*, p. 454.

168. Letter of Dr Mahendra Lal Sircar, LLD, CIE, to the Chief Secretary to the Government of Bengal on the Age of Consent Bill dated 4 March 1891, reproduced in C.Y. Chintamani, *Indian Social Reform*, pp. 248–54; and Mahendra Lal Sircar on the 'Earliest Marriage Age', *Calcutta Journal of Medicine*, July 1871, reprinted in Chintamani, *Indian Social Reform*, pp. 255–60.

169. *Ibid.*, pp. 248–52.

170. *Ibid.*, p. 253.

171. *Ibid.*

172. *Ibid.*, p. 254.

173. *Ibid.*

174. Dagmar Engels, 'The Changing Role of Women', p. 273.

175. *Dainik O Samachar Chandrika*, 15 and 17 January 1891, cited in Sen, 'The Age of Consent Bill', p. 171.
176. *Ibid.*, 11 January 1891.
177. *Bangabasi*, 7 March 1891, cited in Engels, *The Changing Role of Women*, p. 289.
178. *Government of India Legislative Proceedings*, April 1891, Appendix A 20, Report of the Select Committee.
179. Vishnu Prabhakar Paraspe, Headmaster, Anglo-Vernacular School, Raja Deulgaon, Submission to Malabari, reproduced in Dayaram Gidumal, *Status of Women*, p. 43.
180. Waman Narayan Bapat, Tehsildar, Chandur Taluk, Submission to Malabari, reproduced in Dayaram Gidumal, *Status of Women*, p. 47.
181. *Samachar*, 18 February 1891, cited in Engels, *The Changing Role of Women*, p. 289.
182. Tanika Sarkar, 'Rhetoric Against Age of Consent', p. 1877.
183. A central question that ran through the negative reactions to the Bill was the difficulty of applying it. Who would prosecute? There was great anxiety about 'malicious' prosecutions and therefore it was argued that the right be restricted to the girl, her parents or her guardian (who would not make malicious prosecutions) especially when the husband was being charged (*The Times*, 16 February 1891). As R.C. Mitter pointed out, a husband could not be convicted unless his wife produced incriminating evidence which she was unlikely to provide. If she spoke the truth her position would become like that of a widow; if she did not she committed perjury. Either way the amendment was only going to punish the victim of the offence more severely than the offender himself. Sir R.C. argued that the legislation was badly conceived (R.C. Mitter's Minute of Dissent, 5 March 1891, reproduced in the *Hindu Patriot*, 9 March 1891).
184. Uma Chakravarti, 'Conceptualising Brahmanical Patriarchy in Early India: Gender, Caste, Class and the State', *Economic and Political Weekly*, Vol. 28, No. 14, 1993, pp. 579–85, pp. 584–85.
185. *The Times*, 12 January 1891.
186. Dayaram Gidumal, *Status of Women*, p. 21.
187. *Mahratta*, 29 May 1887.
188. S. Natarajan, *A Century of Social Reform*, p. 88.
189. Dayaram Gidumal, *Status of Women*, p. 119.
190. *Ibid.*, p. 47.
191. *Indian Spectator*, 27 May 1881.
192. Ranajit Guha, 'Chandra's Death', Ranajit Guha (ed.), *Subaltern Studies V: Writings on South Asian History and Society*, Delhi, Oxford University Press, 1987, pp. 135–64.

193. Lancelot Wilkinson MD, 'Introduction' to *An Essay on the Second Marriages of Widows, By a Learned Brahmin of Nagpore*, pp. 9–16.
194. Rosalind O'Hanlon, 'Issues of Widowhood in Colonial Western India', Douglas Haynes and Gyan Prakash (ed.), *Contesting Power: Resistance and Everyday Social Relations in South Asia*, Delhi, Oxford University Press, 1991, p. 64.
195. D.D. Karve, *The New Brahmans*, pp. 227–29.
196. *Gadappa v. Girimallappa, ILR*, 19 Bombay 331.
197. *Yamunabai v. Manirbai, ILR*, 23 Bombay 608; *Bai Mangal v. Bai Rukhmini, ILR*, 23 Bombay 291.
198. Richard Tucker, *Ranade*, pp. 293–98.
199. *Bai Mangal v. Bai Rukhmini, ILR*, 23 Bombay 291; Tucker, *Ranade*, pp. 294–95.

4

Men, Women and the Embattled Family

I

This chapter shifts the focus from external processes shaping gender to social processes which acted directly upon the household, as well as internal pressures which operated within the households of upper castes/classes. Certain elements tied the two processes together. Both external forces in society and internal pressures on the family meant that many levels of social authority were at stake in reformulations occurring during the second half of the nineteenth century; the criss-crossing positions on women that we will see below need to be seen in this larger context.

We have outlined the contestatory nature of class formation in Maharashtra, with its double tensions between castes and between different class segments intensifying pressures on the various strata. As Sangari has argued, 'The conflictual and uneven development of "class" did not make for cultural and ideological coherence — rather it made for a heterogeneity producing contradictory positions and multiple voices,' sometimes even in the same person. In such a transformatory situation the 'necessary reconstitution of patriarchies and modes of authority itself acquired an uneven character; conflict between the traditional authority structures and patriarchies with the emerging modified structure with its own attendant patriarchy' was an inevitable aspect of the period. Problems were compounded because there was a 'need for the Hindu woman's ideality to be measured against caste and class arrangements; from a range of prototypes there had to be a "marking out" of a middle-class private sphere.' Further, in the reconstitution of authority, the colonial state had its own stake in social and material arrangements. In sum, as the processes unfolded the domestic economy was left intact structurally but modified outwardly both by the state and by middle-class reformers.[1] Nevertheless, the family became a major site for conflict engendered by different world-views reproducing the conflicts of the public sphere within it.

The female world had conventionally been limited to the household, which was the focal point of female reproduction, domestic labour and of kinship relations of upper-caste women in Maharashtra as in other parts of the country. The colonial state and the reformers had found that the domestic arrangements of the dominant classes were not easily amenable to radical alteration by the legal changes introduced in the nineteenth century. The process of generating change *within* the household thus became imperative and a female constituency to facilitate the process was identified. Such women were to mediate between the public and the private worlds of the emerging class.[2] First they would publicly demonstrate their acquiescence in the changes recommended by the male social reformers and then help to disseminate the reformed ideas within the female world and also socialise the new generations into the new norms. The 'schooling' of women thus was a major platform of middle-class reform.

The need to school women to make them governable and equip them for wifehood was not new, being a major concern of all extant patriarchies. Brahmanical patriarchy's fear of an unregulated female sexuality's potential to subvert the moral and social order underlay the elaboration of codes whose purpose was to make women of the upper castes in particular, governable. Prescriptions in the texts going back to the formation of caste and class structures had dealt with the essential qualities of women — their *strisvabhava* which is libidinous and the need to get them to perform their *stridharma*, their social roles, by harnessing their sexuality for acceptable ends.[3] Ideology and coercion were both used to achieve social control. Processes of 'schooling', achieved through Shastric 'education', were periodically reformulated and restated as is evident from the eighteenth century text *Stridharmapaddhati*, a Sanskrit text prepared at the Maratha court at Tanjore and commissioned by Dipamba, chief wife of the Tanjore ruler Ekoji. Prescribing the code for the 'perfect wife' whose religious and secular duties converge in service to the husband, the text opens its introductory verses with 'Obedient service to one's husband is the primary duty enjoined by the sacred tradition for women.' The verses outline 'schooling' recommending the proper attitude of the wife to her lord, obedience in matters of principle, and diligent and attentive service. Conventional training of upper-caste wives neatly combined the dual actions of religious duties and the daily chores in the household in the formulation: the wife's service to her husband *is* her worship of god. Two Marathi works designed for a wider audience were written by the same author on stridharma, the code by which women were 'schooled', one aptly titled *Pativratadharma* and its underside titled *Narakavarnana*, written especially to counter what was regarded as a Muslim threat to cultural ideals of Hindu womanhood. Virtuous women, properly schooled, attain a good reputation, immediate happiness in this world, and heaven after death, according to the eighteenth century text.[4] Most importantly, women schooled into stridharma keep their libidinous natures in check.

Apart from Brahmanical patriarchy's conceptualisation of women's nature as libidinous, there was the corollary feminisation of evil itself: the latter includes a recognition of women's agency which is perceived negatively. Women displaying agency as they pursue material and social benefits not 'due' to them by employing the instigative method, or through deceit, also need to be schooled. All intrigues attributed to women in the royal household as well as the households of ordinary men are perceived to adopt either incitement or deceit to gain their ends. Women were thus 'naturally' more prone to disrupting social harmony, being innately quarrelsome. Historical memory of these qualities was powerfully embodied in the figure of Anandi, who masterminded the murder of her nephew during the Peshwai.[5] The power of women to create disorder became a metaphor for ungovernability or *fitna*, a term which originally meant seducing; it was applied in the context of seducing women to elope with other men. It ultimately came to imply sedition. Suppressing fitna had the highest priority for the Maratha state.[6] In its original connotation then, fitna had been peculiarly feminine and had represented ungovernability in the domestic domain. Significantly, disorder in the private domain was the model for disorder in the public domain, rather than the other way around. The schooling of women in the domestic domain was as necessary as the governance of the social domain: conceptually the two were linked.

Since control over women and the desire for schooled women is primary for any patriarchal arrangement the necessity of tutoring women was not in dispute in nineteenth century Maharashtra; women of the upper castes were already being schooled by 'domesticity and Shastric injunction'.[7] However, there was a divergence between the traditional elites and the 'reformed' elites on various issues, including the inherent nature of women, what was required of them, and the kind of training and cultivation they should receive.

Pre-colonial conceptualisations of women, although not static, had been restated rather than dramatically reworked; in contrast, the middle-class reformers both restated and recast notions of womanhood. The reconceptualisation of womanhood in the second half of nineteenth century Maharashtra was 'embedded in the aspirations of the emergent middle class which [was] required to restructure the family, to produce suitable ideologies for the reproduction of households, to relate patriarchal practices to the emerging forms of stratification, and to align personal with general class interests'.[8] In sum there was, because of the special nature of social and economic forces generated by the presence of a colonial state, a need for patriarchies to be reassembled according to the changed circumstances giving rise to various discourses of reform. Thus the colonial encounter was both directly and catalytically mutative for the middle classes.

The discourses of reform on women, especially because the legal reforms relating to the excesses of traditional patriarchal practices had reached a dead-end, came to be concentrated on women's education. The importance of education in order to school women into their new roles, crystallised around them as companionate wives, good mothers, and class socialisers, and was a key theme in nineteenth century discourse.[9] Evident in the writings of the period is the specific function of education in the case of women for whom it was not an instrumental factor as it was for men. Men were to be educated, especially in English, both in the view of the state and its subjects, for jobs. In contrast, it was only in the last fifteen years of the nineteenth century that education for women was perceived as having an instrumental dimension when the colonial state identified the need for trained professional women to service the sectors of medical care and teaching in order to reach out to the female population.[10] Initially, then, education was a tool to 'fashion' a new class of women through appropriate schooling. For the reformers it was also the tool by which women could be converted into moral beings for a changed social order, a new means by which their strisvabhava could be transformed into a suitable variant of the traditional conception of stridharma.

The need for education to 'school' women was directly tied to a new meaning to be given to the home. While the separation between public and private and a division of labour continued to govern the female world centred around reproduction, the role of reproduction was enlarged to encompass the nurture of a whole class and the creation of a new culture. The residences of the middle classes for the reformers became 'homes', an affective and moral unit rather than a space occupied by a conglomerate of individuals, thus acquiring an 'ideological clarification'. Into this reworked female world, which still corresponded to a broad division between public and private as before, the new project of mothering and conjugality was introduced, whose central actor was the young wife, the new woman of the present and the future. The responsibility of turning the older household into a 'home' and creating an affective unit was that of young wives and it was to prepare them for such a responsibility that education was required. Thus, middle-class reformers were giving women a defined and limited 'agency', making them social actors through education for specific purposes.[11]

This new notion of a home was however an abstraction, as many of the accounts of women writing in nineteenth century Maharashtra suggest. Young men, in whose hands the ideological reins of this venture were firmly held, battled an army of kin who actually occupied the household. From this web of relatives young men tried to create two distinct units — the husband and wife, and the mother and child — the new roles for women thus being those of conjugality and mothering. Ideologically the two units were made to stand separate from other kin in the family.[12] In the accounts of Ramabai Ranade, tensions within the home between father and son and between the older women and the young wife were over what husbands expected of their wives. Equally, the process of such an extraction of the husband-wife unit in particular implied that men were battling their relatives to gain full control over their wives so that they could fulfil the new missions set for them.[13]

The roles of women as instruments of nurture and as class socialisers were closely connected. Through women the culture of a whole class of people was to be regenerated; the socialising by proper nurturing of children, especially male children, would lead to organising the culture of both the class and the nation,[14] since it was the dominant class that stamped its culture in any case upon the nation. It was for this task that women had to be prepared through proper attention and education. Addressing the Ninth National Social Conference in the last decade of the century, the well-known but cautious reformer Sir R.G. Bhandarkar outlined the need for women's education thus:

A good many proposals have reference to the condition of the female portion of our society. Gentlemen, one half of the intellectual, moral and spiritual resources of our country is being wasted. If our women were educated they would be a powerful instrument for advancing the general condition of our country. They will bring up every new generation in a manner to perform its duty efficiently and will shed the influence of benign virtues peculiar to them on men and, so to say, humanise them....[15]

Since the task of nurturing and class socialising was unique to women, they therefore needed a special education. A carefully chosen, distinctive, syllabus was imperative and women were not to have the same education as men[16] (the kind necessary for acquiring jobs). Nurturing required a knowledge of medical care, child care, cleanliness etc., and this required a 'domestic economy'-type syllabus; religious and moral instruction and literature were necessary to cultivate the self and the personalities of children. Parvati Athavale, a widow who was lifted out of her obscurity and given a place in the reformist agenda (raising funds for the Widows' Home set up by Karve, her brother-in-law), outlined the features of the new home and the training women required to create it. In a chapter entitled 'Social Questions', Parvati dealt with two categories of women, married and unmarried, and then focused on the former, the 'natural' state for women. Firmly arguing the need for married women to stay home, never seeking 'servitude' outside in the form of employment, she wrote:

Women have to remain at home for its protection. In our homes there is not as much effort as there should be to teach children what in English is called 'good manners'. Our men have little connection with their homes and no special relations with their servants and children. So the responsibility for the right conduct of the family and for the right manners falls now on women. As women are the mothers-to-be of this country it is necessary to give them an education suited to their special domestic life. Such an education should include the first principles in medical care, care of children, cooking, care of the garden, how to keep the house clean, the purchase and care of food, singing, and religious and moral instruction, and such like important subjects... If the mother brings into the home regularity of habits and polite manners, the children and servants will follow her example. The home is a school. The mistress and master are the principal teachers in this school. If the teachers throw aside their dignified position and cease to teach the children that home is sure to be the scene of wild strife....

In many places one sees that the home is to the men merely a place to eat. Men should feel an attraction for their homes as they do in the west... Our children and the man of the house must consider the home his place of joy and comfort. And that this may be so must come from the efforts of the women. Every mistress of the home should know how to beautify the home and how to make the home more healthy. To this end there should be instruction given in all girls' schools on the management of the home... The advantage of female education must show itself in the reformation of the home, if it is to be of any advantage to the country.[17]

Education for women, then, was to be a 'private acquisition' first to school them and thereafter to create appropriate personalities, familial social relations, and households, and in a more general sense, a 'moral basis' for the everyday life of the emergent middle class.[18]

A corollary of women as nurturant mothers and class socialisers in the new domestic ideology of the middle class was the model of the companionate wife marking a break from the traditional notion of the wife as primarily a ritual and sexual partner of the husband. Like the nurturant mother the companionate wife too needed to be carefully schooled to fit the role. Dayaram Gidumal outlined the means by which the companionate wife could be created: 'Do not starve women's intellect, shut them out of the light, opportunities for acquiring self knowledge, self awareness and self control. They will not only become your helpmates but your better halves'.[19] The notion of the 'companionate' wife was however an abstraction, and at this point still being constructed. A product of the social needs *and* the imagination of upper-caste reformers, its contours remained vague, making young wives aspire to live up to such a model but also causing them intense heartache because it was never very clear to them what exactly their husbands expected of them. Men on the other hand were eloquent in their descriptions of the companionate wives they were seeking. Karsondas Mulji, a prominent reformer whose own marriage was far from companionate,[20] wrote:

Look at the picture of a woman who delights the heart of a man who overpowers him by her pure love; observe her traits: she walks gently, she speaks only melodious words. She is both mild and guileless. She neither sits idly nor wanders here or there. She neither eats or drinks like a glutton, but like a temperate woman. By her good and amiable disposition her smiling face is suffused with love. From her lips only kind and affectionate words come out as from good trees we get only fragrant flowers and sweet fruits. She carries out all her husband's wishes and passes her time peacefully and happily. In all her work she uses her god given intelligence and tries to remain virtuous in all her deeds. Her heart is fully virtuous and the perennial spring of ardent love ever flows from it.[21]

The disappointment of the men whose expectation from wives remained unfulfilled was also eloquently expressed:

Where is the Hinduani, wise and pure who can quote *Shakuntala* and the *Merchant of Venice*, play the Sitar or Sarangi and sing divinely? Every educated Hindu would like to have such a Kumud [the heroine of the famous nineteenth century Gujarati novel *Saraswati Chandra* by Goverdhan Das Tripathi], such a lovely maiden for his wife. But where are these phantoms of delight in Hindu society? They exist in the brains of those who have read Kalidas and Shakespeare, but otherwise we know them not (anonymous Hindu male, 1884).[22]

These are women who are self-consciously fashioned figures, crafted by middle-class men to be the objects of a new notion of conjugality. The major problem about transformed notions of conjugality in the nineteenth century, unfortunately, was the difficulty of making such powerful images of 'sweet womanhood' come alive. While men of the reforming elite identified education as the means by which such visions of womanhood could be actualised (women needed literacy especially in order to know *what* they should embody), the institution of marriage hinged on early marriage, which implied that young wives went to their husbands with very little education, if any at all.

It was this major contradiction that led to the phenomenon of the husband as teacher for the first generation of married couples among the reformers. It was a process fraught with many tensions as documented in autobiographies and letters by a few of the first 'victims', the young wives themselves. Kashibai Kanitkar for example, wrote that she felt compelled to be educated because she overheard her husband remarking that he could never share a meaningful existence with an illiterate wife.[23] Her husband Govindrao, who was sixteen when she was married to him at nine, was from a wealthy family and had an 'English' education. Conscious of her plain looks and humiliated by her rejection, Kashibai began to secretly teach herself how to read and write and received some assistance from Govindrao.

The project did not, however, have the sanction of her in-laws (being a private venture to win the affections of her husband), so she had to hide her attempts to acquire her skills. Since young wives lived under extreme surveillance within the household, she would often be caught out and humiliated in public. Bridging the gap of many years of slow learning that men had access to but which was squeezed into a few stolen moments in the case of the young wives, they found that far from being regarded as partners in a companionate marriage their husbands often heaped further abuse and humiliation upon them. Kashibai's husband dismissed her attempts to learn English remarking that it was impossible for a 'stone' to learn anything.[24] Sheer grit and the desire for dignity and respect kept Kashibai going and she went on to become a well-known writer and an intellectual who ultimately outstripped her husband's writing skills, but there was much heartbreak in the process. But from Kashibai's example we can see that given the traditional taboos against female literacy and the power relations within the family in extant forms of patriarchy, the male fantasy of a companionate marriage was a new source of power that husbands wielded over their wives.

Similarly Anandibai Joshi,[25] who went down in Maharashtrian consciousness as the best known example of an educated, professional female had a hard time in her early years. She was married at nine to a 'mature' widower whose erratic and unconventional career was amply expressed in his relationship with his young wife through whom he partly achieved his own ambitions. At one stage his educational demands on his wife led him to leave her to negotiate the streets alone in Bombay so that she might attend school while he went out of town. Anandibai recalls that she faced harassment including obscene remarks and gestures from men, forcing her to go back to her parents.[26] The case of Ramabai Ranade, whose relationship with her famous husband has been regarded as a model to be followed by all 'respectable modern' women,[27] is also noteworthy. When she began to receive an education members of the household subjected her to severe harassment which her husband could not, or did not, do anything to stop.[28]

Part of the tension inherent in the early experiments with educating young wives to be companionate partners was the dissatisfaction of a new generation of men with the existing structures of marriage and the lack of choice that they faced as individuals in a situation of repressive collectivities. The frustrations arising from these institutions were transferred upon the young wife as in the case of Govindrao Kanitkar, Kashibai's husband, who was disappointed at being 'saddled' with a woman regarded as unattractive.[29] She was not the kind of woman who was the object of attention of an English-educated male sensibility. Further, the non-consensual marriage combined with pre-pubertal marriage for girls meant that men old enough to be fathers could be husbands as in the cases of Ramabai Ranade and Anandibai Joshi. A companionate marriage, at least in the late nineteenth and early twentieth centuries, was virtually an impossibility. Non-consensual marriage also made male desires about finding romantic love difficult to fulfil within marriage. All these elements went into the many contradictions clustering around the notion of companionate wives for which women could be 'schooled' through education. The process of extracting a husband-wife unit, who shared a companionate marriage, out of the larger family structures and social institutions within which the middle-class male was located, remained a non-starter for most of the nineteenth century.

The project of education for women faced great opposition from within upper-caste societies since traditional codes and taboos relating to the subject were still very strong. Female education had been viewed as not just redundant (learning being associated in tradition with sacred knowledge, which was a closely guarded preserve) but reprehensible. Its association with widowhood in traditional beliefs is significant as widowhood was the most dreaded state for women. Ramabai Ranade and Kashibai Kanitkar both record this taboo as the reason why they had been kept illiterate in their parental homes.[30] There was also a great fear (prevalent across regions) that literacy would give women the means by which they could engage in clandestine correspondence, set up liaisons with men[31] or even elope with them and thus cause fitna. Widely-shared fears such as these in the household, given its internal power structure, made many women themselves ambivalent about education and often made it a new source of power between men and women — it was one more way by which women had to please their husbands. It is important to bear in mind that the project of education for women was largely executed within a patriarchal structure in which women were caught as subjects — rarely were they actual agents. When women did not have to pick up education at their husbands' behest they had to ensure that it remained a secret, to the extent of even mispronouncing words that they knew perfectly well because this would give them away.[32]

Further, the relationship of education to 'schooling' women rather than equipping them to utilise it in any way, or empowering them, remained the core of the new domestic ideology. In this it was not radically different from the traditional schooling of women to absorb the ideological premises of Brahmanical patriarchy, which was required in order that they accept the sum of social practices that were operating in the nineteenth-century: child marriage, early motherhood, the possibility of co-wives, widower husbands as old as fathers, as well as step-children often as old as them, and also the ever-present recourse to violence against women. Upon this traditional value system which all women were schooled in, the new focus on education was an add-on; the new domestic ideology, even from its best proponents, muted the extreme features of extant patriarchal arrangements but did not begin afresh since none of the middle-class reformers wanted a major overhaul. Traditional pativrata merely became for example 'the pure love shining forth' from the devoted wife. The new wife still accepted the unquestioned authority of her husband. For the reforming elite of Maharashtra the excesses of traditional patriarchy were reprehensible but it was from the field of tradition and its notions of womanhood that new notions were to be forged. Patriarchy was both to be reformed and preserved. Women, educated schooled women, thus 'became the subjects and the vehicles through whom *both* the retention and modernisation of newly defined Hindu patriarchal forms were achieved'[33] as our examples will show.

II

I begin an account of the 'schooling' of women among certain sections of the emerging professional class with Anandibai Joshi, who became a legend in her own time in western India. Born in 1865 into a high-status Chitpavan Brahmana household, which had been prosperous but was by then in somewhat straitened circumstances, Anandibai appears to have had a conventional childhood, 'schooled' into accepting as natural the traditional Brahmanical patriarchal practices. However, she was permitted access to rudimentary literacy as a school was located within a part of the house she lived in. Being a vivacious and spirited girl, she picked up enough reading to be shown off by her father to visitors, much to their horror. Anandibai clearly missed the presence of a nurturing mother and recalled later her mother's physical aggression towards her and wrote that, if she had children, she would ensure that they received a loving upbringing.[34]

In the nineteenth century 'childhood' was all too brief in the case of women. Anandibai was married at nine following a period of great anxiety for her parents, very common in the lives of women who have left accounts of their early years. This was because of the Brahmanic injunction that girls must be married before they menstruate. Anandi was a well built girl and the public gaze, which never let Brahmana parents forget that the community was keeping track of the need to uphold social norms, aroused the characteristic fears in the parents.[35] (Similarly, Parvati Athavale records that her quick growth and the family's insecure financial situation led to great anxiety about organising a marriage for her since the women in the village had begun to remark on her unmarried status. Finally a husband was found for Parvati but the man was lame, and only modestly employed.[36]) Being poor added to the general anxiety and finally a match was arranged for Anandi to a widower, Gopalrao Joshi, many years her senior.

The rest of Anandibai's life was dominated by her husband and the travails she experienced, (including physical violence at his hands) have been attributed to Gopalrao's eccentricity.[37] We suggest, however, that his behaviour was not *individually idiosyncratic*. There are numerous examples dotting the accounts of women in which fathers, husbands, brothers behave like Gopalrao Joshi did. Clearly they were not individual acts of eccentricity but located in the structure of patriarchy which put women under the power and authority of certain men. But at the same time it was also structural in another sense, being an expression of the fragmented, decentred, individuals characteristic of the new middle class who often did not know what they wanted. Men of these classes were ambivalent about the norms and values of their traditions without being clear about the changes that were necessary. The only certainty they displayed was the authority they wielded over their wives. Gopalrao Joshi's 'behaviour' suggests that as men found that *they* had to change they both experimented with women and burdened them with their own contradictions. Anandibai's biography tells us that Gopalrao had talked about educating his young wife even as the marriage was being settled.[38] Whether he wished this to be a form of 'schooling' that was merely designed to make Anandi a suitable wife or not, Gopalrao exercised his marital rights according to traditional practice. Anandibai had her first and only child at fourteen, but the child did not survive. (She wrote later that a child's death did not affect the father but that the mother did not want to see it die. This may have been a statement based on her own personal experience of the way the death of her child affected her but did not have the same effect on Gopalrao.[39]) Although we are told that Anandi was 'well developed', and in normal health before she married, she was unable to have more children after this early pregnancy and there are innumerable references that in later years she suffered severe ill-health; she died finally of consumption at the early age of 22.

Gopalrao's obsessive ambition for Anandibai may have been a consequence of guilt that he suppressed about the early motherhood and trauma that Anandi experienced on his account. By the time she was fifteen Gopalrao had corresponded with missionaries abroad seeking help for his wife's education in America and finally she left, at the age of 17, to study medicine in Philadelphia.

As the first 'Hindu' woman to travel to America and to enrol for a course in medicine there, Anandi became visible in India and made a dramatic impact on American women. At around the same time Pandita Ramabai was leaving for England to attempt to pursue a similar course. The two, who were distant cousins, finally met in America when Anandibai graduated.

The years Anandi spent in America have been sedimented in public memory as 'heroic'. Racked by ill-health but sticking closely to traditional customs, Anandibai was the embodiment of Hindu womanhood. This made an impact on American women too, who admired her courage and traditional virtues.[40] Her sponsors do not appear to have been shocked by such views as her defence of child marriage and in India this ensured that she would be regarded as a true daughter of India, an upholder of the 'national' culture. Before Anandibai left America to return to India she had been joined by Gopalrao (who in a characteristic instance of middle-class ambiguity now publicly berated university education for women as disruptive of family life).[41] Anandibai already had a job waiting at Kolhapur which unfortunately she never took up. She died a few months after her return — a tragic denouement to a life that had come to be celebrated throughout India.

Two aspects of Anandibai's life are striking: the first is the troubled relationship of the husband-wife unit, almost an exclusive one separated from the usual larger kin group of most upper-caste households. (Gopalrao's job in the postal department and his mobile existence coupled with his extreme 'individuality' may have contributed to the domestic structure.) The second was the way Anandi became an icon for the virtues of ideal Hindu womanhood. Public memory of the very middle class that was investing in 'companionate' marriages erased her experiences at the hands of her husband and kept alive only her Hindu womanly qualities. In private correspondence with her husband she refers to the fact that their relationship had witnessed much violence, that even as a young wife of ten she had been hit by Gopalrao with pieces of wood, had chairs flung at her, and had been threatened with abandonment. She bore the violence of one expression of patriarchy to uphold another, writing that she did not leave Gopalrao because it would have tarnished her father's honour. Only death could be a resolution to such a stormy existence. At twenty she recalled some of her anguish in a letter to her husband:

I pleaded with you to end my existence. There is nothing in the law to stop such things against women. If there are any [laws/rules] they work against women. Therefore I had no option but to bear everything silently. A Hindu woman has no right to speak even a word against her husband or to advise him. She has only the 'right' to allow her husband to do what he wants and remain silent.[42]

Anandibai had been well schooled into internalising the ideology of traditional patriarchy even though she was aware of other norms of conjugality.[43] On her part she continued to evoke female guilt but deployed it as a sort of armour, using it sometimes to soften her critique of Gopalrao's behaviour and sometimes to sharpen it. Her letters to Gopalrao simultaneously speak of what women suffer in marriage and of her sorrow at not being able to 'please' Gopalrao and make him 'happy' What is notable is that she did not exonerate Gopalrao's violence towards her even as she used the conventional mode of a wife writing to her husband and expressed the usual wifely sentiments in them. While she reminded him of what she had suffered at his hands she did not indict him directly even in private letters, merely letting him know that she had experienced anguish.[44] But by using the double mode she helped to construct the image of Gopalrao as an eccentric man rather than a husband who had been violent with his child wife as he had complete power over her. Anandibai's life exemplifies the point I wish to emphasise: the new educated woman did not, and was not expected to, shed the unique virtues of chaste, suffering, Hindu womanhood. Further, the 'companionate' marriage of new domestic ideologies was one-sided; it gave the husband the right to have expectations and desires but denied them to the wife. (It is significant that it was roughly at the same time that Rakhmabai was challenging child marriage and declining to accept forced conjugality, thereby rejecting the valorised model of suffering Hindu womanhood. Rakhmabai too demanded the right to a companionate marriage like the new class of men but, as we have seen, this met with hysterical opposition.) For Anandibai Joshi and many other young wives of her generation there was no major transformation wrought by 'education'. Anandi was so well 'schooled' that she made it possible for the contradictions of the new conjugality to be erased. It is not surprising that she should be valorised for being a 'good wife' above everything else. When she returned to India she was given a noticeably warm welcome, but when she died soon after, the emotions overflowed; she was given what was probably one of the most honoured and traditional funerals received by a woman in Poona. And it was in the characteristic garb of the married woman, and adorned by the signs of the sumangali, that she was cremated. The newspapers summed up public emotion thus:

Although Anandibai was so young, her perseverance, undaunted courage and devotion to her husband were unparalleled. We think it will be long before we shall see again a woman like her in this country. We do not hesitate to say that Dr. Joshi is worthy of a high place on the roll of historic women who have striven to serve and to elevate their native land.[45]

Clearly the native land was honoured in the eyes of the world through its pativrata wives. Even in far-off America her life and death were summed up as a model of Hindu womanhood 'inspired by the code of Manu'. 'Until death she was patient of hardship, self-controlled... striving to fulfill that most excellent duty which is prescribed for wives'.[46] Public adulation for Anandibai Joshi is a reflection of the values cherished by sections of the middle classes in the nineteenth century. She had shown that intrinsically there was nothing dangerous in women's education; rather that it was perfectly possible to reconcile a professional training, overseas travel, and close interactions with western women with Hindu wifely virtues. Before Anandibai left for America she had publicly defended her need to travel abroad for her medical studies, as well as her plans to go alone, without her husband.[47] She had also successfully carried out her resolve to leave as a Hindu and return as a Hindu. While in America she had defended the Hindu child marriage system.[48] Anandibai had conclusively proved that well schooled Hindu wives were in no danger of losing their religion or their values.

Finally, we may also note that the public adulation for Anandi was a recognition of her defence of tradition and Hindu patriarchal practices even though she herself was one of its victims. When we recall that at that very moment both Rakhmabai and Pandita Ramabai were in different ways challenging 'Hindu' patriarchy, Anandi was a powerful counter to these women: the recalcitrant wife whose 'education' was the source of her desire for a companionate marriage and the disavowal of her conjugal obligations, and the subversive widow who renounced her religion and publicly denounced Hindu patriarchal practices. Anandi's compliance with Hindu patriarchal practices was balm to Hindu society; Hindu conjugality was being vindicated at the moment of its severest stress.

Another, more congenial, example of the companionate marriage valorised significantly by both the reformist and traditional elite was the case of Ramabai Ranade — the most 'perfectly schooled' wife who has left an account for us of the process and values that the new Hindu domestic ideologies[49] sought to inculcate into the wife. It began on a tense note, being one of most unwillingly accepted marriages that have been documented for the region. However, it went on to become one of most celebrated examples of 'conjugality' that middle-class reformers had envisaged for reasons that will be evident in the following account.

Ranade had, initially, been one of the most visible supporters of the crusade for widow remarriage in Maharashtra. In 1873 when Ranade was 31, his first wife, whom he had married when he was thirteen, died following a prolonged illness. Immediately thereafter he began to receive telegrams persuading him to marry a widow. It is worth noting that nobody expected him to remain a widower; both the reformers and his family, especially his father, expected him to remarry immediately, the only question was whether the bride would be a young pre-pubertal virgin, or a 'virgin' widow. Using a mix of subterfuge, emotional blackmail and moral coercion, Ranade's father made sure that his son capitulated and married eleven-year-old Ramabai within a month of the death of his first wife.[50] The father had effectively subverted any possibilities of Ranade's practising his reformist ideals and at the same time facilitated the completion of the traditional requirements for Brahmana males as outlined by Manu: 'A twice born man, versed in the sacred law, shall burn the wife of equal caste who dies before him. Having thus, at the funeral given the sacred fires to his wife who dies before him, he may marry again... and dwell in his own house during the second period of his life.'[51]

Coerced thus, Ranade retreated from the festivities. The reformers however were deeply let down and became the laughing-stock of Brahmanical society. Whatever Ranade did thereafter continued to be judged by this early failure to measure up to his ideals.[52] This controversial beginning to the marriage also gives us a clue to the relationship between Ramabai and Ranade. Following the ceremony, Ranade retreated without partaking even of the ceremonial dinner and locked himself in his room. After Ramabai's father left and she went up to Ranade and their 'room', her 'education' began.[53]

Much has been made of this event, celebrated in public memory. It has been seen as evidence of the reformist zeal for women's education. That, however, is only part of the meaning that may be attributed to this 'extraordinary' beginning of conjugal relations. But let us stop for a moment and consider the circumstances: the bridegroom is a 31-year-old officer in the courts, the bride is a young, most likely pre-pubertal, girl of eleven. What could a mature prominent man of 31 do with a girl young enough to be his daughter?[54] With a wife too young to understand his confused feelings, share his intellectual and social interests or be the object of his 'romantic' yearnings in any way, short of brutally consummating the marriage what would one do in such a situation except to begin teaching the illiterate wife the alphabet? One agenda for raising women's status was nullified — the other more possible one, that of women's education, was a natural and almost inevitable substitute.

At a more substantive level the circumstances were ideal for the process of 'schooling' the young wife. The great difference in age which certainly put the young wife in the 'authority' and awe of the husband was an important aspect of 'schooling' women to be good wives and ultimately intelligent partners through education. The pair of mature husband and young wife was the only situation in which women could really be 'schooled' through education within the household in the nineteenth century. It was not easily achievable with daughters as they were married very young — too young to properly accomplish anything with. Further, one had to consider the potential marital home where the process of education was likely to be abruptly terminated. (Since each marital home was unique, schooling into it was also to be uniquely organised.) In the case of couples closer to each other in age, attempts at educating the wives lacked the 'authority' and awe that older husbands had. Since education was in any case not an instrumental need, and further, women's agency was not the motivating factor, many of the ventures in learning followed a different course. Lakshmibai Tilak (married at 11 to the 18-year old Narayan Tilak) had her first lessons at 17 at her husband's hands, abruptly dissolving into an uncontrollable fit of laughter. The first day's lesson was climaxed by the husband tearing the books to shreds.[55] As Lakshmibai describes it, the lesson failed because, first, she was not 'young' and, second, Tilak was no stranger to her. Reading between the lines it is also apparent that Lakshmibai was laughing at Tilak's authority as teacher over her. Lakshmibai was never 'schooled' and certainly not through education. (Ultimately Lakshmibai learnt not only enough of the alphabet to read widely but also to become one of the most celebrated writers of memoirs in Marathi.)

Ramabai Ranade's awareness of her very vulnerable situation in the conjugal home, given the nature of the conflict over the marriage, would have added to the sense of awe that Ranade aroused in her. Writing about his personality, as recounted to her by women of the household, she described his 'serious nature', even in childhood.[56] His inability to make decisions about his own life despite his 'public figure' status, had made him deeply unhappy and humiliated him in public. There was his genuine grief, which young Ramabai was acutely conscious of (she records that he wept every night for almost a year[57]), over his first wife's death. These would have been chastening elements shaping Ramabai's own responses in the early months. She had also been well schooled in traditional practices. Born in a high status, very orthodox jagirdar family which was well known (Ranade had insisted that his new wife was to be from just such a family even as he resisted his father's pressure for a quick remarriage[58]), she had been carefully brought up but guarded against picking up even the basics of literacy. This is because her father's sister had learnt just enough to read and utter some *stotras* (such as the Venkatesh Stotra) but was widowed early. The widowhood was attributed to her violating the taboo on women's learning and it was decided that teaching girls how to read and write brought ill-luck. Ramabai records the horror this example generated among the women. 'When the women heard of this they came to fear even the thought of reading or writing so it was inevitable that all our girls should be completely illiterate'.[59] It was also no wonder until she herself learnt how to read that the relationship between reading and *knowing* was a mystery to Ramabai.[60] Ramabai started married life with the firm conviction, shaped by her own mother's belief which had guided all her actions, that to a wife her husband was God. Ramabai recounts the parental relationship which was the model for her own:

My father was a person of strong convictions and awesome temper. None in the family dared to utter a word when he was present. My mother suffered a lot in the early days but she won his confidence and pleased him by quiet endurance and modest demeanour. She believed that the husband should be everything to the wife, a god and a guru. She had even taken the *guru-mantra* from him and used to recite it with great devotion.[61]

Before she left her parents' house for her husband's, Ramabai's father had taken her aside and reminded her of the patriarchal code — that she must never bring dishonour to her father's name. He had said:

You are my daughter. Let your demeanour be worthy of our family. Put up with everything patiently, however unbearable it might be.... You are fortunate. If you cultivate forbearance, you will rise to your real worth and prove worthy of the family you were born in. Remember my words. If I ever learn that you have behaved contrary to this I shall never bring you back to your mother's home again.[62]

After recounting her father's words Ramabai sums up her own reaction to this powerful message, a violation of which would mean banishment from the mother's house — the only emotional space a girl had:

My father was a man of firm determination. I knew he would do what he declared. His words impressed me deeply. I decided to engrave on my mind's tablet the principles he gave me and act accordingly. It was not an easy thing....[63]

Armed thus with a positive role model and a set of injunctions, Ramabai was well schooled into the central motif of a woman's training — pleasing her husband and conforming to his authority. At the same time it may be noted that when Ranade broke the taboo operating in her home against education he was also creating the *basis* of a relationship with her. Through learning, she thus discovered a way of pleasing him and receiving his attention. The enterprise of education was the new way of bonding between the husband and wife within the traditional marriage practices, especially in the situation prevailing between Ramabai and Ranade. It was the only means by which the husband-wife unit, the ideal of new domestic ideologies, could be extracted from the larger family unit in which both were actually still enmeshed.

That Ramabai's interest in the educational agenda began and survived only as a way of 'pleasing' Ranade is evident from her account of its various stages. After about two months of personally devoting attention to Ramabai's elementary education and unable to devote more than a couple of hours to her education at night,

Ranade decided to provide her with a female teacher who would come in during the day and take her through a school curriculum. Since she was still a child in many ways and not enthusiastic about acquiring learning for its own sake, Ramabai's 'schooling' immediately ran into trouble. She writes:

And that was the end of everything. Who was going to listen to that teacher? More than half an hour would be spent in looking for the books and slate. The teacher was also a young thing. How could she control me ?...[64]

Six months later Ranade discovered that Ramabai had made no progress beyond what he had originally taught her. When he upbraided the teacher for failing in her responsibilities she flashed back angrily that all labour was wasted upon Ramabai anyway since she lacked the necessary discipline to learn anything, being a rustic. The teacher also handed in her notice and quit. A thoroughly chastened Ramabai burst into tears at the sight of a humiliated Ranade who merely picked up a book and began to read without saying a word to her.[65] Sobered by the event, Ramabai applied herself with more diligence and later offered of her own accord to learn English (of which more later) but continued to tie her learning skills to Ranade's approving presence. Many years later when they were residing in Bengal and he wished her to learn Bengali she remarked that she would do so only if *he* taught her.[66] Ramabai's 'schooling' extended beyond the formal educational processes. To be the companionate wife of a prominent public figure she had to learn to share his interests and identify with his activities. Significantly, however, throughout Ramabai's recounting of the activities she shared with Ranade her own enthusiasm for or investment in the issues is never dwelt upon: they are always described as things Ranade suggested or wished her to do. Fairly early on in the 'companionate' stage of their marriage, when Ramabai had just graduated to adulthood, she once, and only once, acted on her own in an attempt to seek the approval of the women in Ranade's family as well as the 'orthodox' women of the community. The incident related to Ramabai's accompanying Ranade to a public session where a woman, Annapurnabai, rendered Puranic stories to a mixed audience. Among those attending the session was Pandita Ramabai, a thoroughly 'disreputable' character in the eyes of the orthodox, including

Ramabai Ranade's female kin. Some of the orthodox women manoeuvred to make the 'reformist' women sit along with men since they were perceived to be fraternising with them anyway. Caught between her husband's desire for the conjugal couple to go to public meetings together and the disapproval of the womenfolk, Ramabai Ranade pleaded a headache and returned home rather than be publicly ostracised by the orthodox women.[67]

When Ranade returned home and caught Ramabai out in her lie the matter became a severe test of their relationship. As Ramabai recalls the event, the meaning of 'schooling' and the strategies a husband conventionally had recourse to, without using violence, become clear. Ranade communicated his severe disapproval by punishing Ramabai with a studied silence. As Ramabai massaged his feet at night (as usual) she suddenly noticed his rejection of her presence:

I felt sleepy as I sat there massaging his feet. When I realised that he was only pretending to sleep and that there was no chance of his talking to me I became miserable. I wept for a long time. Never before had he done this. If I had done something wrong I would beg forgiveness. But [this time] I could not utter a word. The heart may grow all humble; but one's proud nature still resists *supplication* [emphasis added]. I thought of all this a thousand times but still could not say a word... The whole night passed like this. Neither of us could sleep. When dawn broke he got up and went out. I could not bear such punishment and broke down in tears...[68]

Finally a chastened Ramabai begged forgiveness and promised never to do such a thing again. Ranade was silent for a while and then said:

You do something silly to begin with and then get agitated. It upsets me too. Can one be happy to *see one's dear behave contrary to one's inclination* [emphasis added]. Once the direction is clear you should keep to it firmly. Please don't do this again.[69]

Ramabai immediately resolved *never* to do anything against her husband's wishes. In her own words, 'I felt that there could be no greater punishment than his refusal to speak to me. And throughout the rest of my life I never gave occasion for such punishment again'.[70] She was 21 at the time this incident occurred and had been married to Ranade for 10 years — long enough to realise the place of 'disapproval' in their relationship. It is evident that the general ideological direction was continuously reiterated by those in charge of schooling women. The guiding hand made clear that certain forms of activity were given the official seal of approval, others were placed beyond the pale. As Corrigan and Sayer conclude, 'This had cumulative and enormous cultural consequences for how women identified themselves and their place in the world'.[71] In Ramabai Ranade's case the 'schooling' continued throughout her life in different ways. Her reading was carefully guided; it comprised the publications of the Dakshina Prize Committee, works which were written by Brahmana men focusing on themes approved of by other scholars like them.[72] (For example Phule's ballad on Shivaji with its unconventional interpretation was not accepted by the committee as we saw earlier.[73]) Later, the reading of the *Raghuvamsa* is recorded by Ramabai along with the information that Ranade would carefully explain the *slokas* to her.[74] This was clearly the ideal text for the ideal relationship. A noticeable silence on Ramabai Ranade's familiarity with, or conscious introduction to, radical English works like those Phule was reading or Kashibai Kanitkar was expected to read and comprehend[75] indicates the carefully restricted nature of the 'schooling' of wives by husbands within what may appear to be an extended educational agenda.

Ramabai would also accompany Ranade on his tours, where she attended to his personal needs, cooking special savouries, looking after the camp inmates, writing his letters for him, receiving instructions and reporting their completion twice a day, and finally massaging his feet with ghee at night. Sometimes they played chess together while the servant massaged his feet. These special occasions when the 'schooling' was uninterrupted by the presence of the other kin, when the husband-and-wife unit was actualised in experience, were the happiest days for Ramabai — cherished more than the days at 'home'.[76] And in these moments Ramabai experienced also the godliness of her husband, and tears of reverence and love would well up from her heart. In Ramabai's own words: 'When I was alone, I often thought that although I regarded him from the point of view of an earthly relationship there was such divine power and godliness in him'.[77] Here then was the perfect example of a woman who regarded the husband as God. The new domestic ideology had pulled off a real feat as a traditional model of womanhood provided a suitable extension into the nineteenth century from a 'thousand year old tradition'.

From the point of view of the domestic ideologies being outlined by the reformers the Pygmalion situation provided by the traditional marriage system with an older husband and a child bride was not a disadvantage; it might even be regarded as an ideal way to shape the 'perfect' wife according to the requirements of the emergent forms of patriarchy. It gave men a time when the wife was totally under their 'guidance' and control, when she was pliant, malleable and obedient.

The transition from one set of patriarchical practices to another was eased because it was only the externalia of schooling that were different in the overlapping patriarchies. The central motif of obedience to the husband and the acceptance of his authority remained the basis of the 'companionate' model too. It was the endeavour of the 'reformers' to extract consent from women to this new incarnation of patriarchy. Trained to please husbands and approve their actions, 'new' women like Ramabai Ranade provided early models of consent for the emerging variations of patriarchy. Ramabai for example accepted Ranade's norms in every arena of her life (she identified so completely with Ranade that she frequently refers to 'our party' when she mentions the reformers).[78] She echoed his concerns, executed his suggestions on how to expand the arena of consent by holding meetings of upper-caste women and setting up units of the Arya Mahila Sabha, and finally after his death, by creating the Seva Sadan,[79] an institution for women which was launched to train women to fulfil their domestic, social and national responsibilities. She abstained from going beyond the agenda set out by Ranade during his lifetime; thus while others like Kashibai Kanitkar and Pandita Ramabai attended the Congress sessions in Bombay, Ramabai Ranade stayed away as Ranade disapproved of women's participation in 'politics'.[80] Her first speech in English at a prize distribution ceremony in a girl's school is a representative example of the very limited agenda. She dwelt on the need for humility in order to dispel the notion that education made women unruly, callous and immodest, and reiterated the need for the educated woman to be 'all the more gentle and obedient to husband and elders'.[81]

It is not surprising that Ramabai Ranade was regarded as the embodiment of Hindu wifely virtues by those who inherited

Ranade's political and social mantle. In the foreword of her book *Amchya Ayushatil Kahi Athavani* (*Our life together*), Gokhale wrote:

This is probably the first book written in this manner about a husband by his wife. It is but proper that Vahinibai [Ramabai] should have written it for she occupies a unique position among our women today. She spent twenty-seven years as a comrade, inseparable as a shadow of that saintly personality. Her innate lustre was heightened by education and by the ennobling company of her husband. Her mind is forever engrossed in Rao Sahib... It is important to refer to one or two things which cannot but make a deep impression [on us]. A deep love between husband and wife is often found in western society. That is a relationship of equality. But even when there is a similar deep love, that the wife should devote herself wholly to the service of the husband and consider this as the fulfilment of her life is a special characteristic of women in the East, particularly of India. This characteristic is a fruit of the culture and tradition of thousands of years and here [in Ramabai] we have a beautiful specimen of it. This fundamental characteristic remains unaffected in women like Vahinibai, although the pattern of their life may be modified by new education, new ideas and new environment.[82]

In Ramabai Ranade's example the reformers found the model of the new Indian womanhood, schooled so perfectly by her husband that she could reproduce the male voice exactly and was thereby representative of the type of womanhood who could be 'modern' without losing the traditional Indian wife's virtues. Women thus became the means by which newly-defined Hindu patriarchal practices came into being through their acceptance by women who consented to the agendas set by men of their class. There was no essential contradiction between traditional Brahmanical patriarchy and new forms of it, regarding women. Hindu wifely virtues just got a new lease of life. The characteristic quality of Indian womanhood then came to be the ability to survive any modernising onslaught and keep its essence.

III

There was another side to the contentious presence of multiple and overlapping forms of patriarchy when they were ideologically opposed to each other in nineteenth century Maharashtra, and that was the manner in which these were expressed within the household, specifically in the female domain. Ramabai Ranade's account of life with her husband is thus also significant for a latent oppositional narrative indicative of the not so successful slide from the values of traditional patriarchy to the new domestic ideology of a class segment. While this was not her intention, Ramabai Ranade captures also the contradictions and tensions within a family where women of different generations and differing degrees of relationship to the 'men' of the house find themselves playing out their relationship to each other in a changing situation. Looking at this suppressed narrative of mostly nameless and some named women (as portrayed by the central figure of the new family, the young wife), one can see that the period as a whole, when the battle between traditional patriarchy and its transformed version was unfolding, was deeply confusing for women — despite the essential similarity of 'wifely' virtues in the two forms of patriarchy.

It is clear from a range of male writings that many male reformers portrayed the conflict of values as a case of women themselves resisting change; we often come across the familiar 'women themselves are the oppressors of other women' theme in such writing.[83] This is also how Ramabai Ranade portrays the tension between women in the home, an echo of Ranade himself who sees the conflict as one of women who uphold traditional values and 'resist' change through their obduracy.[84] A close look at the female domain within the Ranade household suggests that there were complex issues at the heart of the conflicts. While these conflicts were expressed as ideological, they had, at their base, a fundamental materiality.

The major crisis points in the self-consciously crafted narrative of the conjugal couple in the Ranade household centred round the actions and speech of the female affinal kin of Ramabai. There were 'eight to ten' of them who resided in this household,[85] all of whom save three remain hazy as Ramabai does not describe them. The three female kin that she does individualise out of this 'group' are all, significantly, widows at the point when the crisis erupts. Among them Durga, the only one of the female kin to be named, is clearly the most powerful. Although she is not in any way the focus of Ramabai Ranade's account, which is built unambiguously around the great Ranade, Durga succeeds in pressing herself upon the narrative to reveal the underside of patriarchy and the tussles generated by it. She calls for more attention than she gets in passing, mostly in negative terms, from Ramabai Ranade because she does appear to be the third figure in a triangular relationship between Ranade, Ramabai and herself. As portrayed by Ramabai Ranade it is Durga who represents the figure of tension in the necessary transformation of the traditional household into an affective unit, the home of the conjugal couple. The ever-present widowed dependent kin could easily disrupt the creation of the conjugal unit in the eyes of a young wife. But another way of interpreting Durga is to see her relationship to both Ramabai and Ranade as a playing-out of the contradictions inherent in the life of a Brahmana widow in the nineteenth century.

Durga was Ranade's only full sibling, born two years after him. In their childhood she is represented as overtly the brighter and the more lively of the two, even as his opposite in verbal skills and general disposition. Certainly she had extraordinary 'natural' intelligence for it to be regarded as part of family folklore. Indulged by her father and by 'too much praise', she was regarded as growing into a 'termagant' who was aggressive and dominating.[86] There was both sibling rivalry and affection in the relationship, with the two sharing games and a common circle of friends. However, while Ranade went to school, Durga did not: but this did not in any way affect her observation and pragmatic understanding which come through in the narration of Ranade's childhood.

When Durga was nine she was married. The same year their mother had died during her eighth confinement and within eighteen days their father married again. (Her brother was married soon after the father's remarriage.) We get no glimpse of Durga's marital household or her life there in Ramabai Ranade's account, as the narrative is about her brother. (But in a letter to a friend written in 1870, Ranade commiserated with him on family troubles and also mentioned his own distress at a situation in which his poor 'orphan sister is kept away from me for months together'. Whether this was because she was in her marital home which was repressive and did not permit interaction with the natal household or because Ranade was away from his family home and could not devote any attention to his sister is not clear.)[87] What is interesting is that while Durga is described as being indulged by her father and clearly sharing a close relationship with him, her brother hardly ever spoke to his father directly, getting things said for him by others.[88] As the years proceeded Ranade went to Bombay to be educated, where he did extraordinarily well and thereafter entered 'service'. During the same period Durga was widowed at the age of 21 and appears to have returned to live in her father's household. From the fact that she returned to her father's house, less likely if she had a son, and the fact that there are no specific references to children, she appears to have been childless. When Ranade was widowed at the age of 31, Durga was firmly ensconced in her father's household and a central figure in it.[89] This position, possibly as the most important woman in it, may have been facilitated by the presence of a stepmother as young as herself as its nominal mistress. In a household where there were only older female kin who would all have been related by blood to Durga, many of whom would have mothered her, she would be the 'insider' in relation to the young stepmother. Taking over the complete reins of the household may also have been easier in the case of widows because their lives were unpunctuated by childbirth and they were therefore always available to perform the full range of female duties in the household.

Available thus and uniquely located as an insider where all other women were outsiders, Durga appears to have also become the natural mediator between the various segments of the family, especially in a situation where the father and son did not communicate; she appears to have mediated both between generations and between the male and the female domains. However, it was not merely her structural location but her personality and the circumstances of her life that converted her into a power-broker of sorts. We see something of this in the first crisis referred to by Ramabai Ranade, Ranade's remarriage, which preceded her own entry into the household.

The father's orthodoxy, the cause of the crisis with Ranade, appears to have been of a very high order; his insistence on Ranade's immediate remarriage to a young girl and his anxiety about a potential marriage with a widow may of course have also been a strategy of survival. He had a young family through his own second marriage who would have to be looked after and 'settled' by Ranade after his own death.[90] Doing so would become extremely difficult if Ranade pursued his ideals since outcasting was a very real and very powerful weapon that would fall upon the whole family. In the exclusive discussions that preceded Ranade's remarriage, Durga figured both as a subject and a witness. Although everyone was dismissed by the father to enable a frank discussion with the son, Durga refused to have herself shut out and listened at the door.

Significantly, one of the arguments raised by Ranade to stall a remarriage was that Durga had been a widow since 21 and no one considered that *she* should remarry. As he put it, 'I am not young any more: I am thirty-two years old. I can certainly lead a life of thought and retirement. Durga is younger than I and has been a widow since she was 21. You do not love her less than you love me, in any way. And yet no one thinks of her. Why am I being urged to marry? If you think it would be good for her to lead a life of restraint it should apply equally to me.'[91]

This is the only record that the family had of the conversation between father and son and it was Durga's version, passed on in later years to Ramabai Ranade.[92] Whether this allusion to Durga was a serious view of Ranade's is not clear because there is no evidence to suggest that when he became the head of the household, he attempted to have Durga remarried. In any case it would have been too late by then since she would have been 32 or so and Ranade may have carried a double sense of guilt about her status and his own failure to marry a widow placed in a situation like her. What is interesting is that Durga herself included a reference to the double standards operating between men and women when she passed on the account. In any case Durga continued to lead a life of 'restraint' while her elder brother was not required to, indeed not allowed to. The open acceptance of male sexuality and the denial of female sexuality was a naturalised aspect of the moral order of Brahmanical society. However, whether it was 'naturalised' by the women themselves in any simple or direct manner needs to be explored. What we do see in our narrative are two related features; one an expression, fairly frequently stated, of hostility towards men, especially against the master/conjugal partner heading the household. The second was a deep-seated fear of the power of the wife of the head of the household. She, it was felt, would marginalise other women by becoming the premier influence in the life of the master through her sexual and affective power over him as well as the legitimate claim she had to his material assets. All other categories of women, mostly widows in our case, were recipients of his 'charity'. In such a situation the conjugal duo was quite naturally the object of close scrutiny, even of sustained surveillance. The women of the household made it a point to know what was going on in the private space of the central pair and they did so as a 'team'.

Denied a 'legitimate' home, widows like Durga might well attempt to ensure their own place where one could be found. Durga's forceful character begins to register as Ramabai Ranade's narrative of her early years with her husband unfolds. She was clearly in charge of the kitchen and the accounts of the household,[93] possibly the real mistress of the Ranade household at the time of Ramabai's marriage. Significantly, she was called 'Akkasaheb',[94] an index of her special power in the family. Ranade himself relied on her ability to handle crises of various kinds in the household and shoulder a 'man's' responsibility within it, for example, keeping a concerned watchful eye on the grief-stricken stepmother at the father's death to ensure that she did not commit suicide, and even cope with the death rituals while he himself stayed away because he could not bear the trauma.[95] Finally, the father's separate household was merged with the son's and the father's family shifted to Poona where Ranade was located.

It is at this stage that the tension in the household between the women, portrayed as 'traditionalist and obdurate', and Ranade, as well as within the female domain between the older women and the young wife Ramabai, openly surfaced.[96] It was overtly expressed as a conflict over the young wife's education, especially her English education, the company she kept and her participation in her husband's social life.[97] But it also had strong overtones of the anxieties generated by the new location and changed dimensions of the household. What power alignments, material arrangements and familial relationships the new situation was going to throw up and how its various components were going to realign themselves were questions yet to be resolved.

In Ramabai Ranade's rendering of the tension between the older women and herself the cause of the disapproval was threefold: the process of the new forms of schooling focused on learning, the learning of English from the *mleccha* Miss Herford, and finally Ramabai Ranade's association with the young and infamous Pandita Ramabai, who had crossed the threshold of the home, to which all women and especially widows were confined, and stepped into the public space reserved for men.[98] These women, now the representatives of the elders and patriarchs, threw into relief the authority residing in this group as they witnessed but were unable to prevent traditional codes being violated as there was now a new 'master' in the house; it was his wife who was violating the codes in order to please her husband. As the women came to recognise their inability to actually dictate what values were going to be upheld they are likely to have noticed the change following the death of the father. The deeply patriarchal nature of this change is significant. As long as Ranade's father was alive the son accepted every expression of his father's choice, of course, but also regretted inviting Vishnu Shastri Pandit and his new widow-bride to a meal when his father was visiting the son's home because this action offended him.[99] Now, after the death of the father, Ranade had suddenly taken to doing what he considered 'right' because there was no patriarch opposing him — only a bunch of women whom 'he' fed and housed, as one of the old widows put it.[100] It was Ranade who was the new patriarch now and so could do as he pleased.

Ramabai Ranade represents the elder women as blind traditionalists; Durga is described as the most intelligent of the women who knew the value of education but was obstinate, proud and hot-tempered by nature, believing that everything 'old was gold'; she struggled hard to exert her influence over Ramabai Ranade, alternately cajoling and haranguing her about her activities and frequently comparing her 'outrageous' behaviour with the modest and endearing conduct of Ranade's first wife. The content of many of these sessions, interestingly, was an incitement to Ramabai that men's authority could be subverted, and even that the wishes of husbands were not sacrosanct: rather it was really family tradition — the Brahmanical code — that was important to a woman. Durga clearly identified with the Brahmanya of the Peshwai.[101]

The 'activity' of education especially its non-instrumental dimension, was in any case seen as frivolous, as was the joint attendance of the husband and wife at public meetings. In Durga's own words here is the traditional Brahmana woman's analysis of the relations between men and women:

Even if the men want you to do these things you should ignore them. You need not say no but after all you need not do it. They will then give up out of sheer boredom. Your parents are orthodox and respectable. Your father and mother have a great sense of decorum. It is such a pleasure to look at them. The women of their family are not supposed to learn even Marathi — let alone English. But you — you are outdoing even the European women.[102]

And since Ramabai continued to act according to Ranade's expectations Durga complained to the other women:

It is she herself who loves this frivolousness of going to meetings. Dada is not so keen about it. Men always say such a lot of things. But should she not have a sense of proportion of how much the women should actually do? If men tell you to do a hundred things, women should take up ten at the most. After all men do not understand these practical things...

What use is the education of women after they are able to read a few sacred books? It's just a fad of his, that's all. He was so much after the first *vahini* (brother's wife, i.e., his first wife) too about this reading and writing. But she, poor thing, was very docile. She put up with such a lot of scolding from him just to please us. That good woman never turned frivolous like this and never gave up our old ways. That is why this large family of more than twelve people could live together in a respectable way. With not so much as the smallest gesture did she ever indicate that *she was the mistress of the household*[103] [emphasis added].

A power struggle in the female domain within the larger household for the position of mistress is evident from this passage, although there were clearly many other issues at stake.

The anxiety and anger about a new mistress is a running theme in the verbal expression of the politics of the household. Older women feared the power of the young 'second' wife over the husband and her ultimate 'enthronement' as the undisputed mistress of the female domain. The oldest widow in the Ranade household captured the complex emotions of fear, anger, and hostility about the young wife during a moment of high tension when the latter had asserted her 'authority', and unilaterally communicated a family lapse to the master:

The widowers' wives are always tell-tale witches. They always curry favour by tale-telling... She is gaining a new trait everyday... Two or three 'nannies' in the house have now become a nuisance [to her]. Let her drive them out and be rid of them. Then let the Sahib and Memsahib sit together on chairs, books in hand. I have noticed that lately she has come to feel that she is the mistress of the house. The servants should obey her alone.[104]

And to Ranade who tried to defend his wife's position by providing her with his protective mantle the old lady said:

There is no need to stand up for your wife in this way. She is not being branded is she? If she is so precious and delicate, keep her safe with you;

put her on a pedestal and worship her like a goddess. You consider yourself very wise just because you have learnt some English. But this is no wisdom. If you are fed up with us you need not insult us by taking sides with your wife. We would prefer to be told to leave the house.[105]

It was to some extent the tenuous position of widowed female kin in relation to the wife in any household that generated so much tension about the position of the 'mistress'. Called upon to be putative mistresses of the household when experienced wives were not available or not free to wield such a position, these 'stand-ins' were expected to hand over the reins of authority when they had served their purpose. Anxiety about the mistress would be heightened by the demarcation between categories of women caused by the new type of schooling given to the wife and new forms of conjugality cementing the relationship between the master of the home and his wife. This accounts for the repeated allusions to 'mistress' used pejoratively, to reading and sitting together — described by old Tai Sasubai, the eldest widow in the house, as 'love which had crossed all limits. Wives must now sit close to their husbands as though their clothes were knotted.'[106] Further, the position of the wife as mistress implied the servility of all other women to her — also an anxious thought for elder women schooled in traditional Brahmanical patriarchy who were insecure about what forms of domestic arrangements emergent patriarchies would make: in sum, the English-educated mistress was a fearful prospect. As Durga said to Ramabai Ranade when she began to be taught English by Miss Herford: 'You are turning yourself into a "Madam" by learning English. It would be only fitting to the pomp of a madam that she should have her food upstairs. After all we are here, downstairs, all the slaves and servants of my lady.'[107]

At the stage that these feelings were expressed Durga would have been forty and Ramabai Ranade around twenty-one. For some years following the relocation of the Ranade household Ramabai alone, as the wife and possibly potential mistress, had been carefully schooled by her husband, an activity that separated this one woman from the rest of the female kin who were left within the ideological moorings of a traditional patriarchy which these older women had been schooled in. Durga's father for example had been so strict about maintaining the separation between the public and the private domains that he had refused to speak to his wife for days because she had continued to stand in the courtyard when a clerk came in to have a drink of water.[108] The domestic ideology of the reformer, by focusing on the young wife and leaving the others to live according to traditional norms, was bound to produce a conflictual ideological situation in the household. And we must recognise the difficulties for women schooled in one set of patriarchal norms to suddenly drop them according to the whims of the 'patriarchs'. The 'elder' women may also have been resentful of the change of values required of them with every change of the patriarch heading the household.

There were also material arrangements at stake in the division of labour in the household. Since education had no instrumental use for women, although it did have a social value for the new class, it was naturally perceived as fruitless to women who were *required* to render other forms of labour in the household. Conventionally it was the senior women who organised domestic labour, allotting tasks within it. Apart from the natural resentment against one of its members who could spend time reading and attending meetings while they continued to perform 'menial duties', the new domestic ideology also separated women in terms of their world-views. At least in the Ranade household the embryonic female intelligentsia was not enabling the penetration of new values, which was part of the agenda of female education, into the female domain but producing anxiety and conflict. The tensions in the female world meant also that women were forced to choose between its warring factions; if you had the emotional sustenance of one you lost the other. Even the well-schooled Ramabai, wanting to please her husband but longing also to be accepted in the female world, slipped once with the disastrous results we have already described. On her part she inevitably resolved the conflict by choosing decisively to go with the master of the house, recognising the tacit requirement of Ranade that one whom he looked upon as his 'own' should be able to do just what *he wished* without being told so.[109]

Once the conflict of interest was decisively resolved and Ramabai Ranade gradually but inevitably moved into the position of the mistress of the household, secure in the support of her husband, the elder women were edged out and they more or less disappeared from the narrative. Only Durga remained as a character who continued to be mentioned, still called upon in a crisis like Ranade's critical illness[110] (when he was out on tour accompanied by his 'own' family), or when the family was faced with social outcasting and she worried about how the *shraddha* rituals would be conducted for the dead.[111] She remained a member of Ranade's 'other' family of stepmother and stepbrothers while Ramabai Ranade presided over his 'real' home. There may have then been a natural reconciliation between the women with relationships coming full circle when their respective places were resolved[112] and they finally achieved the bonding that had eluded them in early years. The last mention that Durga gets is when Ranade was terminally ill. Durga organised prayers in the temple for her brother while Ramabai silently prayed for her husband. A widow of long standing, Durga then consoled the terrified Ramabai, tormented by her impending widowhood, with traditional codes of acceptance. 'God is with us,' Durga said. 'He will take care: *anushthanas* are going on in the temple of Ambabai. She will look after all. You should trust in her and be at peace. Don't lose heart. When you are alert and about, it gives us courage. You are the Lakshmi of the house. You should not let tears soil your eyes at such a moment.' Since Ramabai Ranade's narrative ends with her husband's death we[113] do not know how the two women related to each other in their final years. By then Ramabai had not only been undisputed mistress of the household but also the natural heir to Ranade's mission. As we have already indicated, she completed the task of disseminating the new domestic ideology both through her own person and through the institution she helped to create. The female protagonists of traditional patriarchal practices had inexorably faded away at least in this one household.

One of the notable silences in Ramabai's account of the politics of the female domain and the figures that inhabited it relates to the experience of widowhood. This appears to be a significant omission, particularly when Ramabai Ranade was mortally afraid of being widowed herself and regarded widowhood as a tragic state.[114] It is doubly noticeable because Ranade's name was at one point synonymous with the widow remarriage movement. Yet at no point do we get a direct reference to the way the widows in the Ranade household perceived and experienced widowhood. We do not know whether Durga, the youngest of these widows, wore the signs of widowhood such as the tonsured head. There is, however, a telling sentence in the account which captures the essence of widowhood and might give us a clue to the politics of the female domain. While journeying to Simla on an official visit the Ranade couple were accompanied, among others, by Durga. At Jaipur the party came upon a number of skilled artisans carving figurines of stone. Ramabai describes how Durga 'greatly admired a small image of Lakshmi-Narayana' and then adds with compelling wifely authority 'which *we* bought for her'.[115] Ramabai's association of herself with Ranade as 'we', sharing access to his resources from which Durga was excluded, is a powerful reminder of the materiality of relationships within the household and the deep divide between a wife and a widowed kinswoman. The latter may be permitted to 'manage' it as Durga had done for many years but was not 'entitled' to it. We may recall Ranade's ruling as judge in a case where a widowed daughter had obviously sought a right to support in her natal household: while there could be a moral duty on the part of her natal male kin to provide such support, the widow could not claim a legal right to it.[116]

In a significant essay Sangari argues that women cannot ever name their 'interests' in the cultural codes of patriarchy. These may sometimes be expressed laterally but never directly.[117] In Durga's person and through the references, veiled and open, to the 'mistress' of the household articulated by the widows in Ranade's family we have a powerful example of this crucial characteristic of patriarchy — whether traditional or its transformed variant. Tensions in the female domain were not merely personal or ideological but also deeply material.

The juxtaposition of different sets of patriarchal practices within a given society may be seen to have produced both conflict and a happy co-existence. While men had a certain choice in opting for one or the other variant of patriarchal codes, or even a blend, women had less choice in the matter even though we can see them asserting themselves *within* the structure of patriarchal institutions. It would be mechanical on our part to make an easy association of the new woman as relatively 'liberated', or less enmeshed by patriarchal structures, or consider that those women who were in traditional structures of patriarchy were more in its stranglehold. From the Ranade household it is possible to discern that the reverse situation could obtain. While the carefully schooled new woman considered her husband a virtual god, Durga, the traditional widow, knew how to carve out a powerful place for herself within existing forms of patriarchy by manipulating its premises. (I use the word 'manipulation' rather than 'subversion' *consciously* because actions which do not change the relations and work within patriarchy are not subversive of it. Also, Durga gained a relative advantage, not an absolute one.) She was almost contemptuous of male authority even as she proclaimed the need to adhere to its form. She also 'opted', in a sense, for traditional patriarchal norms because it gave some women a certain power within the household over other categories of women. It permitted women to 'arrogate' to themselves compensatory power within the domestic domain, serving patriarchal ends in the process, because this power had been a way of schooling younger women. Its ideology also gave them more meaning and acceptance of their 'wasted' lives. Further, traditional Brahmanical patriarchal practices had in a sense 'inherited' the consent of women. The oppressive practices had been invisibilised as aspects of 'tradition', 'custom', 'honour' and religious practice. And most notably we need to recognise that pre-existing patriarchal forms were perceived by both men and women as demarcating upper-caste, especially Brahmana, women from castes below them and thus as being a necessary aspect of class order and social stability: women then would and did resist its reformulation.

It was the privileging of the emergent forms of patriarchy over its traditional variants within the same generation and same household that produced intra-familial tensions amongst women and confused them about their ideological position. Durga epitomised the traditional values of her father and had been respected for upholding the Brahmanya, but was an anachronism in her brother's household which had found new ways of defining 'respectability' for elite women. It was only natural that she, and women like her, would resist readily consenting to the new form of patriarchy which in any case concentrated its energy on the wife, who needed to be schooled into becoming a companionate wife and nurturant mother. For the widow who could be neither, despite all the rhetoric, there was less concern shown by the new domestic ideology except to consider making them wives. The expectation of a quick production of consent among widows requiring them to switch from one articulation of patriarchy to another, was not easy because there was no husband to demand it of them. Since the husband was the pivot of traditional patriarchy as well as its variant, his demand for conforming to one or his disapproval of another legitimised which form of patriarchy the wife must consent to as exemplified by Ramabai Ranade.

We must not however conclude from Ramabai Ranade's example that emergent forms of patriarchy met with no resistance from wives. As we have suggested earlier, the whole business of 'pleasing' husbands and living up to their notions of womanhood could well have appeared to be among the *visible* forms of patriarchy which women might resist and instead prefer to live by tradition where patriarchal practices were rendered invisible within the general framework of religion, custom, and family traditions. While traditional patriarchy had the sedimented consent of women who saw themselves as upholding social and community norms by living in certain ways which marked them off from others below them, the new patriarchal requirements were more difficult to mask, especially in the early stages before women were schooled into it. We have the example of Lakshmibai Sardesai, the wife of the well-known historian of Maharashtra, G.S. Sardesai, employed in the princely state of Baroda at the turn of the century. She records two attempts at making her do what she did not want to by her husband as part of the new domestic ideology. One was the fad among the new professional class of men to put their wives through a formal course in 'nurturing' — a nursing and midwifery course which her husband suggested.[118] Clearly, men considered that a casual and unstructured picking-up of nurturing skills was insufficient for an important feminine task. Fortunately for her, Lakshmibai was required to actually nurture a baby niece whose mother had died, so that gave her an excuse for not conforming to her husband's plans for her.

The second occasion had to do with the 'fashioning' of a new self by an emergent class. Sardesai desired that his wife give up wearing the conventional nine-yard sari and take on the creation of an appropriate apparel for the nineteenth century middle-class woman, cutting across regions: the six-yard version of the sari regarded as more modern, more modest and the really respectable way to 'cover' the female body. Lakshmibai hated it, and argued vociferously against it with her husband, but finally gave in. However, the mother-in-law was so outraged by the daughter-in-law's transformation that she threatened to leave her son's house during a visit and actually left because the son refused to change his position. But a few days after the mother-in-law had gone Lakshmibai Sardesai quietly reverted to her traditional nine-yard sari. In the following postscript to the episode Lakshmibai records: 'Apparently my husband either did not notice or decided not to say anything'.[119] Earlier she had recorded that she had already disappointed her husband and made him angry by failing to learn English as he desired, since she did not have 'enough time and energy for it'.[120] Using her Marathi effectively, Lakshmibai put into writing her own view of what was happening between husbands and wives in a secret 'voluminous' diary which her husband only discovered after her death. Fortunately for us, he had it published, but only as a 'supplementary' account to his own autobiography.[121]

We can see that at least some wives, among other categories of women, did not fully endorse the view Ramabai Ranade held about women necessarily accepting male authority when she recognised that all women knew that they had to do what men desired in order to please them.[122] Schooling to 'please' men under the emergent forms of patriarchy was still tenuous and the household remained an embattled space between men, between women, and between men and women. It was being subjected to double pressures: from forces in society working externally and its echo within the family working internally. Neither patriarchal forms nor cultural practices were satisfactorily settled for the new elites. Gender relations continued to be reworked, and dynamically tied to social processes as class and nation were being born.

NOTES AND REFERENCES

1. Kumkum Sangari, 'Relating Histories: Definitions of Literacy, Literature, Gender in Nineteenth Century Calcutta and England', in Svati Joshi (ed.), *Rethinking English: Essays in Literature, Language, History*, New Delhi, Trianka, 1991, pp. 32–123, pp. 37–40.
2. Gail Pearson, 'The Female Intelligentsia in a Segregated Society — Bombay, a Case Study', in M. Allen and S.N. Mukherjee (eds.), *Women in India and Nepal*, Canberra, Australian National University Press, 1982, pp. 136–54, pp. 136–38.
3. Uma Chakravarti, 'Conceptualising Brahmanical Patriarchy in Early India: Gender, Caste, Class and State', *Economic and Political Weekly*, Vol. 28, No. 14, 3 April 1993, pp. 579–85.
4. Julia Leslie, *The Perfect Wife*, pp. 20–21.

5. Sudhanwa Deshpande, 'Theatre and Nationalism: The Plays of Krishnaji Prabhakar Khadilkar', M.Phil. thesis under preparation. Also see Kumkum Sangari, 'Consent, Agency and the Rhetorics of Incitement', *Economic and Political Weekly*, Vol. 28, No. 18, 1993, pp. 867–82, especially pp. 872–77 for an account of Kaikeyi's agency, represented, and sedimented, as incitement in public memory.

6. Sumit Guha, 'Fitna in Maratha Theory and Practice', paper presented at the Nehru Memorial Museum and Library, 15 September, 1993.

7. Kumkum Sangari, 'Relating Histories', p. 58.

8. *Ibid.*, p. 56.

9. See for example Himani Banerji, 'Mothers and Teachers; Gender and Class in Educational Proposals for and by Women in Colonial Bengal', *Journal of Historical Sociology*, Vol. 5, No. 1, March 1992, pp. 1–30, p. 3.

10. Gail Pearson, 'Female Intelligentsia', pp. 139–40. In 1884 Ramabai made an eloquent plea before the Hunter Commission for the education of women in order to train them as teachers, nurses and doctors. A few years later the Lady Dufferin Fund was set up to train women as doctors (Manisha Lal, Ph.D. thesis under preparation, University of Pennsylvania).

11. Himani Banerji, 'Mothers and Teachers', pp. 2, 7, 27.

12. Parvati Athavale describes the shift in the structure of families in the early twentieth century thus: 'Formerly there were large families but now the "king", the "queen" and the "crown prince" seem to be all that is wanted' (Parvati Athavale, *The Hindu Widow*, pp. 136).

13. Based on a reading of Ramabai Ranade's *Reminiscences*. See discussion on pp. 216–24 below.

14. Himani Banerji, 'Mothers and Teachers', p. 3.

15. C.Y. Chintamani, *Indian Social Reform*, p. 178.

16. *Ibid.*

17. Parvati Athavale, *The Hindu Widow*, pp. 134–36, 141.

18. Himani Banerji, 'Mothers and Teachers', p. 4.

19. C.Y. Chintamani, *Indian Social Reform*, p. 105.

20. B.N. Motivala, *Karsondas Mulji: A Biographical Study*, Bombay, Karsondas Mulji Centenary Celebration Committee, 1935, pp. 361–65.

21. *Ibid.*, p. 366.

22. Dayaram Gidumal, *Status of Women*, pp. xcix-c.

23. Y.D. Phadke, *Women in Maharashtra*, Delhi, Maharashtra Information Centre, 1989, p. 23.

24. Sarojini Vaidya, *Shreemati Kashibai Kanitkar: Atmacharitrani Charitra*, Bombay, Popular Prakashan, 1991, pp. 75ff.

25. The information on Anandibai Joshi is derived from various sources. These include Kashibai Kanitkar's biographical account of the former's life which also contains letters written by Anandibai Joshi to various persons including her husband Gopalrao Joshi (Kashibai Kanitkar, *Dr. Anandibai Joshi: Yanche Charitra va Patre*, Bombay, Manoranjan Grantha Prasarak Mandali, 1912). A recent biographical novel (S.J. Joshi, *Anandi Gopal*, tr. and abridged by Asha Damle, Calcutta, Stree, 1992) is useful in reconstructing the 'legend' surrounding Anandibai's tragic life and death. The life of Anandibai as perceived and documented by an American woman who met her in America was published in 1888 and contains useful contemporary material on Anandibai's American location (Caroline Healey Dall, *The Life of Anandabai Joshee*, Boston, Roberts Brothers, 1888). The cross-currents that brought Anandibai and Pandita Ramabai together and Anandi's American sojourn are detailed in Pandita Ramabai's *The High Caste Hindu Woman*, Philadelphia, printed by Ramabai Dongre Medhavi, 1888, pp. i-viii, and Sister Geraldine's *Letters and Correspondence of Pandita Ramabai*, (A.B. Shah ed.), Bombay, Maharashtra Board for Literature and Culture, 1977.

26. Women's particapation in learning was regarded as a sign of kali yuga (Dall, *The Life*, pp. 85–86; Kashibai Kanitkar, *Dr. Anandibai Joshi*, pp. 41– 42).

27. Sarojini Vaidya, *Shreemati Kashibai Kanitkar*, p. 163.

28. Ramabai Ranade, *Ranade: His Wife's Reminiscences*, translated by Kusumvati Deshpande, Delhi, Publications Division, 1963, pp. 47ff.

29. Susie Tharu and K. Lalitha, *Women Writing in India: 600 BC to the Present*, Vol. I, Delhi, Oxford University Press, 1991, p. 256.

30. Ramabai Ranade, *Reminiscences*, p. 38; Sarojini Vaidya, *Shreemati Kashibai*, p. 20.

31. Kashibai Kanitkar, *Dr. Anandibai Joshi*, p. 25. Also see Tanika Sarkar, 'A Book of Her Own, A Life of Her Own: Autobiography of a Nineteenth Century Woman', *History Workshop Journal*, No. 36, 1993, pp. 35–65, p. 57.

32. Sarojini Vaidya, *Shreemati Kashibai Kanitkar*, p. 75. The traditional prejudice against education continued to be reiterated by fiery nationalists, not just by the older generation of patriarchs, although it was now dressed up in the content of education rather than mere acquisition of literacy skills. Tilak for example mounted an attack on the Huzurpaga school set up by the reformers in 1884. He

accused it of following a syllabus which would train women to be clerks rather than to become good housewives and *great* mothers. All that was required in the case of women's education were reading and writing skills and study of carefully selected Shastric texts (Y.D. Phadke, *Women in Maharashtra*, p. 12).

33. Kumkum Sangari, 'Relating Histories', p. 57.
34. Dall, *The Life*, pp. 17–21; Kashibai Kanitkar, *Dr. Anandibai Joshi*, pp. 17, 12–13
35. *Ibid.*, p. 17; S.J. Joshi, *Anandi Gopal*, pp. 2–3.
36. Parvati Athavale, *The Hindu Widow*, p. 8.
37. See for example S.J. Joshi, *Anandi Gopal*, p. vii; Jayant Raghunath Joshi, 'Anandibai Joshi: Triumph and Tragedy', *Span*, December 1988, p. 15; Meera Kosambi, 'Reality and Reflection. Personal Narratives of Two Women in Nineteenth Century Maharashtra', in Kumkum Sangari and Uma Chakravarti (eds.), *From Myths to Markets: Essays on Gender*, Shimla, Indian Institute of Advance Study, Forthcoming.
38. S.J. Joshi, *Anandi Gopal*, pp. 8–9.
39. *Ibid.*, pp. 103–06; Dall, *The Life*, p. 32.
40. Pandita Ramabai, *The High Caste Hindu Woman*, pp. ii–v; Dall suggested that American women could learn from Anandi's wifely conduct (Dall, *The Life*, p. 116).
41. Gopalrao publicly stated that higher education for women made them 'unfitted' for the domestic duties of wives and mothers (Dall, *The Life*, p. 123); S.J. Joshi, *Anandi Gopal*, p. 188.
42. Kashibai Kanitkar, *Dr. Anandibai Joshi*, pp. 188–89, translated for author by Madhu Malti Deshpande.
43. S.J. Joshi, *Anandi Gopal*, p. 211; It is significant that Anandibai wrote a long account of Savitri in one of her letters to Mrs. Carpenter extolling her virtues of complete obedience and loyalty to her husband (Dall, *The Life*, pp. 64–68).
44. Anandibai's letters, conveying distress at Gopalrao's volatile behaviour and his expressions of anger in his letters to her, begin and end with wifely and loving phrases. Between the conventional beginning and end Anandibai however revealed other emotions and responded to his accusations, sometimes with a fairly spirited defence of herself and her actions. In a typical letter she began with 'I am your loyal wife, still I have not been able to give you anything. Since the kind God has sent me to this earth in the form of a woman, I am accepting with obedience and equanimity whatever he has given to me.' Then she proceeds to take up the substantive issue in Gopalrao's letter to her where he has been critical of a photograph Anandibai sent him in which she is not wearing the

conventional nine-yard Maharashtrian-style sari but the 'Gujarati' or Hindustani style. From Anandibai's letter to Gopalrao it appears that not only has Gopalrao castigated her for changing the manner in which the sari is worn but also because the draping of the *pallu* has revealed too much of Anandibai for his liking. Anandibai's response includes disbelief at the fact that he has been unnecessarily critical, and being double-faced for saying one thing to her when she left for America and another when he wrote to her. She nominally 'concedes' that she had committed a 'mistake' by not telling him in advance that she would change to the Gujarati/Hindustani style, but also makes clear that she had to change into it for practical reasons, and finally that she did what she thought was right. She also pointed out with sarcasm that it was 'after all *our country's dress*' (emphasis added) and made clear that *she* did not think it was flashy or bad. Then she reverts to the conventional female sentiments towards a husband with phrases like, 'I am not unhappy for myself but I am unhappy from the depth of my being because you are not getting anything from me. It was not my intention to hurt your dear heart' (Kashibai Kanitkar, *Dr. Anandibai Joshi*, pp. 186–89), translated by Madhu Malti Deshpande. Given the double voice she had to use in her relationship with Gopalrao it is not surprising that she considered the summer of 1883, which she spent with her 'aunt' Mrs. Carpenter soon after her arrival in America (who was a loving mother figure for Anandibai), 'as the happiest in her life, living among those who really loved her' (Dall, *The Life*, p. 96).

45. While Anandi was critically ill the Poona papers had issued daily bulletins on her condition. Anandibai had reverted to an undiluted Brahmanic ideology, objecting to the maidservant stepping on the mat near her bed (Dall, *The Life*, pp. 181–83) so it is no wonder that 'all' Poona valorised her and prayed for her (*Gyanachakshu*, 2 March 1887, tr. from Marathi by Pandita Ramabai and cited in the *The High Caste Hindu Woman*, p. vi).

46. Pandita Ramabai, *The High Caste Hindu Woman*, p. iv.

47. Catherine Healey Dall, *The Life*, Boston, pp. 82–91.

48. *Ibid.*, p. 109; Pandita Ramabai, *The High Caste Hindu Woman*, pp. iii-iv.

49. The discussion on the 'schooling' of Ramabai Ranade, the pressures the new domestic ideologies generated among Brahmana households, the 'politics' of the 'family' and the materiality of the 'politics' in this section and the next are based on a reading of Ramabai Ranade's *Reminiscences*. This book has been extensively

used by other scholars but mainly to describe the focus on women's education by reformers in the nineteenth century.

50. Ramabai Ranade, *Reminiscences*, pp. 32–37; Richard Tucker, *Ranade*, pp. 78– 81.

51. *Manu*, V, 167–69.

52. We do not know whether Ranade seriously intended to marry a widow or considered the alternative of remaining a widower. It is significant that Ramabai Ranade does not dwell on this dimension of the issue of the remarriage of Ranade.

53. Ramabai Ranade, *Reminiscences*, p. 37.

54. More than a decade later Karve described his decision to marry a widow as based partly on 'humanitarian' grounds but also because he was 'terrified' of marrying a girl young enough to be his daughter (D.K. Karve, *My Life Story* in D.D. Karve, *New Brahmans*, p. 39.)

55. Lakshmibai Tilak, *I Follow After: An Autobiography*, tr. by E. Josephine Inkster, London, Oxford University Press, 1950, pp. 65–66.

56. Ramabai Ranade, *Reminiscences*, pp. 21–23.

57. *Ibid.*, p. 28.

58. *Ibid.*, p. 34.

59. *Ibid.*, p. 38.

60. *Ibid.*, p. 39.

61. *Ibid.*, pp. 29–30.

62. *Ibid.*, p. 49.

63. *Ibid.*, pp. 39–40.

64. *Ibid.*

65. *Ibid.*, p. 40.

66. *Ibid.*, p. 126.

67. *Ibid.*, pp. 105–107.

68. *Ibid.*, p. 107.

70. *Ibid.*

71. Philip Corrigan and Derek Sayer, *Great Arch*, 1985, p. 6, cited in Himani Banerji, 'Mothers and Teachers', p. 5.

72. Ramabai Ranade, *Reminiscences*, p. 47.

73. Rosalind O'Hanlon, *Caste, Conflict and Ideology*, p. 179.

74. Ramabai Ranade, *Reminiscences*, p. 92.

75. Rosalind O'Hanlon, *Caste, Conflict and Ideology*, p. 112; Kashibai Kanitkar was 'required' to read Mill's *Subjection of Women* by her husband as soon as she was literate in English (Y.D. Phadke, *Women in Maharashtra*, p. 23).

76. Ramabai Ranade, *Reminiscences*, p. 91.

77. *Ibid.*, p. 94.

78. *Ibid.*, pp. 54–55.

79. *Ibid.*, pp. 220–24.
80. In her later years Ramabai Ranade may have made up for her obedient and pliant behaviour during her husband's lifetime as she became a supporter of Tilak's militant stance on nationalism which was a contrast to Ranade's moderate position (Susie Tharu and K. Lalitha, *Women Writing in India*, Vol. 1, p. 282). The shift is significant because Tilak in his characteristic style, had even referred to the Reformers as eunuchs like Shikhandi (Wolpert, *Tilak and Gokhale*, p. 37).
81. Ramabai Ranade, *Reminiscences*, p. 97.
82. *Ibid.*, pp. 10–11.
83. One reformer proclaimed that it was 'the female that in India, directly or indirectly, offers the greatest resistance to the cause of social reform (Dayaram Gidumal, *The Status of Women*, p. cviii). Another was of the opinion that it was women who were responsible for early marriage since they were impatient to experience 'the fun of having festivities' (Dayaram Gidumal, *The Status of Women*, p. lxxi).
84. Ramabai Ranade, *Reminiscences*, pp. 49–50, 76, 89–90.
85. *Ibid.*, p. 47.
86. *Ibid.*, pp. 19–22.
87. Tucker, *Ranade*, p. 72.
88. Ramabai Ranade, *Reminiscences*, pp. 24, 41. An important aspect of this text is the conflict between the orthodox father and the reformist son in the Ranade household. The relationship between them was extremely complex and tense and needs further work as a theme since it will reveal a great deal about the relationship *between* men in a patriarchal context.
89. *Ibid.*, pp. 34–36.
90. *Ibid.*, p. 36.
91. *Ibid.*, p. 34.
92. *Ibid.*, p. 36.
93. Durga had been made literate, along with her stepmother, by her father partly to maintain household accounts (*Reminiscences*, p. 47).
94. Ramabai Ranade, *Reminiscences*, p. 21.
95. *Ibid.*, p. 45.
96. *Ibid.*, p. 47.
97. *Ibid.*, p. 48ff. It is important to note that this was the only area where a difference of values is recorded. There would be little difference in other arenas as the upholding of Brahmanical caste norms and endogamous marriages was never under question by the reformers. In this context Ranade's statements that one was unconsciously influenced by the traditions in which one was born, by the very milk drunk at the mother's breast, is an eloquent

reminder that there was a common culture that he and the more orthodox Brahmanas shared (Tucker, *Ranade*, p. 81).

98. *Ibid.*, pp. 48ff, 79ff.
99. *Ibid.*, pp. 40–42.
100. *Ibid.*, p. 100.
101. *Ibid.*, pp. 83ff.
102. *Ibid.*, p. 84.
103. *Ibid.*
104. *Ibid.*, p. 100.
105. *Ibid.*, p. 101.
106. *Ibid.*, p. 89.
107. *Ibid.*, p. 70.
108. *Ibid.*, p. 88.
109. *Ibid.*, p. 108.
110. *Ibid.*, p. 131.
111. *Ibid.*, p. 138.
112. *Ibid.*, p. 197. Ramabai recounts that when she required surgery, causing Ranade great anxiety, Durga made arrangements for a close friend of Ranade's to be present to keep him 'company'. Here she enacts her role as a considerate sister looking after her brother's emotional needs. At the same time the established nature of the conjugal relationship is taken for granted. Ramabai in turn describes how she agreed to Ranade's decision on the proper treatment for her because it was a wife's 'sacred duty to see that her husband had to suffer nothing on her account… That was her highest bliss and her sacred rule.' In an extraordinary role reversal, Ramabai Ranade epitomised the new domestic ideologies by concluding that Ranade would not be able to bear the burden of sorrow if she died first. Therefore if one of them had to go it should be him rather than her. Here was a very new way of looking at widowhood (*Ibid.*, pp. 196–97).
113. *Ibid.*, p. 211.
114. *Ibid.*, pp. 120–22, p. 129.
115. *Ibid.*, p. 110.
116. *Ibid.*; *Bai Mangal v. Bai Rukhmini, ILR*, 23 Bombay 291.
117. Kumkum Sangari, 'Consent, Agency and the Rhetorics of Incitement', p. 873.
118. G.S. Sardesai, 'Excerpts from Mai's Diary', in D.D. Karve, *The New Brahmans*, pp. 120–21.
119. *Ibid.*, pp. 121–22.
120. *Ibid.*, p. 120.
121. *Ibid.*, p. 119.
122. Ramabai Ranade, *Reminiscences*, pp. 76, 84, 90.

5

On Widowhood: The Critique of Cultural Practices in Women's Writing

Much historical writing on the nineteenth century has looked at what impelled social reform, why men were inspired to intervene in social processes, and how action on these was executed on various fronts. Since social reform was for many years synonymous with the widow reform movement, the issue of the 'status' of the widow has almost been overworked in writing. This has produced a striking imbalance because we know very little of what women, especially widows, had to say on the subject of widowhood. I propose to look here at the writings of women.[1] As women were drawn into literacy and education to school them to be companionate wives and fitting mothers, they began to use their newly acquired skills to articulate their understanding of the 'status' of women, and especially the 'plight' of the child widow among the upper castes. It is important to take note of the issues highlighted by them not merely to expand the arena of our concerns but to shift the attention of history from 'knowledge' about widowhood produced by men to the experience of widowhood as described by women.

The sample of women's writing that I present below is representative rather than exhaustive and the focus is more on unpublished or lesser-known material but it is supported by some of the writing of women which feminist scholars have begun to take note of in recent years. I am, however, not dealing with the writings of women, whether known or unknown, who consented to traditional cultural practices in relation to widowhood, i.e., to women like Durga and the unnamed older women in Ramabai Ranade's household, or Parvati Athavale's mother (see below), because my interest in this work lies in the formation of a critique of enforced widowhood and the extant forms of Brahmanical patriarchal practices. And finally, since women's writing was both describing the experience of widowhood and also outlining the structure of relations in which that experience may be located, the purpose of this chapter is to present the writing of women *and* draw out its implications.

The reformist discourse on widowhood, especially on the miseries of the child widow (outlined in Chapter Two), had become widely influential by the late nineteenth century in western India. The body of writing in journals and pamphlets by those engaged in the widow 'remarriage' movement, some of which was extremely impassioned, was supported by the publication of the first novels in Marathi: Baba Padmanji's *Yamuna Paryatan* (*The Journey of Yamuna*) and H.N. Apte's *Pan Lakshyant Kon Gheto* (*But Who Cares*).[2] Both dealt with oppressive practices for women, climaxed by widowhood, but the latter in particular was widely influential because of its graphic and moving portrayal of the experiences of a young widow whose attempts at retaining her dignity are cruelly terminated by her forcible tonsure. But although these writings were crucial in drawing attention to the young widow's plight it is important to recognise that the male reformist discourse was essentially a humanist rhetoric which was confined to a description of the oppressive cultural practices that spelt the social death of the upper-caste widow. The analysis of men had in the main concentrated on the place of custom and the 'aberrations' of tradition,[3] rather than the structural elements in which the upper-caste widows' social death was located. Male writing had tended also to exonerate religion, and to carefully distinguish custom from religion. Most significantly, there was a complete silence on the crucial issue of the material and ideological arrangements of Brahmanical patriarchy which underpinned the practices associated with widowhood among the upper castes.[4]

From the sample of writing presented below it will be evident that women absorbed the humanist rhetoric but, in important ways, added to it and went far beyond it. From their accounts we can see that as women were being schooled to perform their roles in the transformed patriarchies of the emerging classes in the late nineteenth century, and even as they were schooled to provide consent to the new ideologies, they also resisted the limitations of the ideologies to lay bare the full range of oppressive practices imposed upon all women, but particularly upon widows. They used their skills of reading and writing to intervene in debates which often bypassed them or were conducted by men on their behalf. There is a sense in which they went public in a variety of ways, from expressing themselves in essays written in schools to writing to the newspapers and even publishing full-length monographs on the oppression of women. What is significant is that, almost always, the motivation for writing came from the miseries of widowhood among the upper castes but the actual writing then went far beyond this to provide an embryonic critique of patriarchal power.

A typical example of women writing on widowhood is a prize-winning essay by Sushila Devi[5] who combines the liberal reformist position on the problem of widowhood, concerns about widows being led 'astray', and the conventional solutions for widowhood with a sensitive rendering of the anguished relationships between mothers and daughters, and the ambivalent relations between mothers-in-law, daughters-in-law and the wider community of female kin. The core of the essay, written in 1907, is set as a narrative of a young girl who is married at nine to a 'mature adult male of 40'. Immediately thereafter the new bride gets a taste of her changed status as she is broken into the 'distrust system' in which a man is always represented by the older womenfolk as a wolf in sheep's clothing and always to be shunned. The woman is made out to be still worse in this system. She is a 'burning fire' so dangerous that to glance at one, even during the day, causes destruction to man.[6]

Since she is too young for the marriage to be consummated the girl is described as being forcibly 'ripened' by the mother-in-law, who feeds her well with 'cream and curds', like 'fattening a pigeon before the kill'. But when the girl is widowed everyone's overriding concern is with the inability of the beautiful and youthful widow to keep her widowhood 'sacred'. The surveillance of the women begins at the funeral itself. As they mourn the death of the husband the female mourners begin to recount the misdeeds and lapses of other widows. The poor mother of the widow is so pained by the 'distrust system', and the idea that female nature is more evil than good, so ingrained in the Hindu mind (an obvious reference to the notion of strisvabhava of the Brahmanical texts), that she begins to feel that it would have been better if the widowed daughter had died when she was born.[7] Sushila Devi's description of the mother's feelings provides us with an intuitive decoding of the 'consent' of women to patriarchal practices.

Transformed into a household drudge, always at the beck and call of others in the house, the widow is the first to rise and the last to retire. For the mother-in-law who had 'nourished' the daughter-in- law only a while ago the girl now becomes a viper. 'To harbour a young widow is like cherishing a viper. One does not know when it may sting the hand that gives it milk,' says the mother-in-law repeatedly. Finally it is only death (through neglect and overwork) that brings peace to the anguished widow. For everyone else the widow's death is a relief,[8] especially since the family honour of both households, the natal and the affinal, has been upheld through a 'sacred' widowhood.

Sushila Devi's prize-winning essay, which relies heavily on the narrative style to capture the experience of widowhood, drops this style and adopts a pragmatic stance when it proceeds to outline solutions. According to her, child widows in India are comparable to the 'old maids' or 'spinsters' of Europe who have been unable to find husbands; she suggests that the lives of child widows can be made 'pleasant' and 'endurable' through a cultivation of the mind and of their artistic skills. Education of women, especially widows, is thus crucial. Through it widows can escape 'drudge labour' and become productive, useful members of society.[9]

What is notable about Sushila Devi's essay is that she is acutely aware of the cross-currents in Hindu society on the issue of widow remarriage. Realising that while some reformers are in favour of the marriage of widows, most upper-caste Hindus are strongly opposed to it, and that consequently not enough men are coming 'forward' to marry widows, she herself advises that the happiness of widows should not be staked solely on remarriage. Finally, she argues for a return to the spaces women were believed to have had as *Brahmavadinis* (women scholars, versed in the *Brahman*) in Vedic India.[10] Sushila Devi thus simultaneously evokes a double image of control, one traditional, the ancient renunciatory model, the other the educated, creative existence prevalent in the west, which enables the assertion of a developed self-control and releases energy for a useful purpose for the benefit of society. From her account of 'spinsters' in the west and Brahmavadinis in ancient India and the degraded status of widows in the nineteenth century, it is evident that Sushila Devi is advocating a careful handling of the 'problem' of widowhood, skilful cultivation of the self through education and useful industry, thus granting a limited agency to widows who would conduct themselves with propriety and win the respect of their society.[11] This position, that widows could in a sense 'sublimate' their sexuality, pre-figures Gandhi and was an important strand in the 'nationalist' resolution of widowhood. The widows' energies here get channelised into serving the nation.

Much more polemical and hard-hitting is the analysis of Tarabai Shinde who wrote *Stri Purusha Tulana* in 1882.[12] Tarabai's father was a member of Jyotiba Phule's Satyashodhak Samaj and was prominent in non-Brahmana politics, but Tarabai herself made only a single venture into the public domain when she published her critique of patriarchal double standards. Tarabai's work is unique for its style and the quality of its polemics. The text itself was written in reaction to a criminal case involving a young Brahmana widow, Vijayalakshmi, who was charged with murdering her 'illegitimate' infant at birth. The sessions court sentenced her to hang for moral depravity although the higher courts took a more lenient view and commuted the sentence to transportation for life. Vijayalakshmi's case was widely discussed with strong views being expressed, mostly by men.[13]

Tarabai was the only woman who intervened in this discussion with *Stri Purusha Tulana* but the text she wrote went far beyond the immediate circumstances of the trial, and the predicament of widows, to take on patriarchal practices itself. Tarabai's work begins with a lambasting of the position that only women's bodies were 'home to all kinds of vices', a stock theme in male writing from the Brahmanical texts onwards but now given a hysterical edge through the circumstances of the Vijayalakshmi case. Because the entire focus of the attack was on the poor widow and not on the man who fathered the child, Tarabai asks pointedly, 'Or have men got the same faults as are found in women?' She thus contests head on the position held from the time of Manu that women are innately lascivious and sinful,[14] a position that continued to have wide currency in the nineteenth century as is evident from Tarabai's opening statements.

Tarabai's account of widowhood and of the double standards of men with regard to it is scathing:

Once women have lost their position as wives they have to hide their faces and spend the rest of their lives shut away in a dark corner. So why don't you hide your faces when your wives have died, shave off your beards and mustaches and go off and live in the wilderness for the rest of your lives? Oh no not you! One wife dies and you just get in another on the 10th day itself.[15]

Describing the travails of widowhood Tarabai attributes them squarely to men by addressing them as the perpetrators:

Once a woman's husband has died not even a dog would swallow what she's got to. What's in store for her? The barber comes to shave all the curls and hair off just to cool your eyes. All her ornaments are taken away ... She's stripped and exposed in all sorts of ways as if she belonged to no one; she becomes a widow-pot hidden in the corner. She's shut out from going to wedding receptions women go to — And why all these restrictions? Because her husband has died![16]

According to Tarabai men were directly responsible for the social codes which oppressed widows. But more importantly they are culpable on the count of sexually enticing the widow. Tarabai's version of the fall of widows and the trap they are led into is thus described from the woman's standpoint; it springs, according to Tarabai, from the woman's gullibility and desire to be loved. Tarabai differentiates between the emotion of love, the fulfilment of which women seek, and men's emotions, which are confined to lusting after women, seeking pleasure and taking no responsibility for the consequences. This accounts for women like Vijayalakshmi going wrong:

Even when women do horrible bold things they're still better than you. First of all you find all sorts of ways to get her captivated. Then once you've got her she puts complete trust in you and begins to love you ... she deserts her stridharma, the most priceless jewel she has in this world and offers her life to you. How is she to understand your dirty tricks? How long does this love of yours last? Till your lust is satisfied. When she is pregnant you throw all the misery and responsibility upon her and go into hiding... There's this poor doe, her face like death under the burden when she goes to ask that tiger of a man what to do; he'll answer as if he's respectability itself 'What do you mean what should we do? You did it, you take the consequences ...' What can the poor woman do? In the end she gives up in despair. To save her honour she even gets herself an abortion. She takes up her bundle of shame and goes off to prison. Some women take their lives, others go into exile....[17]

In Tarabai's view the miseries of enforced widowhood and the lapses of the widows from stridharma are attributable to the structures men have created and the advantage they can take even of the enforced celibacy of widows. But what is notable is that despite her direct contest with patriarchal norms Tarabai does not outline alternatives which would help women step out of marriage altogether, nor does she explicitly argue the case for economic independence. She exhorts men to be courageous to enable widows to remarry and to treat them with affection. Since remarriage was contingent upon men rising to the occasion, Tarabai challenges men to live up to the 'heroic self-images' they have created for themselves. She says, 'Seeing as you're such almighty heroes why is it so impossible for you to pull widows out of this pit of shame? Why can't you break some caste rules, put the *kumkuma* back on their foreheads and let them enjoy the happiness of marriage again?'[18]

Tarabai's agenda for widowhood is linked to her understanding of women, and the kind of marriage they are seeking; she argues for an ideal, loving marital relationship in the place of an unequal one. But at the same time in her bitter tirades against men she even seeks governmental intervention in order to 'discipline' them.[19] Throughout *Stri Purusha Tulana* she simultaneously exposes men and shames them as well as appeals to them to make a better world for women. Her polemic resists and contests that of men, creating a dissonance on all issues but particularly with regard to the sensual nature of women. She shares the reformist view of some men on the need for widow marriage (while exposing their complacency and cowardice in not going far enough). Unlike the male reformers she does not confine widow marriage only to child widows. In Tarabai's view all widows require a home and a husband to love.[20] Thus she rejects unambiguously the social and sexual death of widows. However, she confines the recovery of the widow from social death only to a social personhood as contained within marriage. Tarabai successfully exposes patriarchy but is not quite successful in conceptualising an alternative to it. Nevertheless her critique was one of the most important pieces of writing on gender in the nineteenth century, indeed a unique one that dismantled male discourse on women and widowhood and provided an alternative. Such a discourse was bound to be marginalised. Tarabai did not write anything else for the rest of her life. What she had written was bitterly criticised[21] and was concealed from public view.

While Tarabai's polemical and impassioned critique was marginalised, women's voices could not be completely stifled. Between 1884 and 1891, as a fierce debate raged in western India in particular over the custom of child marriage and enforced widowhood, an important intervention in the discussion was made by a woman who clearly sought anonymity by writing under the pseudonym of 'a Hindu Lady'. This debate had originated, as we saw earlier, in Behram Malabari's initiative in seeking the opinions of a wide cross-section of people. What is important for us here is that it was restricted operatively only to men in order to suggest legislation on increasing the age of marriage, especially for girls. Malabari had sought submissions from various 'public' figures across India including Ranade, Mandlik, Bhandarkar, Phule, and a large number of men from the professional class.[22] The absence of women from this 'public' discussion is striking, particularly when we recall that by the early 1880s women's forums such as the Arya Mahila Samaj were in existence. Further, the Hunter Commission had sought the opinion of women who had testified before it on what they looked forward to in a new educational programme. Among the women who had testified was Pandita Ramabai[23] but, most importantly, by 1882 Tarabai had already published her scathing attack on male power, social customs, and the oppression of women. The absence of women who could speak for themselves rather than have men speak for them is notable. It can only be read as evidence of nineteenth century men's reluctance to concede agency to women, thereby consigning them to be the subjects of a discourse in which men almost had a natural right to decide their fate by virtue of their concern for them.

It is not as if women did not want to speak. Tarabai's work is a permanent testimony to the desire of women to speak on their own behalf and contest the point of view that men were projecting. Ramabai was writing, speaking and travelling across the globe in order to communicate her understanding of the oppression of Hindu women as well as a need for change. Kashibai Kanitkar had written her essay titled 'Women: Past and Present' which was published in the *Subodh Patrika* in 1881 and by 1884 she had begun writing her first novel *Rangarao*.[24] Thus there was a climate in which women wanted to speak to men and women around them, using every available form of communication, and yet they were not being included in the public discourses of the time.

It is in this context that two letters to the *Times of India* in May and September 1885 by the 'Hindu Lady' assume significance. This Hindu Lady was Rakhmabai who, as we know, was in 1885 already embroiled in a court case as she was contesting the practice of child marriage and the burdensome obligations it imposed upon women. Perhaps it was because she was already the subject of a dispute that she sought anonymity for her viewpoint, or perhaps it was because the reformers regarded women as having no opinion of their own and left them out of the public debates, and she wished to communicate what was an informed opinion based on personal experience.

Something of this tension between women like Rakhmabai, Tarabai, and Pandita Ramabai and the 'Reformers' comes through in all their writing. Rakhmabai's first letter[25] more or less opens with the sense of betrayal at the apathy and the lack of moral courage among people which makes real reform so difficult, and the rest of the letter is punctuated with similar sentiments.[26] Her own account is a contrast to the submissions made by the reformers to Malabari, even the testimony of her stepfather, because she describes what child marriage has meant for her personally. And because she wrote from experience, although the letter she sent to the *Times of India* in June 1885 was supposed to be about child marriage *and* enforced widowhood, she never managed to get down to the subject of enforced widowhood, having so much to say on the issue of child marriage. She then wrote a separate letter on enforced widowhood a few months later.

Rakhmabai outlines the distinctive ways in which the custom of child marriage affects women, even though she recognises that both men and women are affected by Hindu social customs. In her view, these customs did not burden men with half the difficulties they entailed for women because marriage did not impose any insuperable 'obstacles' in the course of their studies. Here she dwells upon a crucial aspect of child marriage which relates to the loss of power that affects only women, in making decisions regarding education following marriage. This loss of power was of fundamental importance to Rakhmabai as it meant the loss of both mental and physical freedom for the girl. Whatever possibilities a girl might retain with respect to learning even after marriage, were she to have a liberal husband or in-laws, are however abruptly terminated when the girl begins the reproductive cycle of childbirths, most often when she is fourteen.

Rakhmabai deals at some length with the power relations in the household of the in-laws as the full complement of oppressive practices are operative here. Unpaid labour is extracted from the daughter-in-law who is worse off than the servant because the daughter-in-law has no bargaining power. And despite her parents being her natural guardians she is abandoned by them as they will not provide support to her once she is married. Rakhmabai also describes the use of physical violence as part of the disciplining process which operates within the affinal family to ensure she becomes a compliant member of the new household. Her insightful description includes a recognition that the young husband, should he wish to intervene, is unable to do so because he himself is not a free agent as he is as yet economically dependent on his family. If he is not sympathetic he, of course, joins in the oppression.

Hindu women were thus, in Rakhmabai's opinion, worse off than beasts on the one hand and playthings and objects of enjoyment on the other, unceremoniously thrown away when their temporary use was over. She is particularly pungent when she turns her attention to the relationship between women's oppression, social customs and Shastric sanction. Since all the writers of the Shastras were men they have produced 'knowledge' which ensures that women are believed by men to be 'unclean' but yet created specifically for their gratification and special service. This 'knowledge' about women which devalues them has led to women devaluing themselves.

On a personal note, Rakhmabai describes how child marriage has destroyed the happiness of her life as it obstructs what she prizes above everything else — study and mental cultivation. That this viewpoint, which Rakhmabai represents through her obstinate refusal to consummate her marriage, is unique, is evident when she separates women from men, even supposedly sympathetic men who 'cannot in the least understand the wretchedness we Hindu women have to endure'. No wonder then that women would have to turn to the government, given the narrowness of the social reform base and the isolation of people like Malabari. Since the opposition to reform was so vocal, by the 1880s Rakhmabai, who was clearly monitoring the formation of 'public' opinion, was also deeply disappointed that the leaders of the Hindu community, instead of being aroused to a sense of their duty, had dashed the hopes of women like Rakhmabai to pieces. Painfully aware of the display of anti-reform sentiments of the Hindu community, Rakhmabai recognises in her letter to the *Times of India* that the government would be most 'chary to pass a law if the very community for whose welfare the law has to be enacted protested it so strongly'. She thus recognises the limits of the government's reformist agenda. There is a circularity of argument here but it does not reflect the limitations of Rakhmabai's analytical ability as much as an understanding of the overwhelming odds against women. But even as she recognises these odds, Rakhmabai rejects as specious the arguments of Mandlik and other nationalists that it is humiliating to ask for help from the government and that it endangers 'our freedom of action'. She also demolishes the argument of the anti-reformers that a few educated persons cannot decide for the people as a whole by pointing out that when Manu drew up his celebrated code he was working in similar circumstances. Manu's code, she thus suggests, had emanated from as restricted a social group as the reformist legislations being recommended in the nineteenth century.

Rakhmabai concludes her letter on child marriage by suggesting certain legal measures which are comprehensive, far-reaching, and bold in their conceptualisations, following the proposals of Malabari in spirit. The first, and most strikingly personal, provides an exit for women like her by suggesting that 'any marriage' performed without the sanction of the government, if disputed within a certain period, should be null and void. The boldness of her suggestions is cloaked before and after by conventional statements that women often make, such as the difficulties of a young unknown girl like her attempting to draft legislation which would affect the 'whole country'. But what is significant is that she claims the authority to proceed with making recommendations because as someone who has experienced misery and has had her life destroyed by the evil custom of child marriage, she cannot rest till she carries her appeal to the government on behalf of the young men and women of India. And because most women have not intervened in the public debate it is important not to read their silence as assent or infer from it that women do not suffer as a consequence of the 'evil' customs. Breaking the silence of women,

Rakhmabai made her appeal not merely on her own behalf but also on behalf of 'my suffering sisters' as she put it. Addressing the 'gentlemen' dominating society she said:

Because you *cannot* [emphasis added] enter our feelings do not think we are satisfied with the life of drudgery that we live, and that we have no taste for, and aspiration after, a higher life...[27]

This in essence was Rakhmabai's position; women too aspired to mental and physical freedom, study and mental cultivation. These represented a higher life which domesticity and early motherhood made impossible. She was convinced that the regeneration of India that the men desired and was being associated superficially with material progress was actually contingent upon the regeneration of the Indian people, particularly the coming generations. That would ensure that India would revert to its once proud position, its old lost glory.

In her second letter on widowhood, published in the *Times of India*[28] a few months later, Rakhmabai used a mixture of sarcasm, allusions to medieval forms of barbarism, and devastating irony in critiquing the discourse of the anti-reformers as she outlined the degradation of Hindu widowhood. What is most striking however is that her critique is based on the experience of widowhood among the upper castes, especially Brahmanas, not the practices prevalent among the Sutars, certainly not the experiences of her own mother. It appears that Rakhmabai identified herself with a certain class, and within that a specific reformist circle — something that may have been typified by the women in the Arya Mahila Sabha. On the whole the letter is suggestive of the way in which women absorbed the reformist discourse (with all its limitations) but inscribed it indelibly with the stamp of their own insight which came from *feeling* the oppressiveness of being a woman. Rakhmabai's letter addresses certain questions which do not normally appear in the writing of nineteenth century men on the subject of widowhood. However, these issues are often a response to the 'popular' opinion on women and widowhood which were crucial components of the existing beliefs and ideologies of Brahmanical patriarchy. For example, a stock argument which had the sanction of the Shastras and was kept alive by the shastris was that men were 'pure by nature', and if necessary could be purified by penance. In contrast women were 'by nature unclean' and must therefore be rightly debarred from anything sacred.[29] Rakhmabai cites this widely prevalent opinion and notes that while her 'educated countrymen' will not use these puerile arguments in public they hold them privately. What surprises Rakhmabai is how men never question these opinions even though they ought to know that since these 'dicta were formulated by men they were of necessity one sided'. As far as Rakhmabai is concerned there is little doubt that since it was men who constructed women as inherently bad they did so because this would legitimise their having privileges and women being denied basic rights.

Thus, for Rakhmabai, a double standard of morality between men and women was a consequence of men monopolising legislative and religious power which they used to their own advantage, and their representation of women as inherently bad was essential to legitimising the double standards. Most men, in Rakhmabai's view, accepted the brutal injustice against Hindu widows, while they themselves quickly remarried, even if they had something of 'that unconvenient commodity' called a 'conscience', because the Shastras and shastris had naturalised a dual set of practices as following from the distinctive nature of women.

Rakhmabai classifies widowhood into different categories based on the age at which women enter widowhood and the differences in the manner in which they experience and cope with it. This distinction is important to Rakhmabai because one of the points on which she takes issue with the shastris (or the religious law-givers as she calls them) is that they have dictated the *same* practices upon widows regardless of whether they are six or sixty. Thus, children who do not know what wifehood is must experience the tortures of widowhood — torture which she compares with the Inquisition, except that the tortures of the Inquisition are temporary. Since, on the other hand women live under a permanent Inquisition the tortures of widowhood end only with the death of the widow. While the system of oppression is dictated by the 'butcher-priests', the agents of the persecution, the perpetrators of the social exclusion imposed on the widow are the members of her 'own' family. Widows are consigned to perform menial work, subjected to rigid austerities, live on coarse fare and all this is a consequence of their economic vulnerability as 'dependents' of their relatives.

One of the striking features of Rakhmabai's analysis of widowhood is the manner in which she 'deconstructs' the ideologies by which a Hindu woman laments her daughter's birth, but particularly what makes her wish her daughter dead when her son-in-law dies. When the child widow appeals to her mother at the agonies she is subjected to her mother answers:

My darling, you were married to a very rich husband when you were four years old. But consequences of your guilt in your former life have pursued you here and therefore you have lost your husband. The joy and happiness of this world is therefore shut out to you. Misery is your lot. You must never think of taking part in the world and its joys. Your life must be therefore devoted to the observance of fasts and the practices of austerities. Do therefore darling follow thy husband...[30]

These statements from the mother come not because the mother does not feel the anguish of her daughter but because this is the only explanation she has and the only comfort she can offer the young widowed daughter.

The mother's feelings and the manner in which ideology is extended by women, the apparent consent they provide but the reality behind what we may mistakenly read as complicity are linked in Rakhmabai's writing to her perception of most women as effectively having no choice and no agency. This is in contrast to the manner in which she represents men as they rehearse similar arguments to their young daughters and granddaughters. Although the statements they make are similar to the ones the mothers make, men, even old men, quickly remarry (even before the ten conventional days of mourning are over) and yet are 'philosophically' rigid in the cases of widowed daughters or granddaughters. But because these men are implicated in the double standards that they perpetuate even their similar statements have a different ideological edge to them. In Rakhmabai's words the 'affectionate' father consoles his daughter:

My darling, fate has ordained this widowhood for you and what human effect can upset the decree of fate! This is punishment for the sins of your previous birth and you can only expiate your sins by a life of austerity and devotion. Give up, dear, *the vanities of this world* [emphasis added], and live a life of purity and preserve the reputation of your family.[31]

Thus while the father lives in this world he exhorts his widowed daughter to be 'in the world but not of the world'. Apart from conscious perpetuation of an ideology which gives the male privileges that it denies women it is significant that Rakhmabai represents the men as evoking family honour.[32] Men share in the construction and perpetuation of patriarchal ideologies, women are its subjects in Rakhmabai's understanding.

Rakhmabai also deconstructs the statements of a renowned champion of Hinduism, one of the foremost leaders credited with much wisdom and keen judgement, and reveals its ideological underpinnings:

The patriot seems to have lost himself completely when this gentleman held forth for the pure and noble life which widows of India led and which, if my memory serves me right at this distance of time, was in his opinion such a balm to their souls, such an incentive to self-abnegation, that widowhood was more a blessing than a misfortune from a spiritual point of view...[33]

Rakhmabai tells the reader that she cannot understand how this patriot's 'keen judgement' can comprehend only one aspect of the question. The 'dry light of his cold philosophy' is unmoved by the wails of the widows which have failed to reach the heart of this gentleman who has however publicly insisted that justice must be done to the 'people of India'. She implies that the patriot's notion of people does not include women and she herself has used the letters column to speak publicly on behalf of her 'sisters', the Hindu widows, whom she describes as 'unbeloved of God and despised of man — a social pariah and a domestic drudge'[34] — and exhorts the government to intervene through legislation to end their miseries.

II

In contrast to the men and women who wrote about widowhood from outside the framework of experience the writing of the widows themselves was deeply personalised rather than polemical. A set of essays written in 1910[35] by young widows of the fifth and sixth form[36] at the Widows' Home in Poona is significant for the insight it gives us into the *feelings* of widows in contrast to *knowledge* about them. The collection is illustrative of the easy slide that occurs in the essays between widows as objects and widows as subjects; the form of the writing itself reflects the difficulty of maintaining a distinction between the two when the writer is herself a widow.

Some of these accounts begin in the third person. But when it comes to emotional passages recounting the sufferings of the widow they slip into the first person. For example Radhabai Inamdar begins her essay with, 'There is no humane heart which will not feel for a widow ...' She sustains the use of the third person for the bulk of the essay but shifts to the first person in the middle with 'There is no end to the tale of "us" miserable widows ... Our cries have no value.' She returns to a more objective expression when she speaks of each person needing someone to listen to their tale of misery but falls again into the first person when expressing the anguish of 'us widows who are in the slough of despondency and the bog of widowhood who will die like vermin if we are not lifted out of the bog'. Finally she exclaims piteously: 'We are now the waste products of the world, let it be put to good use. Our industry will add wealth to the country.'[37]

Even those widows who did not actually slip into the first person were not writing about widowhood as an object of analysis but of widowhood as the subject of experience; in writing about themselves the dominant emotion they express is of being entrapped, a situation that no one else really cared about. 'But who cares?' was a continuous refrain.[38] Believing that no one cared convinced the widows that only those who had experienced widowhood could know how miserable it was.

Radhabai Inamdar for example used Tukaram's verses to illustrate her conviction that the experience of widowhood was so unique and incomprehensible that no one who was not a widow could understand what it was like to be one. Language itself was incapable of expressing the experience of widowhood. Tukaram's metaphor came closest to expressing the inexpressible — 'How a fish can sleep under water can only be learnt by being born a fish'; similarly, 'we widows alone can realise the pain,' says Radhabai.[39]

Struggling painfully to express the inexpressible, the widows nevertheless movingly describe the vulnerability, the lack of dignity and personhood of the widow, and her dependence upon others who have the power to humiliate her. These were experiences that the widows felt were unique to their own lives, the pain that others could not even imagine. What is ironical is that while the widow experienced, in their view, an 'excess' of pain, they were regarded by others as if they were not human at all but like a 'stone without feeling and without emotion'. Harper's description of a widow as a lifeless thing, an 'it' or an animal (*prani*) may be recalled here.[40] Widows were routinely spoken of as if they did not exist;

derogatory references would be made to them by others in their presence without the slightest concern for their feelings.[41]

The abject and powerless situation of the high-caste widow was continually reiterated through everyday expressions of power such as a routine subjection to verbal 'lashings',[42] denial of adequate food,[43] surveillance, performance of drudge labour, and even physical assaults.[44] What made the upper-caste widow's condition so precarious and put her in the power and control of others was her 'dependence' on these very people, particularly if she had no son. In western India, unlike Bengal where the widow had tenuous rights in the husband's property during her lifetime, she had no control at all over coparcenary property. The Mitakshara system merely granted her a vague notion of maintenance: the widow supposedly had some kind of a right to food, clothing, and shelter, contingent upon 'good' behaviour.[45] Whether this was actually enforceable under the pre-colonial Peshwai needs to be explored but that the lack of a definite notion of rights led to incidents of sati is suggested in the Peshwai offering pensions to the relatives of widows to maintain them, a practice briefly supported by the early colonial state in western India.[46]

In any case, questions of law in the context of widowhood among the upper castes seem to be less relevant than the prevalence of social and cultural norms. This is strikingly evident in the essays of the widows in the Poona Home. The fact that they focus so much on a perceived sense of deprivation of the basic survival needs of food, clothing, and shelter is important. Questions of legal title hardly figure; what does appear in their writing is actual practices flowing from social and cultural norms about widowhood.

In reading the essays of the widows it might be useful to explore the concept of entitlements.[47] This could be a key to understanding the way in which they perceived themselves and their ambiguous location in the household where they were being sheltered. Here, the concept needs to be looked at both in its objective material form and the cultural values that perpetuate differential entitlements, even within the same gender, in the same household.

To begin with, as Sen has pointed out, the concept of entitlement is typically legal whereas household distribution is typically not governed by law. Nevertheless, Sen has convincingly argued the case for extending the concept to be used for distribution within the household.[48] The case for social and cultural norms with respect to entitlement is relevant for all women but is especially so for the widow. Since widows were regarded, even in the law, as having only a claim to 'maintenance' the question of how much of the resources they actually got, is crucial — especially to the sense of worth that accompanied it. As Papanek suggests, entitlements to food, etc., within the household represent the social consensus about the value of specific categories of persons as expressed in the norms governing 'who gets what and why'. In the case of the widow we may put it better as 'who does not get what and why'. Ideas about entitlement are clearly part of a larger cultural 'repertoire' containing many other ideas about the relative value of persons; they constitute a part of a system of beliefs about distributional justice.[49] The widow's lowest allocation within the household is an outcome of her social dispensability and of her marginal status therein.

Cultural ideas about widowhood in upper-caste Hindu society enhance the power of the family to make minimal allocations to the widow. Ideas about entitlement to the widow are also linked to ideas about self-deprivation for religious reasons. The low entitlement of the widow is thus not merely culturally sanctioned but also sanctified in spiritual terms since she is meant to fast often, pursue the ascetic model and devote herself to the memory of her dead husband. Ideas about self-sacrifice and self-restraint, which in any case are widely prevalent with regard to women, are redoubled in the case of Hindu widows, and they play a crucial role in formulating an ideology of low or minimal entitlement to the widow. These points may be borne in mind in the description of widowhood provided by the widows in their essays.

From the accounts of the widows at the Widows' Home in Poona it is apparent that those who 'sheltered' or maintained the widow did so on sufferance rather than in accordance with any respect for the widows' right to entitlements. There are repeated references to the widows as 'burdens'; widows were made to feel that by their continued existence they were eating into resources which 'belonged' to others and which they were not entitled to.[50]

The question of who should or who did maintain the widow in Maharashtra was also conditioned by personal behaviour and the circumstances of individual families rather than a close adherence to legal provision. Widows often stayed on in their natal families especially if they had been widowed before they had made a formal entry into the husband's home. If the in-laws never came to collect her after the death of their son there does not appear to have been any way that the natal family could ensure the maintenance of the sonless widow by the affinal family. In such a situation, the widow might stay on in her natal family but she could be on sufferance here too.

Nevertheless, widows did make a distinction between their affinal and natal kinsfolk. Sakhubai Apte wrote that parents often suffered more than their widowed young daughters who were probably too young to comprehend what it meant to be a widow. But Sakhubai also recognised that once the child widow became an adult, the natal family's attitude to her often changed. Henceforth the family considered that in the widow they had got 'a servant to work for them', even though they continued to feel sorry for her.[51]

The perceived lack of status of the widow in her father's house is described by Sakhubai:

If her married sisters come to visit the parents they are treated like guests while the widow is made to 'toil' for them ... Even her sisters do not help her. Her brothers and their wives taunt her. In the absence of her parents the poor widow becomes the slave of her sisters-in-law. Even loving brothers begin disrespecting her...[52]

It is evident from some of the essays that the natal household was not necessarily a more comfortable or welcoming place than that of her affinal family. But if her condition was so precarious in her natal home, according to Radhabai, it was 'ten-fold' worse in her father-in-law's house.[53] Sakhubai recognised that in the father-in-law's house people had 'full power over the widow'. Everybody treated her not only as drudge labour but also as the cause of the husband's death and the source of their misfortune.[54] According to Radhabai:

There is not a particle of feeling for her in that house. She is treated like a low class maid servant. She has to spend the whole of her life in servitude to her sisters-in-law. If she dies, even in the midst of such low and hard work, people are glad of it. As a widow a woman is unclaimed property. She has no value...[55]

The widow's dependence on others for her physical survival was evident from her sense of helplessness: she had no alternative that she could see. She had to submit to her fate like 'a cow in the hands of a butcher',[56] an analogy used by our essayists repeatedly, and bear the insults and humiliation of a life of ceaseless labour in return for the maintenance provided to her. Drudge labour, extracted from the widows, is a *leitmotif* in the writing of the widows:

A widow is worked like a menial... if she but stops for a few minutes, just to take a breath her mother-in-law throws a volley of abuses, intermixed with filthy accusations...[57]

She does not get her two meals a day ... She is made to work like a coolie.[58] After her husband's death a widow does not get sufficient food and clothes; if poor she has to work near the fire in the kitchen... she is overworked like a slave from Africa.[59]

The accounts of the widows suggest that the widow's association with labour, in part the labour all women performed, was perceived as harder and more menial than that of other women. The phrase 'like a low-class servant'[60] is expressive and was a likely outcome not just of the labour performed but of power relations within the family which reduced the widow to a more abject and degraded status than other women. Further, the fact that the widow's labour was demanded by, and rendered to, others (in a household which the widow could not regard as her own) made the performance of such labour more humiliating, causing the widows to see themselves as 'low class maid servants' and 'slaves'.

Other factors added to the quantum of drudgery. Unlike wives, widows were free from birth pollution and from feeding and child-care preoccupations. Wives, subject to both, would be exempt from labouring at particular times. Widows, on the other hand, were always available except for periods of menstrual pollution.[61] Further, because they were excluded from ceremonial and ritual obligations, and even from witnessing such events, the widows felt that there was nothing but ceaseless labour in their lives.

Being without 'encumbrances' and a fixed place in the family, widows were also regarded as 'mobile' labour and could be sent from one household to another as the need arose. From accounts of the Karve household and other nineteenth century biographies it appears that the careers of many professional young men, who came to constitute an important segment of the middle class, were built upon the free labour of the widowed women of their families. These widows were farmed around to labour and manage houses as substitutes for dead wives, or as support labour for young or sickly wives. As more men went to the cities to study and pursue professions, women's labour was needed to make such moves possible; widows in the family were the most expendable and were therefore much in demand. Both Karve and his friend Joshi, who shared common housing, had a succession of widowed relatives to run the kitchen for them.[62]

Thus, while affinal and natal kinsfolk sometimes shunted a widow from one household to another because of their unwillingness to maintain her, it was not uncommon for contesting claims to be made for the labour of the widow. This was the case with Anandibai Karve. Widowed at eight, she stayed on in her natal family for about three years until her in-laws sent for her. Although they said that they regarded her as a substitute for their dead son it was evident that her labour was what was valued.[63] Anandibai's parents were not very happy about sending her but they were poor, and had two other widowed daughters. Anandibai consented to go as it would mean one mouth less to feed, thus relieving some of the pressure on her father.

Anandibai's parents-in-law were economically more stable than her parents but her mother-in-law had had 20 childbirths. Only the first two and the last three had survived but it is likely that the mother-in-law would have been worn out with pregnancies, childbirths and child care. Moreover, she was also asthmatic, so Anandibai took over all the work outside the home. In her own words:

I had seen my parents get work done by day labourers in our orchards and fields and I soon began to supervise similar work in my new home...[64] I did all the minor chores in the house, the preparation for the worship of the gods, cleaning the courtyard, sprinkling a mixture of water and cow dung over it... We had no well; our water supply was from an irrigation channel passing through the compound and I had to get up at 4 o'clock in the morning to fill all the pots with water as otherwise it became muddy because of all the cattle and human beings who crossed it. Sometimes I got very weary of all this work and thought about my parental home and cried. But I also knew that there was no relief possible... Sometime during the first year my husband's brother's wife gave birth to a baby and I had to do much more work than before. The next year when I was twelve I was looking after all the cattle, milking the cows and buffaloes, feeding the bullocks, cooking breakfast for the farmhands and more. I went daily to the fields to supervise the farmhands work and to pluck green grass for the calves and when I came home I had to wash clothes and then clean the dinner plates too. I was busy from early morning till late in the evening.[65]

When Anandibai was about 22 she went home on a special visit to her parents since her elder sister was very ill and found that her widowed brother, Narharpant Joshi, who lived in Bombay and had a small child, required someone to replace his dead wife in the communal kitchen run by Karve.[66] Anandibai's brother was a member of this communal household consisting of 13 or 14 persons. Narharpant had sent a letter to his family from Bombay asking for help and Anandibai was despatched directly from her natal household without seeking her affinal family's 'approval'. Anandibai wrote that she did not know the details of what happened as 'from that day my contact with my parents-in-law ended and I never again went back. I do not know whether they tried to get me back and what my father told them ...'[67]

In Bombay Anandibai continued to labour in different circumstances:

The humid, warm climate was very exhausting. I had to cook for over a dozen people either in the morning or in the evening. In my house, or in the house of my parents-in-law we hardly ever ate *roti*: preparing rice is easy by comparison. But in Bombay roti had to be prepared everyday... I was not very happy in Bombay...[68]

Anandibai also looked after her brother's young son. When Ramabai opened the Sharada Sadan, a home for widows, in 1889, Anandibai joined as a day student. She took her young nephew along with her each day. Anandibai found it difficult to study along with all the housework and childcare, so it was suggested that she join the Sharada Sadan as a boarder. At her brother's residence however her labour could not be spared and at the same time her parents also pressed their claims to it. Feeling cornered, Anandibai finally appealed to Ramabai who, according to Anandibai, 'rose to the occasion'. Realising that there were competing claims for Anandibai's labour, she offered Rs 50 a year to Anandibai's father to enable him to hire a servant so that Anandibai could reside in the school and carry on her studies.[69]

From Anandibai's account it is evident that the labour of the widow was a crucial determinant of where she resided and who 'sheltered' or 'maintained' her. If neither her parents nor her in-laws were willing, or 'able', to maintain her, a widow simply went to work in the house of anyone, including strangers. As Ambubai Bapat said in her essay:

If she [the widow] be the daughter of a rich man he feeds her, if the widow of a rich man his family feeds her, but if both her relations are poor she is forcibly shaved and compelled to become a cook in profession having no means of support.[70]

An unclear notion of a widow's entitlements and an unending life of drudgery were most clearly associated with the sonless widow, but particularly with the child widow. If a widow had a son she could look forward to a time when the son became a shareholder in the property, if he had any, or would take over the support of his widowed mother.[71] But as Harper pointed out in his study of Havik Brahmanas,[72] the sonless widow remained a 'dependent' widow right through her life, 'passing a long term of life in perfect misery', according to Varubai Ranade in her account of widowhood.[73]

Brahmanical patriarchy's conceptualisation of the widow as a woman who was sexually and socially dead[74] but physically alive is reflected in the description of the everyday experiences provided by the widows of the Poona Home. As women who continued to live after the death of their husbands they had to be 'maintained'. But along with, and in return for, such investment in their survival went the full utilisation of their labour. A common charge against the widow, expressive of the relationship between her and those who fed her, was, 'She is a drone, she wants to be fed without doing any work'.[75] Illness among widows, for example, was hardly ever regarded as real and was seen as an excuse to avoid having to work. In the eyes of those who fed them this was a subversion of the unstated code in which the widow provided labour in return for food and shelter.[76]

Along with the recognition of the widow's physical existence was the anomaly of her sexual and social non-existence, unlike other women and men in her household. Widows thus had to be marked off from other women; they had to be shut off from the male gaze and from their own sexuality. The essays of the young girls echo the anomalous position of the widows. Ambubai Bapat describes the condition of the widow without support who is forced to labour in the homes of others and may be seduced by the men of the house:

If both her relations are poor she is forcibly shaved and compelled to become a cook in profession having no means of support. If she be young there is fear of being misled by wicked masters ... Young widows have to pass through the ordeal of chastity, temptations which gods cannot withstand.[77]

To mark widows off from all others in the household, but especially women, they were given a distinctive appearance and an ascetic code which they were required to follow. To safeguard their chastity, measures like eating less, eating cooling foods, fasting often, and sleeping on the floor were prescribed and routinely practised and were meant to reduce their sexual drives. These restrictions reiterate the low entitlement of the widows, completing the circle of material and cultural elements within the same structure. In male discourse ascetic practices were part of cultural tradition, 'the lofty pitch of moral training' of the 'patient and single life' as typified by the widow. It was an institution that the Hindus needed to be proud of, not one to be regretted.[78] However, it is significant that the widows themselves perceived these practices as *deprivations*. According to them the 'widow is *compelled* to fast as often as the calendar will dictate'(emphasis added).[79] Others conveniently regard it as a 'sin to eat two meals a day, or to ask for anything in the world'.[80] Clearly, in the view of the widows these expectations are aspects of normal human behaviour and widows are normal human beings like everyone else.

The most effective means by which the widows' 'virtue' was to be preserved however was not left to ascetic practices, nor the widow's control of her sexuality; it was not left, also, to her good sense, but to a tightly monitored system of surveillance mounted upon her.

The surveillance of the widow was total as it normally involved watching her every moment of the day to ensure that she worked in return for her maintenance, but also so that she did not go 'astray'. It involved subjecting every single action of hers to scrutiny, 'protecting' her virtue and ensuring that she did not 'steal' time. In the widows' own words:

People attribute wicked motives to every one of her actions ... If she but smiles they say it must be with some immoral motive. If she shows unwillingness to have her head shaved they level filthy accusations against her.[81] If she stealthily looks into a mirror her mother chastises her ...[82] If she happens to dress herself she is immediately asked for whom she has been doing this ... If she be late in returning from the river-side where she is sent to wash clothes, she is immediately suspected of immorality and assaulted...[83]

She is closely watched [in case] she speaks of ill treatment to any visitors; children of her husband's brothers are set to guard her. They overhear a word or two and distort the story into a regular complaint against their parents. The poor widow is then taken to task ...[84] If she can read and write and takes a book in her hand just to relieve her mind of all distressing thoughts, she is called shameless. If she adjusts her hair [if unshaven] she is accused of flirtations or the desire to flirt.[85] If there be no work for her, there are mothers-in-law who would mix up rice and dal and ask her to separate them simply to keep her engaged. She must not go out, she must not speak to anybody ...[86]

The policing of the widow at close quarters was done, among others, by the women and children of the household, especially sisters-in-law and their children. This added to the power which other women in the family had over the widow with regard to allotments of food and other basic needs. Such powerful and continuous surveillance was most degrading especially since the widows already regarded themselves as being subject to the male gaze and as victims of the predatory nature of men. The problem thus lay not in the widows but in lascivious men. As one widow wrote:

Owing to her husband's death there remains no support to her. What then? The wicked ones have an excellent opportunity. They covet her; she is in constant fear of these wretched men. She has to protect her reputation, she has to remain moral. She gets confused. She bows her head. 'Oh God to whom shall I go for protection? How shall I save myself? Come oh lord; run quick, do protect this cow from the butcher' ... such is her state of mind... they prefer death ...[87]

It is evident from the accounts of widows that neither ascetic practices nor bodily mortification or surveillance designed to keep their sexuality under check, nor social rules to keep male sexuality in control were considered capable of preventing 'illicit' relationships. The structures of control were completed by the enforced shaving of widows, a sign both of castration and defeminisation.[88] Referring to it as 'that ceremony', widows invariably describe it as *enforced*. To the widows the practice was an assault; it was the most humiliating aspect of their existence, far worse then all the other miseries they experienced. Signifying castration in the symbolic system, it had a most violent effect upon the widow; the physical violation it involved was akin to rape both of the body and the mind. The widows express a whole complex of emotions about their degradation.

The greatest of all miseries, the culmination of the enormities of custom is the forcible shaving of a Brahmana and other high caste widows. The cruel and pernicious custom is horrid beyond conception. [The widow] is simply helpless; she must submit to that cruel inhuman operation. She often faints, she is dumb founded, tears flow in a flood ... but nobody cares. Her caste people think they have achieved a great success as soon as she is disfigured. What demonical work...[89] A widow is not allowed to speak to a male stranger but she is forced to go alone into a closed room to get herself shaved by a low class barber. Bravo to such relations [who force her]. Who can describe her 'happiness' in such a seclusion? She is like a cow in the power of the butcher...[90]

In the southern Maratha country there are many sacred places, among them is Narsinghvadi. This is the place where widows are taken for being shaved. Huts are raised on the banks of the river [which] have no roofs and no doors ... to such places widows are taken and made to sit in front of the barbers to be shaved. They cry but nobody listens to them and they are forcibly shaved. If a girl-widow stands at the door along with her brothers and sisters she is called shameless, while in such an open space ... she is exposed to the mercy of the barber. Shame to such men and to their sense of modesty.[91]

The experience of physical violation had implications at the subconscious level leading to severe trauma in some cases. Pundalik, who went on to become a Gandhian worker in his later years, was nine when his mother was tonsured. He describes movingly his mother's brutal entry into the state of widowhood:

For nine days none of us was allowed to go to mother's room. On the tenth day she had to face the ordeal of becoming sacred according to the traditions of the Hindu religion. This proved to be such a shock that she went completely out of her mind. At night she had to be locked up. She used to cry out during her fit of insanity 'What is a head? It is only a vegetable marrow put on one's shoulder.' Mother lived only for three months after father's death.[92]

Pundalik's mother was not a young childless widow. Even so, her trauma was too much for her to take. Such trauma was not uncommon. Ambubai Gumaste, a widow herself, described the experiences of another young widow:

This custom is a demon in Hindu society. A girl of 13 or 14, so tender and so young, is pushed before a barber ... In the house of a rich man there was a widow of about 11 or 12. He decided upon getting her forcibly shaved. She cried and piteously begged to be excused from that horrid operation but no one heeded her prayers. She was shaved. She [then] refused to take food and died. What to say to such brutes who would stoop to such meanness...[93]

The trauma of the enforced tonsure and the experience of such a brutal defeminisation ritual is described by another widow as a 'mania' men indulged in leading to a terrible depression that was beyond her powers of description.[94]

It is apparent from the essays of the widows that they unambiguously rejected the humiliating practices they were subjected to. Those who apparently 'consented' were actually coerced, as is evident from Anandibai's account of how she 'agreed' to have her head shaved.[95] The symbolic system associated with such practices, whether of tonsure, or pollution, or inauspiciousness, or danger, was clearly irrelevant to the essayists; in their eyes the practices were all similar as they degraded the widow. The belief system which endorsed, or provided the rationale for, such practices was treated with scorn. The tonsure for example was believed to be essential to the happiness of the husband as without it he would be steeped in night-soil and tortured by anxiety about her chastity. A young widow described the kind of beliefs put forward to enforce certain customs:

And the reason people give consists of one word — 'customs'. 'It is an established custom' they assert. 'Our family Gods will not bear its violation'. 'How long' they add 'would you steep her husband in night soil, in the lower world? When she is made a shaved recluse, there would be no immoral temptation.[96]

She then goes on to express her scorn for such beliefs:

But who has discovered that the husband of the widow is thrown into a pit of night soil unless she is shaved? Who will guarantee that all shaved widows will remain moral?[97]

The essays are a sharp critique of custom, society, and religion. They stand in contrast to the widely prevalent view among men that widows were strongly in the grip of religious belief. For example, in the view of Narayan Bhikaji (a deputy collector from Nasik), widows attributed all calamities to sins committed by them in former lives and looked to happiness in the future by conducting themselves piously,[98] a formulation reminiscent of the Brahmanical texts. The widows at the Poona Widows' Home, through their own experience, understanding, and through exposure to a reformist discourse on widowhood, raised certain questions about the role of religion in legitimising oppressive customs governing widowhood. They understood also that it was these customs and norms that made even the parents of widows regard them as polluting, inauspicious and dead for all ceremonial and social purposes. Radhabai captured the complexities of the parental dilemma thus:

Some people will ask me how it is possible for her own parents to give [the young widow pain]. I say yes, it is the social customary law that compels them to do so. God knows when we widows shall see the effacement of such cruel superstitions. Even a father dare not accept the sandalwood paste and flowers arranged by his own dear widowed child for the worship of his idols. Even her own dear mother dare not accept food at her hands.[99]

Parents were themselves the victims of a cruel system which made them apparently complicit in the oppression of their widowed daughters. Even the most sympathetic and compassionate of Brahmana fathers was unable to protect his young daughter or ward from the ignominy of public chastisement meted out to them by family priests — the real enforcers of Brahmanical patriarchal codes at the community level.[100]

The widows, in turn, recognised that the cruel customs were perpetuated by the custodians of the sacred law — 'hard hearted' men who flaunted broad 'caste marks' on their foreheads threatened and abused them,[101] and enforced their 'superior' authority, overriding the concessions sympathetic guardians sometimes permitted to the widows. It was the priests who, in the final reckoning, ensured the social death of widows.

The culpability of the Brahmana priests was apparent to the essayists on the basis of their experiences and personal observations. The reformers, however, were not quite so unambiguous. In fact, many Brahmana reformers found it necessary to work within existing structures. They accepted punishments imposed upon them by the community of Brahmanas led by the priest, even as they consciously performed actions that were regarded as breaches of caste norms. Some strands of the male reformist discourse had placed considerable importance on locating the precise originary moment of the oppressive practices. This was the Muslim 'invasion of India'. It appears from the essays of the widows that their parents and families, and teachers at their institution, had ascribed the abject state of Hindu women as exemplified by the widow, to Muslim rapaciousness and barbarity. By the turn of the century this view was well entrenched and deeply cherished by middle-class Hindu society functioning in part to exonerate their own complicity in such customs. Thus, practices like early marriage, sati, purdah, the denial of education were all attributed to the 'fear of Mussalmans abducting women', especially 'good looking widows'.[102] The disfigurement of young widows by tonsure too was linked to the 'need' to 'protect' their chastity. Such an explanation possibly reflects attempts made by the ideologues around the widows to make them feel that the offensive customs had a rationale, that it was defence of the 'community' or 'nation' and 'necessity' that drove Hindus to create the customs which the widows found so repugnant. Such paternalistic notions of the disfigurement of widows, 'for their own good', did not however fully convince all the widows. At least one of them was unconvinced of the validity of such a singular explanation,[103] erasing so completely the guilt of the men around her — especially since there was ample evidence of predatory Hindu men looking for victims among young widows even in their 'disfigured' state.[104]

The essayists were painfully aware of the state of social death to which they had been condemned. Desperate to be rescued from such a situation, Radhabai Inamdar spoke for all widows:

If people want to drag us out of this slough of despondency, this bog of widowhood, if they do not wish to see us die like vermin, [and] they still wish to recognise us as human beings they should give widows some training, some education to make them useful. It is not possible to turn all widows into under graduates or graduates, but it is possible to turn them into nurses, midwives, or industrial assistants. We are now the waste products of the world. Let it be put to good use. Our industry will add wealth to the nation.[105]

In Radhabai Inamdar's poignant plea, the relationship between the sexual and social death of the widow and her unrecognised drudge labour is clear. In her understanding, the return of widows to a suitable social role implied not marriage so much as recognised *productive* labour. This would lend meaning to the lives of widows, transforming them from 'waste products' to useful citizens, contributing like others to the 'wealth' of the nation. Unfortunately, as Radhabai recognised in her desperate plea, the recovery of most widows from social death lay outside their power and in the hands of others. In the meanwhile, was there scope for resistance, for not submitting 'like a cow in the hands of a butcher'?

A few acts of resistance on the part of widows are recorded in stray writings from the early part of the twentieth century; all of these are acts of non-compliance with the enforced shaving of the hair. It is significant that the resistance should have been expressed thus: the widows' refusal of the tonsure was a rejection of the state of social death it symbolised. Even a moderate like Parvati Athavale (see pp. 278–281 below) exhorted that widows must not submit to the 'compulsory rite' of shaving and that they should assert 'their right to their own heads', refusing to subject them to the barber. She herself gave up the rite at the age of 42, showing great courage and defiance of social norms in doing so as she became the target of ridicule and the subject of unsavoury remarks.[106] The refusal to have the head shaved was often the only act of open resistance on the part of the widow who might never, for the rest of her life, express her volition again.[107] But some widows went further. Such was the case of a nameless widow whose acts of defiance were recorded in passing by her brother Pundalik in his account of his life. This widow was the daughter of another nameless widow whose traumatic tonsure and subsequent insanity we have already referred to. Sobbing as she breathed her last, the widowed mother died clutching the young widowed daughter in her arms, fearing for what the daughter must suffer. The mother's anxiety was amply borne out. The family's fortunes soon went into a severe decline within a few years after the death of the parents. Pundalik's widowed sister was witness to the humiliation of her married sister Gita at the hands of her husband who was also her maternal uncle. Beaten severely one night and unwilling to take the degradation she was subjected to, including the introduction of a prostitute into the household by her husband, Gita committed suicide. This was within months of their mother's death.[108]

These experiences may have shaped our nameless widow's resolve to fight for her survival. As the fortunes of her natal family went from bad to worse, her condition grew more precarious. An unscrupulous brother Gopal, who had gained control of the property, did not give the widowed sister enough for her maintenance and she was left to fend for herself while Pundalik went off in pursuit of a revolutionary life. Finally in desperation she decided to file a suit against her late husband's brother and called Pundalik from Belgaum to help with the legal formalities. There was not enough money to file a suit. Gopal refused to give her any money till she gave him a receipt for all the money she had received as maintenance since her widowhood while she was living in her father's house.

Pundalik's attitude (despite his patriotic impulses) was that his widowed sister should live with her husband's people. He strongly disapproved of her going to a court of law to get money for maintenance. In an attempt to settle her in her dead husband's family, Pundalik entered into negotiations with them. Finally, it was decided that the sister would live with her in-laws. However, the in-laws were very orthodox people and would not allow a widow who had not shaved her head 'according to the ancient Hindu custom' to live in their home. Pundalik tried his best to persuade his sister to shave her head but she was adamant and refused to 'consent'. Pundalik then left her with the in-laws hoping that the matter would resolve itself after he returned to Belgaum. But two or three days later the widowed sister took a night train without informing anybody and returned to her unoccupied ancestral natal house.

Without resources once more, the widowed sister heard that a 'destitute' could declare oneself as such and then file a pauper suit. Her brother was horrified at the idea of declaring themselves as paupers but she went ahead anyway and finally won her suit for maintenance 'retroactively' from the date of her husband's death. She went on to live alone, keeping her hair and her independence, on the allowance she had won by going to court: her revolutionary brother went on to become a Gandhian social worker, but the widow never again appeared in his memoirs. She remained a nameless widow who anonymously pursued a lone battle for survival and dignity.[109] It must be borne in mind that acts of defiance or open resistance were not easy for most widows as these implied taking on the ideologies of upper-caste widowhood. The anonymous widow's battle just cited required exposing cultural practices, paternalistic ideologies, and material arrangements which could reduce women to destitution and yet demand the upholding of 'family' honour. Widows could not, therefore declare their denial of consent to Brahmanical patriarchy's ideology of widowhood. It would perhaps have been easier to manipulate the structures to gain a measure of power — that is, become complicit, or appear to become so, in the arrangements and thereby attempt to gain control over an otherwise tenuous situation. It was to provide an alternative to the miserable lives of widows that institutional support and a meaningful location in society were sought by Pandita Ramabai. Only an institution which would take the widow out of her marginal location in the family, whether natal or affinal, would make it possible for widows to collectively resist oppressive practices and not leave it to individual effort and individual solutions.

III

Pandita Ramabai and Parvati Athavale, two Brahmana widows, who were involved in providing institutional support to widows in western India, also wrote on widowhood but analysed its structures and conceptualised the woman's question in noticeably different ways. Through their writing[110] I want to show how new forms of consent were being produced among widows to domestic ideologies of a certain class and how a critique of the same ideologies of the upper castes were being formed at the time.

Parvati Athavale might be regarded as the typical widow, fully schooled in the Brahmanical ideologies prevalent in nineteenth century Maharashtra and located squarely in its material structures. However, she was drawn into the moderate reform programme in the last decade of the nineteenth century through the marriage of her widowed sister Anandibai to Professor D.D. Karve. After some years Parvati began an education and finally joined the institution which Karve set up for widows. She gradually became one of its major fund-raisers and travelled alone, first in India and then all the way to America, as part of her effort at raising money. She wrote her autobiography in 1928 in Marathi, dedicating her book to all the 'brothers and sisters' who were working for the welfare of women, especially widows.

Parvati was an 'adult' widow with a son, a category that was not the 'object' of the Reformers' attention. Her younger sister Anandibai was, on the other hand, a virgin widow and that distinction alone accounted for the 'remarriage' of one and not the other. Parvati had been widowed at nineteen, by which time she had had three childbirths but with only one child that survived. Her husband left her no property and had no home of his own and no relatives or in-laws to whom she could go, so she went back to her parents' home. There were three widows among the daughters of the family, leaving a major sense of burden upon the parents.[111] According to prevalent customs whereby a man's corpse had to be accompanied by the hair and the bangles of the widow, Parvati underwent what she describes as 'that ceremony',[112] the mandatory tonsure, which had a traumatic impact on her young son. For the sake of her parents and her son Parvati states that she put on a brave front and tried to cope with her widowhood.[113]

In Parvati's own understanding her sister's 'remarriage' to Karve was an event that changed the 'whole course of her life'.[114] While it had the support of Parvati's father and brother, her mother had not approved as she 'belonged to the old way of thinking'.[115] Further, she was deeply fearful that the other widowed daughters might follow Anandibai's example. To ward off such a possibility the mother did not want to leave Parvati at Anandibai's home when she went on a pilgrimage and insisted on taking her along, even though she might have been exposed to cholera. The mother's position was that if Parvati remarried it would mean a stain on the family's honour. It would be better to go on a pilgrimage and die of cholera.[116] After much manoeuvring Parvati finally moved to her sister's residence in Poona, overtly to facilitate an education for her son. But the new location gave her the opportunity to first study and then join Karve in his work of providing institutional support to widows.

These developments were of critical importance in the life of Parvati. In a chapter titled 'The Change in My Opinion',[117] Parvati describes the way in which she graduated from sharing with many other women a commonsense everyday ideology on widowhood to acquiring a new 'service' orientation. Living in Poona and 'gaining an education' had included walking to the Widows' Home with

Professor Karve, and talking to him about the 'condition of widows in India', and what 'means could be adopted for their relief'. The process of education and interaction with the Karves raised certain questions in Parvati's mind about the real meaning of 'the country of India, her national life and what is needed to be done for the national uplift'.[118] This sentiment wherein 'nationalism' for middle-class women came to mean 'serving the people', rather than concentrating their energies on throwing out the British, was not unique to Parvati and was shared by Anandi Gopal and Pandita Ramabai, among others. Thus while many men were preoccupied with 'political' and social issues, women were both influenced by, and were allotted an important role in, the formation of a service orientation by the new paternalist ideologies emerging in the nineteenth century.

Parvati insightfully distinguishes between the line of 'independence' and 'equality' being pushed by the 'Reformers', as part of their public activity and support for nationalism, and the 'special calling' she imbibed from Professor Karve's service to the motherland. In her understanding she could serve her motherland by bringing a ray of hope to the unhappy daughters of India — the widows. Thus she would redefine her higher spiritual duties.[119] What is significant is that for Parvati this was also a way of handling the problem of her latent sexuality. It would enable her to withstand the temptations of entering married life and was a way of sublimating her sexual drive. She rationalised this decision to remain a widow as a means by which one could be of service to the extended family of the nation, rather than being of 'use to one family only' as she put it.[120]

Parvati describes the decision to serve the 'country', and remain a widow, as one that *she* took, consciously.[121] I want to suggest, without in any way undermining Parvati's assertion of female agency, that the agency itself was structured by nineteenth century paternalist ideologies for the specific category of widows, through a normative resolution of a major problem. No one, not even nineteenth century Reformers, advocated or even approved of the remarriage of the adult widow who had 'tasted the joys of married life'[122] (a euphemism for a consummated marriage in nineteenth century discourse). Therefore widows like Parvati had no means by which they could re-enter married life. Traditional Brahmanic ideology had prescribed an ascetic religious life for them; the new paternalist ideologies were engaged in the formation of a 'service to the nation' code. However we must assert that Parvati found the new ideologies less oppressive and more meaningful and therefore *chose* it in preference to traditional Brahmanic ideology.

Parvati's statements, devoted to outlining a suitable agenda for women, were shaped directly and indirectly by ideologies which best suited her situation, temperament, and caste and class location.[123] Since Parvati had had the rare experience of living in American homes, she wanted to make certain comparisons and alert women about the direction that their lives should take. What Parvati suggests as the proper code for women is an outline of the new 'Hindu' bourgeois domestic ideology that changing class, professional and familial structures were throwing up.

At the very outset Parvati naturalises the sexual division of labour where men work outside the home to procure money and women remain in the home 'for its protection'.[124] Women were also the mothers-to-be of the country and were to be trained accordingly. This was necessary to ensure that women rather than servants were its actual mistresses.[125] Further, the home was to be made the place of joy and comfort for tired husbands so that they felt like coming home to it.[126] Apart from managing the home and being compassionate, married women were to also help in social work. Female education was linked entirely to a reform of the home, if it was to be of advantage to the country.[127] Parvati was strongly disapproving of women seeking outside 'servitude' as she describes employment.[128] Service within the home and to the husband must be and remain the norm for Indian women. She expanded on the subject thus:

If by freedom from servitude is meant freedom from men and a life of independence from them, then that freedom is *unnatural, impossible, disastrous and opposed to the laws of right living* [emphasis added]. In India there are certain legal rights that women have yet to obtain... But their freedom from suffering can best be accomplished by co-operating with men. In order to escape servitude to their husbands they must not accept the servitude of outside employment. Our sisters in this country must learn a lesson from the sorrowful condition of European women who have obtained their material liberty... [But in] Europe there is now a strife between men and women. Women have entered into the occupations of men and at times made themselves strangers to the home, *the sacred place for their duties* [emphasis added]. We do not want such conditions in

India... In India every woman must place before her mind the ideal of being the best sister, the best mother, and the best wife. For women there is greater servitude in outside employment than there is in married life. There is no reason why women should not choose the servitude of love to that of money.[129]

Outside employment for women, according to Parvati, resulted in the loss of the 'riches' of domestic life and also of spiritual riches. In Parvati's formulation it was through domestic servitude that women would find the path to bliss. Through this re-creation of a familial ideology Parvati distanced herself from an understanding, and a critique, of patriarchy. In privileging the married state Parvati reiterated both the traditional Brahmanical ideology of giving a central place to the wife and the nineteenth century male reformers' focus on the wife as the object of considered attention. Was Parvati expressing a sense of regret that she had not fully experienced the joys of domesticity or a desire for a life that could have been hers? Had Parvati, even as she pressed herself into the service of the nation, at the same time accepted the devaluation of the woman as the widow? In the final analysis it appears to me that Parvati could not step beyond the limits of the new family ideologies to take a long hard look at the sole option it provided for a widow like her, or to question the formation of a single model of companionate wife and nurturant mother in the case of other women.

While Parvati began her life as the typical widow, Pandita Ramabai, as we shall see later in this work, began and remained the most untypical widow of her times. Her writing on widowhood in the *The High Caste Hindu Woman* is marked by two features: first, it is almost self-consciously *not* drawn from her own experiences as a widow of which we never get a glimpse;[130] and second, her understanding of widowhood is located in her understanding of the upper-caste woman's status in society. Thus her writing on widowhood is analytical, insightful, and sharply presented, unlike much of the writing discussed here which flows out of the pens of our writers in a jumble of statements and pleas for help, and is invariably based on personal experience. However, in her letters and correspondence Pandita Ramabai writes movingly about specific and generalised oppressions suffered by widows who came to seek shelter in the institution she set up for them.[131]

The analytical frame that Pandita Ramabai used in her discussion may be partly ascribed to the kind of text she was creating, which was aimed at a wide audience of primarily non-Indians whose help she hoped to enlist for her work in setting up a widows' home.[132] She did not restrict herself to the oppression of widows but tried to show how widowhood, for the upper castes especially, was to be seen as part of an integral whole rather than an aberration in an otherwise acceptable structure. She divided her book into chapters on childhood, married life, and widowhood corresponding to the stages in a woman's life, telling us in her 'prefatory remarks' that such a division corresponded to the way the 'Sacred Laws'[133] divided a woman's life. But even in using this conventional device she overturns the logic of the Sacred Laws, which simply follow the division of man's life into *brahmacharya* and *grahastha* and the respective duties in each stage, and builds a continuum of oppression which reaches a climax in the state of widowhood. She displays masterly control when she lays bare the ideologies and practices of widowhood. In this, she is able to draw both from texts, to which she has a unique access for a woman of her times through her knowledge of Sanskrit, and an acute observation, having looked at things with a woman's sensibility, of practices prevailing in different parts of the country. Further she draws upon an understanding of historical knowledge which nineteenth century men had access to through books, newspaper articles and the spoken word.[134] Her understanding of the stratification of the texts into earlier and later is crucial to the arguments she builds up about the prevalence or otherwise of particularly oppressive practices. But unlike most men writing on the same theme she uses it to draw attention to the need for textual sanction, even if it meant interpolating something into the earliest texts, in order to legitimise and sediment ideologies as new practices expanded the field of control over women.[135] An important dimension of Pandita Ramabai's analysis is to probe, as she herself had gradually come to do over the years of her intellectual growth, the ideologies by which Brahmana men dominated society.

The distinction between the way she perceives the existing ideologies which rationalise widowhood in Brahmanism and most other widows' perceptions is evident even as Ramabai opens her discussion on the subject. While Parvati, echoing her mother and other women, presents it as attributable to a neutral 'fate',[136] Ramabai tells us about the patriarchal ideology prevalent all over

India which is to regard widowhood as a punishment for crimes committed by the woman in her previous birth, including disobedience or disloyalty to her husband. The length of her widowhood would be determined by the magnitude of the 'crimes' being punished.[137] Ramabai then grades widows according to whether they are mothers of sons or childless. Observant and analytical as she is, she points to one category, the older widow, who draws respect which all older people get but which is enhanced because she has withstood temptations and persecutions.[138] The aged widow is at the opposite end of the spectrum from the child widow upon whom falls the greatest abuse and hatred of the community.

Ramabai outlines the social practices that degrade the widow such as the common term used to refer to both the widow and prostitute.[139] The young widow is the object of suspicion and is closely guarded because she might ruin the family's honour through her 'lapses'. In order to make her less attractive to a 'man's eye' she is disfigured and made to fast so that her youthful nature and desire are repressed.[140] The anxiety about family honour[141] makes even her own parents, who otherwise sympathise with her, reproduce the entire set of oppressive social and cultural practices. Faced with an unending cycle of degradation, with no possibility of employment, the high-caste Hindu widow has no options and no exit from the dark tunnel in which she is trapped. The only 'alternatives' available are suicide or prostitution[142] which are not real choices, because they are forced upon what may appear to be her circumstances but are actually a consequence of 'cruel customs'.

Having outlined the unending humiliation and miseries of high caste Hindu widowhood,[143] Ramabai turns her attention to the programme of reform being suggested by the 'Sudharaks'. What is striking is how clear-eyed Ramabai is about the limitations of their single-point agenda. In her view the Reformers were being simplistic in assuming that by establishing the system of remarriage 'all the wants of the widow' would be met. While she agreed that the system needed to be introduced for the infant widows who *wished* to marry, this measure alone was insufficient and incapable of meeting their wants. Further, because she knew upper-caste society so well, she was convinced that widow marriage among high castes would not become an approved custom in the immediate future. Conventional beliefs were too strong to disappear overnight, men lacked the courage to marry widows, and there was a great gap between advocating something and actually doing it oneself.[144] She is scathing in her dismissal of the hypocritical men. In her words:

I have known men of great learning and high reputation who took oaths to the effect that if they were to become widowers and wished to marry again they would marry widows. But no sooner had their first wives died than they forgot all about the oaths and married pretty little maidens...[145]

Of course Ramabai was objective enough to recognise that men failed to live up to their stated ideals because of the tremendous power of the weapon of excommunication and of emotional blackmail. There would be few men who had the courage to make sacrifices and withstand social pressure; those who had it could feel so overwhelmed by the burden of transgressing social customs and the persecution suffered at the hands of the community that a desperate few took their own lives.[146] Ramabai ends the discussion of remarriage by pointing out that it was not always an available option nor would it always be desirable.[147]

The limitations of the remarriage agenda may also be understood by looking at what Ramabai wrote about *niyoga*, the practice by which a widow cohabited with her dead husband's brother to raise offspring for him. In discussing niyoga Ramabai brings in a remarkable perspective which is completely missing from all the discussions on the 'Vedic Age'. This was a clarity about niyoga which was not to be confused with a general principle recognising the widow's right to remarry. Ramabai described the specific function of niyoga which was to provide offspring to the dead husband because dying without male offspring was the greatest tragedy that could befall a man for it would deny him immortality.[148] Niyoga was firmly located within a patriarchal structure, not something that dealt with a widow's needs and certainly not her general right to remarry.[149]

The ancient past was not so golden after all. A survey of the textual prescriptions for men and women gave Ramabai an opportunity to dramatically highlight the double standard of morality contained in them. She arranged her material from *Manu* to show how a widow was to fast, emaciate her body, refraining from even mentioning the name of another man, but a widower was to complete the funeral rituals for his dead wife and then marry once more.[150]

Ramabai's writing on widowhood is also continuously interspersed with an account of how priests have created consent and why women are 'willing' agents in a self-destructive act like sati. Ramabai writes:

[The widow] was conscious of the miseries to which she would be subjected now that she had survived her husband. The momentary agony of suffocation in the flames was nothing compared to her lot as a widow. She gladly consented and voluntarily offered herself to please the Gods and men...[151]

Ramabai like feminists today, looks closely at the notion of a 'voluntary' sati,[152] recognising that many occasions were not directly a result of coercion. She wrote:

The act was supposed to be altogether a voluntary one, and no doubt it was so in many cases. Some died for the love, stronger than death, which they cherished for their husbands. Some died not because they had been happy in this world but because they believed with all the heart that they should be happy hereafter, some to obtain great renown, for tombstones and monuments were erected to those who thus died... others to escape the thousand temptations and sins and miseries which they knew would fall to their lot as widows...[153]

The 'voluntary' sati was ideologically and materially structured to display female agency in certain constructed ways. It is not surprising after all that Ramabai should have been so controversial: she had done some real decoding of patriarchal ideologies which had legitimised the cultural practices prevalent in the nineteenth century.

To conclude this discussion of women's writing on widowhood I want to draw out the implications in the issues addressed by women as well as their silences on certain issues. I also want to highlight the contrasting manner in which certain issues were addressed by men and women. It is striking that men writing on widowhood rarely attacked male power in the home and in society. Their focus was usually on notions of 'tradition', 'customs', and 'superstitions', which are treated as abstractions, that had a certain autonomy and staying power, to perpetuate them. This way of presenting 'tradition' is also shared by some of the women writers. However, in the writing of women like Tarabai, Rakhmabai, and Ramabai, who make a critique of male power in varying degrees, 'traditions' and 'customs' are not mere abstractions but continue through the agency of men and women. In Rakhmabai's writing the unequal manner in which Hindu social customs apply to men and women is specifically noted,[154] suggesting a recognition that Hindu social customs are an articulation of patriarchal structures as they are not gender-neutral.

Also, the double standard of morality operating on men and women is integrated into the writing of women like Tarabai, Rakhmabai, and Ramabai. This distinguishes their understanding of social and cultural practices from moderate critiques of custom by women like Parvati, as well as most men who rarely, if ever, specifically highlight the issue of double standards. Consequently, in the writing of Tarabai, Rakhmabai, and Ramabai there is a certain forthrightness in naming the oppressive forces and the power of men to perpetuate the oppressive structures. And having named the oppressive forces, and recognised their hold, women's writing is often pessimistic because there is both a sense of having to battle too many institutions and powers at the same time with very little support.[155] A critique of the failure of the Reformers and a sense of betrayal at their lack of courage is also unique to women's writing.

Women's writing, especially the writing of Rakhmabai and Ramabai, discusses the relationship between women, particularly the question of women against women or what should be identified as the politics of the household, very differently from men's writing. In women's writing it is a powered relationship between women who are *hierarchically* placed. Those wielding power are related to the husband under whose custody the young wife or widow is placed.[156] Thus, while men sometimes shifted the onus of the oppression of some women and exonerated themselves,[157] women's writing tried to show how some women were *complicit* with men in oppressing other women. It is significant that the writing of women also tried to grapple with why women consented to certain practices which degraded them. There is an attempt to understand for themselves and their readers, especially in the work of Ramabai, how women's consent is produced, a distinctive feature of women's writing which is absent in the writing of men.

The manner in which the sexuality of the widow is treated is also distinctive in women's writing where the widow is seen as being vulnerable to predatory men, or her own natural impulses which can lead to her being seduced by men who escape both the responsibility for their actions and the ignominy which falls entirely on the widow.[158] Women's writing focussed instead on the protection the widows required from men on the prowl but was strongly opposed to the severe strictures imposed on widows.[159] In the extraordinary and devastating description of a young girl wife who is soon widowed, cited earlier, Sushila Devi pointed out the paradox of female sexuality which was to be ripened one moment and crushed at another:[160] female sexuality is, in this passage, portrayed as an object of use in which men are the agents, women the passive objectified beings. In such a repressive situation it was inevitable that the widows were unable to express their own needs. All the young women in the Poona Widows' Home dwelt upon the sexuality of the widow as making her more vulnerable.[161] In my reading of the sources I have found only one widow who guardedly acknowledged her own latent sexual needs in a letter to her mother when she decided to run away from home and surreptitiously remarry a reformer. She explained her decision as a way in which she could ensure that she did not 'go astray'.[162]

Finally, but most significantly, men rarely recognised the labour performed by widows, which as we have just seen was a major theme in the writing of the women, particularly widows. It is hardly surprising then that men's discussion of the 'problem' of widowhood never outlined its distinctive cultural codes within the context of production relations and patriarchal structures, or analysed it in terms of the relationship between caste, gender, and labour. This restricted discussion on widowhood, even when it was recognised that widowhood was different among upper and lower castes, established the parameters within which women themselves framed their own discourses. Tarabai's polemical writing could sense the working of patriarchal power but could not clearly see its relationship to other structures of inequality.[163] Thus, while women sought to express themselves outside the discourses of men they were effectively limited by them. What women managed to do however was to step out of the boundaries of the discussion by dealing with issues obliquely. They brought in issues which men had hardly addressed, for example, economic independence, the extraction of labour from widows, gainful employment and a right to control their own lives. They also did the reverse, which was to contest men's judgement of certain issues as central to the problem of widowhood, such as the sexuality of the nubile widow.[164]

Further, they imbued certain terms like 'nation' with a distinctive meaning. For some of the widows this was a place which could solve *their* problems and patriotism was to be demonstrated by working to change the quality of life for the widow.[165]

Given the limited nature of men's understanding of the larger context in which widowhood was located, despite the expanded but marginalised way women wrote about widowhood, it is not surprising that the Reformers hardly changed anything for the widow in the late nineteenth and early twentieth centuries. They were unable to attack either caste or patriarchy, so the structure in which upper-caste cultural codes for women were located remained intact. The problem of the upper-caste child widow finally sorted itself out not so much through the intervention of the Reformers or through the large-scale remarriages of widows but because the age of marriage gradually went up. Women began to be educated and as certain occupations opened up for them the 'destitute' widow could find ways to support herself. Without breaking up the relationship between caste, gender and labour, structural changes occurred within the upper castes which reduced the magnitude of the problem of the upper-caste child widow by the second half of the twentieth century.

NOTES AND REFERENCES

1. The writings of women in this chapter, especially those of the widows themselves, are subjective testimonies. In the context of understanding these testimonies it may be useful to draw from the work of Teresa de Lauretis who suggests that experience is a particular kind of consciousness to be distinguished from reason and knowledge. According to her, experience is the process by which subjectivity is constructed for all social beings. It is through this process that one is placed in social reality, and so it is that one perceives and comprehends as subjective (in the sense of originating in oneself) those relations — material, economic, and interpersonal — which are in fact social, and in a larger perspective historical (Teresa de Lauretis, *Alice Doesn't*, Bloomington, Indiana University Press, 1984, p. 159).

2. Meenakshi Mukherjee, *Realism and Reality: The Novel and Society in India*, Delhi, Oxford University Press, 1985, pp. 28–30,

pp. 85–91; Sisir Kumar Das, *A History of Indian Literature*, Vol. VIII, Delhi, Sahitya Akademi, 1991, pp. 115, 299–300.

3. For an extended discussion of the reinvention of tradition in which the 'status' of women in the ancient past was projected as very high in the writings of nineteenth century men but according to whom serious aberrations later led to women's degradation, see my paper 'Whatever Happened to the Vedic Dasi: Orientalism, Nationalism, and a Script for the Past', in Kumkum Sangari and Sudesh Vaid, eds., *Recasting Women: Essays in Colonial History*, Delhi, Kali for Women, 1989, pp. 27–87, especially pp. 50–52.

4. Uma Chakravarti, 'Gender, Caste and Labour: the Ideological and Material Structure of Widowhood', *Economic and Political Weekly*, Vol. 30, No. 36, September 9, 1995, pp. 2248–57.

5. Sushila Devi's essay entitled 'The Ideal of Hindu Womanhood with Practical Suggestion for its Realisation' won the Gaekwar prize and was published by the Civil and Military Gazette Press, Lahore, in 1907. The longish essay of some 60 pages was not the only work of Sushila Devi to have been published. Her other publications include 'The Cosmopolitan Hinduani: Indian Stories in English', '*Uttam Acharan Siksha*: Eight Lectures in Hindi Chiefly Intended for Hindu Women', and the 'Life of Queen Victoria' which was written under the order of the Director of Public Instruction, Patiala, for distribution in girls' schools. Sushila Devi ran an institution for widows entirely managed by 'ladies' and called the Hindu Widows' Industrial School. The institution provided instruction in 'plain and fancy' needlework to Hindu widows of respectable families to enable them to earn a 'quiet living' at their own homes.

Although Sushila Devi lived and worked in North India I have included her work here partly because as a Gaekwar prize-winning essay, this work is likely to have circulated in central and western India, especially since a pan-Indian context existed to the discussion on women's status and the enforcement of oppressive practices upon widows. This is reflected even in Sushila Devi's description of widowhood which shows familiarity with the cultural practices confined to peninsular India and draws upon them to flesh out the full range of practices imposed upon widows.

Sushila Devi was herself a 'cosmopolitan Hinduani' in the values she had absorbed and projected, enlightened and modest at the same time. She had been educated in England and travelled in Europe. In Munich an artist had expressed a desire to paint her but as a 'Hindu' wife she had refused to pose for a man. The artist who respected the high values of Hindu womanhood had then painted

her from memory. Sushila Devi had fully absorbed the rhetoric of
nineteenth century 'enlightened' men with its inevitable component
of a great, ancient Hindu past where women were educated and
knowledge was available to 'all classes', not confined to the chosen
few. Sushila Devi believed that women had at that time held the
power entrusted to them most sacredly, and thereby uplifted the
Hindu race. They attended public ceremonies and took part in the
great sacrifices of the day. With their 'judgement formed through
proper training, the accomplished maidens, glowing with youth and
health, chose their partners in life by the Svayamwar ceremony.'
Thus by the combined efforts of both men and women 'our beloved
Bharat' had excelled, according to Sushila Devi, in 'spiritual
prosperity as well as social and material prosperity'. Despite this
full-scale reproduction of the construction of a glorious past, when
Sushila Devi gets down to dealing with the present she drops the
rhetoric (but not the domestic ideologies of the nineteenth century)
and draws upon female experience and female popular discourse to
discuss widowhood. This had relevance for western India as much
as for the rest of India and for this reason her work has been
included in this discussion.

6. Sushila Devi, *The Ideal of Hindu Womanhood*, p. 28.
7. *Ibid.*, pp. 30–31. A.S. Altekar in his widely influential work, *The Position of Women in Hindu Civilisation* (Delhi, Motilal Banarasidas, 1987, p. 5, first published in 1938) used a similar argument but in a somewhat circular manner. According to him parents felt unhappy at the birth of daughters because of the miseries a possible widowhood in the future might entail.
8. *Ibid.*, pp. 33–34.
9. *Ibid.*, pp. 55–56.
10. *Ibid.*, pp. 57–58.
11. *Ibid.*, pp. 32, 55–56.
12. Tarabai Shinde, *Stri Purusha Tulana*, tr. and ed. by Rosalind O'Hanlon as *A Comparison Between Men and Women, Tarabai Shinde and the Critique of Gender Relations in Colonial India* (with an Introduction), Madras, Oxford University Press, 1994.
13. *Ibid.*, pp. 1–2, 93, 96.
14. *Ibid.*, p. 75.
15. *Ibid.*, p. 88.
16. *Ibid.*, pp. 89–90.
17. *Ibid.*, pp. 117–18.
18. *Ibid.*, p. 85.
19. *Ibid.*, pp. 97, 118.
20. *Ibid.*, pp. 96–97, 117–18.

21. *Ibid.*, p. 59.
22. Responses to Malabari's initiative were published in Dayaram Gidumal, *Status of Women in India*, and include the reactions of the established figures of nineteenth century western India.
23. These developments are discussed in detail in the next chapter.
24. Susie Tharu and K. Lalitha, *Women Writing in India*, Vol. II, p. 256.
25. The *Times of India*, 26 June 1885.
26. Although Rakhmabai displays a sense of betrayal for the failure of men of her class background to push reform she excludes Malabari from among those men who lack the 'courage to withstand adverse reactions from the anti-reformers'.
27. The *Times of India*, 26 June 1885.
28. The *Times of India*, 19 September 1885.
29. Julia Leslie, *The Perfect Wife*, pp. 22–34. She shows the antecedents of popular ideologies in ancient Brahmanical texts and their reiteration in texts compiled in the eighteenth century which would have the effect of refurbishing the circulation of Brahmanical ideologies at a 'popular' level.
30. The *Times of India*, 19 September 1885.
31. *Ibid.*
32. We may recall Ramabai Ranade's father also evoking family honour to ensure suitable behaviour when she was leaving her natal home after marriage to live in her husband's home (see Chapter 4, p. 218–19).
33. The *Times of India*, 19 September 1885.
34. *Ibid.*
35. These essays appear to have remained unpublished. The collection of essays was addressed to Sir Herbert Risley by B.A. Gupte from Calcutta on 27 April 1911, requesting that they be published in book form. The essays were written in Marathi by widows who were inmates at the Poona Widows' and Orphans' Home and prizes of Rs 12 were offered. The manuscript sent by Gupte to Risley was a translation from the original in Marathi and was entitled 'Position of Widow: Experiences of Widows and Other Girls'. Gupte hoped that the published version of the essays could be submitted to the government for its consideration in order to make the law of cruelty to animals applicable to the forcible shaving of young and minor widows. The essays in typescript form are currently located in the India Office Library, London (Eur. Ms. D. 356). Hereafter the Ms. is cited as Radhabai Inamdar et. al., *Position of Widows*. Page numbers cited will follow the pagination in the original typescript.
36. It is difficult to estimate the age of the widows since it was common

for the widows to go to institutions such as the Poona Home at different moments in their life and only then begin their education. See Parvati Athavale, *Hindu Widow*, p. 22.

37. Radhabai Inamdar et.al., *Position of Widows*, p. 3.

38. H.N. Apte's title in his book on widowhood provides the girls a phrase to express their sense of marginalisation.

39. The writing of the girls attempts to describe the anguish of their everyday lives and they use any phrases or metaphors that help them to express themselves. They are probably aware that the essays will have a limited readership so they are noticeably forthcoming in describing their experiences and in communicating their sense of despair. The essays of the girls are in marked contrast to the writing of widows like Pandita Ramabai, Anandibai Karve, or Parvati Athavale who are 'reformers' in their own eyes. The latter attempt to conceptualise and provide a structure to the experience of widowhood as they are consciously speaking to an audience — they know they are publishing, unlike the girls in the Widows' Home.

40. Edward Harper, 'Fear and the Status of Women', *South Western Journal of Anthropology*, No. 25, 1969, pp. 81–95, p. 90.

41. Radhabai Inamdar et al., *Position of Widows*, p. 27.

42. *Ibid.* Any and every situation would be an opportunity to indulge in abuse and taunts. Bhimabai Kale describes how even the occasional illness of the mistress of the house in which the widow was being 'sheltered' could bring forth barbs like 'Why is she [the widow] not taken ill instead? This useless burden, who wants to feed her? (p. 10). Another widow recounts that taunts and abuses would include wishing the death of the widow: 'Who cares for her? She is Lakshmi turned into a broom. Let her die, it will be a relief' (p. 14).

43. Radhabai Inamdar et al., *Position of Widows*, pp. 5, 9, 11, 26, 28; the widows show an acute awareness not just of what they were given to eat but also the manner in which they were treated as they were being given the meal. 'When insulted the food is like poison' (p. 8).

44. Radhabai Inamdar et al., *Position of Widows*, p. 26.

45. D.N. Agarwal, *A Textbook of Hindu Law*, Allahabad, Ram Narain Beni Prasad, 1960, pp. 35, 205ff; B.D. Sirvya, *Hindu Woman's Estate (Non-Technical Stridhana)*, Calcutta, Butterworth and Company, 1913, pp.7–8. We must note that a very large number of widows were child widows whose husbands themselves would have died at a young age while they lived in a joint family and therefore held undivided coparcenary property. The child widow's vulnerability in the Mitakshara system came from this situation

since she had no right to seek a partition of the property; all she
was entitled to 'legally' was maintenance.

46. K. Ballhatchet, *Social Policy*, p. 28.
47. Hanna Papanek, 'To Each Less than She Needs: From Each More than She Can Do: Allocations, Entitlements and Value', and Amartya K. Sen, 'Gender and Cooperative Conflicts', in Irene Tinker, ed., *Persistent Inequalities: Women and World Development*, New York, Oxford University Press, 1990, pp. 162–84 and 123–49.
48. Sen, 'Gender', p. 140.
49. Papanek, 'To Each', pp. 169–74.
50. Radhabai Inamdar et al., *Position of Widows*, pp. 10, 14.
51. *Ibid.*, p. 27.
52. *Ibid.*, p. 28.
53. *Ibid.*, p. 1.
54. *Ibid.*, p. 27.
55. *Ibid.*, p. 1.
56. *Ibid.*, pp. 14, 15.
57. *Ibid.*, p. 26.
58. *Ibid.*, p. 9.
59. *Ibid.*, p. 23.
60. *Ibid.*, p. 1.
61. See M.K. Indira's biographical novel, *Phaniyamma* (tr. from the original in Kannada by Tejasvini Niranjana, Delhi, Kali for Women, 1989) for a graphic, real-life account which depicts the ceaseless labour performed by a widow who is always available to perform heavy labour since she does not reproduce.
62. Anandibai Karve, *Maze Purana*, tr. and ed. by Kaveri Karve, in D.D. Karve, *New Brahmans*, pp. 58–79, 67.
63. *Ibid.*, p. 64.
64. *Ibid.* Here we have a significant reference to the double position of the Brahmana widow simultaneously sharing the class power of her kinsmen and rendering managerial labour from which other young married women were exempt. As a member of a class Anandibai was required to assert her class power over those who laboured for this Brahmana family. The widow's own powerlessness is thus relative. What the widows perceive is the loss of power they suffer in widowhood which separates them from other women: further, they see only their own labour, not that of others belonging to a different class.
65. *Ibid.*, pp. 64–65.
66. The communal kitchen was set up as a way of cutting costs. However, the women clearly regarded the labour, put in by them into such a household, more like that of a servant woman since

cooking would be done for larger numbers without the moderating influence of such people being regarded as family.

67. Anandibai Karve, *Maze Purana*, in D.D. Karve, *New Brahmans*, p. 67.

68. *Ibid.*, p. 68.

69. *Ibid.*, p. 69.

70. Radhabai Inamdar et al., *Position of Widows*, p. 6. See also pp. 26–29. The 1864 census records for Bombay list 1,795 Brahmanas (among 30,604 Brahmana residents in Bombay) as domestic servants. At least some of them are likely to have been destitute widows without means of support since it appears to have been the only 'profession' open to them (census data from Christine Dobbin, *Urban Leadership in Western India*, p. 8).

71. However, during the interim period widows had a hard time at the hands of those who controlled the family's resources. According to Ambubai Bapat, the young widowed mother had to protect her infants 'like the young ones of a cat being taken from one corner to another corner for shelter' (Radhabai Inamdar et al., *Position of Widows*, p. 6). Another widow describes the situation of the widow with children thus: 'The anxiety of educating her sons and getting her daughters married, and the distressing thought of starvation staring the face, the complete want of provision for medical treatment during illness add to the mental suffering of the widow compounding the loss of the husband' (p. 26).

72. Edward Harper, 'Fear and the Status of Women', p. 90.

73. Radhabai Inamdar et al., *Position of Widows*, p. 25.

74. Uma Chakravarti, 'Gender, Caste and Labour', pp. 2248–49.

75. Radhabai Inamdar et al., *Position of Widows*, p. 6

76. *Ibid.*

77. *Ibid.*

78. Dayaram Gidumal, 'The Status Of Women', pp. lxxv, lxxvi, lxxxi.

79. Radhabai Inamdar et al., *Position of Widows*, p. 2.

80. *Ibid.*, p. 11.

81. *Ibid.*, p. 6.

82. *Ibid.*, p. 10.

83. *Ibid.*, p. 26.

84. *Ibid.*, p. 27.

85. *Ibid.*, p. 28.

86. *Ibid.*, p. 5.

87. *Ibid.*, p. 15.

88. Uma Chakravarti, 'Gender, Caste and Labour', p. 2252.

89. Radhabai Inamdar et al., *Position of Widows*, p. 2.

90. *Ibid.*, p. 15.

91. *Ibid.*, p. 11.
92. N.C. Katagade, 'Pundalik' in D.D. Karve ed., *New Brahmans*, pp. 195–97.
93. Radhabai Inamdar et al., *Position of Widows*, p. 19.
94. *Ibid.*, p. 23.
95. Anandibai Karve, 'Maze Purana' in D.D. Karve, *New Brahmans*, pp. 65–66.
96. *Ibid.*, pp. 14–15.
97. *Ibid.*, pp. 14–15.
98. Dayaram Gidumal, *Status of Women*, pp. 9–10.
99. Radhabai Inamdar et al., *Position of Widows*, p. 1.
100. *Ibid.*, pp. 8–9.
101. *Ibid.*, p. 8, 25. Many of the essayists describe an incident which appears to have been recounted to them by the father of a young widow. A Brahmana father was celebrating some occasion in his home to which the 'house priests' had been invited for a meal. The Brahmana father had a young widowed daughter who had been tonsured. Unaware, or unmindful, of her 'inauspicious' status, she ran about playing with the other children, when she was sighted by a Brahmana priest. He immediately ordered her out of sight; when the little girl asked him why she must go in when her friends were allowed to be present she was told that it was because she was a 'shaved widow'. She was then sent off to a dark corner to eat her food while her father looked on miserably, unable to prevent the girl's humiliation.
102. *Ibid.*, pp. 5, 7, 20.
103. *Ibid.*, p. 20. The same widow had no doubts at all about the double standards prevalent with regard to explanations about denial of education to girls on the grounds that it would spoil them. If the same education did not spoil boys why would it spoil girls, she asked pertinently. Double standards with regard to tonsuring are also condemned by another widow: when men don't tonsure themselves at the death of their wives why should widows have to do so, she asks with asperity (p. 7).
104. *Ibid.*, p. 2.
105. *Ibid.*, pp. 3–4.
106. Parvati Athavale, *Hindu Widow: An Autobiography*, first published in 1928, reprinted at Delhi, Reliance Publishing House, 1986, p. 47.
107. Interview with Gomati, New Delhi, 1988. Widowed at 16 at around the year 1924, she had led a conventional widow's existence until she went to live with the family of 'Sister' Subbalakshmi who had set up a widows' home in Madras. She was deeply unhappy

while living with her natal kin but submitted to the widow's fate except for finding the strength, she herself 'does not know from where', to refuse to have her head shaved.

108. N.C. Katagade, 'Pundalik', in D.D. Karve (ed.), *New Brahmans*, pp. 201–203.

109. *Ibid.*, pp. 226–27.

110. Parvati Athavale, *Hindu Widow*, and Pandita Ramabai, *The High Caste Hindu Woman*, 1888.

111. Parvati Athavale, *Hindu Widow*, pp. 14–15.

112. *Ibid.*, p. 15.

113. *Ibid.*

114. *Ibid.*

115. *Ibid.*, pp. 15–20.

116. *Ibid.*, p. 20.

117. *Ibid.*, pp. 27ff.

118. *Ibid.*, p. 27.

119. *Ibid.*, p. 29. Characteristic of the new spirit of service and a high-caste woman's unique understanding of patriotism is an account Parvati provides of how a young Bengali patriot tried to force Parvati to return forthwith to India when he found her washing dishes as a maidservant in the house of an American. The self-styled patriot told Parvati that her actions were making 'us Indians extremely ashamed' of her and that it was a stain on her Brahmanahood. Parvati responded by saying 'I have as much national pride as you have'; she was in America to raise funds for the widows' home, not to enjoy herself. What could be more patriotic than acting on behalf of the widows? She ultimately got brow-beaten into promising that she would return only because a severe disagreement between a Bengali and a Maharashtrian in a foreign land would give the wrong signal about India: nationalism then was unity, apart from meaning service for her (pp. 102–107).

120. *Ibid.*, p. 30. Here Parvati is both prefiguring and echoing Gandhi who had a similar resolution of the problem of young widowhood: service to the nation as the extended family.

121. A major display of volition and agency for Parvati was her discarding the signs of widowhood at the fairly mature age of 42. In a chapter which is devoted entirely to the subject of how and why she discarded the signs of widowhood Parvati contested the traditional Brahmanical ideology's requirement of the tonsure. In Parvati's view this was a rite that compelled the widow to renounce worldly things. She recommended that widows refuse to submit to the barber's razor when they reached the age of 'discretion'. Instead they should assert their rights to their own heads, let their hair grow and 'take

their place in human relationships' as they did before widowhood. She knew that such a display of 'volition' on the part of widows would be criticised but it was important nevertheless because it would enable the widows to adopt a way of living that they themselves felt was right. For Parvati the crucial reason why widows must do so was because the rite itself was false since it had been associated with a *sannyasi's* outward manifestation of an inner state, a withdrawal from the world. The widow should tonsure her head only if she herself wished to enter the renunciatory state, 'wished to renounce worldly living *of her own accord*' (emphasis added). As the practice existed it was a violation of the woman's body and that too by a stranger. Parvati not only gave up the tonsured head but vigorously campaigned for doing so. It was the only issue over which she was critical of the so-called Reformers for not doing enough, but what she wanted them to do was to take on the shaving of the widows rather than leave it to the barbers.

Throughout the discussion on the tonsuring of a widow's head Parvati was making a strong statement on the right of the widow to choice, to agency, and for customs and rites to correspond to meaning behind the symbolic actions. As she ended her discussion of the theme of forced tonsure she appealed to the agency of the widows by urging them to take the lead against the unjust custom, which in the name of religion, sorely pressed upon them (pp. 46–54).

130. Ramabai Ranade, *Reminiscences*, p. 82.
131. Sister Geraldine, *The Letters and Correspondence of Pandita Ramabai*, edited by A.B. Shah, Bombay, Maharashtra State Board for Literature and Culture, 1977, pp. 241–242, 247, 280–83, 285–89.
132. Pandita Ramabai Saraswati, *The High Caste Hindu Woman*, pp. 1, 118–19.
133. *Ibid.*, p. 11.
134. Ramabai refers to the controversy regarding sanction for sati in the Vedic texts which she describes as an interpolation, citing Max Muller's work on the question of interpolation. She also cites from articles published in journals and newspapers (pp. 79, 87–90).
135. Pandita Ramabai, *The High Caste Hindu Woman*, pp. 74–75.
136. Parvati Athavale, *Hindu Widow*, p. 26.
137. Pandita Ramabai, *The High Caste Hindu Woman*, p. 69.
138. *Ibid.*, p. 70.
139. *Ibid.*, p. 83.
140. *Ibid.*, pp. 82ff.
141. *Ibid.*, p. 85.
142. *Ibid.*, p. 86.

143. *Ibid.* Ramabai is one of the few women writers who are conscious of distinctive cultural norms operating on widows according to the position occupied in the hierarchy by the caste to which the widow belongs. It was because she did not subsume all widows into the same structure that she titled her book *The High Caste Hindu Woman* and outlined the specific practices for the widow of the upper castes in her chapter on widowhood. She also recognised that oppressive practices like shaving the head which were unique to the Brahmanas were spreading to the lower castes as the lower castes took 'great pride in imitating their higher caste brethren'. This awareness of sanskritisation is notably rare in nineteenth century writing and is evidence of Ramabai's keen sociological observation (p. 82).

144. Pandita Ramabai, *The High Caste Hindu Woman*, pp. 90–91.

145. *Ibid.*, p. 91.

146. *Ibid.*, p. 92.

147. *Ibid.*, p. 93.

148. *Ibid.*, pp. 70–72.

149. *Ibid.* Ramabai cites while discussing niyoga the example of a custom among the Jews who also used a system of 'appointment', to raise up 'seed for the deceased husband' of the widow (p. 71).

150. Pandita Ramabai, *The High Caste Hindu Woman*, pp. 72–73.

151. *Ibid.*, pp. 75–76.

152. Kumkum Sangari and Sudesh Vaid, 'Institutions, Beliefs, Ideologies: Widow Immolation in Contemporary Rajasthan', *Economic and Political Weekly*, Vol. 27, No. 3, April 27, 1991, pp. WS 2–18.

153. Pandita Ramabai, *The High Caste Hindu Woman*, pp. 76–77.

154. The *Times of India*, 26 June 1886.

155. *Ibid.*; *Times of India*, 19 September 1886; Pandita Ramabai, *The High Caste Hindu Woman*, p. 93.

156. Rakhmabai, The *Times of India*, 26 June 1886; Sushila Devi, *The Ideal Wife*, pp. 32–34.

157. Dayaram Gidumal, *The Status of Women*, pp. lxxi, cviii.

158. Tarabai Shinde, *Stri Purusha Tulana*, p. 117.

159. Pandita Ramabai, *The High Caste Hindu Woman*, pp. 84–85, Radhabai Inamdar et al., *Position of Widows*, pp. 6, 15.

160. Sushila Devi, *The Ideal Wife*, pp. 29–32.

161. Radhabai Inamdar et al., *Position of Widows*, pp. 6, 15.

162. Letter from Dhankore Bai to Madhavdas Raghunathdas, reproduced in B.N. Motivala, *Karsondas Mulji*, p. 209; letter from Dhankore Bai to her mother, *Ibid.*, pp. 211–12.

163. Tarabai had pointed out, as Pandita Ramabai also did, that enforced widowhood which had been restricted to the upper castes in the

past was now spreading to the lower castes (*Stri Purusha Tulana*, tr. by O'Hanlon, p. 75, and *The High Caste Hindu Woman*, p. 82). Even one of the young women in the Poona Widows' Home had remarked on enforced widowhood as an aspect of the upper-caste practices which did not operate on Shudra women who could remarry. Their lives were therefore not as miserable as those of upper-caste women, according to Ambubai Gumaste (Radhabai Inamdar et al., *Position of Widows*, p. 19).

164. See Chapter II, pp. 82ff.
165. Radhabai Inamdar et al., *Position of Widows*, pp. 4, 29; Parvati Athavale, *Hindu Widow*, pp. 29, 49, 105.

PART THREE

I have tried to outline in this work the complex factors working at a transitional historical moment which can help us understand the relationship between structure and agency with particular reference to gender. Women of a specific caste and class location were subject to multiple pressures in nineteenth century western India such that their agency was shaped by certain material and ideological structures. Although it is not being suggested that women's agency was so determined that they had no volition or individual will, the discussion in Part II has attempted to lay out the range and complexity of institutions within which women were located and within which they could, or sometimes had to, act, or be acted upon. We have also seen that even in a transitional moment the lives of women were more circumscribed than those of men so that *effectively* women had fewer choices than men. Their agency tended to be articulated in certain ways and it has been my attempt to probe these through discussions on law, the state, the family and religious and cultural institutions.

I want now to draw my explorations to a close by looking at the relationship between structure and agency, or a life and a time, through the person of Pandita Ramabai, the most visible of nineteenth century women in Maharashtra and yet, necessarily, the most controversial upper-caste woman of her times. A question that has occurred to me is: did the fact that Ramabai was a Brahmana widow have something to do with why she was so controversial? Was the upper-caste widow in the nineteenth century structurally so located that the gender question for a certain class was most sharply articulated through her? Did her location mean that her choices were even more limited than those of other women and that therefore when such a woman became an agent rather than a subject, when she took control of her own life and that of other women like her,. she came into conflict with established structures of authority? Through Ramabai's life I hope to show something of the 'conflictual and uneven resolution' of the gender contradictions of her time for a particular class of women. Through an account of her struggle one may recover also a sense of the struggle, potential and actual, of many women of her time.

6

Structure and Agency: A Life and a Time

A close look at Ramabai's life[1] and work reveals that it was unique in relation to the social location of many Brahmana men of the nineteenth century. Born into a Chitpavan Brahmana family and thus capable of sharing in the social power of the Brahmanas, Ramabai's father had, however, begun to suffer the consequences of non-conformism.[2] Brahmanical structures were tightly organised and internally coherent; social and ritual power was available to one within that structure only if its basic premises and contemporary practices were accepted. Ramabai's father's experiences with Brahmanism in western India both shaped her life and directly fed into it; the break with Brahmanism was therefore inevitable and almost predetermined, given the extraordinary nature of his life and the legacy she inherited.

Ramabai's father, Anant Shastri Dongre, was born and trained as a Sanskrit scholar in the last days of the Peshwai.[3] During the four years when he studied under a teacher attached to the Peshwa's court he had been deeply impressed by the sight of his guru teaching Sanskrit to Varanasibai, the wife of the last Peshwa Bajirao II. When the British took over Poona and the Peshwai territories, Anant Shastri returned to his home in Malherambi (Mangalore). He made an abortive attempt to teach his wife Sanskrit but failed due to family disapproval. Following the Brahmana convention of seeking patronage for the pursuit of learning and teaching from the court, Anant travelled to Mysore where he was rewarded handsomely. After ten years he travelled to other centres such as Banaras and Nepal, combining pilgrimage and the accumulation of knowledge with the search for patronage. On his way back to Mangalore, at the great pilgrimage centre of Paithan, he chanced

upon another travelling Brahmana who was on the look-out for
grooms for his two young daughters. On finding Anant Shastri (by
then a widower of forty-four) a suitable match for the older of the
two girls, the nine-year-old Lakshmibai was given to him in
marriage. Anant Shastri took his young bride home and attempted
once more to teach Sanskrit to a woman, this time to his second
wife.[4]

While Lakshmibai proved an able pupil, Anant Shastri's action
was regarded as 'heretical', and a confrontation with family and
established Brahmanical authority quickly ensued. Many years later
Ramabai recapitulated Anant Shastri's battle for democratising
sacred learning:

My father though a very orthodox Hindu and strictly adhering to caste
and other religious rules was yet a reformer in his own way. He could not
see why women and people of the shudra caste [could] not learn to read
and write the Sanskrit language and learn sacred literature. He thought it
better to try the experiment at home instead of preaching to others. He
found an apt pupil in my mother. She devoted many hours of her time
in the night to the regular study of the sacred Puranic literature and was
able to store up a great deal of knowledge in her mind.

The Brahmana pandits living round about my father's village tried to
dissuade him from the heretical course following in teaching his wife the
sacred language of the gods. His extensive studies in the Hindu sacred
literature enabled him to quote chapter and verse of each sacred book
[which gave such authority]. His misdeeds were reported to the head priest
of the sect to which he belonged and the learned Brahmanas induced the
guru to call this heretic to appear before him and before the august
assemblage of the Pandits to give his reasons for taking this course, or be
excommunicated ... [5]

Ramabai's father had thus found that the sanction for teaching
the Peshwa's wife did not extend to ordinary women. However, he
participated in a long-drawn-out debate about scriptural sanction
for women learning Sanskrit and provided an impressive amount
of evidence from the *smritis* and the epics. He succeeded in staving
off excommunication and became known as an 'orthodox reformer'.

Nevertheless, he decided to move to the forest and set up an
ashrama with his young wife where he could teach according to his
convictions; it was here that Ramabai, the youngest of his children,
was born and where Lakshmibai brought up her young family. The
family ran out of the economic support they had relied upon

thirteen years after the ashrama was set up since everyone who came to it had to be fed and looked after. Anant Shastri was thus obliged to leave the ashrama and take up a pilgrim's life once more when Ramabai was only six months old. They travelled around as *pauranikas*, public narrators of the Puranas at temples or other sacred spots, and received gifts of food, clothes and flowers from the people to whom they narrated the stories.[6]

It was during these travels across the country in search of *mukti* (salvation) that Ramabai's learning began. Since her father was by now too old to teach, Ramabai was taught Sanskrit by her mother, (or picked up what she heard as her father taught her brother),[7] doubling the unconventionality of the venture. The difference in Ramabai's early experiences from those of the new Brahmanas is striking. Men like Ranade, Telang, and even Tilak went to school to avail themselves of the new opportunities provided by English education. Their families invested in such an education because it was imperative to the pursuit of a career in the administration or the judiciary. They all learnt English literature, history, mathematics and western philosophy.[8] In contrast Ramabai and her brother trained for no profession; unconventional though it was to teach a woman, Anant Shastri's family still carried on with the traditional ideals of the truly religious vocation prescribed for the Brahmanas — teaching, worship, and living off gifts. How rare this ideal was is evident even for a time as far back as the sixth century B.C. because it was the basis of the critique of contemporary Brahmanism by the Buddha.[9] In the nineteenth century especially, following the unprecedented militarisation and secularisation of the Brahmanas in western India it appears to have been, to put it mildly, clearly unusual, almost certainly unique.

For many years the Dongre family lived thus on the margins of society pursuing a way of life which was peripatetic, a sort of combination of the *vanaprastha* and *sanyasa* stages outlined by the traditional Brahmanical texts. Anant Shastri reworked these stages, first running an ashrama with his wife and then taking his family in a collective quest for mukti. The collective quest was most unusual as in the normal course Ramabai would have had a very different life. The 'normal' householder compulsions of living within the tight grip of caste and kin had been consciously 'renounced' by Anant Shastri's family because of their claustrophobic control over individuals, compelling them to be part of a system of oppressive practices. They also tried to escape becoming victims of such a system, which their resistance would have made them.[10] In search of space for themselves, the entire family tried to create an alternative existence by living away from the stranglehold of Brahmanical society. They managed to succeed only partially because even in their unusual existence, caste norms had to be upheld, especially with regard to marriage. Ramabai's elder sister was married, according to convention, as a child; the marriage was tragic, as the groom refused to abide by the arrangement agreed upon of living as a member of Anant Shastri's family[11] and devoting himself to learning. Drawing upon this unfortunate experience, Anant Shastri did not arrange a similar marriage for Ramabai. This was a unique aspect of Ramabai's life — she remained unmarried far beyond the acceptable limit for Brahmana girls. Such an arrangement would have been impossible had it not been for Anant Shastri's peripatetic existence. One can see in Ramabai's future life the same search for space, the need to cut away from oppressive practices and carve out a meaningful existence.

The alternative existence adopted by Ramabai's family also entailed great physical hardship. Her old father became too feeble to direct the reading of the *Puranas* by his children. Unfortunately, the family was not equipped to do anything else and menial work was proscribed for Brahmanas. At the same time, severe famine struck Madras presidency, the area in which the Dongre family then lived. Like the rest of the poor, the Dongre family too wandered from place to place in search of sustenance. As the family was too proud to beg, the strain was severe. Following days of eating leaves and wild berries, Anant Shastri determined to end his life by performing[12] the *jal samadhi* like Jnaneshwar and Muktabai's parents, but died of exhaustion even before the ritual could be formally undertaken. Ramabai poignantly recalled the last moments many years later:

I shall never forget his last injunctions to me. His blind eyes could not see my face, but he held me tight in his arms, and stroking my head and cheeks he told me in a few words, broken with emotion, to remember how he loved me and how he taught me to do right and never depart from the way of righteousness. His last loving command to me was to live an honourable life, if I lived at all, and serve god all my life....'As you are the last of my children, you are dearest to me' he said. 'I have given you into god's keeping, he will guard you'.[13]

Ramabai was soon to witness more suffering. Worn out through privation, her mother was unable to stand the painful loss of her husband and the rigours of starvation during the famine years. Ramabai helplessly watched her mother on the verge of death and finally in a desperate bid to save her, went out to beg for food, only to find that it had come too late to save Lakshmibai. Unable to eat the piece of *bajri* (*roti* made of millet) Ramabai brought her, Lakshmi became unconscious and died a few days later. Srinivas and Ramabai had the utmost difficulty in carrying their mother to the cremation-ground and performing the appropriate death rituals. With the help of two sympathetic Brahmanas, Ramabai and Srinivas personally carried their dead mother's bier. Ramabai's small stature meant that she had to carry the bier upon her head in order to reach the burning ghat and complete the last rites.[14]

Writing about the months when, as a young woman of 16, Ramabai suddenly lost both her parents and her elder sister, she described the gradual erosion of faith in the traditional gods following the trauma:

I cannot describe all the sufferings of that terrible time. My father, mother, and sister, all died of starvation within a few months of each other. My brother and I survived and wandered about still visiting sacred places bathing in rivers and worshipping the gods and goddesses in order to get our desire. We had fulfilled all the conditions in the sacred books and kept all the rules.... For three years after the death of our parents and eldest sister we walked more than 4000 miles on foot without any sort of comfort, but the gods did not appear to us. After years of fruitless service we began to lose our faith.... We still continued to keep the caste rules, worshipped the gods and studied sacred literature as usual. We wandered from the south to the north as far as Kashmir and then to the east [reaching] Calcutta in 1878.[15]

The visit to Calcutta proved momentous. Ramabai and her brother met the intellectual elite, including pandits and reformers, and were welcomed and feted by them. These were the halcyon days of Ramabai's public life as she appeared as a godsend to the reformers,[16] providing them with a living embodiment of their perception of ancient Indian womanhood. To them Ramabai represented the recovery of the lost figures of Gargi and Maitreyi, women who were learned in Sanskrit at a time when women did not have learning of any kind and those who wished to learn still had to do so secretly. The euphoric reception she received also suggests that the second half of the nineteenth century was in some senses a historical conjuncture ripe for a Ramabai to appear. There was already a space for her, especially in Calcutta. For 50 years or more reformers had been talking of the glory of ancient Hindu womanhood, with its figures of Gargi and Maitreyi. Ramabai easily fitted into that space as ancient womanhood thus came alive in her person. She stepped into that already prepared frame and captured the public gaze.[17]

In later years Ramabai also recalled two landmarks of her Calcutta sojourn: she was asked to lecture on women (among the topics she lectured on was female emancipation, the education of women and the 'Rise and Fall of the Aryan Race')[18] and was advised by the leading Brahmo reformer, Keshub Chandra Sen, to study the Vedas. Ramabai describes her encounter with Sen thus:

K.C. Sen and his family showed great kindness to me and when parting he gave me a copy of one of the Vedas. He asked if I had studied the Vedas. I answered in the negative and said women were not fit to read the Vedas and were not allowed to do so. It would be breaking the rules of religion, if I were to study the Vedas. He could not but smile at my declaration of this Hindu doctrine. He said nothing in answer but advised me to study the Vedas and Upanishads... New thoughts were awakening in my heart. I questioned myself, why I should not study the Vedas and Vedanta. Soon I persuaded myself into the belief that it was not wrong for a woman to read the Vedas. So I began to first read the Upanishads, then the Vedanta and the Veda. I became more dissatisfied with myself...[19]

At the same time, in order to lecture on the duties of women according to the Shastras, Ramabai had to first study the Shastras herself. The reading of the 'forbidden' texts had some unintended consequences. It is ironic, but characteristic, that reformist men let Ramabai into their charmed circle, pointed out to her their vision of high Hinduism, set an agenda for her in relation to uplifting other women, but did not conceive of a situation in which Ramabai could go beyond it according to her own understanding. Her reading of the Dharmashastras led her to question the fundamental propositions of Brahmanic Hinduism. She writes:

While reading the Dharmashastras I came to know many things which I never knew before. There were contradictory statements about almost everything. What one book said was most righteous, the other book declared as being unrighteous... but there were two things on which all those books the Dharmashastras, the sacred epics, the Puranas and modern poets, the popular preachers of the present day and orthodox high caste men were agreed, that women of the high and low caste, as a class were all bad, very bad, worse than demons, as unholy as untruth and that they could not get moksha [like] men. The only hope of their getting this much desired liberation from karma and its results, that is countless millions of births and deaths and untold suffering, was the worship of their husbands. The husband is said to be a woman's god; there is no other god for her. This god may be the worst sinner and a great criminal; *still he is her god* and she must worship him.... The woman is allowed to go into higher existence (only) thus far but to attain moksha or liberation she must perform such great religious acts... by which she will be reincarnated as a high caste man, in order to study Vedas and the Vedanta and thereby get the knowledge of the true Brahma and be amalgamated in it. The extra-ordinary religious acts which help a woman to get into the way of getting moksha are utter abandonment of her will to that of her husband.... The woman has no right to study the Vedas and Vedanta and without knowing them no one can know the Brahma; therefore no woman can get moksha.Q.E.D.[20]

Analysing the Dharmashastras for herself, Ramabai became deeply conscious of the contempt with which women of all castes and men of the lower caste were regarded. The rules did not permit the Shudras to perform the same religious acts as the upper castes. They too, like women, were exhorted to serve the upper castes faithfully and then they would be reborn as high-caste men. The low-caste untouchables must lead degraded lives and after repeated births in such conditions, perchance after faithfully serving the high castes as their bondservants with *contentment*, they might be reborn into a higher caste and then gradually be 'uplifted'.[21] Struck by the common degradation of women and the low castes, about which the Shastras were unanimous, Ramabai's early Brahmanic socialisation was deeply shaken. She documents her growing awareness thus:

I had a vague idea of these doctrines of the Hindu religion from my childhood but while studying the Dharmashastras they presented themselves before my eyes with great force. My eyes were gradually opened: I was awakening up to my own hopeless condition as a woman, and it was becoming clearer and clearer to me that I had no place anywhere as far as religious consolation was concerned. I became quite dissatisfied with myself. I wanted something more than the Shastras could give me but I did not know what it was that I wanted.[22]

It was precisely these oppressive features of Brahmanic Hinduism that her father had attempted to escape from. Sheltered during her wandering years from the stranglehold of an oppressive ideology, and imbued with the fervour of her father's quest for salvation, Ramabai had little direct experience or even definite knowledge of the social power of Brahmanism. The travails of the wandering years followed by the failure of the family's collective search for salvation had been one aspect of her trauma. Now followed the further erosion of a spirited young woman's faith in her traditional religion. Before she could recover or resolve her growing sense of alienation, Ramabai suffered another severe blow; her brother Srinivas also died following a sudden illness.

All alone in the world for the first time with the last of her close kin taken from her, homeless and without economic support, Ramabai accepted a marriage proposal from an acquaintance in Sylhet.[23] Bipin Behari Medhavi, a friend of her brother Srinivas, was active in debates on the reform of caste and religious beliefs. He was of a different caste, a Shudra, and in accepting the proposal Ramabai chose to break decisively with tradition. By making a *pratiloma* marriage, she was defying Shastric injunctions which viewed such a marriage with horror. What is significant is that she did so consciously, even though there were other offers from fellow-castemen. One such highly 'qualified' Brahmana suitor, a Sanskrit scholar but also a 'modernist' from Maharashtra, an officer in the Bombay Civil Service, travelled to Assam to press his proposal.[24] From a contemporary account it is apparent that some learned Brahmana men regarded themselves as 'fitting' partners for Ramabai with whom an intellectual kinship could be established while upholding caste norms. And yet unlike them, Ramabai chose to cross the caste divide, describing it simply thus: 'Having lost faith in the religion of my ancestors I married a Bengali gentlemen of the Shudra caste'.[25]

Ramabai and Bipin Behari were married according to the Civil Marriage Act as neither of them believed in traditional Hinduism. The marriage was subjected to much criticism and Bipin Behari was promptly excommunicated. Tragically, the marriage was brief as Bipin Behari died within two years and Ramabai was left alone once more, but this time with a baby girl to support.[26] Like Vassitha in the Buddhist narrative who lost all her kin and, maddened with grief, turned to the Buddha for support,[27]

Ramabai's own search for meaning in life and for solace was now intensified.

Her early life on the margins of society, though unusual, was uncontroversial because the family was unknown. However, once she had stepped into the limelight in Calcutta her unconventional past began to be viewed with some suspicion, especially as her unmarried status at 22 was inexplicable in a society where even the Brahmo reformers such as K.C. Sen were wont to marry off their daughters around adolescence.[28] It is not surprising therefore that a great deal of speculation about her 'status' circulated as authentic information about her. One view was that Ramabai was not married because she was dedicated to Krishna as a child[29] — this explained her unmarried status. Another assumption was that she was a 'child' widow.[30] Both these speculations indicate notions of womanhood among the Hindu middle classes in the nineteenth century: women must be either given in to a religious community or widowed, if they were not married. Now, with actual widowhood, Ramabai became visible in a different way.

Her break with traditional codes now reached a decisive point. Her early life, unusual as it was with her late marriage, had, however, been compensated by her learning; her image had thus been one that could be played into the nineteenth century reformist agenda. Her cross-caste marriage was unprecedented (all the male reformers were still marrying very much within caste) but it was probably intellectually 'acceptable' in the reformist circles of Bengal, especially the Brahmos (although it was viewed with horror by traditional Hindu society). With widowhood however Ramabai became potentially a dangerous figure. Her life was henceforth subjected to much greater surveillance by a public that was unused to seeing women except in the domestic space. Ramabai refused to stay in the domestic space; she refused also the traditional role for the widow, that of withdrawal from society. Instead, following widowhood, she turned once more to a 'public' career, this time with a focused mission of serving the oppressed women of India. Her background, her life choices, her personality and her career now catapulted her into the public gaze, making her the most controversial Indian woman of her times.

On her part Ramabai began cautiously; like widows in Bengal she wore white and cropped her hair close. Left to fend for herself and her baby, without an income or property (her husband does not appear to have left Ramabai with any assets and is described as coming up the hard way, with Ramabai clearing off some of his debts), Ramabai decided to return to western India, the home of her ancestors.[31] The moderate reformers in the Prarthana Samaj like Ranade and Bhandarkar had invited her back and promised to provide support for her.[32] Ramabai arrived in Poona in 1882 and worked with this group of reformers, setting up a chain of Arya Mahila Sabhas. Here, a certain class of women could meet and discuss issues relating to the larger body of women.[33] She continued to narrate the Puranas, but this time to a new urban middle-class audience, and to propagate the objectives of the Arya Mahila Sabha.[34] She also appeared before the Hunter Commission and made a fervent plea for the introduction of facilities for the education of women, with special training for them as teachers and doctors so that they could serve other women.[35] But the task with which she most identified — the setting-up of a widows' home for high-caste Hindu widows, whose oppression was the subject of much concern — made little progress. She had fitted into the reformers' agenda but as yet there was no substantial move on their part to act in setting up the widows' home.

The sense of social isolation was compounded by the absence of religious moorings. Her peculiar location as a woman without any close kin in a world of male reformers 'intellectually' engaged in transforming Brahmanical Hinduism without addressing central questions, all well established in professions and surrounded, in the main, by docile and loving women, needs to be borne in mind. Ramabai's search for personal fulfilment as well as her struggle to understand, and conceptualise women's oppression from her own position as a woman were vastly different from the motivations and worldview of the men around her.

As a widow, Ramabai was also vulnerable in a way no man could ever be. Poona was orthodox and could be vicious in its 'defence' of Brahmanic Hinduism. Except in the sheltered atmosphere of like-minded reformers Ramabai's public appearances, speaking on behalf of women, were too threatening and she was often shouted down by aggressive men. Documenting one such lecture, Tagore wrote from Poona that the present-day Bargis (Maharashtrians) turned rowdy as soon as she got up to speak and that she had to sit down without finishing her speech.[36] Even Ramabai's extraordinary courage must have been severely tested by such incidents.

The scorn with which Brahmana women treated Ramabai (and which she could not have been unaware of) also increased her sense of alienation from the dominant elite of Poona. This is graphically described by Ranade's wife (in her memoirs about her famous judge-husband), who was exhorted to be kind to the sorrowful Ramabai. She records that other women in her family and neighbourhood regarded her as a wretched convert (long before she became a Christian). Unable to accept her background, they railed against her:

We cannot tolerate such sacrilege. What an accursed thing. Her father had turned her into a devotee and wedded her to the heavenly bridegroom Shri Dwarkanath. And yet this wretch married a Bengali baboo and polluted herself. And did she at least build a home for herself after that? No fear. She brought utter ruin on everyone connected with her and is now out to pollute the whole world.[37]

Apart from the very fact of the widow occupying a public space, her speech was also dangerous. The Arya Mahila Sabha was regarded as an institution set up to do away with the domination of men. Ramabai was reported as arguing that according to existing social practices women had to obey men, or be treated like slaves, without being cared for at all. They toiled without end all day. They had to serve their husbands hand and foot, even when they themselves were tired, and still be prepared to receive kicks and blows at the slightest pretext. It was believed that the Pandita only exhorted women to free themselves from the tyranny of men at these meetings in the Arya Mahila Sabhas, causing horror to the orthodox, both men and women.[38] Thus even if Ramabai was a Brahmana woman herself she had no 'community', no social base and no real emotional bonds to fall back upon. Ranade's wife describes how, despite the approval and support of her husband, she was caught in a dilemma and, in trying to seek the support of her female kin, reneged once in public on her association with Ramabai.[39] While Ranade could, through his disapproval of his wife, force her to continue her relationship with Ramabai, the fragility of such a relationship was probably no consolation to Ramabai herself.

These experiences heightened Ramabai's vulnerability. Despite her public location she was alone and dependent upon the charity of the reformers even for her daily needs. The sense of urgency, both at the personal level and in connection with the work that she wished to pursue — the setting-up of a widows' home — was not shared by the reformers. The religious search, too, had remained unfulfilled. Throughout the years of hardship when the family had wandered about, they had collectively been sustained by their search for mukti. The intensity of those early experiences had left a lasting need in Ramabai to find religious meaning in her life. Her tragic losses had added to this quest. Her association with the Brahmos and the Prarthana Samajists — a variant of the Brahmos in Maharashtra — did not fill the void. Recalling her state of mind during this period, Ramabai wrote:

I was desperately in need of some religion. The Hindu religion held out no hope for me. The Brahmo religion was not a very definite one. For it is nothing but what a man makes for himself. He chooses and gathers whatever seems good to him from all religions known to him.... The Brahmo religion has no other foundation than a man's own natural light and the sense of right or wrong which he possesses in common with all of mankind. It could not and did not satisfy me...[40]

What Ramabai appears to have been in need of was not some abstract notion of God but a figure that she could express an intense devotion to, one that could satisfy her both intellectually *and* emotionally. In an earlier age she may have found satisfaction among the Bhakti saints. In the nineteenth century, however, the Bhakti tradition itself had been absorbed within a larger Brahmanic Hinduism and does not appear to have been perceived as a distinctive alternative to it.[41] Also, Ramabai was a product of nineteenth century social forces, a widow who had a social agenda on widowhood. Her need and search was thus for a solution that could simultaneously accommodate her social agenda as well as her personal quest for religious fulfilment.

It was at this point that Ramabai first came into contact with Christian missionaries. Her own unfulfilled searches had made her susceptible to outside influences. At the same time her public visibility, would have brought her to the notice of Christian missionaries. They began to woo her as a potential catch.[42] On her part, Ramabai had read a Bengali translation of the Gospel according to Saint Luke, one of the most moving renderings of

Christ's life, which made an immediate impact upon her. Attracted by its content, she had considered becoming a Christian, but she wrote later that her husband did not like the idea of her becoming 'publicly baptised', thus joining the 'despised Christian community'.[43] Now in Poona, a missionary, Miss Hurford, taught her English and introduced her to the Bible in Marathi

But the most crucial influence in the move to Christianity, came from someone who shared her own background, Nilkantha Goreh, known after his conversion as Father Goreh. A Chitpavan Brahmana like Ramabai and a 'true' seeker too like her, Goreh had found personal fulfilment in Christ rather than in Christianity as it was institutionalised. He spent his later years wandering around like Ramabai's father, having found his faith in Christ though not a community among the Christians.[44] It was following Ramabai's reading of a book written by him that she became 'intellectually' convinced[45] of the truth of Christ but this was still in the future. As suggested earlier, while in Poona (with its strong Brahmanical ambience) Ramabai's lifework had crystallised and come to focus on the need to provide practical support to battered and oppressed child widows. One such victim, a young widow of 12 who had been married at the age of five and been widowed a few days later, was brought to her in 1882. Regarded as the killer of her husband, she had been thrown out by her in-laws. Ramabai took the young widow into her home and began to form an idea of a widows' home. She wrote:

As I looked on that little figure, my vague thoughts about doing something for my sisters in a similar condition began to shape.... I began to place a plan for starting a home for Hindu widows before my countrymen and to ask for their help. For six months or more I tried my best to get help but could not...[46]

Disappointed thus in her 'countrymen', she decided to build up her own skills and make contact with people 'outside'. In order to get a medical education as a preliminary step, she made up her mind to go to England 'if the way opened'.[47] Through contacts in the Church of England Mission in Poona she finally found an opening and in early 1883 she left for England. In order to raise money for her passage she wrote and published the *Stri Dharma Niti*, a book about 'morals' for women.[48] Dedicated to the memory of her deceased husband and in many ways a contrast to *The High*

Caste Hindu Woman which she wrote after her conversion, it represents the reformist approach to Hindu womanhood and is indicative of the close links she had with her moderate, male Brahmana associates. However, even this early work carries her unique stamp; in my view it is less about the companionate wife and more about women's self-cultivation even as they performed the roles of wife and mother. The writing and publication of the book to raise money, a practice she continued for some years, is also evidence of her uncertain economic position. She was probably one of the first known women who wrote and lectured for a living in the nineteenth century.[49]

On her voyage to England, Ramabai was accompanied by her three-year old daughter Manoramabai, and Anandibai Bhagat, a friend. Till she left, the competing pulls of the Prarthana Samajists and Christianity do not appear to have been resolved; she had publicly stated at Pandharpur in November/December 1882 that she had no intention of becoming a Christian.[50] Anxious about her independence, Ramabai also made sure before she left that she should not be beholden to the missionaries in England who were arranging her stay and education, by organising support for herself as a teacher of Marathi.[51]

However, Ramabai's visit to England was crucial in decisively resolving the tension she had been experiencing about religion in favour of Christianity. She was warmly welcomed by the sisters at Wantage where one of them, Sister Geraldine, became her spiritual mother. Thereafter she always referred to her as *Ajibai* or Grandmother.[52] Ramabai's decisive move to Christianity appears to have followed her introduction to the 'rescue' work carried on by the sisters in London. She was particularly moved by her meeting with women who had once been inmates at the 'Rescue Home', an institution for 'fallen women', who were now so 'completely changed', and so filled with love for Christ and compassion for 'suffering humanity', that they had gone on to devote their lives to the service of the sick and the infirm. Ramabai was drawn to the service aspect of Christianity.[53]

At this point in her life she was still in search of her 'mission' rather than the philosophical aspects of faith. What appealed to her about Christianity was that it drew people into action. In this she thus differed from other high-caste Brahmana men such as Goreh or even Waman Narayan Tilak who were drawn to Christianity on rational and philosophical grounds. She was also struck by the fact that Christians, regarded as outcastes by Hindus, were attempting to help those 'unfortunate women who were degraded in the eyes of society'.

> I had never heard or seen anything of the kind done for this class of women by the Hindus in my country.... The Hindu shastras do not deal kindly with these women. The law of the Hindu commands that the king shall cause fallen women to be eaten by dogs in the outskirts of the town. They are considered the greatest sinners and not worthy of compassion.[54]

Notions of sin and redemption appealed to Ramabai, particularly after she heard the story of Christ's meeting with the Samaritan woman and his message to her on the nature of true worship. To Ramabai, Christ then became the divine saviour, one who could 'uplift' the downtrodden women of India. It was after this, according to her official account of her move into Christianity, that she made a decisive break with the religion of her ancestors and was baptised along with her daughter on 29 September 1883.[55] Adrift emotionally since the loss of her natal kin and a religious seeker for as long as she could remember, she finally sought an anchor in Christ for her emotional and religious needs.

Ramabai's traumatic experiences were, however, not yet over. If anything they intensified. What is significant is that the otherwise courageous and honest Ramabai suppressed, in her own testimony, one of the most painful experiences of the last few months of 1883, immediately before and after her conversion. This silence is eloquent and suggests that she could not, even in later years, deal with the anguish of these days during which her companion, who saw herself as a daughter to Ramabai, killed herself, either fearing conversion or regretting a baptism that had already occurred. The episode is difficult to reconstruct because it is only alluded to by Max Muller in whose house Ramabai stayed after her own baptism.[56] There is also a brief account of Anandibai's death in a letter written by the Mother Superior of St Mary's Home, Wantage, where Ramabai and Anandibai were living. It was here that Anandibai, in what was believed to have been a fit of temporary insanity, took poison and died after a few hours of intense suffering. Sister Geraldine, who compiled the letters to, from, and about Ramabai, also noted that the shock occasioned by the death of

Anandibai brought Ramabai to experience a great sense of sin and to prepare with great humility for her baptism.[57]

Max Muller's account captures Ramabai's state of mind with much greater sensitivity than the official version of the sisters at Wantage.[58] Muller recounts the tragic months of September and October:

But even then her tragedy was not yet ended. She had declared to the sisters that grateful as she felt for their kindness she would never become a Christian because, as she often said, a good Brahmani is quite as good as a good Christian. Her friend, however was frightened by the idea that she and Ramabai would be made Christians by force; and to save Ramabai and herself from such a fate she tried one night to strangle her (Ramabai). Failing in that she killed herself. It was after this terrible catastrophe at Wantage that Ramabai came to stay with us at Oxford, and such was her nervous prostration that we had to give her a maidservant to sleep every night in the same room with her. Nor was this all. After all the arrangements had been made to enable her to attend medical lectures at Oxford [where she was visiting the Mullers] her hearing became suddenly so much affected that she had to give up the idea of a medical career.[59]

The events as recorded by Max Muller starkly convey Ramabai's trauma; even the dramatic collapse of an already impeded hearing seems to be connected with the double stress of the conversion and the suicide of a friend for which Ramabai may have felt responsible. Years later, writing her *Testimony*, Ramabai merely records that she knew full well that her conversion would displease 'her friends and countrymen', and goes on to say that she has never regretted having taken that step.[60] But the anguish she felt led to a withdrawal. She shrank from being a public figure and wanted to work quietly and unobtrusively. She was pained by the knowledge that many eyes were upon her and her 'future work'.[61]

Father Goreh's support was instrumental in her recovery from the trauma. Goreh had convinced her that the theism of the Prarthana Samajists was no different from Christianity. She wrote later that 'his humble "sweet voice" had pierced my heart', and she recognised that only he had the power to turn her away from the Brahmana religion.[62] Max Muller also recounts a more pressing concern that led Ramabai to Christianity. She had told him that it was not so much that she felt her former religion was entirely false or mischievous but that she could no longer stand quite alone. She needed support. She wanted particularly to be able to worship together with those whom she loved and who had been kind to her.[63]

The outcry in India following the news of her conversion was immediate and characteristic. The supposedly liberal reformist press in the hands of Brahmana men was particularly vociferous and swung from eulogising her to damning her for her 'fickleness' which was portrayed as *'peculiarly female'* [emphasis added]. The editor of *Indu Prakash* complained:

We were all taken with awe and wonderstruck by her charms of appearance [!] and the fluent tongue wielding the language; her modest and intelligent speeches, all so sweet and juicy, all now gone and wasted. Oh Pandita Bai. You are after all a woman, whatever your culture and achievement be — you are thus rendered a woman helpless. We however wondered, how you could take so many years to become 'holy'. You have disappointed a number of friends and admirers, be assured.[64]

The *Indu Prakash* also wrote mockingly of Ramabai's so-called religious quest:

Pandita Ramabai was in the first instance a Hindu, then she became a Brahmo, now she has become a Christian. This shows and proves she is of unstable mind. We should not be surprised if she becomes a Muslim soon. She has only to meet a Muslim Kazi who will convince her that his religion will give her peace and salvation.[65]

The honeymoon with the liberals was clearly over, as the double condemnation of Ramabai contained above indicates. What could very well have been perceived as a 'rational' choice on Ramabai's part, and as evidence of her ability to decide for herself *despite* being a woman who was subject to multiple pressures, her decision is turned into an act of fickleness 'natural' to women. But, significantly, the editorial also echoes a sense of injury at Ramabai's failure to fall in line with the liberal reformist agenda in the creation of a new kind of woman: educated, but pliant. Unlike Brahmana conservatives such as Tilak, who defined the nation in exclusivist terms, and had ideologically placed themselves against British imperialism while regarding Christianity as its handmaiden, the reformists had no such ground for opposing Ramabai. Her choice of religious belief could not be critiqued on 'rational' grounds. It was explicable only in terms of the limitations of the reformers' liberal position embedded within a patriarchal ideology, tied inextricably with their upper-class/caste position.

Only Phule defended Ramabai and did so publicly. He argued that Ramabai, as a truly educated woman, had seen for herself the bias of the Shastras towards the low castes and women and therefore could not but break with Brahmanic Hinduism. He castigated newspaper editorials for their denunciation of Ramabai's conversion. He suggested that the hysterical reaction of the male writers was because they were unwilling to accept a situation where women had taken to writing and expressing their dissent in print.[66]

In sharp contrast to Phule were the conservatives, who lashed out at Ramabai calling her a *batli* (impure, fallen, polluted), and accused her of committing a grave and unpardonable sin against Hindu society.[67] She was regarded as having fooled everybody. The anger of the middle-class Hindu intelligentsia across the country at Ramabai's renouncing Hinduism for Christianity was partly because they could no longer use her as an example of an educated, 'Hindu' woman who fully endorsed 'Hindu' culture. It was also partly because women had no right to choose to break from Hinduism anyway. Even Vivekananda and Ramakrishna denounced her. For Ramakrishna, Ramabai was too ambitious — she represented a kind of egotism and idealism which was not 'good' as it was a mere pursuit of name and fame.[68] Vivekananda on the other hand could see the potential gains that Ramabai could have brought to his 'cause' if she had remained a Hindu. Ramabai would go on to make quite an impact on America but how much more would be gained if an Indian woman, in Indian dress, preached the religion which fell from the lips of the rishis of India. A great wave would inundate the whole western world, he had said. 'Will there be no women in the land of Maitreyi, Lilavati, Savitri, and Ubhayabharati, who will venture to do this?' he had mourned.[69] The significant point is that after her conversion Ramabai represented not the glory of the ancient Maitreyi but a discordant voice who spoke for the subjugated woman of nineteenth century India.

In September 1884 Ramabai joined the Women's College, Cheltenham, as a student and as a teacher of Marathi. The new role envisaged for her as a teacher, and possibly as a public lecturer addressing students and assemblies of women and men (in order to provide her with an income), threw her into the first of her many brushes with Church authority. It is important to point out that Ramabai never at any point in her post-conversion life, became a *pliant* tool in the hands of the missionaries. Too independent for the Church, she had a relationship with various segments of Christianity, in India and in England, marked by considerable tension. Among the missionaries, distrust of her as a person never quite ended.

The first early brush was symptomatic of her volatile relationship with the Church which was patriarchal and racist. It was precipitated by the suggestion that Ramabai should teach young English men and women Indian languages and philosophy in order to help establish an understanding of India in them. The Bishops of Lahore and Bombay reacted sharply to this suggestion and dismissed it on the grounds that it would create a scandal in India if a woman were to teach men.[70] When Ramabai was told that the suggestion had been shot down by people who were 'eminently' fit to judge the situation in India, she was furious. She refused to accept that any set of English men, however long they may have lived in India, could be better judges than her. She rejected outright their notion of a code of behaviour befitting an 'Indian woman'. She was, after all, the daughter of a woman who had taught the inmates of an ashrama, so it was unlikely that such an argument would be convincing to her. Further, she strongly believed that by accepting the rationale of the bishops she would be acting against her father, mother, brother and husband who had 'approved of young girls speaking in mixed assemblies'. She argued that the bishops' reactions betrayed a lack of trust in her, but most importantly it was against her understanding of God who, she believed, was neither male nor female. This understanding had been central to her acceptance of Christ. Ramabai concluded that imposing Church authority on this matter would infringe her personal liberty.[71] Clearly it was a matter not just of faith but of principles.

Surprised by the fierceness of Ramabai's arguments, the sisters at Wantage, attempted to make a subtle distinction between her lecturing to mixed assemblies in India 'to arouse the conscience of men about their oppression of women'[72] and doing the same in England (where presumably no conscience needed to be stirred). The latter, they held, could not be justified on any ground.

The clumsy approach of the Church authorities to the question of the propriety of Ramabai teaching English men was merely a facade. At the core of the proposition was the fear that the status of a 'professor' might go to Ramabai's head and make her more difficult to 'control'. The utility of such a 'vain' person, who refused to accept that as a Christian she must also accept the authority of the bishops, was held suspect by the Anglican Church.[73] The confrontation with the authorities of the Church of England which failed to break Ramabai's independent spirit was summed up by her thus:

I have a conscience and a mind of *my own* [emphasis added]. I must myself think and do everything which God has given me the power of doing.... I have with great effort freed myself from the yoke of the Indian priestly tribe so I am not at present willing to place myself under another similar yoke by accepting everything that comes from the priests as authorised command of the Most High. Can you, or your friends prove that giving lessons to boys is wrong? I am not [that] anxious to give lessons to men, but I am anxious to do away with all kinds of prejudices which deprive a woman in India of her proper place in society.... I do not think I shall say anything on behalf of my liberty [but] as far as I know from the time I have had a real liberty, I have not acted as a lawless woman. When people decide anything for me without consulting with me about it I do of course call it interfering with my liberty and am not willing to let them do it. Would you feel bound to accept every word or rule which comes from the bishop as an expression of the will of the Most High? Perhaps you would... but I do not, and will not.[74]

The Anglican Church's attitude to Ramabai, a 'native' of a country ruled by the English, was a combination of colonial arrogance and racial contempt. It was, at the same time, a recognition of the need to have her as a pliant instrument for the Church's missionary agenda. Ramabai was unwilling to play the role they found for her and at one stage instilled in them the fear that she would quit Christianity rather than give up her right to think for herself.[75] She turned the tables on them and found fault with the conventional approach of the missionaries who went out to teach those of whose 'language and philosophy and modes of thought they are utterly ignorant, with whom they have no sympathy'. This was in contrast to the apostles of old, especially St. Paul, who 'became to the Jews as a Jew, to the Greeks as a Greek'. She was critical especially of the missionaries concentrating their arguments on the errors of Hinduism. Let the missionaries put themselves in the place of the Hindus and see from their point of view and then think whether they would like their own Christianity learnt by the Hindus merely to have its errors and weak points exposed.[76] She also disagreed with the understanding prevalent among missionaries and others in England that it was only worthwhile educating the upper strata of Indian society. When a low-caste convert Marathi girl was not accommodated for a course of study in England on the grounds that she was of low caste and therefore would not be accepted as a 'teacher' when she returned to India, Ramabai argued:

Why would we think others low and ourselves great? We are the same in God's sight are we not? Perhaps, the humblest shoe-maker is greater in his sight than a proud Brahmin. Our Lord Himself was born a humble carpenter and he did all things for the humble in spirit. Is it not so ?[77]

It was Ramabai's ability to argue and turn the arguments of the authorities round on themselves that was so devastating. She was just too 'self-reliant' for them. This self-reliance was demonstrated not only in non-theological matters but also over issues central to Christian philosophy. She had a long drawn out dispute over the miraculous birth of Christ as well as the concept of the Holy Trinity. During this discussion she refused to accept the view that the Anglican Church in particular represented the sole treasury of truth whereas all other Christians were followers of false doctrines. She infuriated Sister Geraldine, her mentor in the Anglican Church, who turned 'mad with rage' when she argued that the latter had no right to characterise dissenters as 'heretics', since she herself belonged to a heretic church in the eyes of the Roman Catholics.[78]

It is not surprising, therefore, that the missionaries who had thought that they had gained a prize catch when they converted her were deeply disappointed and annoyed. She was variously described as someone whom the devil was attempting to get hold of, or as too self-reliant, which in the case of a 'neophyte was intensely dangerous'.[79] There was great anxiety also that if she returned to India too soon Christianity would lose its hold over her completely.[80]

Ramabai's refusal to allow the missionaries to dictate the nature of her relationship to God, to India and to Hinduism were at the heart of the reproaches they directed against her. Her lifestyle, (for example, following a vegetarian diet), was regarded as caste prejudice and evidence of her false pride.[81] In response she argued that she liked to be called a Hindu, 'for I am one', and wanted to

keep all the customs of her forefathers as far as she could, as long
as they were not hurtful to her neighbours.[82] She went on to say
decisively that she would not allow anyone to 'lay hands on my
personal liberty'. Declaring that she had a mind strong enough to
resist 'meaningless social customs' which deprived a woman of her
proper place in society, she had refused to accept a decision of the
Church to disallow her to teach men. She described the bishops'
position as a personal insult to her which she would not accept.[83]
Unable now to pursue her study of medicine, thwarted in her role
as teacher and refusing the authority of the Church to interpret
God to her, Ramabai decided that it was better to have the 'shade
of an old tree, or the meanest hut', rather than be dictated to. For
Ramabai, faith had to be consistent with conviction, with the inner
voice which she often used to great effect in any controversy, or
with conscience which would at all times guide one's actions, and
was above any authority or anyone's belief.[84]

Perhaps the dual burden in Ramabai's relationship with the
Anglican Church, in which she had to accept the direct colonial
mentality of the Church and its male authority structures, as well
as its missionary ambitions, explains her decision to go to America
in search of support for her work in India. The Anglican
missionaries were ambivalent about her going. She became the prize
catch, the rare Indian jewel, whom America stole from England.[85]
Yet, they felt it was better that she went since they had been unable
to make her work within their framework of priorities. But they
made some attempt to hold on to Manoramabai, the Pandita's
daughter. The missionaries may have recognised that ensuring a
degree of pliancy in an adult, even if she was a woman without
definite support, was difficult to achieve. Training one from
childhood onwards might have better success. Ramabai's
continuous travels in America and her preoccupation with
lecturing, writing and raising funds meant that she found it difficult
to keep Mano with her. The sisters at Wantage were more than
happy to have her and later tried to resist the child's return to her
mother. Ramabai, however, was adamant that Mano must grow
among her own people, live like them so that she could serve them
and decide for herself what her particular religious beliefs within
various Christian sects must be. The missionaries were quite
scornful of the Pandita's ideas, describing how Mano's early
cultivated training was ruined when she returned to India and how

much like a "little pig" she was thanks to her mother's peculiar notions about a simple Indian upbringing.[86] The Anglican missionaries were not sympathetic to Pandita Ramabai's attempts to integrate in her life and work a commitment to her own people and culture with a deep faith in Christ.

This lack of space to manoeuvre different aspects, needs and beliefs was a continual problem that Pandita Ramabai faced in her life. The Anglican missionaries demanded that she work in a kind of structure and were suspicious of her 'Indian' side; the Brahmana intelligentsia with whom she tried to work later were deeply suspicious of her 'Christian' side. Wedged between the two, Ramabai alienated first one set of people and then another.

Ramabai went to America ostensibly to attend the graduation of a distant cousin, Anandibai Joshi, in 1886,[87] and stayed on for two years travelling from coast to coast. From her experiences it would appear that a certain 'secular' support was available to women pursuing professional and social goals. This came from women's groups such as the Christian Temperance Union, the Suffragettes, and the Abolitionists (of slavery) who mobilised women for social change.[88] Anandibai Joshi's medical education had been facilitated through the intervention of Mrs Carpenter and Dr Rachel Bodley, and a number of women provided hospitality and support to Ramabai during her two-year stay in the United States.[89] During this period Ramabai addressed hundreds of meetings, sometimes as many as four in a day, and travelled over 50,000 kilometres, doing an incredible amount of 'writing, speaking travelling, entertaining, and thinking' as part of her effort to collect money for the Widows' Home.[90]

Ramabai was apparently the first public figure from India to solicit funds for setting up social institutions back home. A few years later Vivekananda, too, would do the same, using a very different strategy and for a very different agenda. Ramabai appealed to the American women as women, to help the oppressed widows of India. It was to publicise their miserable state that Ramabai wrote her best-known work *The High Caste Hindu Woman*. The book was widely sold; proceeds from its sales helped to repay the Wantage sisters for their support in England (this would end her obligation to them) and to set up a fund for the opening of a widows' home in India.[91] At the same time the book functioned to disseminate information about the plight of the high-caste Hindu widow. It resulted in the formation of the American Ramabai Association to provide funds for the opening and continued maintenance of the Widows' Home in India. When she finally set sail for India from San Francisco in 1888 she had completed the initial task of raising funds, but was clearly nervous about the road ahead which, she wrote, 'seemed dark, unknown, and so difficult' that she felt almost as if she were going back to a strange people.[92] It was not without reason, because her actions continued to be independent and defiant, plunging her repeatedly into controversy.

Ramabai's visible achievements during the years she spent in America and the drive with which she proceeded to set up the home for widows, could not but impress the elite of Bombay and Poona. She called her home Sharada Sadan, the home of learning. The disappointment and opposition expressed even by the reform party at her conversion, melted, at least for the moment, since Ramabai had succeeded where others had not even seriously begun, in setting up such an institution. Ramabai desired to open and run the widows' home with support from Brahmana men, some of whom she had worked with in 1882-83, since the concept of such an institution was still somewhat unorthodox and required public support from at least a section of the communities from which the high-caste widows were to be drawn. Sharada Sadan was inaugurated in March 1889 in Bombay, with Mrs Kashibai Kanitkar presiding over the function. Characteristically, Ramabai's initiative was hailed by the press as an indication that 'native' society was alive and vigorous. The 'race' that had produced her had nothing to despair, proclaimed a journalist in the *Bombay Educational Record*.[93]

In the first three years the number of inmates in Sharada Sadan gradually rose. Ramabai continued in her role as champion of women's issues and participated in the annual Congress meeting held in Bombay in December 1889. Speaking before an assembly of 2,000 delegates, including 10 women, at a time when the liberal Ranade considered it undesirable that women should take part in politics, she pointedly drew the attention of the men to the way they had marginalised women. 'It is not strange, my countrymen,' she said, 'that my voice is small, for you have never given a woman the chance to make her voice strong'.[94] A few days later she took a strong stand at the meeting of the third National Social Conference on the humiliation of child widows. On the issue of introducing a regulation banning the tonsuring of widows, Ramabai argued that women should be left to decide for themselves 'freely' whether they wished to be tonsured. Recognising the agency of women, she insisted that a widow must decide how she would live: if she wished to have her head shaved she should be allowed to do so. But at the same time Ramabai made it amply clear that although she had come across a great number of widows she had never yet met one who was *willing* to have her head shaved. Driving home her point, she demanded to know from the men whether any of them would have their heads shaved on the death of their wives. Using the by-now common arguments of the nationalists of their right to free speech, about which a great deal had been said in that very hall, she ended by demanding the *same* privilege for women. On her part, she said, she was convinced that if Indian women were given the opportunity to decide for themselves they, like the women of Sparta, would then join their husbands in the defence of their people.[95]

Ramabai's understanding of patriarchy, her ready wit and quick repartee also came in extremely handy when she was faced by hostile men and women. When the Age of Consent controversy created a polarisation among elites, with the militant nationalists championing tradition, Ramabai drew back the attention of the audience to the real issues that needed focusing on: the rights of women. At a women's convention in Bombay, women reformers such as Kashibai Kanitkar and Ramabai were charged with sacrificing family relations. A woman participant demanded to know from Mrs Kanitkar if she would like her son-in-law to be sued in a court for infringing the conditions laid down in the Bill. While Mrs Kanitkar fumbled for a suitable reply Ramabai shot back, 'Never mind the son-in-law, his life is not worth more than that of the daughter'.[96] Despite unsympathetic audiences Ramabai continued to weigh in with her opinion on any issue that affected women, even if she was shouted down. And, in a characteristic reformulation, she redefined loyalty and patriotism in terms of the worship of mothers rather than some tokenist display of loyalty to the 'Queen'.[97] Finally, her pragmatic approach to social and national questions is revealed in her advocacy of Hindi as the most effective language for the nation.[98]

Within the Sharada Sadan Ramabai tried to provide the widowed inmates with a new understanding of themselves. Over the years, particularly after she moved to Kedgaon, she experimented with ideas that could provide women with space to grow and be self-sufficient, a sort of female community for women of all castes (unlike other institutions where only Brahmana women were admitted), providing a sanctuary for them within the larger society which was dominated by men.[99] Since widows had been regarded as social outcasts and were expected to lead joyless lives, Ramabai attempted to return them to the larger social body, as well as to help them build a new and meaningful life. Within three months of the opening of Sharada Sadan she noted a change in the nature of her girls who had happy times singing together with Ramabai in the evenings, enjoying the simple joys of just being alive.[100]

Significantly, Ramabai's attitude to the remarriage of widows was very different from that of the male reformers as we have already seen. It was just one way of returning widowed women to society but not the only way since, in her view, they were not merely sexual beings whose sexuality posed a threat to the social order. There were a number of ways by which widows could live, as teachers, nurses, or workers. At Mukti Sadan in Kedgaon her girls did everything from weaving, dairy farming, cooking, gardening, running a printing press and even farming.[101] What she did insist upon was that all categories of women, including widows, were to be fully integrated into the social community in which no woman was regarded as inauspicious. When her first student, the child widow Godubai (named Anandibai after her marriage), was to be remarried to Dr Karve, a grand reception was attended by fifty or sixty widows who had organised the whole function.[102] By integrating widows into society, Ramabai was reconceptualising widowhood and womanhood in a way that most male reformers could never think of.

It was probably this unique social vision, born out of a personal understanding and based on her own experiences, that led to what was almost an inevitable conflict with Hindu society, including the 'reform party'. In setting up Sharada Sadan, the Ramabai Association of America had decided that it should be 'secular', with no religious teaching of any kind. Further, a number of the Brahmana male reformers were appointed to the Advisory Board which functioned also as the Managing Board. Evidently, although the Ramabai Association had been generous with its support, it was not free of male authority structures; it had put Ramabai in charge of the women but placed the reformers in authority over Ramabai. (As represented by the latter, however, it was Ramabai who had refused to function without 'absolute power'.) Over a period of time Ramabai found herself obstructed over basic decisions, even on the subject of which girls could be admitted since such decisions were made by the 'Managing Board'.[103] Apparently, the Ramabai Association of America wanted to work within notions of existing social norms and so, both in America and in India, men were put in charge of the Widows' Home. In November 1890, a year after the Sadan was opened, Ramabai moved to Poona since Bombay was proving too expensive. Orthodox Poona maintained a more effective surveillance of the Sadan and soon a series of controversies arose about the impending or actual conversion of Brahmana widows in the institution. Brahmanical society in Poona became hysterical. Deep-seated fears about what an institution for widows, where they were to be educated and made useful, would do to Hindu society, partly explained the lack of enthusiasm for setting up such an institution. The fact that the institution was headed by a Christian woman had added to the anxiety but now the rumours about conversion gave a hysterical edge to the fears. That widows, the dregs of Hindu society, should have the audacity to seek conversion was unthinkable. This would imply a recognition of women's agency — a right to determine the course of their own lives which even the reformers were unwilling to grant them, but which Ramabai insisted on. Further, such an assertion of choice was a rejection of the moral order of Brahmanism. It would also be a declaration by the widows that they found Brahmanical patriarchal practices unacceptable and therefore they wished to break from them. The attack on Ramabai by Tilak and others was virulent: not only was she a Christian but she was in charge of an institution housing young women away from the control of male kin. In recalling the controversy over Ramabai's own conversion and about the widows in Sharada Sadan, we need to note that other women, like Lakshmibai Tilak, who converted (following their husbands) did not arouse such strong emotions. Their conversion was regarded as natural. It was only women who decided for themselves who were perceived as dangerous.

The entire 'conversion' controversy brought to the fore the hypocrisy of upper-caste Hindu society. While the conservative among them were not uncomfortable about the degradation and humiliation inhering in widowhood, the reformers went along with the idea of an institution because it would provide a home for their social outcasts. But even they did not want an open recognition of the widows' abandonment of their ancestral faith since this was tantamount to a critique of Brahmanical patriarchal tradition within which they had comfortably accommodated their own agenda of reform.

Ramabai summed up the Board's limited agenda and her relationship with it thus:

We must never expect to give anything better than food and raiment, and teach a few letters to the girls. I had from the beginning intended in all sincerity to give my girls full religious freedom. I would not prevent them from reading the sacred books of their own religion, so too I did not mean to prevent them from reading the Bible if they wished to do so fully understanding what they were doing. I would never have tried to decide then not to induce minors to learn my religion against the wishes of their parents and guardians... but now as the case stands I shall be obliged to let the girls have full freedom regarding their ancestral religion and prevent them from reading the Bible even if they or the guardians wish me to let them know something about Christianity. Here my conscience smites me.[104]

Ramabai found out the hard way that along with American funds went conditions, that there were no funds without controls. The members of her Board who reacted sharply to her position, on practising her own faith on the premises without having to shut the doors against her girls[105] (who otherwise had free access to her rooms), in their turn were insecure about how the widows of their communities would react to religious ideas other than their own and did not want to antagonise Brahmana men from whom they (the Board members) were drawn.[106] At the core of the controversy was the question: who has custody of women? Can women be permitted to decide for themselves? Clearly the reaction over the conversions indicates that men were not willing to give up their control over the women of their community even when they had little use for them otherwise.

The controversy regarding conversions finally ended with the reformers on the Board, including Ranade and Bhandarkar, resigning.[107] For a while many high-caste widows were withdrawn. But as long as there was no other institution, upper caste widows who had no home had perforce to be sent to the Sharada Sadan.

Ramabai describes how even when rancorous attacks were being made against her and her institution, the orthodox neighbours of a poor Brahmana widow who was being persecuted by her relatives, pointed to the Sharada Sadan as the place for her to go. Ironically, it was Ramabai Ranade (whose husband was on the Board and who went on to resign) who brought in the young widow, accompanied by her child. The girl had been so miserable that she did not want to think twice about going to Sharada Sadan. The account of this event suggests that it was a number of 'orthodox' Brahmana women who spearheaded this move; they went to Ramabai Ranade's house and got her to act with the support of two 'orthodox' widows in the house who had earlier been very critical of the Pandita.[108]

The threat posed by Ramabai's institution, given her refusal to submit to an agenda set by middle-class reformers, finally led to the setting-up of a widows' home in Hingne by D.K. Karve in 1896. Karve had married Godubai in 1891. Godubai had been Ramabai's first student in Sharada Sadan and was among those who had shown an interest in Christianity. Karve made strategic use of the panic among the Brahmana community of Poona following the conversion controversy to set up his own institution (and push the cause of widow remarriage as well). As Karve recognised, 'From the orthodox point of view, even the remarriage of widows was not so objectionable as their conversion to Christianity'.[109]

Karve's institution was very cautiously administered and his work on widow remarriage was strictly separated from the institution he set up for widows. Its regulations were so framed that a widow of the school who remarried had to leave it. Further, the institution was open only to Brahmana widows.[110] In Karve's institution Brahmana reformers finally found the perfect institutional answer to their project for young widows: a widows' home safely in the hands of a moderate, respectable, Brahmana man — a marked contrast to that 'disastrous' first experiment they had supported, an institution in the hands of a defiant widow herself.

Looking back at the controversy over the possible conversion of widows from the vantage-point of today, how do we understand Ramabai's action? It has been suggested that with her conversion, particularly after the confrontation with the Board of Advisers, Ramabai ceased to influence her society.[111] This view is only partially tenable. It is possible that Ramabai could only have

influenced Brahmanical society in a certain way if she had remained
a Hindu widow. But the argument can also be turned around —
how far could she have gone in her own life and in her
conceptualisation of society and of women's place in it, if she had
remained a Hindu widow, contained within the agenda set by men
of her caste and class? Ramabai had tried to work within certain
norms even if she did not agree with them. For example, she made
arrangements for the widows at Sharada Sadan to pursue their caste
practices; cooking and living arrangements followed caste rules at
all costs, even if they affected Ramabai personally.[112] But as the
preceding account indicates, there were *real* constraints on an
independent woman like her which made it difficult for Ramabai
to work within certain structures of authority.

Further, it is necessary for us to understand, *without prejudice*,
that as a deeply *religious* woman with social concerns Ramabai's
dissatisfaction with Hindu social practices led her to find fulfilment
in Christianity.[113] Thereafter she insisted on the right of all,
including the widows at Sharada Sadan, to have the same choice.
While she believed in the higher value of Christianity and wished
to proselytise, she did not approve of intolerance and sectarianism.
She continued to have very close relations with Godubai (Anandibai
Karve) who had expressed an impulsive desire to become a
Christian but finally remained a Hindu. Many years later Godubai,
who regarded Sharada Sadan as her 'mother's home' and returned
to it to have her first child, went on to describe her own religion
as Ramabai's, service to others.[114] Characteristic of the combination
of Ramabai's acceptance of others' beliefs and her own desire to
lead them to the 'truth' she had found, was an incident recorded
by Ramabai Ranade. After a forty-year association with the latter
during which she had remained an active Prarthana Samajist,
Pandita Ramabai preached Christianity to her, even as she lay
dying.[115] Clearly Pandita Ramabai never gave up trying, although
it was not the primary basis of a relationship with people she came
in contact with.

She clung to the principle of free will despite the awareness that
it would annoy those whose feelings she cherished as, for example,
when she insisted that Manorama, her daughter, must decide for
herself when she became a major which particular sect of the
Christian church appealed to her.[116] Ramabai's position on religion
was summed up as 'neutrality in Sharada Sadan in matters of

religion along with liberty', the right to exercise choice in matters of faith.[117]

If the break with Brahmanical/Hindu society came it came consciously, but it was also inevitable, given Ramabai's personality and the work she set out to do. Further it is also necessary to bear in mind that the years of the controversy over the working of Sharada Sadan coincided with the peak of the struggle between various factions within the Poona elite. Tilak had used every issue of gender or religion to consolidate his base among the upper castes and had successfully wrenched leadership away from the moderate reformers. The marginalised reformers were caught on the horns of a dilemma. They broadly supported Ramabai's work but, in the face of the conservative assault upon them, did not wish to be marginalised further. The reformers' break with Ramabai was inevitable, given their own larger concerns of continuing to stake their claim for social leadership in Maharashtra against Brahmanas like Tilak. By the last decade of the nineteenth century the struggle among contending parties to define the social and national agenda had reached a flash-point. The years of the controversy at Sharada Sadan also coincided with Vivekananda's address to the Chicago Parliament of Religions, and his public denial in the USA of oppressive practices imposed on widows in India. Vivekananda's travels in the US to collect funds for his work were a counter to the appeals Ramabai had earlier made.

The controversy in America between the followers of Vivekananda and the members of the Ramabai Association was noteworthy because it raised certain issues which have resurfaced in Indian politics. The question that was at the heart of the controversy was: were widows in India oppressed and deprived of their rights? The basis of Ramabai's lectures and writing had been to make amply clear that widows *were* oppressed in Brahmanical society. She had aroused American women's sympathy for, possibly even guilt about, their 'sisters' on the other side of the globe. Vivekananda's lecture (that triggered off the controversy) was about the status of women in India. In January 1895 Vivekananda's lecture on 'Ideals of Womanhood — Hindu, Mohammedan and Christian' was reported in the *Daily Standard Union* of January 21.[118] The ideal of womanhood, according to Swamiji, centred in the Aryan race of India, the most ancient in the world's history. In that race men and women were priests, or 'co-religionists'. But with the advent of a distinct priest class the co-priesthood of the woman took a step back. It was the Semitic races which first proclaimed that women had no voice. The degeneration of women's status over time throughout the world was however ultimately replaced by another ideal of womanhood: in the west it was the wife, in India the mother.[119] Then followed the remark that set off the controversy: in India woman has enjoyed property rights for thousands of years. Here (in America) a man may disinherit his wife, in India the whole of the estate of the deceased husband must go to the wife, 'personal property absolutely, real property for life',[120] the Swami proclaimed.

The Swami then went on to outline the spirituality even of the act of reproduction. The Aryan was one who was born through prayer, the non-Aryan one who was born through sensuality. So deeply was this recognised in India that there was adultery in marriage unless marriage was consummated in prayer. The secret of the Aryan race lay in chastity.[121]

After this 'stupendous speech' Vivekananda wrote that the men did not quite appreciate his lecture but the women were ecstatic about it.[122] However, women of the Boston circle of the Ramabai Association contested the Swami's emphatic statement on the property rights of widows.[123] In the course of the controversy both sides brought in the opinions of European scholars, Rhys Davids for Vivekananda and Max Muller for Ramabai, to establish the 'honesty' of the two Indians.[124] While the controversy ran its course without either side giving in, what is significant is that, the recurrent theme of India's image came up. The attack on Ramabai was directed at the 'poor opinion' of India that she evoked in the American mind so that American papers were replete with statements such as 'Widows are not allowed to marry again, and are left to starve and drudge'.[125]

Another point made was about the acceptance of funds. The Swami was represented by his followers as making a distinction about taking money from distant countries of an alien faith which respectable high-caste Hindus would be repelled by and the 'voluntary, free will offering from people of calm judgment, intellectually convinced of the importance of the work' he was doing.[126] Throughout the controversy Vivekananda was reported as reiterating that widows were not oppressed; if they did not remarry it was because there was a scarcity of men,[127] that even if old men married young girls and then died leaving them widows, 'if the husband was wealthy it was all the better for the widow the sooner he died.' He was also reported to have said, 'I have travelled all over India, but failed to see a case of ill treatment mentioned.' He later corrected the report by saying that while he denied that all widows were ill-treated some cases of ill-treatment might occur. These, however, were sporadic and exceptional. He repudiated the statement that the ill-treatment of widows was an accepted and traditional part of Hindu custom.[128]

Throughout the controversy both sides were careful not to have either Ramabai or Vivekananda directly making references to each other. It was their viewpoints about Indian women, especially Indian widows, that were in contest. Further, the issue of Indian women was somewhat rhetorical for Vivekananda — an aspect of India's great tradition and its ability to provide spiritual solace to the west — but the Swamiji had a grand agenda in which opinion about widowhood was important only to the extent that it did not prick the bubble of spiritual greatness. In keeping with this mode of reconciling what might be an uncomfortable reminder of the mundane concerns of widows, Vivekananda's supporters argued that Ramabai had misrepresented, wilfully or otherwise, the condition of widows as decreed by Hindu religious law and custom. The truth, instead, according to Swamiji's supporters was that the life of the Hindu widow, rich or poor, young or old, was one of religious asceticism, that is to say, of poverty and self-denial.[129] The widow's life, by custom, was one in which spiritual and moral values were held supreme and therefore it was, by custom, austere. Outsiders (read the American public) were unaware of this fact but to those who *understood it* the widow's life was entirely different from that portrayed by Ramabai. Widows in Hindu society represented an informal order of nuns; in India the life of spiritual renunciation, which the widow undertook, was universally considered to be a far more exalted and fruitful life than that of matrimony. And most importantly, it was argued, the remarkable fact was that the widow, whatever her previous disposition may have been, often developed the prized qualities of endurance, fortitude, selflessness and serenity. 'Devoting herself to religious practices she became spiritually alive'.[130] On the sticky question of the widow's rights to inheritance, it was argued that the Swamiji should know, he had studied law; but to clinch the issue it was held that the status of the Hindu mother was so high and unassailable that the Hindu lawgivers never thought of legislating specifically for her support by her sons.[131]

Given this construction of Hindu widowhood, it is not surprising that Ramabai was bitter about India's spiritualists. Travelling in north India, a year after Vivekananda's storming of America, Ramabai's ire was in full evidence, especially in Banaras, Mathura, and Brindavan where widows lived out their 'ascetic' existences: at these centres where 'sublime' philosophies were daily taught, she found that widows were oppressed, neglected and (sexually) exploited without any 'Mahatma championing their cause'. The image of India in the west surfaced once more and she appealed to the 'learned brothers and comfortable sisters' there that they take a good look, beyond the poetry, into the prose of women's lives and decide for themselves (after living like them as beggars, going in and out of their dirty huts), about the nature of the fruits of the 'sublime philosophies'.[132]

The reality of the widow's life was not a matter that could be settled in America and in any case the Swami said different things about caste and women's status to Indian audiences. Even in America Vivekananda, probably for tactical reasons, decided to take donations for Sasipada Banerji's home for widows in Calcutta,[133] scoring a point about more 'patriotic' attempts at social work than Ramabai's efforts in Poona. The controversy is notable for the larger question of gender versus nation; taking funds from people, especially women, whose guilt about not being 'womanly' enough or spiritual enough had been evoked by Vivekananda with his exhortations to them to invest in their own spiritual regeneration and that of the west as a whole, was respectable and patriotic. Ramabai's strategy, on the other hand, was undignified and by implication unpatriotic because it tarnished the image of the proud and noble Hindus, whose history and culture were the oldest, and whose spirituality was untarnished even if they were materially impoverished.

Vivekananda's strong disapproval of Ramabai's conversion to Christianity and her appeal on behalf of Hindu widows were aspects of cultural nationalism that obscured oppressive Hindu social practices and gender contradictions, especially when addressing a western audience. A complex of pressures was simultaneously working on Ramabai and her attempt to integrate a range of positions in her own life and work. The intersection of caste, class, religion and gender had, by the end of the nineteenth century, worked to form a particular construction of the nation which was exclusivist in orientation. Ramabai and her standpoint on gender and religion could not be accommodated in this construction and so she became the 'betrayer' of her nation because the nation itself came to be viewed in terms of a predominantly Hindu ethos. Ramabai's direct and indirect experiences with liberal and radical Hindu nationalists alienated her from her original social moorings and reduced the space for her intervention and participation in the contemporary agendas of her male counterparts in western India. After the abandonment by 'liberal' Hindus, Ramabai appears to have gradually turned away from the upper-caste intelligentsia in Poona and Bombay and broadened the arena of her operations. The famine of 1897 proved to be decisive in the shift. Ramabai recalled the last famine in which her own parents had died. The memory of human beings forced to fend for themselves, a situation in which many women, especially widows, were abandoned, and the great danger to young women from predatory men as they wandered about in search of food, made her decide to rescue as many girls as she could.[134] Travelling into Central India where the famine was severe, she brought, at first a few, and then hundreds, of girls back to Mukti Sadan in Poona. However, some prominent citizens comprising Europeans, Parsis and Mohammedans who were horrified by the 'rabble' she brought in to live in the Sadan, objected on the ground that there would be problems of civic amenities and sought municipal intervention. Not to be thwarted, and demonstrating a high degree of initiative, she moved all the famine-stricken girls to Kedgaon where she had a plot of land.[135] It was here that she set up the institution that occupied her for the rest of her life. By now Hindus showed less interest in what she did; rescuing poor starving girls was not a matter to be concerned about even if they were certainly to be converted into Christians. Only Tilak, consistent with his earlier position, objected. It mattered to him that any Hindu girl, upper caste or lower, rich or poor, became Christian, although there is little evidence that Hindu social reformers themselves did anything concrete for famine victims. They may of course have exhorted and criticised the government for not doing enough. Even the American Ramabai Association did not approve of the move to Kedgaon as it put the institution out of the reach of the upper castes for whom it had been intended.[136] Resourceful as ever, Ramabai turned to Australia for financial support.[137]

Ramabai's sense of alienation from groups and institutions around her was heightened by a decisive confrontation with the colonial state. Until the plague episode Ramabai had steered clear of the colonial government, although its existence and patriarchal bias had come in for a scathing attack during the Rakhmabai controversy. Pointing to the interlocking nature of patriarchies and distinguishing between Christianity and the British government, she had denounced the latter's judicial decree sending Rakhmabai to jail. Noting the compact between the British government and the male population of India, she said that there was no hope for the women of India, whether they be under Hindu or British rule.[138] In 1897 however Ramabai became embroiled in a controversy that brought on the wrath of the colonial state and the Anglican missionaries. (This is an episode which some of Ramabai's missionary supporters and biographers usually pass by in their accounts of her life and work.) The government's anti-plague measures were unpopular with many Brahmanas, those of Poona in particular, with many charges of high-handedness, and invasion of homes being levelled by Indian leaders against the authorities. Ramabai, characteristically, was concerned as always with the gender dimensions of the measures and the sexual hazards faced by girls from the state's employees. She wrote to the *Bombay Guardian* criticising the plague measures and the government's handling of the epidemic. She gave details of one of her girls who, on mere suspicion of plague, was forcibly taken to the segregation camp and later abducted by one of the watchmen. The letter created a furore and the matter was taken up by a member of the British Parliament. She repeated the charges a few months later, accusing the British authorities of not recognising that 'Indian women were modest' and needed special consideration. In any case she wished to know if the English woman 'poor though she may be' would like to be exposed to the public gaze and roughly handled by male doctors. Was the Indian woman not as modest as the English, she queried. The Indian woman had deserved better treatment at the hands of the Governor and the Plague Committee, Ramabai asserted.[139]

Furious at the charges, the Governor of Bombay, Lord

Sandhurst, dismissed them as grossly inaccurate and misleading without even conducting an enquiry. This provoked Ramabai once more to write to the *Bombay Guardian*, this time taking on the 'Honourable' Governor himself for playing upon the supposed failings of the 'Orientals' of not substantiating their charges. But as Ramabai sharply pointed out the 'Occident' could also boast of such people, including the 'worthy' Governor, who had made certain charges against her without offering any proof of their truth. Since the letters she was writing were being published in a newspaper edited by the American missionary Alfred Dyer, she appealed to the 'conscientious Christian public' in the name of truth and justice to decide whether Lord Sandhurst had done the proper thing by dismissing the charges she had made.[140]

Unfortunately for Ramabai, at least on this occasion the conscientious Christian public in the Anglican Church, including her dear friend Sister Geraldine (Ajibai), stood by the colonial state and regarded her letter as childish, sensational and seditious. She suggested that Ramabai had contributed to the agitation which culminated in the murder of Ayerst and Rand, two officials believed to have acted brutally towards the people. The *Christian Patriot* warned her that she was treading a dangerous path, and other 'Christian well-wishers' in England suggested that she make a written recantation of the statements in her letter.[141] Ramabai, however, stood her ground and for a while it was believed that she was close to arrest.[142] Unfortunately, Sister Geraldine, did not really understand either the stand Ramabai had taken while in England, or this one back on her native soil, and believed that her actions had put her at a disadvantage vis-a-vis the government.[143]

Ramabai's persistence with her charges and her refusal to be brow-beaten by the colonial state or a section of the missionaries (which earned her some respect from her old adversary Tilak) was a contrast to the behaviour of Poona Brahmana men. While in England to give evidence before the Royal Commission on Finance, Gokhale had, on the basis of accounts sent to him from Poona, suggested that the conduct of Ayerst and Rand had been high-handed. When Gokhale returned an enquiry was instituted into his allegations but his 'friends' were no longer willing to substantiate his charges. They besought him not to reveal their identities. Finding that, except for Ramabai, everyone had retreated, Gokhale decided to tender an apology.[144]

By 'the turn of the century Ramabai's alienation from her erstwhile middle-class compatriots, the Hindu nationalists, the colonial state, as well as the Anglican missionaries, was complete. Unable to fit into anyone else's agenda, she was often castigated but sometimes grudgingly admired. The gradual shift away from the middle-class base in which Ramabai had worked initially, and for a while even after she adopted Christianity as her faith, had an unfortunate consequence: the possibilities of a dialogue between her and middle-class reformers, and between reformist Hinduism and Indian interpretations of Christianity, were reduced.[145] Increasingly, in her later years, Ramabai turned inwards much more to a gospel-based Christianity (while retaining a distance from any particular denomination) and then to an emotional rather than 'intellectual' relationship with Christ.[146] In 1905 Mukti Sadan was visited by a Pentecostal Christian preacher and following this the Ramabai community of women experienced an 'awakening'. They 'spoke in tongues', there was much weeping and hysterical laughter as part of the 'Revival'.[147] At least for a while this form of worship, described as 'mass hysteria', may have expressed the feelings of Ramabai and her girls. It did not last long and the institution reverted to its quieter forms of worship, singing Marathi *kirtanas* composed by the Christian poet Waman Narayan Tilak.[148] Ramabai learnt Greek and Hebrew in order to provide a more authentic Marathi translation of the Bible, which then 'her girls' would print in the press at Mukti. This was her last piece of work as she grew increasingly hard of hearing. When she died in 1922 she had experienced tragedy anew: Manorama had died unexpectedly a few months earlier. The Marathi press gave her a typical obituary, admiring her initiative and spirit but bemoaning her adoption of Christianity.[149] The ambivalence persisted. Perhaps the most liberal summing-up she got was from D.K. Karve, the husband of her first widow pupil at Sharada Sadan, who had taken Brahmana widows into safe custody following Ramabai's decisive split with Hindu society in 1893. When Ramabai's centenary was being celebrated in 1958 he said reflectively, 'It was our own fault that this great woman, like Dr Ambedkar, was lost to the Hindu religion'.[150] Perhaps this is one way to read Ramabai's stormy relationship with her society. But equally perhaps this is too simple a reading of Ramabai's complex interaction with her times.

EPILOGUE

If we look closely at the history of individuals and of a region such as Maharashtra in the late nineteenth and early twentieth centuries we can see that recourse to the theme of 'betrayal' of a culture and of the country was a highly emotive way of marginalising certain individuals and their points of view. It was also a way of establishing others as the 'truly authentic' spokespersons of their people. In the Poona Deccan region the label of 'betrayers' was easily applied and was a construct of Tilak who at the height of the Age of Consent controversy had gone so far as to say that the moderate Reformers should form themselves into a separate nationality. If this was Tilak's reaction to the Reformers' moderate agenda for the improvement of the condition of women *without* transforming the real bases of Brahmanical patriarchy, what chance did Ramabai have of inclusion in the embryonic nation as defined by Tilak? She had rejected a whole set of oppressive practices which she saw as integral to Hinduism and had thus rejected the culture of the dominant class of her time. Branding her a betrayer was intended to marginalise her as a person as well as suppress her critique of Hindu society.

It was possible to 'sediment' the image of Ramabai as a 'betrayer' because in the constructed perception of a certain class (comprising mainly the upper castes) Christianity was regarded as a handmaiden of imperialism and was conflated with colonialism. A conversion to Christianity then became a betrayal not just of ancestral 'religion' but of the nation because the nation is *ipso facto* 'Hindu'.

And it is because the 'nation' has come to be viewed, even by those who regarded themselves as secular, in terms of a predominantly Hindu ethos that there has been a certain ambiguity about Ramabai's place in Indian society. If it was not so, it would be apparent that neither the conversion to Christianity nor her use of funds from American supporters nor her advocating Christianity to others can make her a 'betrayer' of the nation. Ramabai's conflict with the colonial government, her understanding of the manner in which colonial patriarchy interlocked with indigenous patriarchy to tyrannise women and her conflict with the Anglican Church should indicate that her focus was at all times on the women of India living under oppressive structures and practices. On our part we need to recognise that it is time to break down the false divide on 'loyalty' to the nation created by those with little concern for its oppressed sections or those for whom there could be only one oppressive relationship, that between the colonising and the colonised. As Phule argued, was it patriotic to oppress one's own people, the lower castes, while one might be eloquent in opposing the colonial government?[151] It was not that Phule and Ramabai betrayed the nation — rather they were the ones who were betrayed — as were their concerns — by the 'narrow' basis of a nationalism which itself was merely a construct of upper caste men.

NOTES AND REFERENCES

1. For a theoretical discussion of agency in the context of gender see Kumkum Sangari, 'Consent, Agency and the Rhetorics of Incitement', *Economic and Political Weekly*, Vol. 27, No. 18, 1 May 1993, pp. 867–82.

2. At least from as early as the sixth century B.C. the Buddhist texts describe the existence of two types of Brahmanas, the ascetic Brahmana and the *grahastha* Brahmana. The former was the 'ideal' type, as he had the minimum of material possessions and devoted himself fully to the pursuit of salvation. The grahastha Brahmana was the 'deviant' Brahmana who was indistinguishable from the rest of society as he pursued the same material goals as everyone else. By the nineteenth century the ascetic type of Brahmanas were almost extinct as a category and it was they who were now regarded as the deviants by the rest of the Brahmanas. For a more extended discussion of the ascetic Brahmana see Uma Chakravarti, *The Social Dimensions of Early Buddhism*, Delhi, Oxford University Press, 1987, pp. 39–46. From the writing of Ramabai and early biographies of her, it appears that Anant Shastri Dongre tried to live out the 'ascetic' type of existence in terms of his search for truth but combined it with the grahastha type since he lived as a 'family' man even in his later years. The contradictions of the two types of life took their toll on the family as the discussion here shows.

3. Nicol Macnicol, *Pandita Ramabai*, Calcutta, Association Press (Y.M.C.A.), 1926, pp. 5–6.

4. *Ibid.*, pp. 6–7.

5. Pandita Ramabai, *A Testimony of Our Inexhaustible Treasure*, Kedgaon (Poona), Ramabai Mukti Mission, 1907, (1992 reprint), pp. 10–11.

6. *Ibid.*, pp. 12–13.

7. Pandita Ramabai Saraswati, *The High Caste Hindu Woman*, p. xi; Max Muller, 'My Indian Friends', in *Life and Letters of F. Max Muller, Edited by his Wife*, London, Green and Company, 1902, Vol. II, p. 125.
8. See for example the accounts of five Brahmana families in D.D. Karve, *New Brahmans*.
9. Uma Chakravarti, 'Renouncer and Householder in Early Buddhism', *Social Analysis*, No. 13, May 1983, pp. 70–81.
10. Pandita Ramabai, *Testimony*, pp. 11–12.
11. Pandita Ramabai, *The High Caste Hindu Woman*, pp. 62–63.
12. Macnicol, *Pandita Ramabai*, p. 25.
13. *Ibid.*, pp. 25–26.
14. Pandita Ramabai, *The High Caste Hindu Woman*, p. xiii.
15. Pandita Ramabai, *Testimony*, p. 16.
16. B.C. Pal, *Memories of My Life and Times*, Calcutta, Bipin Chandra Pal Institute, 1973, pp. 305–06.
17. Uma Chakravarti, 'Whatever Happened to the Vedic Dasi: Orientalism, Nationalism and a Script for the Past', in Kumkum Sangari and Sudesh Vaid, *Recasting Women*, p. 33.
18. Padmini Sengupta, *Pandita Ramabai Saraswati: Her Life and Work*, Bombay, Asia Publishing House, 1970, p. 69.
19. *Testimony*, p. 22.
20. *Ibid.*, pp. 18–20.
21. *Ibid.*, p. 20.
22. *Ibid.*, p. 21.
23. *Ibid.*, p. 22.
24. The suitor, according to Bipin Chandra Pal's memoirs, was Shreepad Babaji Thakur who was fluent in English, having been to England to pass the Civil Service Examination. He spoke at a meeting in Sylhet on comparative philology and enthralled his audience. However he had not gone to Sylhet to speak on comparative philology but had visited it incognito to press his proposal of marriage to Ramabai. He had tried to lecture from the same platform as Ramabai and 'conquer' her if possible by establishing a 'strong intellectual kinship with her'. B.C. Pal writes that the whole venture was abortive as Ramabai refused to attend his lecture. The unsuccessful suitor for the hand of the famous Pandita then saw no reason to conceal his identity any further and went back to Bombay after revealing it. B.C. Pal's account suggests that Bipin Behari Medhavi too pursued Ramabai with tenacity, following her from Sylhet to Dacca, before she agreed to marry him (B.C. Pal, *Memories*, pp. 306–7).
25. *Testimony*, p. 22; Sister Geraldine, *The Letters and Correspondence of*

Pandita Ramabai, Bombay, Maharashtra State Board for Literature and Culture, 1977, pp. 17–18.

26. Dall, *The Life of Dr Anandabai Joshee*, p. vi; Sister Geraldine, *Letters and Correspondence*, p. 18.
27. I.B. Horner, *Women in Primitive Buddhism: Laywomen and Almswomen*, Delhi, Motilal Banarsidass, 1975, p. 196.
28. Heimsath, *Indian Nationalism*, p. 96.
29. Ramabai Ranade, *Reminiscences*, p. 82.
30. B.C. Pal, *Memories*, p. 307.
31. *Letters and Correspondence*, p. 18.
32. *Testimony*, p. 24.
33. Ramabai Ranade, *Reminiscences*, p. 83; D.G. Vaidya, 'The Arya Mahila Samaj: Extracts from the History of the Prarthana Samaj', Bombay, Prarthana Samaj, cited in Padmini Sengupta, *Pandita Ramabai Saraswati*, Bombay, Asia Publishing House, 1970, pp. 348–51.
34. Ramabai Ranade, *Reminiscences*, p. 83; Sengupta, *Pandita Ramabai*, p. 351.
35. *Education Commission, Bombay, Vol. II*, September 1882; Pandita Ramabai, *The High Caste Hindu Woman*, pp. xvi–xviii.
36. *Rabindra Racanabali*, Vol. 13, centenary edition, Calcutta, West Bengal Government Publication, 1961, pp. 101f.
37. Ramabai Ranade, *Reminiscences*, p. 82.
38. *Ibid.*, p. 83.
39. *Ibid.*, pp. 105–06.
40. *Testimony*, pp. 23–24.
41. See Chapter 1 p. 12 of this work.
42. C.E. Gardner, *Life of Father Goreh*, London, Longman Green and Company, 1900, pp. 274–76; Sengupta, *Pandita Ramabai*, pp. 116–17.
43. *Testimony*, p. 26.
44. Max Muller, 'My Indian Friends', pp. 47–65.
45. Pandita Ramabai, *Testimony*, p. 26.
46. *Mukti Prayer Bell*, Kedgaon, Ramabai Mukti Mission, September 1907, cited in Macnicol, *Pandita Ramabai*, p. 59.
47. Sister Geraldine, *Letters and Correspondence*, p. 18; Pandita Ramabai, *Testimony*, p. 24; Pandita Ramabai, *The High Caste Hindu Woman*, p. xviii.
48. Pandita Ramabai, *Stri Dharma Niti*, (first published 1882), Kedgaon, Pune, Ramabai Mukti Mission, 1966 (reprint). The government had bought six hundred copies of the 1882 edition for distribution in schools (*Letters and Correspondence*, p. 18).
49. The *Subodh Patrika* reported (12 and 19 November 1882) the gift

of purses at her public recital of the *Puranas*. The Cheltenham College Magazine reported in September 1884 that Pandita Ramabai's expenses had sometimes been defrayed by princes such as the Nawab of Junagarh (see Sengupta, *Pandita Ramabai Saraswati*, p. 98).

50. Gardner, *Life of Father Goreh*, p. 275.
51. Pandita Ramabai, *Letter to Sadashiv Pandurang*, 1883, cited in Sengupta, *Pandita Ramabai*, p. 129.
52. *Letters and Correspondence*, p. 24.
53. Pandita Ramabai, *Testimony*, pp. 25–26.
54. *Ibid.*
55. *Ibid.*
56. Max Muller, 'My Indian Friends', pp. 127–29.
57. *Letters and Correspondence*, p. 11.
58. It appears that an unposted letter Anandi Bhagat had written to her old schoolmaster in Poona was found among her things after she died. It was included among the letters published by Sister Geraldine in the *Letters and Correspondence of Pandita Ramabai* (pp. 11–14). Although we do not get biographical details of Anandi Bhagat from this letter we do get an 'insight' into her state of mind while she was in England. The letter is a mixture of longing to go back to India and a justifying of her decision to come to England. She says that her mind is always looking forward, like a bird, to 'my India', but there are frequent references to England, its progress and its beauty. There are references also to money she had to pay for her board in England, and a scholarship she got from the government which had to be repaid. She was insecure and lonely as she could not understand why her brothers to whom she had been writing, were not replying. She was emotionally dependent on 'Pandita Bai' who loved her like her own daughter Mano, with a mother's love. The mixed feelings, and the ambivalence about home where her family and friends were and England where she was being educated, would have multiplied with the conversion and made her feel she would lose all her kin. An exit from her new place in England would be difficult as she was so far away from home. Ramabai's guilt and sense of loneliness following Anandi's death were probably the reason why she did not write about it. Five years later when she was returning from America to India she recalled that earlier journey when she and Anandi Bhagat had set forth from home to be educated. She wrote to Sister Geraldine that she greatly missed Anandibai 'that dear faithful friend', and she hoped that Anandi rested in peace. 'It seemed very sad to return without her', wrote Ramabai (*Letters and Correspondence*, p. 212).

59. Max Muller, 'My Indian Friends', pp. 127–28.
60. *Testimony*, p. 26.
61. *Letters and Correspondence*, p. 22.
62. Gardner, *Father Goreh*, p. 275.
63. Max Muller, 'My Indian Friends', pp. 128–29.
64. *Indu Prakash*, 22 October 1883.
65. *Ibid.*, 19 November 1883.
66. *Satsar*, September 1885, reproduced in Y.D. Phadke, *Collected Works of Jotiba Phule*, Bombay, Maharashtra Rajya Sahitya ani Sanskriti Mandal, 1991, pp. 345–62.
67. *Ibid.*; N.C. Kelkar, *Lokamanya Tilak Yanche Charitra*, Tr. by D.V. Divekar as *Life and Times of Lokamanya Tilak*, Delhi, Anupama (reprint), 1987, p. 223.
68. *Gospel of Shree Ramakrishna*, p. 377, cited in Padmini Sengupta, *Pandita Ramabai*, p. 163.
69. *Selections From Swami Vivekananda*, Almora, Advaita Ashrama, 1946, p. 356.
70. *Letters and Correspondence*, pp. 38–45.
71. *Ibid.*, pp. 48–51, 25.
72. *Ibid.*, pp. 51–52.
73. *Ibid.*, pp. 43, 76.
74. *Ibid.*, p. 59.
75. *Ibid.*, pp. 55, 78.
76. Cheltenham Ladies College Magazine, Autumn 1885, Spring 1886, cited in Padmini Sengupta, *Pandita Ramabai*, p. 49.
77. *Letters and Correspondence*, p. 119. Ramabai's ability to rise above her Marathi Brahmana background, which she was conscious of and on occasion could evoke with pride, is notable (*Letters and Correspondence*, p. 60.)
78. *Ibid.*, pp. 33, 159–60, 169–70.
79. *Ibid.*, pp. 75–76.
80. *Ibid.*, p. 40.
81. *Ibid.*, pp. 100–101.
82. *Ibid.*, p. 109.
83. *Ibid.*, p. 124.
84. *Ibid.*, pp. 126, 33. The Church hierarchy was anxious about Ramabai's independence for less erudite reasons, too. At one point while she was at Cheltenham, away from the Sisters, Ramabai went to meet a Brahmana male friend in Bristol. This caused the Sisters at Wantage much embarrassment as the gentleman had been a sort of 'attache' to the Pandita (*Letters and Correspondence*, p. 20). There is a certain anxiety here about Ramabai's conduct which was 'improper' in the eyes of the Sisters if it included interaction with

men. For Ramabai England thus became a place of restrictions, rather than of freedom and liberty (See Inderpal Grewal, *Home and Harem: Nation, Gender, Empire and the Culture of Travel*, Durham, Duke University Press, 1996, pp. 179–229.

85. *Letters and Correspondence*, p. 99, 406, 300.
86. *Ibid.*, pp. 116, 196–99, 240, 256. The case of Father Goreh's motherless baby daughter might bear out the point of the missionaries making up for their inability to control the high-caste converts by taking over the children. Lakshmi Goreh, Nilkantha's wife, had died two days after the birth of the baby. The infant was then looked after by a missionary couple, taken to England, trained there and, many years later, returned to do mission work in India. Ramabai's fight to keep her child despite the difficulties she faced is a contrast to Goreh, who, as a man, may have considered himself unable to bring up his child himself (for Lakshmi and Nilkantha's child see C.E. Gardner, *Life of Father Goreh*, pp. 87–88).
87. *Letters and Correspondence*, pp. 165–66.
88. *Ibid.*, pp. 407–8; Helen Dyer, *Pandita Ramabai: The Story of Her Life*, London, Morgan and Scott, 1900, p. 23. Among those who gathered around Ramabai in Boston were the prominent social reformer Francis Willard and the Unitarian minister Edward Everett Hale (Edith L. Blumhofer, 'Pandita Ramabai and Indian Christianity: A North American Perspective', unpublished typescript).
89. Pandita Ramabai, *The High Caste Hindu Woman*, p. 11.
90. Sister Geraldine, *Letters and Correspondence*, pp. 181, 219–20. Dall describes one such meeting at which six hundred people were in the audience and listened to Ramabai with rapt attention. Dall also records that Ramabai had a certain piquancy and originality, not found elsewhere (Dall, *The Life of Dr Anandabai Joshee*, p. 135).
91. *The High Caste Hindu Woman*, pp. xxi–xxiv; *Letters and Correspondence*, pp. 212–14.
92. *Letters and Correspondence*, p. 184.
93. *Indu Prakash*, 11 March 1889 and 18 March 1889; *Bombay Educational Record*, cited in Padmini Sengupta, *Pandita Ramabai*, p. 184.
94. *Report of the Fifth National Congress*, p. 155, cited in Padmini Sengupta, *Pandita Ramabai*, p. 193.
95. *Times of India*, 30 December 1889.
96. Cited in Padmini Sengupta, *Pandita Ramabai*, pp. 206–7.
97. *Ibid.*
98. *Indu Prakash*, 6 May 1889.
99. *Letters and Correspondence*, pp. 238, 247, 314, 342.

100. D.K. Karve and N.M. Patwardhan, *Dhondo Keshav Karve: Atma Vritta Va Charitra*, Pune, Hingne Stri Shiksha Sansthan, 1956, p. 119.

101. *Letters and Correspondence*, p. 392.

102. D.K. Karve, *Atma Vritta Va Charitra*, p. 117.

103. *Letters and Correspondence*, pp. 269, 271–73.

104. *Ibid.*, pp. 268–69.

105. *Ibid.*, pp. 264–65.

106. *Ibid.*, p. 269.

107. N.C. Kelkar, *Lokamanya Tilak Yanche Charitra*, English translation, p. 221.

108. *Letters and Correspondence*, pp. 275–77. The sister-in-law referred to here was probably Durga 'vahini', described as an old orthodox type in Pandita Ramabai's letter. The action of the orthodox widows in bringing the destitute and oppressed widow to Sharada Sadan suggests that the 'traditional' system had no institutional or alternative structures where a widow could safely find shelter.

109. D.K. Karve, *Looking Back*, Poona, Hindu Widows' Home Association, 1939, pp. 60–61.

110. D.D. Karve, *New Brahmans*, pp. 75–76. Vithal Ramji Shinde reported that he had wanted his sister to join the institution but Karve declined to take her on the ground that the time was not yet ripe for admitting non-Brahmana widows due to the need to maintain pollution taboos (Sister Geraldine, *Letters and Correspondence*, p. xxvi).

111. N.C. Kelkar, *Lokamanya Tilak*, p. 223.

112. Sister Geraldine, *Letters and Correspondence*, pp. 249.

113. In this context we may recall Vidyasagar's disillusionment with Hindu society. Towards the end of his life, in a high state of despondency, he told a visitor from Maharashtra that Hindus as Hindus would never accept social reform (C.Y. Chintamani, *Indian Social Reform*, p. 189).

114. D.D. Karve, *New Brahmans*, pp. 72–74, 70.

115. Nicol Macnicol, *Pandita Ramabai*, p. 130.

116. Sister Geraldine, *Letters and Correspondence*, pp. 196–97. The Pandita told Catherine Dall that she did not belong to the Church of England, nor to any other church. She had made that a precondition when she was baptised. She believed in the Bible and she insisted on believing in it in her own way (Dall, *The Life*, p. 133). In this context Blumhofer's suggestion that Ramabai was closer to popular 'movements' that swept Christian societies rather than restricting herself to any particular Church is useful in

understanding Ramabai's location within Christianity (Blumhofer, 'Pandita Ramabai', unpublished manuscript).

117. *Ibid.*, pp. 264, 310.
118. Marie Louise Burke, *Swami Vivekananda in America: New Discoveries*, Calcutta, Advaita Ashrama, 1966, pp. 557–59.
119. *Ibid.*, pp. 541–44.
120. *Ibid.*, p. 544.
121. *Ibid.*
122. *Ibid.* Vivekananda cultivated his image for the 'ecstatic' effect he had upon his audience and considered it worth his while to invest some of the funds he collected for a scarlet dress and turban (Burke, *Swami Vivekananda*, pp. 39, 398, 412). In this he may be contrasted with Ramabai who made a dramatic impact through the starkness of her everyday apparel — the white sari of the widow. Nevertheless she looked 'strikingly beautiful' (Dall, *The Life*, p. 130).
123. *Ibid.*, pp. 554–57.
124. *Ibid.*, pp. 556, 562.
125. *Ibid.*, pp. 552, 558, 560.
126. *Ibid.*, pp. 561–62.
127. *Ibid.*, p. 567.
128. *Ibid.*, p. 569.
129. *Ibid.*, p. 587.
130. *Ibid.*, pp. 588–89.
131. *Ibid.*, p. 589.
132. *Letters and Correspondence*, pp. 313–14.
133. Marie Louise Burke, *Swami Vivekananda*, p. 593.
134. Pandita Ramabai rarely, if ever, directly referred to women's sexuality. It appears in her writing as a latent issue, almost invariably in the context of the special vulnerability of young girls to sexual exploitation by predatory men who were always on the look–out for opportunities to seduce women. In this kind of somewhat flattened handling of the issue of female sexuality she was not unique, as it is characteristic of all the writing of women of a certain class and socialisation. Pandita Ramabai's attitude to women's sexuality reflects a mixture of reticence and the need to have to talk about an uncomfortable subject. Although it is not prudish it does seem to have a certain ascetic reserve generally, unless it relates to the dangers women face from men.
135. *Letters and Correspondence*, p. 345.
136. *Ibid.*, p. 372.
137. *Ibid.*, pp. 374, 384.
138. *Ibid.*, pp. 176–78.
139. *Ibid.*, p. xxviii.

140. *Ibid.*, pp. xxviii-xxix.

141. *Ibid.*, p. 348.

142. Brahmana officials of the Government raided Ramabai's institution under the pretext of searching out plague cases (*Letters and Correspondence*, p. 379).

143. Sister Geraldine considered the statement made by Ramabai not only 'ill judged and foolish', putting her at a disadvantage with the government, whom one ought to always be loyal to, but actually seditious. Ramabai's statement had thus brought her into 'severe disfavour and suspicion with the ruling power'. Interestingly, according to Sister Geraldine, this put her at a disadvantage even with her Brahmana fellow-countrymen who were angry with her for embracing Christianity. They got their opportunity to harass her as they were in the employ of the government as Sanitary and School Inspectors and meted out harsh measures against her (*Letters and Correspondence*, pp. 300, 348).

144. S. Natarajan, *G.K. Gokhale: The Man and His Message*, p. 2, cited in Padmini Sengupta, *Pandita Ramabai*, p. 256.

145. Ramabai's position during the years immediately after her conversion was close to that of what today we may call a secular humanist. (*The Missionary Review of the World*, cited in Edith Blumhofer, 'Pandita Ramabai'). She also tried to argue for an incorporation of 'Indian' features into the practice of Christianity. For example, when the question of the use of a cross was being discussed she resisted it as unnecessary. She also argued that if it was to be adopted at all it should not have a Latin inscription but a Sanskrit one, which was the most beautiful and oldest language of 'my dear native land' as she put it (*Letters and Correspondence*, p. 28).

146. Ramabai wrote that the dry discussions about sects and differences did not interest her. She had the 'peace that passeth all understanding' (Sister Geraldine, *Letters and Correspondence*, p. 335).

147. Sister Geraldine, *Letters and Correspondence*, pp. 389–92; Padmini Sengupta, *Pandita Ramabai*, p. 277.

148. Padmini Sengupta, *Pandita Ramabai*, p. 277.

149. *Kesari*, 11 April 1922.

150. S.M. Adhav, *Pandita Ramabai Centenary Souvenir*, p. 19, cited in Padmini Sengupta, *Pandita Ramabai*, p. 328.

151. *Satsar*, September 1885, reprinted in Y.D. Phadke, *Collected Works of Jotiba Phule*, Bombay, 1991, pp. 345–62; Rosalind O'Hanlon, *Caste, Conflict, and Ideology*, pp. 202–203.

Bibliography

Agarwala, D.N., *A Text Book of Hindu Law*, Allahabad, Ram Narainlal Beni Prasad, 1960.

Altekar, A.S., *The Position of Women in Hindu Civilisation*, Delhi, Motilal Banarsidass, 1987 (Reprint).

Anon., *An Essay on the Second Marriage of Widows by a Learned Brahmin of Nagpore* (With an Introduction by Lancelot Wilkinson), no publisher, 1841, manuscript in National Library, Calcutta.

Anon., *Marriage of Hindu Widows Advocated by the Pathare Reform Association*, Bombay, Indu Prakash Press, 1869.

Arundale, George (ed.), *Annie Besant, Builder of New India: Her Fundamental Principles of Nation Building*, Madras, Theosophical Publishing House, 1942.

Athavale, Parvati, *Hindu Widow (an Autobiography)* tr., Rev. Justine E. Abbot, Delhi, Reliance Publishing House, 1986.

Ballhatchet, Kenneth, *Social Policy and Social Change in Western India: 1817–1830*, London, Oxford University Press, 1957.

Banerji, Himani, 'Mothers and Daughters: Gender and Class in Educational Proposals for Women and by Women in Colonial Bengal', *Journal of Historical Sociology*, Vol. 5, No. 1, March 1992, pp. 1–30.

Bandhopadhaya, Sekhar, 'Caste, Class, and Culture in Colonial India', *Indian History Congress Symposia Papers: 1*, Delhi, 1992.

Baudhayana, Dharmasutra, tr.,George Buhler, *Sacred Laws of the Aryas*, Part II, Delhi, Motilal Banarsidass, 1975 (Reprint).

Behere, N.K., *The Background of Maratha Renaissance in the 17th Century*, Bangalore, The Bangalore Printing Press, 1946.

Besant, Annie, *Speeches and Writings*, Madras, Natesan and Co., n.d.

———, *Birth of New India: Collection of Writings and Speeches on Indian Affairs*, Madras, Theosophical Society, 1917.

Bhagwat, Vidyut, 'Marathi Literature as a Source for Contemporary Feminism', *Economic and Political Weekly*, Vol. 30, No. 17, April 29, 1995, pp.WS. 24–29.

Blumhofer, Edith L., 'Pandita Ramabai and Indian Christianity: A North American Perspective', unpublished manuscript.

Broughton, Thomas Duer, *Letters Written in a Maratha Camp During the Year 1809*, London, John Murray, 1813.

Burke, Marie-Louise, *Swami Vivekananda in America: New Discoveries*, Calcutta, Advaita Ashram, 1966.

Carroll, Lucy, 'Law, Custom and Statutory Social Reform: The Hindu Widow's Remarriage Act of 1856', in J. Krishnamurty (ed.), *Women in Colonial India: Essays on Survival, Work and the State*, Delhi, Oxford University Press, 1989, pp. 1–26.

Cashman, Richard, *The Myth of the Lokamanya: Tilak and Mass Politics in Maharashtra*, Berkeley, University of California Press, 1975.

Chakravarti, Uma, 'Renouncer and Householder in Early Buddhism', *Social Analysis*, No. 13, May 1983, pp. 70–81.

———, *Social Dimensions of Early Buddhism*, Delhi, Oxford University Press, 1987.

———, 'Conceptualising Brahmanical Patriarchy in Early India: Gender, Caste, Class and State', *Economic and Political Weekly*, Vol. 28, No. 14, April 3, 1993, pp. 579–85.

———, 'Women, Men and Beasts: The Jataka as Popular Tradition', *Studies in History*, Vol. 9, No. 1, N.S., 1993, pp. 43–69.

———, 'Gender, Caste and Labour: The Ideological and Material Arrangements of Widowhood', *Economic and Political Weekly*, Vol. 30, No. 36, September 9, 1995, pp. 2248–56.

Chandra, Sudhir, 'The Problem of Social Reform in Modern India: The Study of a Case', in S.C. Malik (ed.), *Dissent, Protest and Reform in Indian Civilisation*, Shimla, Indian Institute of Advanced Study, 1977, pp. 250–62.

———, 'Whose Laws: Notes on a Legitimising Myth of a Colonial Indian State', *Studies in History*, Vol. 8, No. 2, N.S., 1992, pp. 189–211.

Chintamani, C.Y. (ed.), *Indian Social Reforms: Being a Collection of Essays, Addresses and Speeches*, Madras, Minerva Press, 1901.

Choksey, R.D., *The Last Phase: Selections From the Deccan Commissioner's File (Peshwa Daftar), 1815–1818. With an Introductory Note on British Diplomacy at the Court of the Peshwa*, Bombay, Pheonix Publishers, 1948.

Chowdhry, Prem, 'Customs in a Peasant Economy: Women in Colonial Haryana', in Kumkum Sangari and Sudesh Vaid (ed.), *Recasting Women: Essays in Indian Colonial History*, Delhi, Kali for Women, 1989, pp. 302–36.

———, *The Veiled Woman: Shifting Gender Equations in Rural Haryana 1880-1990*, Delhi, Oxford University Press, 1994.

Conlon, Frank, *Caste in a Changing World: The Chitrapur Saraswat Brahmans 1870–1934*, Delhi, Thomson Press, 1977.

Crawford, A., *Our Troubles in the Poona and the Deccan*, Westminister, Constable and Company, 1897.

Dall, Caroline Healey, *The Life of Dr. Anandabai Joshee*, Boston, Roberts Brothers, 1888.

Das, Sisir Kumar, *A History of Indian Literature*, Vol.VIII, Delhi, Sahitya Akademi, 1991.

Deleury, J., *The Cult Of Vithoba*, Poona, Deccan College Post-Graduate Resarch Institute, 1961.

Desai, Sudha V., *Social Life in Maharashtra Under the Peshwas*, Bombay, Popular Prakashan, 1980.

Deshpande, Sudhanwa, 'Theatre and Nationalism: The Plays of Krishnaji Prabhakar Khadilkar', M.Phil. thesis under preparation.

De Lauretis, Teresa, *Alice Doesn't*, Bloomington, Indiana University Press, 1984.

Dirks, Nicholas B., *The Hollow Crown: Ethnohistory of a Little Kingdom*, Cambridge, Cambridge University Press, 1987.

Dobbin, Christine, *Urban Leadership in Western India: Politics and Communities in Bombay City, 1840-1885*, London, Oxford University Press, 1972.

Dumont, Louis, 'The Conception of Kingship in Ancient India', *Contributions to Indian Sociology*, No. VI, December 1962, pp. 48-77.

Dyer, Helen, *Pandita Ramabai: The Story of Her Life*, London, Morgan and Scott, 1900.

Engels, Dagmar, *The Changing Role of Women in Bengal: c.1890–1930 With Special Reference to British and Bengali Discourse on Gender*, unpublished Ph.D. thesis, School of Oriental and African Studies, London.

———, 'The Age of Consent Act: Colonial Ideology in Bengal', *South Asia Research*, Vol. 3, No. 2, November 1983, pp. 107–35.

Enthoven, R.E., *The Tribes and Castes of Bombay*, Vol. III, Delhi, Cosmo, 1975 (reprint).

Fillozat, Pierre-Sylvain and Vasundhara Fillozat, *Hampi-Vijayanagar: The Temple of Vitthala*, New Delhi, Sitaram Bhartia Institute of Scientific Research, 1988.

Fukazawa, Hiroshi, 'State and Caste System (Jati) in the Eighteenth Century Maratha Kingdom', *Hitotsubashi Journal Of Economics*, Vol. 9, No. 1, June 1968, pp. 32–44.

———, *The Medieval Deccan: Peasants, Social Systems and States, Sixteenth to Eighteenth Centuries*, Delhi, Oxford University Press, 1991.

Gadgil, D.R., *Poona: A Socio-Economic Survey: Part II*, Poona, Gokhale Institute of Politics and Economics, 1952.

Gardner, C.E., *Life of Father Goreh*, London, Longmans, Green & Company, 1900.

Geraldine, Sister, (Compiler) *The Letters and Correspondence of Pandita Ramabai*, Bombay, Maharashtra State Board for Literature and Culture, 1977.

Ghose, J.C., *The English Works of Rammohun Rŏy*, Calcutta, Bhawanipore Oriental Press,1885.

Gidumal, Dayaram, *The Status of Women in India or A Handbook For Hindu Social Reformers*, Bombay, Fort Publishers, 1889.

Gokhale, Balkrishna Govind, *Poona in the Eighteenth Century: An Urban History*, Delhi, Oxford University Press, 1988.

Gokhale-Turner, Jayashree, 'Region and Regionalism in the Study of Indian Politics: The Case of Maharashtra', in N.K. Wagle (ed.), *Images of Maharashtra: A Regional Profile of India*, London Curzon Press Limited, 1980, pp. 88–101.

Guha, Ranajit, 'Chandra's Death', Ranajit Guha (ed.), *Subaltern Studies V: Writings on South Asian History and Society*, Delhi, Oxford University Press, 1987, pp. 135–65.

Guha, Sumit, 'Fitna in Maratha Theory and Practice', paper presented at Nehru Memorial Museum and Library, September 15, 1993.

Gune, V.T., *The Judicial System of the Marathas*, Poona, Deccan College, 1953.

Hardiman, David (ed.), *Peasant Resistance in India*, Delhi, Oxford University Press, 1992.

Harper, Edward, 'Fear and the Status of Women', *South-Western Journal of Anthropology*, No. 25, 1969, pp. 81–95.

Hassan, Syed Sirajul, *The Castes and Tribes of the Nizam's Dominions* (1920), Delhi, Asian Educational Services, 1989 (Reprint).

Heimsath, Charles H., 'The Origin and Enactment of the Indian Age of Consent Bill, 1891', *Journal of Asian Studies*, Vol. I, No. 4, 1962, pp. 491–504.

———, *Indian Nationalism and Hindu Social Reform*, Princeton University Press, 1964.

Horner, I.B., *Women Under Primitive Buddhism: Laywomen and Almswomen*, Delhi, Motilal Banarsidass, 1975.

Inamdar, Radhabai, et. al., *Position of Widow: Experiences of Widows and Other Girls*, Manuscript submitted to the Director of Ethnography, Calcutta, 1911, Eur. Ms. D. 356, India Office Library.

Inden, Ronald, *Imagining India*, Oxford, Basil Backwell, 1990.

Indira, M.K., *Phaniyamma*, tr., Tejaswini Niranjana, Delhi, Kali for Women, 1989.

Johnson, Gordon, 'Chitpavan Brahmins and Politics in Western India in the late Nineteenth and Early Twentieth Centuries', in Edmund Leach and S.N. Mukherjee (eds.), *Elites in South Asia*, Cambridge, Cambridge University Press, 1970, pp. 95–118.

Joshi, Raghunath, 'Anandibai Joshi: Triumph and Tragedy', *Span*, December 1988.

Joshi, S.J., *Anandi Gopal*, tr. and abridged by Asha Damle, Calcutta, Stree, 1992.

Joshi, Svati (ed.), *Rethinking English: Essays in Literature, Language, History*, Delhi, Trianka, 1991.

Kadam, V.S., 'The Institution of Marriage and the Position of Women in Eighteenth Century Maharashtra', *Indian Economic and Social History Review*, Vol. 25, No. 3, 1988, pp. 341–70.

Kanitkar, Kashibai, *Dr. Anandi Gopal: Yanche Charitra va Patre*, Bombay, Manoranjan Grantha Prasarak Mandali, 1912.

Kane, P.V. *History of the Dharmashastra*, Poona, Deccan College Post-Graduate Research Institute, 1941, Vol.II, Part I.

Karve Anandibai, 'Maze Purana', tr. and ed. by Kaveri Karve, in D.D. Karve, *The New Brahmans: Five Maharashtrian Families*, Berkeley, University of California Press, 1963.

Karve, D.D., *The New Brahmans: Five Maharashtrian Families*, Berkeley, University of California Press, 1963.

Karve, D.K. *Looking Back*, Poona, Hindu Widow's Home Association, 1931.

———, and N.M. Patwardhan, *Dhondo Keshav Karve:Atma Vritta Va Charitra*, Pune, Hingne Stri Shiksha Sansthan, 1956.

———, 'My Life Story', D.D. Karve (ed.), *New Brahmans: Five Maharashtrian Families*, Berkeley, University of California Press, 1963.

Karve, Irawati, 'On the Road: A Maharashtrian Pilgrimage', *Journal of Asian Studies*, Vol. 22, No. 1, November 1962, pp. 13–29.

Katagade, N.C., 'Pundalik', D.D. Karve (ed.), *New Brahmans: Five Maharashtrian Families*, Berkeley, University of California Press, 1963.

Keer, Dhananjay, *Jotirao Phooley: Father of the Indian Social Revolution*, Bombay, Popular Prakashan, 1964.

Kelkar, N.C., *Life and Times of Lokamanya Tilak*, Delhi, Anupam Publications, 1987 (Reprint).

Kolenda, Pauline, 'Widowhood Among "Untouchable" Chuhras', in Pauline Kolenda, *Regional Differences in Family Structure in India*, Jaipur, Rawat Press, 1987, pp. 289–354.

Kolhatkar, W.M., 'Widow Remarriage in India', in C.Y. Chintamani (ed.), *Indian Social Reform*, Madras, Minerva Press, 1901.

Kosambi, D.D., *Myth and Reality: Studies in the Formation of Indian Culture*, Bombay, Popular Prakashan, 1962.

Kosambi, Meera, 'Glory of Peshwa Pune', *Economic and Political Weekly*, Vol. 24, No. 5, 1989, pp. 247–49.

Kosambi, Meera, 'Reality and Reflection: Personal Narratives of Two Women in Nineteenth Century Maharashtra', in Kumkum Sangari and Uma Chakravarti (eds.), *From Myths to Markets: Essays on Gender*, Shimla, Indian Institute of Advanced Study (forthcoming)..

Kumar, Ravinder, *Western India in the Nineteenth Century: A Study in the Social History of Maharashtra*, London, Routeledge & Kegan Paul, 1968.

Leslie, Julia, *The Perfect Wife: The Orthodox Hindu Woman According to the Stridharmapaddhati of Tryambaka Yajavan*, Delhi, Oxford University Press, 1989.

Leopold, Joan, 'The Aryan Theory of Race', *Indian Economic and Social History Review*, Vol. 7, No. 2, June 1970, pp. 271–97.

Ludders, Berlin H, *A List of Brahmi Inscriptions*, Varanasi, Indological Book House, 1973 (Reprint).

Macnicol, Nicol, *Pandita Ramabai*, Calcutta, Association Press (Y.M.C.A.), 1926.

McCormack, William C., 'Caste and the British Administration of Hindu Law', *Journal of Asian and African Studies*, Vol. 1, No. 1, 1966, pp. 27–34.

Manusmriti, tr., George Buhler, *The Laws of Manu*, Delhi, Motilal Banarsidass, 1984, (Reprint).

Masselos, J.C., *Towards Nationalism: Group Affiliations and the Politics of Public Associations in Nineteenth Century Western India*, Bombay, Popular Prakashan, 1974.

Misra, B.B., *The Indian Middle Classes: Their Growth in Modern Times*, London, Oxford University Press, 1961.

Motivala, B.N., *Karsondas Mulji, A Biographical Study*, Bombay, Karsondas Mulji Centenary Celebration Committee, 1935.

Mukherjee, Meenakshi, *Realism and Reality: The Novel and Society in India*, Delhi, Oxford University Press, 1985.

Muktabai, 'Mang Maharachya Dukhavisayi' (About the Grief of the Mangs and Mahars) *Dnyanodaya*, Ahmednagar, 1855, reprinted in Susie Tharu and K. Lalitha, *Women Writing in India: 600 B.C. to the Present, Volume I: 600 B.C. to Early 20th Century*, Delhi, Oxford University Press, 1991, pp. 215–16.

Müller, Max, 'My Indian Friends', in Müller, Max Mrs., (ed.), *Life and Letters of Rt. Hon. Friedrich Max Müller, Edited by his Wife*, London, Longman's Green, 1902, Vol.II, pp. 47–62.

Naik, V.T., (ed.), *Select Writings and Speeches of K.T. Telang*, Vol.II, Bombay, Gaud Saraswat Mitra Mandal, 1916.

Natarajan, S., *A Century of Social Reform in India*, Bombay, Asia Publishing House, 1959.

Nelson, J.H., *A Prospectus for the Scientific Study of the Hindu Law*, London, C. Kegan Paul, 1881.

Nethercot, Arthur H., *The First Five Lives of Annie Besant*, Chicago, University of Chicago Press, 1960.

O'Hanlon, Rosalind, *Caste, Conflict and Ideology: Mahatma Jotirao Phule and Low Caste Protest in Nineteenth Century Western India*, Cambridge, University Press, 1985.

———, 'Issues of Widowhood: Gender and Resistance in Colonial Western India', in Douglas Haynes and Gyan Prakash (ed.), *Contesting Power: Resistance and Everyday Social Relations in South Asia*, Delhi, Oxford University Press, 1991, pp. 62–108.

Oldenberg, Veena Talwar, 'Lifestyle as Resistance: The Case of Courtesans of Lucknow' in Douglas Haynes and Gyan Prakash (ed.), *Contesting Power: Resistance and Everyday Social Relations in South Asia*, Delhi, Oxford University Press, 1991, pp. 23–61.

Omvedt, Gail, *Cultural Revolt in a Colonial Society: The Non-Brahman Movement in Western India: 1873 to 1930*, Bombay, Scientific Socialist Education Trust, 1976.

———, 'Jotiba Phule, the Bahujan Samaj and Women', unpublished typescript.

Pal, Bipin Chandra, *Memories of My Life and Times*, Calcutta, Bipin Chandra Pal Institute, 1973.

Papanek, Hanna, 'To Each Less Than She Needs, From Each More Than She Can Do: Allocations, Entitlements and Value', in Irene Tinker, *Persistent Inequalities, Women and World Development*, New York, Oxford University Press, 1990, pp. 162–84.

Patterson, Maureen L.P., 'Changing Patterns of Occupation Among Chitpavan Brahmans', *Indian Economic and Social History Review*, Vol. 7, No. 1, 1970, pp. 375–96.

Pavate, T.V., *Makers of Modern India*, Jullunder, University Publishers, 1964.

Pearson, Gail, 'The Female Intelligentsia in a Segregated Society: Bombay, A Case Study', in M. Allen and S.N. Mukherjee (ed.), *Women in India and Nepal*, Canberra, Australian National University, 1983, pp. 136–54.

Perlin, Frank, 'Of White Whale and Countrymen in the Eighteenth Century Maratha Deccan: Extended Class Relations, Rights and the Problem of Rural Autonomy under the Old Regime', *Journal of Peasant Studies*, Vol. 5, No. 2, 1977, pp. 172–232.

Phadke, Y.D., *Women in Maharashtra*, Delhi, Government of Maharashtra, 1989.

———, *Social Reform Movements in Maharashtra*, Delhi, Maharashtra Information Centre, 1989.

———, *Collected Works of Jotiba Phule*, Bombay, Maharashtra Rajya Sahitya ani Sanskriti Mandal, 1991.

Phule, Jotiba, *Gulamgiri*, tr. Ved Kumar, Vadalankar, Bombay, Mahatma Phule Charitra Sadhana Prakashan Samiti, 1974.

Pillai, G.P., *Representative Indians*, London, Thacker and Company, 1920.

Preston, Laurence W., 'Subregional Religious Centres in the History of Maharashtra: The Sites Sacred to Ganesh', in N.K. Wagle (ed.), *Images of Maharashtra: A Regional Profile of India*, London, Curzon Press Limited, 1980.

Rabindra Rachanabali, Vol. 12, Calcutta, West Bengal Government, 1962.

Ramabai Pandita, *Stri Dharma Niti* (1882), Kedgaon, Pune, Ramabai Mukti Mission, 1966 (Reprint).

Ramabai Pandita, *A Testimony of Our Inexhaustible Treasure*, Kedgaon, Pandita Ramabai Mukti Mission, Pune, 1992.

Ramabai Saraswati Pandita, *The High Caste Hindu Woman*, Philadelphia, published by Pandita Ramabai, 1888.

Ranade, M.G., 'Introduction to the Peshwa's Diaries', in M.G. Ranade, *Rise of Maratha Power and Other Essays*, Bombay, P.C. Manektala, 1961 (Reprint).

Ranade, P.V., 'Feudal Content of Maharashtra Dharma', *Indian Historical Review*, Vol. 1, No. 1, 1974.

Ranade, Ramabai, *Amchya Ayushatil Kahi Athavani*, tr., Kusumavati Deshpande, *Ranade: His Wife's Reminiscences*, Delhi, Publications Division, Government of India, 1963.

Rege, Sharmila, 'State and Sexuality: The Case of the Erotic 'Lavanee' and 'Tamasha' in Maharashtra', in Patricia Uberoi (ed.), *Social Reform, Sexuality and the State*, Delhi, Sage Publications, 1996, pp. 23–38.

Roy, Sripati, *Customs and Customary Law in British India* (1910), Delhi, Mittal Publications, 1986 (Reprint).

Sangari, Kumkum, 'Relating Histories: Definitions of Literacy, Literature, Gender in Nineteenth Century Calcutta and England', in Svati Joshi (ed.), *Rethinking English: Essays in Literature, Language, History*, Delhi, Trianka, 1991.

————, 'Consent, Agency and the Rhetorics of Incitement', *Economic and Political Weekly*, Vol. 28, No. 18, 1st May 1993, pp. 867–82.

Sangari, Kumkum and Sudesh Vaid (ed.), *Recasting Women: Essays in Indian Colonial History*, Delhi, Kali for Women, 1989.

————, 'Institutions, Beliefs Ideologies: Widow Immolation in Contemporary Rajasthan', *Economic and Political Weekly*, Vol. 26, No. 17, April 27, 1991, pp. WS.2–18.

Sardesai, G.S., 'Excerpts from Mai's Diary', in D.D. Karve (ed.), *New Brahmans: Five Maharashtrian Families*, Berkeley, University of California Press, 1962.

Sarkar, Tanika, 'Rhetoric Against Age of Consent: Resisting Colonial Reason and Death of a Child Wife', *Economic and Political Weekly*, Vol. 28, No. 36, September 4, 1993, pp. 1869–78.

————, 'A Book of Her Own: Autobiography of a Nineteenth Century Woman', *History Workshop Journal*, No. 36, 1993, pp. 35–65.

Seal, Anil, *The Emergence of Indian Nationalism: Competition and Collaboration in the Later Nineteenth Century*, Cambridge, Cambridge University Press, 1968.

Selections From Swami Vivekananda, Almora, Advaita Ashram, 1946.

Sen, Amartya K., 'Gender and Co-operative Conflicts', in Irene Tinker (ed.), *Persistent Inequalities: Women and World Development*, New York, Oxford University Press, 1990, pp. 123–49.

Sen, Amiya, 'Hindu Revivalism in Action: The Age of Consent Bill Agitation in Bengal', *Indian Historical Review*, Vol. 7, Nos. 1–2, July 1980-January 1981, pp.160–84.

Sengupta, Padmini, *Pandita Ramabai Saraswati: Her Life and Work*, Bombay, Asia Publishing House, 1970.

Shinde, Tarabai, *Stri-Purusha Tulana*, tr., Rosalind O'Hanlon as *A Comparison Between Men and Women: Tarabai Shinde and the Critique of Gender Relations in Colonial India*, Madras, Oxford University Press, 1994.

Sinha, Mrinalini, 'Colonial Politics and the Ideal of Masculinity: The Example of the Age of Consent Act of 1891 in Bengal', *Proceedings of the Third National Conference on Women's Studies*, Chandigarh, Indian Association of Women's Studies, 1986, Vol.II, Sub Theme 6.

Srinivas, M.N., *Social Change in Modern India*, Bombay, Orient Longman, 1972.

Steele, Arthur, *The Hindu Castes: Their Law, Religion and Customs*, Delhi, Mittal Publications, 1986.

Sushila, Devi, *The Ideal of Hindu Womanhood, With Practical Suggestions for its Realisation*, Lahore, Civil and Military Gazette, 1907.

Thapar, Romila, *A History of India*, Vol.I., London, Penguin Books, 1966.

Tharu, Susie and K. Lalitha (ed.), *Women Writing in India: 600 B.C. to the Present, Volume I: 600 B.C. to the Early 20th Century*, Delhi, Oxford University Press, 1991.

Tilak, Lakshmibai, *I Follow After: An Autobiography*, tr., E. Josephine Inkster, London, Oxford University Press, 1950.

Tucker, Richard P., 'Early Setting of the Non-Brahmin Movement in Maharashtra, *The Indian Historical Review*, Vol. 9, Nos. 1–2, 1981, pp. 134–59.

———, *Ranade and the Roots of Indian Nationalism*, Bombay, Popular Prakashan, 1977.

Vaidya, Sarojini, *Sreemati Kashibai Kanitkar: Atmacharitra ani Charitra*, Bombay, Popular Prakashan, 1991.

Vanita, Ruth, 'Three Women Sants of Maharashtra: Muktabai, Janabai, Bahinabai', *Women Bhakta Poets*, Special Edition of *Manushi*, Nos. 50-52, January-June 1989, pp. 45–61.

Varde, Mohini, *Dr. Rakhmabai: Ek Aart*, Bombay, Popular Prakashan, 1982.

Verma, Amrit, *Hundred Great Indians Through the Ages*, Campbell-California, G.I.P. Books, 1992.

Vidyasagar, Ishwarchandra, *Marriage of Hindu Widows*, With an Introduction by Aravinda Poddar, Calcutta, K.P. Bagchi and Company, 1976.

Wagle, N.K., 'A Dispute Between the Pancal Devajna Sonars and the Brahmanas of Pune Regarding Social Rank and Ritual Privileges: A Case Study of the British Administration of Jati Laws in Maharashtra 1822–1825', in N.K. Wagle, (ed.), *Images of Maharashtra: A Regional Profile of India*, London, Curzon Press, 1980, pp. 129–59.

Wink, Andre, *Land and Sovereignty in India: Agrarian Politics in Eighteenth Century Maratha Svarajya*, Cambridge, Cambridge University Press, 1986.

Wolpert, Stanley, *Tilak and Gokhale: Reform and Revolution in the Making of Modern India*, Berkeley, University of California, 1962.

Zelliot, Eleanor, *From Untouchable to Dalit: Essays on the Ambedkar Movement*, Delhi, Manohar, 1992.

Index

adultery, and enslavement, 22;
and fire ordeal, 29; and
lower caste women, 29, 41n;
as women's worst offence,
28–29; cases of, 20–21, 45;
early colonial attitudes,
45–46; women, enhanced
punishment for, 20–22
Age of Consent (debate/bill),
84, 105, 123, 144, 165,
175–87, 198n, 327, 341
Ambedkar, 11, 71, 340
Anandibai, 29, 41n, 202
Anandibai, Bhagat, 316, 345n
Anandibai Joshi (Anandi Gopal),
208, 209, 240n, 279, 325,
331, 332; child marriage,
defence, 213; childhood
pressures, 211; education,
212; Hindu womanhood,
icon of, 213, 215; in
America, 212–13; marital
violence, 211–14, 241n, 242n
Anandibai Karve, 116n, 272,
277; and Pandita Ramabai,
267; as Baya, 116n; as
Godubai, 328; labour,
conflicting claims over,
266–68, 293n, 294n;
remarriage of, 116n, 277–78
anonymous widow, struggle of,
275–77
Arya Mahila Sabha, 158, 253,
257, 312, 313

Bahujan Samaj, 67
Bajirao I, 29, 30, 38n, 44, 104
batik, 21, 22
Besant, Annie, xv(n), xvi(n);
conservative views of, xvi(n);
"The Education of Hindu
Girls", xvi(n); Hindu
revivalist agenda of, xii, xiii;
India's past, xvi(n); Pandita
Ramabai, as opposed to, xiii,
xvi; reformers, attitude
towards, xii; widow
remarriage, opposition to,
xii; women, status of, xvi(n)
Bhakti, 9, 11, 34, 53, 65, 103,
314; Chokhamela, 9, 10, 16;
critique of, 11–13, 65;
historical evaluation of, 11;
Pandharpur, 9, 12, 15–16;
protest as well as succour, 10;
sect, Mahanubhav, 9, 34n;
sect, Varkari, 9, 11, 32n;
Varkari sants, social base, 9;
Vithoba, 9, 10, 15–16, 35n;
women sants, 11, 35n
Bhakti sants, Bahinabai, 11;
Eknath, 10, 43; Janabai, 11;
Janadev, 9, 11; Muktabai,
11; Namdev, 9; Ramdas, 12,
103–04; Tukaram, 9, 11, 261
Bhandarkar, 91, 94, 102, 104,
158, 177, 205, 253, 312, 330
Brahmanas, 303, 305–06, 342n;
and *dakshina*, 6, 31, 44–45,

58, 107n; and English education, 57–58, 60–63, 71–73, 79, 99–100, 110n; and anti-reformist, 102–05; castes, lower, opposition to education of, 72–73, other, disputes with, 7, 48–53, 53–55, 108n; Chitpavans, 3, 4–5, 6, 7, 26, 32n, 33n, 50, 62–63, 104; colonial state, conciliation policy of, 43–45, 48, 58–60, crisis under, 51, 92, 96–99, economic power under, 62–64; Deshastha, 3, 4; Hindu Dharma Vyavasthapak Mandal, 90; intellectual elite, leadership struggles, 78–79, 99–106; Peshwai, patronage under, 6, 13, 36n, 37n, strict norms under, 15; Poona Sarvajanik Sabha, 94–96, 101; reformist and orthodox, unity between, 101–02; Vedashastrottejaka Sabha, 94

Brahmanism, 31, 57, 65, 68, 77, 167–68, 178, 188, 303, 305, 308–10, 320, 329; and Bhakti sants, 9–12; anti Brahmanism movements, context of, 92; critique from within, 78–81; history of, 8, Phule's interpretation, 69–71; Peshwai, protected and promoted by, 6, 13, 15, 36n, 37n

Brahmanical patriarchy, 31, 167–68, 188, 279, 280–82, 329, 330; aggressive support to practices of, 178; colonial legal structures, upheld by, 133; conceptualisation of widowhood, 268; consent to practices of, 236, 277; continuity in practices of, 224; discussions of, 246–47, 257; model of womanhood in, 39n; priests as upholders of codes of, 273; Ramabai's critique of, xi, 2; reproductive potential of women, 25; sexuality, female, fear and exaggeration of, 201–02, importance of controlling, 20–22, 29, 31, 39n; widowhood codes, importance of, 23–28; widow immolation, importance of, 30; widow's place in and Phule, 76; women, Brahman, suicide by, 42n; women, codes for, 17, 31; women, monitoring of, 17–18

Brahmos, 311, 314

caste/caste system, and class, 57–58, 61–62, 64; as system of production, 26–27; Bhakti sants, reflection in lives and works of, 9–12; contestations, 48–58, 64, 72, 92, 129, 162; lower castes, education, opposition by Brahmans, 72–73, practices, homogenised under 'Hindu law', 129, 133, 137, reservation and colonial state, 98, 101, suppression under Peshwai, 15–16; panchayats, 49, 134–35, 160–61, 163, 174, 186, 191n, 192n; Peshwai, reinforced by, 13–17; Phule's understanding of, 66–70; reformist ideology, limitations of, 101–05; sanskritisation, 56–57, 65,

67, 92; structure,
Maharashtra, 7, 8, 14, 36n,
51, 64; upward mobility,
aspirations, 39n, 40n, 52,
56–57, 129, 130, 152–53,
155, supression of, 15, 27,
30; women, determinant of
codes for, 17, 20–22, 23–25,
31, 52–53
Chiplunkar, Vishnu Shastri, 4,
90, 100, 102, 104, 112n
Chiplunkar, Krishna Shastri, 79
Christianity, conflation with
colonialism, xiii, xiv;
missionaries, 44, 45, 59, 80,
314, 321, 323, 339–40, 347n
class formation/middle class,
128, 138, 157, 170, 175;
and changing self image,
158; and unified gender
codes, 163; and widow
remarriage, 87; English
education, 61–62; new social
forces, 57–58; recasting
women, 200, 211–12, 233,
280; relationship to caste,
110n; restructuring the
family, 203
colonial state, and Age of
Consent, 175, 185–86; and
'Brahmanophobia', 95–96,
118n; and caste
contestations, 48–57, 58;
and definition of Shudras,
127; and domestic sphere,
200–01; and English
education, 57–62, 109n; and
Pandita Ramabai, 338–40;
and the Rakhmabai case,
170–75; and widowhood,
85; attitude towards
non-Brahmanas, change in, 98;
Brahmanas, conciliation of,

43–48, 58–60, 106n, 107n,
132; coercive power in
favour of Brahmanas,
withdrawing of, 51–52, 92;
gender codes, upholding of,
45–48; law, customary,
tensions with, 134–38,
statutory, formation of,
123–34; women's education,
203, sexuality, complicity in
control over, 187–88
companionate marriage,
206–09, 213–15, 220, 223,
236, 246, 281, 316
conjugality, 123, 128, 134, 138,
139, 141–51, 170, 204, 207,
216, 232; colonial state,
notions of, 135–38;
disciplining the wife, 255;
Hindu law on, 147–48;
marital rape, 176, 177, 181,
182, 184; punishment for
refusal of, 166–75, 195n;
restitution of, 138–51;
wifehood among Hindus,
125–26, 169, 188, among
Shudras, 126–27

Dalit intelligentsia, 11–13
dasi, 11
Deshmukhs, 3
Deshmukh, Gopal Hari, 79, 87,
93, 100
Durga, sister of Ranade, as
widow, material position in
natal family, 227–29, 232,
235, survival strategy and
manipulation, 227–32,
235–36; biography, 226–27;
traditional codes, upholder
of, 230–31; views on men,
230–31

Elphinstone, 43, 58, 59, 60,
106n, 107n, 108n
Engels, Dagmar, 182
excommunication/*ghatasphot*,
19, 23, 28, 29, 41n, 76, 91,
93, 116n, 160, 284, 304, 310

family/household, 200, 201,
203, 208, 213, 224–26, 229,
233, 235, 238
feminist historians, xvii(n)
fitna, 202, 210
Fukuzawa, 13, 14, 15, 18, 22

Garbhadhanam, 19, 178, 179,
181, 183
gender, 29, 78, 92, 94, 166, 238,
252, 301, 302, 336; Age of
Consent debate, 175–87; and
colonial law enforcement,
123–34, 135–37; and early
colonial attitudes, 45–48; and
emergent classes, 158; and
nationalism, 169, 178, 185,
188n, 213, 240n, 241n, 246,
333–34; and new social forces,
43, 45–48; and Peshwai,
17–31; as index of caste
status, 17, 52–53, 55–56; bias
in history writing, xv(n); codes
of, 18, 39n, 40n; double
standards of morality, 235,
250–51, 258, 284, 286, 295n;
relationship with class and
state, xv, 2, with caste and
labour, 22, 287; writing
gender history, xiv; widow
remarriage debate, 81–94
Gokhale, 5, 101, 224, 339
Goreh, Father, Nilkanth, 315,
316, 318, 347n
Guha, Ranajit, 187

history, interpretations of,
Brahmans, reformers and
orthodox, 102–04; Phule's,
69–71; women, origins of
low status, 102, 274
'home'/domestic ideology,
204–06, 214, 216, 219,
225–26, 234; male
constructs of, 210, 233, 236;
new versions, success of,
222–23, 277, 280–81
household/family, 255, 262, 286

Jambhekar, Bal Shastri, 79

Kadam, 20, 27
Kanitkar, Kashibai, 208, 209,
222–23, 240n, 253, 326, 327
Karve, 266, 277–79, 328, 331,
340
Karve, Irawati, 12
Kosambi, D. D., 8, 9, 10, 36n
Kunbis, 7; caste aspirations, 55,
67, 72; *pat* marriages, 26;
Tukaram, 9
kunbina, 21, 22

law, contradictions in customary
and statutory, 134–38;
customary, 123, 125, 126;
Hindu law, 188n, 195n,
application of, 123–27,
170–71, cross-caste
homogenisation under, 129,
133, 137, 162–63,
interpretations of, 129–35,
141, on conjugal rights,
147–50, Rakhmabai's case,
141–51, 159–60, 162, 164;
statutory, 123–24, 128, 147;
widow remarriage, meshing
'Hindu' and statutory, 123–34

Madhavarao I, 6, 28, 30
Malabari, Behram, 88, 160,
    164, 173, 176, 183, 186,
    196n, 253–56, 291n; child
    marriage, initiative against,
    174, 176, 183, 253, 256,
    291n; Hindu caste law,
    limitations, understanding of,
    173–74; on women's consent
    to marriage, 164
Mandlik, 89, 99–100, 102,
    105, 163, 165, 253, 256
Mangs, 7, 67, 72, 73, 74–76
Mahars, 7, 43, 67, 72–73;
    Chokhamela, 9; Peshwai,
    restrictions under, 13;
    traditional duties of, 10
Manu, xvi, 26, 124, 131, 169,
    173, 216, 250, 256, 284
Marathas, 3, 4, 7, 67, 90, 97,
    98, 108n, 109n, 111n;
    Brahmans, disputes with,
    53–55; Peshwai,
    marginalisation under, 7;
    Shivaji, 3, 7, 32n, 70–71,
    103–04, 119; Watandars, 5
marriage, child wife, death of
    Phulmoni, 177–78, 197n,
    'ripening', 248, 287;
    companionate, 206–09,
    213–15, 220, 223, 236, 246,
    281, 316, and one sidedness
    of, 214; consent in,
    Rakhmabai's case, 141,
    145–46, 148–49, 164–65,
    170, 184; endogamy, 20, 55;
    forms of, 26; marital rape,
    176, 177, 181, 182, 184;
    Peshwai, alliances during, 5,
    18, 38n, regulation of codes,
    14, 18–20; pratiloma, 21,
    310; pre-pubertal/child, 18,
    19, 165, 174, 175, 209,

211, 213, 254–57;
    sacramental, 125, 133, 167,
    169; Satyashodhak, 77–78;
    suffering within, Anandibai
    Joshi, 211–14, 241n, 242n

nationalism, appropriating the
    past, 103; gender dimensions
    of, 168, 169, 178, 185, 188,
    213, 240n, 241n, 246,
    333–34; narrow basis of, xi,
    341–42

O'Hanlon, Rosalind, 70

Pandharpur, Brahman control
    over ritual, 12; caste
    distinctions during
    pilgrimage, 12; in Varkari
    tradition, 9; Peshwai control,
    15–16
Pandita Ramabai, 212, 215, 220,
    223, 229, 240n, 253, 254,
    267, 277, 279, 281–86, 298n,
    301, 343n, 345n, 349n; Age
    of Consent debate,
    intervention in, 327; Anandi
    Bhagat, 316–18; and
    Christianity, xi, xii, 314–19,
    331–32, 348n, 350n; and
    Max Muller, 317–18; and
    Phule, 320; and reformers,
    307–08, 311–12, 314, 319,
    328–29, 330, 333; and
    Tilak, 319, 329, 337, 339;
    ancient Hindu womanhood,
    epitome of, 307–08; Arya
    Mahila Sabha, 312–13;
    Brahmanical Hinduism,
    alienation from, 310;
    brother, Srinivas, 307, 310;
    child marriage, escape from,
    306; Church, conflict with,

321–25, 339–41, 346n, 347n; colonial state, confrontation with, 338–39, 341, 350n; conversion, hysterical reaction to, 319–20; daughter, Manorama, 316, 324, 332, 340; Dharmashastras, analyses of, 309. 317; early life, 305–07; efforts for Widows Home, 325–26; father, Ananta Shastri Dongre, 303, 306; history writing, 'suppression' in xi, xiii, xv(n); Hunter Commission, 312; husband, Bipin Behari Medhavi, 310; male aggression, object of, 312–13, 329, 331; marriage, *pratiloma*, 310; mother, Lakshmibai, 304–05, 307; Mukti Sadan, 328, 337, 340; on *sati*, 285; on widowhood, 281–85, 336; Parvati Athavale, 205–06, 211, 239n, 246, 275, 277–82, 296n, 297n; religiosity of, 314, 332, 348n; Sanskrit, learning, 305; Sharada Sadan, 267, 326–29, 332–33, 340; Sister Geraldine, 316–17, 323, 339, 345n, 350n; stigmatised as betrayer, 341–42; "Stridharma Niti", 315; surveillance, as widow, 311; *The High Caste Hindu Woman*, 281, 315–16, 325; Vivekananda, as opposed to, 320, 325, 333, 335–36, 349n; widowhood of, 311–12; widow remarriage, attitude to, 283–84; women and widowhood, reconceptualisation, 328;

women, belief in entitlement to choice, 329–30, 332–33 patriarchy/patriarchies, codes of, 219; consent for new forms of, 247, 249; critiques of, 250, 252, 282, 285–88; ideologies, clash of, 187; interlocking of, 174–75, 341; reassembling of, 203; resistance to new forms of, 230, 233, 236–38; transformation of, 208, 210, 212, 223–25

Peshwai, 2, 43, 45, 46, 48, 62, 104, 185–87, 262, 303; and gender codes, 17–18, 19, 31; and widowhood, 23–28; as *Brahmanya raj*, 3, 5, 27, 29, 31, 36n, 64, 74–75; as Dharmarajya, 14; as financial, military, administrative nexus, 5; Brahmans, patronage to, 6, 13, 15, 36n, 37n; caste hierarchies, reinforced, 13–14; Chitpavan dominance in, 4, 5; non-Chitpavans, marginalisation of, 6, 7; women, adultery by, 20–22, enslavement of, 22

Phule, 64, 80, 98, 100–05, 111n, 113n, 222, 250, 253, 320, 342; and widows, 76–77; Brahman reformers, distance from, 102; caste system, critique of, 65–66, material basis of, 68, origins of, 69–70; democratic ideals, influence of, 66, 112n; education, lower caste women, 73, 112n, 113n; gender, reconceptualisation

of, 77–78; harassment faced
by, 111n, 113n; Hinduism
as expression of Brahmanical
worldview, 68–69; history,
radical interpretation of,
69–71; Hunter Commission,
72; on patriotism, 342;
Ramabai, defence of, 77;
sanskritisation, critique of,
67; Satyashodhak Samaj,
77–78, 96; Tarabai, defence
of, 77; works of, *Gulamgiri*,
68, 112n, *Sarvajanik
Satyadharma*, 77, *Shetkaryaca
Asud*, 77, *Traitya Ratna*, 68
Padwal, Tukaram Tatya, 66–67
Phulmoni, 177–78, 197n
Poona Widows and Orphans
Home, 260, 262–63, 273,
278, 287, 291n, 299n
Prabhus, 7, 15–17, 50, 60–61,
81, 90, 97, 151–53

Radhabai, 29, 41
Ramabai, 30
Ramabai Ranade, 204, 209,
238, 216–37, 243n, 244n,
246, 331–32; *Amchya
Ayushatil Kahi Athavani*,
224; Arya Mahila Sabha,
223; education, 209–17, of
women, views on, 223;
marriage, 216–17; pleasing
the husband, 219, 222–23,
236–37; politics of
household, 225–35; Seva
Sadan, 223; widowhood
views on, 234, 245n
Rakhmabai, 214–15, 254–60,
285–86, 338; as object of
derision, 159, 167, 168–69;
biography of, 151–58;
caste-class location of,

151–53; letters, on child
marriage and widowhood,
254–60; mother, Jayantibai,
155–56; stepfather, Dr.
Sakharam Arjun, 139–41,
143, 156–57, 195n; the
Rakhmabai case (Dadaji vs
Rakhmabai), 138–41, 151,
193n, arguments in, 141–51,
conjugal rights, 141–44,
147–51, 158, consent, the
question of, 141, 145–46,
149, 164–65, 170, 184,
consummation, the question
of, 141–42, 148–49, 158,
167, Hindu law, 159–60,
judgement, 151, 170–71,
property, at the crux of,
161–62, 171, 173
Ranade, 95, 99, 102–04, 158,
186, 216–35, 244n, 245n,
253, 305, 312, 326, 330;
and Pandita Ramabai, 312,
326, 330; as judge, 129–32,
188; Brahman conservatives,
ideological unity with,
101–04, 244, 245n;
limitations as reformer, 93,
186, 188n, 216; patriarchy,
reform of, 216–35
reformers/*sudharaks*, xi, 78–81,
95, 166, 182, 254, 279,
281, 337, 341; agenda,
surpassed by women writers,
247, 252, 260, 285–88,
297n; and Pandita Ramabai,
307–08, 311–12, 314, 319,
328–29, 330, 333; and
anti-reformism, 100,
102–05, 256–57; early
agendas, 78–81; English
education of, 305; failure of,
92–93, 101–05, 166, 186,

188; ideological unity with orthodoxy, 101–02; limited reform of Brahmanical patriarchal structures, xiii, 89, 272–73, 283; on consent, 186, 198n; on widow remarriage, 81–84, 86–93, 99, 249; Prarthana Sabha, 94, 102, 312, 314, 318, 332; Vidhva Vivahottejaka Mandal, 89–90
Rammohan Roy, 82

sanskritisation, 56–57, 65, 67, 92, 127, 298n
Said, Edward, xiv, xvii(n)
sati, 18, 45, 83, 262, 274, 281, 285; abolition of, 82, 123; and colonial state, 47–48, 107n; self-immolation, 30, 52; voluntary, decoding of, 285
Satyashodhak Samaj, 96
Savitribai, 76, 113n, 11n
Sen, 308, 311
sexuality, female, as evil, 202; control over, 20–22, 29, 31, 39, 187–88; fear of, 201–02; *fitna*, 202, 210; focus of debate, 82–84, 86, 115n; suppression of, widows', 82–83, 268–69, 286–87, 328; surveillance of, 17–18
Shinde, Tarabai, 77, 250–54, 285–87, 298n
Shudras, 15, 51, 67, 70, 105, 112n, 126–27, 119n
Sonars, Konkan, Devarajna, 48–53, 108n
stridharma/pativrata dharma, 22, 29, 30, 201–02, 204, 210, 215, 251–52
surveillance, enslavement,

effectuated by, 21; of female sexuality, 17–18; pre-pubertal marriages, ensured by, 19, 211; of widows, 23, 25, 208, 211, 228, 248, 262, 264, 268, 275–77; of wives, 208, 228
Sutars, 61, 151–54, 157–58, 164

Telang, 145–48, 150, 160, 163–64, 174, 178, 186, 191n, 192n, 197n, 305
Tilak, Bal Gangadhar, 97–106, 119, 166, 168, 171, 178–79, 185, 197n, 240n, 241n, 305, 319, 329, 333, 337, 339, 341; and Pandita Ramabai, 319, 329, 337, 339; and untouchability, 105; anti reformism of, 100, 178–79, 197n, 240n, 241n; class position, reflection in politics of, 97–98, 101; nationalism of, 185, 319, 337, 341; on Rakhmabai's case, 166–68, 171; on women's education, 240n; Phulmoni, child wife, on death of, 197n; Shivaji festival, use of, 103–04, 119n
Tilak, Waman Narayan, 316, 340
tonsure, of widows, 23–25, 30, 76, 83, 88, 327; barber's strike, 115n; Brahmanical order, importance for, 25; ceremony, 24; expenditure, 25; resistance and excommunication, 23; symbolic meaning of, 83, 270–71; trauma of, 270–72, 275–76

'untouchable', 7, 8, 9, 16

Vidyasagar, Ishwarchandra,
    81–82, 86, 93, 115n, 116n
Vijayalakshmi, 187–88, 250
Vivekananda, Swami, 320, 325,
    336, 349n; on Indian
    womanhood, 333; on
    women's property rights, 334;
    on widows, 333, 335; on
    widow remarriage, 334

widow/widowhood, adult,
    278–79; and Pandita
    Ramabai, 281–85, 336; as
    opposed to wife, 25, 31, 231;
    ascetic, strict code for
    Brahmans, 23, 30, 92,
    forbidden to lower castes, 15,
    27, 52; child, 82, 84, 87, 89,
    101, 132, 246–48, 252, 259,
    264, 283, 287, 288n, 292n,
    315, 326; demography,
    labour, caste, relationship
    with, 25–27; entitlement,
    262–63, 268–69; experiences
    of, 226–28, 232, 234–36,
    246–47, 249, 251, 257–58,
    261–62, 264, 268, 275–76,
    288n, 292, 294n, 295n;
    ghatasphot, 28, 41n, 76;
    inheritance by, 155; labour,
    extraction of, 248, 258, 262,
    264, 268, 275, 287; Peshwai
    orders on, 24; Phule's
    intervention, 76; predatory
    males, 251, 268, 270, 274;
    problem, nationalist resolution
    of, 250, 279, 280, 288n;
    property rights of, 127, 129,
    130–31, 155, 176, 262;
    reformist discourse on, 247;
    resistance to enforcement,

23–24, 86–87, 115n, 116n,
    248, 275–77; social control
    over, 330; sexuality,
    suppression of, 82–83,
    268–69, 286–87, 328;
    surveillance of, 23, 25, 208,
    211, 228, 248, 262, 264,
    268, 275–77; upper caste,
    247, 257, 262–63, 273, 282,
    288n, 299n, 301, 330
widow remarriage, and caste
    hierarchy, 17, 52; and
    forfeiture of property,
    124–25, 127–30, 155; and
    Shudras, 126; as solution,
    Pandita Ramabai's critique,
    283–84; Brahman reformers,
    position of, 81–84, 87, 88,
    90–91; debate on, 82–84,
    86–89, 91–92, 94, 99, 114n,
    117n, focus on female
    sexuality, 82–84, 86, 115;
    karewa (levirate), 128; *niyoga*
    (levirate), 284; *pat* form of,
    23, 26–28, 40, 52, 130,
    153; programmes, failure of,
    92–93; statutory law,
    contradictions of, 123–24;
    Vidhva Vivahottejaka
    Mandal, 89–90; Widow
    Remarriage Act (Act XV of
    1856), 81, 123–34, 176,
    contradictions in
    interpretations of, 132–33,
    judicial controversy,
    evaluation of, 132–34, lower
    castes, applicability to,
    interpretations, 126–34,
    wifehood, definition of, 126
women, absent voice of, 117n,
    246, 253–54, 256; adultery,
    enhanced punishment for,
    20–21; agency of, 202, 204,

210, 217, 250, 253, 259,
285–86, 296n, 297n, 301,
327, 329; and caste
hierarchies, 17, 52, 55–56;
and Phule, 73–78; as
nurturers, 204–05, 236–37;
body as focus of debates,
180, 250, as nation's body,
180; colonial law, subjects
of, 187; consent, production
of, 199n, 236–37, 259, 285;
domestic sphere, reform of,
201, 203; "educating", 203,
206–10, 214, 217, 219,
222–23; education of,
xvi(n)-xvi(n), 138, 246, 250,
254, 280, 319; enslavement
under Peshwai of, 21, 22;
"immorality", burden of, 45,
85, 135–37; labour and
sexuality, control over,
17–31, 128, 183, 185; legal
systems, multiple subjection
to, 133–38; literacy of, 207,
208, 246, taboo on, 218;
married, property of, 162;
marriage as exchange of, 18,
38, 165–66, prepubertal,
18–19, 165, 175, 209;
patriarchy, complicity in,
29–30, 259, 277, 286;
reconceptualisation, 19th
century, 203; *sants*, 11, 35;
"schooling", 201–06,

209–11, 212–15, 217, 222,
229, 236–37, 238, 246–47;
sexuality, as offence, 22, 39n,
83, fear of, 201–02,
reformers' perception of,
82–85, 86, 115n; statutory
law and lower caste, 133,
136–37; *stridharma/pativrata
dharma*, 22, 29, 30, 201–02,
204, 210, 215, 251–52;
strisvabhava, 201, 248
women writers, on anguish of
low castes, Muktabai, 74–75,
76; on child marriage,
Rakhmabai, 254–56; on
experiences of widowhood:
Ambubai Bapat, 268–69,
294n, Ambubai Gumaste,
272, 299n, Anandibai Karve,
266–68, Bhimabai Kale,
292n, Parvati Athavale,
278–80, Pandita Ramabai,
282–85, Radhabai Inamdar,
261, 264, 273–75,
Rakhmabai, 258–60,
Sakhubai Apte, 264, Sushila
Devi, 248–50, Tarabai
Shinde, 250–52, Varubai
Ranade, 268; on resistance,
Lakshmibai Sardesai, 237–38

Young Poona, 79

Zelliot, 12

Afterword

Eight years after *Rewriting History* first came out, Ramabai's life and times still enthuse me, and I continue to engage with her, think about her and write about her— this, despite the fact that there have been occasional comments from 'native' cultural specialists from Maharashtra who have suggested that 'outsiders' cannot 'really understand', or write with 'authenticity' about the region in which she lived her life. I believe that the politics of cultural uniqueness and its corollary, a possessive territoriality, are a way of refusing to engage with what *Rewriting History* is really about—class, caste and nation through the prism of gender, with a particular focus on the figure of the controversial Pandita Ramabai. The broader context within which I looked at Ramabai and the possibilities and constraints of the choices she could have made (and indeed those she did make), meant that her individual 'story' came only in the last part of the book and formed a 'small' segment of it. Noting this, a sympathetic feminist reviewer pointed to the frustrations of there being too little on Ramabai! *This* is a charge that I accept. Even today, I have not been able to bring a sense of closure to my work on Ramabai and her life. In the last few years I have also found that she interests many others in a range of fields, for example filmmakers, feminist educationists, people interested in the history of Maharashtra who are otherwise 'outsiders', so we continue to talk about her in all sorts of ways. Sabeena Gadihoke, a feminist filmmaker with whom I have shared many conversations about history, became deeply impressed by Ramabai's photographic practices, especially her successful attempts to raise the conscience of the world on the widows of India through the use of photographs. Reading newly completed translations of Ramabai's untranslated works, especially of her travels in the United States (about which she wrote extensively in Marathi), as well as the very insightful account of Ramabai's conversion and understanding of Christianity by Gauri Viswanathan, has not only given me great reading pleasure but also further insights about Ramabai, some of which I dwell on below. Clearly, I haven't quite finished with Ramabai, and perhaps never will at a personal level, regardless of how much gets written about her. But then why did *Rewriting History* have so much on a gendered social history and relatively so 'little' on Ramabai? Let me attempt an explanation.

Rewriting History was written as part of an exercise in examining gender as crucial to class formation, caste contestation and the construction of a national identity: my attempt was to go beyond the focus on the centrality of the woman's question in nineteenth century social reform. At the time I began work on it, the focus of scholarly attention, including feminist scholarship on the nineteenth century, was more or less confined to the bhadralok of Bengal — their concerns, their complex material location, their angst, and, as one reviewer put it, their obsession with themselves, as well as their 'resolution' of the woman's question (which was, interestingly, articulated as a broader, 'nationalist' resolution of the woman's question). It was this that dominated historical writing. By implication then, the [regional] experience of Bengal became *the* experience and resolution of the women's question for all of India! That the bhadralok comprised the three upper castes of Bengal—Brahmin, Kayastha and Baido— was taken for granted and so it rarely needed to be explained. The paucity of work on caste, except for the pioneering and significant work of Sekhar Bandhopadhya, meant that caste had not been a factor in understanding or contextualising questions of gender. This also meant that our understanding of gender—as projected for the whole of India—was so inflected by the writing on Bengal that it was almost indelibly stamped by the imprimatur of bhadralok nationalist concerns. Since I was more interested in examining alternative positions, from a caste and gender perspective during the 19th century, Maharashtra was the most interesting region to explore. Not only was the presence of Phule and the non-Brahmin movement in the second half of the 19th century an important factor in this decision, the critical writings of Tarabai Shinde and

Pandita Ramabai on the women's question settled the issue for me. Also because I wanted to have the caste, class and gender framework, the fact that there was a solid pre-existing body of historical writing on this framework—indeed the framework I wanted to use had emanated from this very body of writing— made it possible for me to focus more on gender and thus expand the lines of enquiry pursued by Gail Omvedt and Rosalind O'Hanlon among others. I could thus explore both Ramabai and other contemporary women like Rakhmabai not only within a gendered social context, but also in the context of caste contestations.

In some ways, my 'move' into the 19th century was almost an accident but also had its own history. From the mid-eighties on, the women's movement and the women's studies movement, along with pressures exerted by feminist activists, have impelled me to examine gender more centrally in my historical work. My historical training had made me a 'specialist' in ancient Indian history, a period that I began to look at afresh, in light of my interest in gender. A major concern of the women's movement was to examine questions of culture, tradition, and religion-based ideology, especially because we were continually confronted by deeply sedimented notions of the 'high' status of women in 'Hindu' culture. Consequently I became interested in the history of how this notion came to circulate and become a part of the nineteenth century writing on the women's question, especially on the construction of the myth of the vedic/Aryan woman. This initial interest in the 19th century took the form of a long paper titled 'Whatever Happened to the Vedic Dasi,' an essay that appeared in *Recasting Women* and which opened up the 19th century for me. 'The Vedic Dasi' had also ended with a brief discussion of how a woman like Pandita Ramabai came to see the ancient past which middle class male reformers, whether of the conservative or reformist kind, were fairly fixated on in the context of the 'women's question'. That brief examination triggered off an emotional interest in Ramabai which has remained with me since then. So when Kali for Women came up with the idea of publishing an archive of women's writing which would include a reprint of Ramabai's *The*

High Caste Hindu Woman, I was asked to write the introduction. I accepted the suggestion with alacrity. As things turned out I did not, in the end, write a conventional introduction to a reprint but, much to the horror of the editors of Kali, instead wrote an extraordinarily long 'introduction' to the life of Pandita Ramabai rather than to *The High Caste Hindu Woman*. In the course of this long and winding 'context' for Ramabai I tried to explore questions of law, class formation and caste contestation, the 'schooling' of women—a term used by Kumkum Sangari to suggest a specific aspect of training women into the requirements of new patriarchies— rather than looking at formal processes of the 'education' of women. Women's writing, however showed that they often went far beyond the agendas set for them by their contemporary male reformers and the complex ways in which they perceived the 'women's question'. The focus was thus shifted from the Ranades, Tilaks, Mandliks, Bhandarkars and Malabaris not only to Pandita Ramabai but to Rakhmabai, Ramabai Ranade, and her sister-in-law Durga—otherwise submerged in her autobiography which focussed on the great man 'Himself'— Anandibai Joshi, Kashibai Kanitkar, Tarabai Shinde and a host of named and nameless widows. *Rewriting History* was written as an account of social processes, of individuals who were part of these processes, and of the possibilities and the limits of those possibilities for women of the late 19th century in Maharashtra.

At the same time there were limits to the processes and individuals that I explored in *Rewriting History* partly because of the nature of the material that I had access to, and partly because of the very processes themselves that limited the body of writing to upper caste women. This, in turn, had to do with the nature of 19th century class formation in Maharashtra. There are no dalit voices in *Rewriting History* except for a fragment of an essay written by Muktabai. The sole piece of writing by Tarabai Shinde appears to be all that we have of an 'A'brahmani voice for the 19th century. However, a notable feature of recent feminist scholarship on Maharashtra is that it has been able to go far beyond the questions originally examined by historians. The rationale of my own interest in Maharashtra from the point of view of a feminist lens has been fully borne out in recent works by Vidyut Bhagwat as well as in Sharmila Rege's works on dalit women's testimonios and on dalit counterpublics. Shefali Chandra's doctoral work on the place of English education for women in Maharashtra in the 19ᵗʰ century, and Sabeena Gadihoke's examination of the photographic practices of Pandita Ramabai in her larger account of zenana photography, among other works, are examples of the range of interest generated by feminist scholars on the history of Maharashtra, an interest that will continue to grow in the years to come.

II

One area of Ramabai's life that I dealt with in *Rewriting History*, though not at great length, was her conversion to Christianity and the controversies surrounding this act as perceived by the Hindu middle class constituency that she had been part of in the early 1880s. Other scholars have also examined the social consequences of her conversion in terms of her work with widows and other marginalized women, particularly her stance on resisting pressure from her funders in America on the question of making public to the widows in Sharda Sadan her deep faith in Christ. Ram Bapat's essay on her relationship to Christianity was perhaps the first serious account of Ramabai's spiritual quest and her religiosity,[1] an aspect of her life that feminist scholars like me perhaps had a late and slow concern with. Like many feminists of my generation who had grown up in households and communities that were embedded in cultural practices that were oppressive, but were regarded as timeless and time-tested, I had a distrust of religion because of its close relationship with the endorsement of patriarchal structures on the one hand, and the demonisation of other religions on the other. Initially, I could not quite appreciate the logic of conversion for anyone like Ramabai who was clearly a feminist in her time; in the case of Maharashtra there was also the example of Phule who seemed to be able to work within the framework of a secular humanism to mount his challenge to the caste system. But as I proceeded to engage with Ramabai, and see her from her own standpoint, I grew to appreciate her deep engagement with religion and her need for both an emotional anchor. Also, her ability to make, and sustain, 'rational' choices in relation to her acceptance of Christianity as well as in engaging in debates within it on matters of religious interpretation, were admirable. *In Rewriting History* I had moved to appreciating Ramabai's spiritual quest and strongly defended that choice in terms of her critique of Hindu socio-religious practices. I had also reacted strongly to the suggestion that Christianity and colonialism were so deeply intertwined that an acceptance of Christianity made Ramabai a comprador, anti-nationalist and complicit in colonialism. Since then, Gauri Viswanathan has published an important work on conversions where Ramabai's relationship to Christianity has been explored with great sensitivity and perceptiveness, providing us with an understanding of a convert's complex relationship to the religion she had 'freely' chosen.[2]

Let us begin with the popular Hindu middle class position that Ramabai's conversion to Christianity made her 'anti-national'. The same middle classes paid no attention to Ramabai's long struggle with the Anglican Church on matters of 'propriety' and of belief, a struggle in which Ramabai refused to compromise on her convictions. For the Anglican missionaries the ideal role for Ramabai was one in which she functioned within the parameters of a '*purdahnasheen*, zenana style community' with no contact with men either to teach them, as she sought to do, or visit or interact with gentleman friends, especially given her background as a Hindu widow. But this is precisely what Indian women were determined to step out of. Ramabai rebutted this position of the Church with one of the most sustained anti-orientalist diatribes in 19th century letters, puncturing all the most cherished notions of women's reform held by English missionaries (p.151). Finally, Sister Geraldine, Rambai's mentor in England, who facilitated her conversion to Christianity but with whom she had serious differences on her understanding of Christan theology, realized the principle that Ramabai was raising in the supposed acts of transgression. And through the power of her counterattack the missionaries were shown up as functioning within a set of contradictions that they were then forcing upon her. Through this controversy Ramabai demonstrated most effectively that just as she had decisively refused to be contained within the agenda of reformers and nationalists in India, she refused to let the Church dictate to her on matters of how she understood the women's question as well as how she sought to enact her role in confronting the structures that contained women across countries.

Another aspect of Ramabai's relationship to Christianity that has been obscured in writings on her is her protracted effort to define a conception of divinity that satisfied her craving for interpretative freedom (p.121). According to Vishwanathan, scholars have accorded relevance to Ramabai's spirituality only to the extent that it illuminated her protest against brahmanical ritualism. But, according to her, Ramabai's search for a moral and theological framework of a social critique of gender disparities in Brahmanism also 'provided her a point of entry into a devastating analysis of British colonialism.' Vishwanathan argues that Ramabai's articulation of doctrinal differences on the focal points of Anglican doctrines was shaped by her belief that other religious groups like the Jews, Non-conformists, Wesleyans, Congregationists, Methodists and others were left out of the Anglican fold in England as decisively as were its colonial subjects (p.121). When Ramabai raised questions of theological inconsistencies in British Christianity and when sister Geraldine, her chief mentor in England, hit back by threatening her with forfeiting divine grace, Ramabai stated firmly that she was convinced that the door of the 'Universal Church' was not shut against her—in any case the Church was not confined within the walls of the Anglican Church. She thus disaggregated religion from political national institutions. Her faith therefore enabled her to take on both nationalism and colonialism according to the issue at hand. At the same time she 'salvaged religious belief as personal testimony from the crude pit of religious ideology, which Ramabai came to see as a product of the instrumental rationality of the colonial English state' (p.124).

One last point that is significant in the context of Ramabai's relationship to Christianity is her affinity to a range of dissenting positions circulating in England against the official theology of the Anglican Church in popular pamphlet literature. Among the arguments made by Ram Bapat is that she remained isolated from non-brahman conceptualisations and movements to challenge Brahmanism in Maharashtra, and by implication was locked into an elite, upper caste Brahmanical social location (p.227). This may be true at the level of alliances in India although she did critique the caste system in her writings. But Ramabai's explorations within Christianity for a faith that could satisfy her, show influences upon her thinking which were drawn from working class English radicalism. Vishwanathan suggests that Ramabai's conversion to Christianity perhaps opened up a 'transnational space of identification that was impossible within the more narrowly confined caste structure' (p.143). Armed with arguments derived from her own understanding and her background, but also her familiarity with sources of heretical thinking which the sisters believed were drawn from mass-based pamphlet literature, Ramabai became a part of the deep sectarian divide in England; her intellectual resistance to religious authority allied her, 'as a colonial subject, with the English masses' disaffection from rule that represented only landed and clerical interests.' Thus, far from conversion to Christianity implicating her in colonialism, Vishwanathan shows that Ramabai's resistance to official authority in the Church—which symbolized Englishness—and her closeness to 'heretical' positions in England, lent itself to strong expressions of anti-colonialism (p.137). This is recognized by Sister Geraldine in her closing account of Ramabai's fraught relationship with the Anglican Church which had initiated her conversion but failed to convince her on points of authority and theology:

> Christian liberty and Christian hierarchical government, with its ramifications and discipline, her mind was unable to harmonise. Then too the very title the "Church of England' was something abhorrent to her. And can we not understand how such a title may seem to the uninitiated foreigners to savour of the inborn arrogance of our insular

nature instead of the sweet humility of the Divine Master? I felt from
the beginning that this was a bone that stuck in her throat.... England
to an Indian has an unsavoury sound....the bitterness that burns like
a fire deep down in the souls of Indian people, which various
circumstances tend to suppress, must out at certain times...with this
feeling burning in their souls the very title the Church of England
would tend to alarm and repel (*Letters & Correspondence*, pp. 404-
406).

I began *Rewriting History* with a sense of unease at the way
Christianity and colonialism have been conflated not only by Hindu
nationalists but also by critics of modernity; this in part explains
why Ramabai has been dismissed as someone who, because of her
conversion, could no longer influence her community. This easy
conflation of Christianity and colonialism has been effectively
broken by Vishwanathan, at least in the case of Ramabai, as is
evident from the discussion above. Even so Ramabai's anti-colonial
stand, especially after the controversy at the time of the plague,
has not really been understood, and I too was almost defensive
when I dwelt on the nationalist's dismissal of Ramabai, even as I
vigorously rebutted the 'nationalist' position. You can imagine my
surprise when a young political activist came up to me in Baroda
after one of my sessions on gendering history and told me that one
of the Chapekar brothers had mentioned Ramabai in his memoirs
as having hidden some firearms for him! As my young friend put it
'what was, or what could have been the connection between the
'convert' Ramabai who had been fiercely attacked by Tilak, and
the Chapekar brothers, who were believed to have been the killers
of Ayerst and Rand and were hanged for their offence? The Chapekar
brothers had set up a society for the removal of obstructions to the
Hindu religion. They were strongly against the conversion of
Brahmins to Christianity which should have made them the sworn
enemies of Ramabai. So how did they end up being linked to her?
Did anger against the British government temporarily bridge the
opposition between the worlds of the Hindu fundamentalist and a
Christian convert who was committed to spreading the faith to
others but, as I had argued in *Rewriting History*, was as nationalist

as anyone else? In *Rewriting History* I had already delineated the
outlines of the fierce controversy that Ramabai generated with the
Anglican Church and the British government because of her public
stance on the plague atrocities. Suddenly, the attacks of Sister
Geraldine against Ramabai's public position on the atrocities of
the British soldiers during the handling of the plague measures,
which she condemned as seditious, took on an altogether different
meaning. Geraldine had also referred to physical searches in
Ramabai's Kedgaon premises (*Letters & Correspondence*, p.379).
So could the officials have been looking for evidence of 'sedition'
such as arms? And what do we make of the Chapekar claim to links
with Ramabai? Was she so angry with the British government for
its brutal and racist measures in 1897 that she was driven by impulse
to collaborate with other hardliners? Perhaps we will never really
know. Ramabai remains something of an enigma even after so
much work on her. And we are constantly discovering new facets
about her as the brief analysis of her varied writings provided below
will indicate.

III

Combining within herself a number of different personas, Ramabai
seems to me to have been the most prolific and sustained woman
writer of her time. As a social reformer, an activist with a capacity
to make important interventions in society, as a traveller, a deeply
spiritual person who found a faith that satisfied her religious cravings,
as someone committed to spreading that faith, and as a person
who interpreted the teachings of the faith she had chosen, as a
person who had to raise funds for the social interventions she tried
to make, and as an institution builder, she had a variety of reasons
that impelled her to write. But all this was later in her career. She
began her career as a writer for very instrumental reasons: as a
woman with no independent resources—women had no right to
property, and she had no husband or other male to support her—
she had no money at all and was dependent on others for her
sustenance; Ramabai was thus forced to find ways of supporting

herself throughout her life. There are poignant references in her writings, particularly in her letters, to being 'manifestly penniless,' (*Letters & Correspondence* p. 164) to paying off debts (p. 184), to juggling the meagre resources that she had (p. 204), and to how wonderful it would be if she could transport some of her father's land to Bombay to set up her home for widows (p. 254). She tried to train herself as an independent professional seeking to join a course in medicine, for which she travelled to England, but that project failed to materialise since she was hard of hearing. She tried to teach, but that led her into controversy with the Anglican Church— and so she remained dependent on the goodwill of others until she raised enough resources to set up her institution for widows. She turned to writing as a way of earning money to maintain a modicum of financial autonomy and that is how she came to write her first piece of work in Marathi, the *Stri Dharma Niti* (1882)—a manual for schooling women into the norms of new patriarchal practices for the emerging middle classes. Fortunately for her, this book was bought in bulk by the education department and was prescribed for girls in schools in Maharashtra. By this time Ramabai had decided to travel to England and the proceeds of the sales of the book were meant to raise money for her passage. Later, all the other reasons that I have outlined above provided the motivation for her writing; nevertheless, the proceeds of some of her writings continued to provide funds for her varied ventures even though they were also meant to disseminate a point of view.

Ramabai used writing to *communicate* to different constituencies for different purposes: to audiences in America to stir their consciences about the oppression of Indian women so that they would generously contribute to the institution she intended to set up for widows—this became her best known work titled *The High Caste Hindu Woman* (1888). She wrote 'travel' articles which went into books in Marathi for audiences back home on what she found interesting while she was in England and America; she wrote letters to the newspapers as part of her interventions in shaping public opinion, she wrote passionate pieces to the British authorities to seek social and legal intervention in the lives of women of India, and she wrote brief accounts of her life and her discovery of Christ for a missionary constituency as part of her work in spreading the faith. She also wrote innumerable letters to a range of people but only one collection has survived which forms an invaluable resource to document Ramabai's life. This collection is a miscellany—of debates on Christianity, on the Anglican Church, on travel, on people she considered worthy of introducing to her daughter Manorama through her letters to her, descriptions of her 'rescue' work in Brindavan and the famine-stricken Central Provinces, her opinion on the Rakhmabai case and the consequent indictment of the British government, and finally her so-called 'seditious' actions in criticising the Governor of Bombay Presidency. It was painstakingly put together by Sister Geraldine and the more I think about the writing of a woman-centred history and the difficulties of sources the more I find myself really moved by Sister Geraldine's preservation of the correspondence and her investment in archiving it. By this act of archiving she made a lasting contribution to our understanding of Ramabai, Christianity, colonialism and the experience of conversion. We may recall that although there was a deep bond between Ramabai and her Ajibai— Sister Geraldine—that bond was marked by severe stresses and tensions and it is fairly clear that Geraldine was ambivalent about Ramabai. In the end these tensions shaped Geraldine's concluding remarks on Ramabai which are both 'honest' and deeply subjective, even as she sought to provide an 'objective' and dispassionate account of their relationship. What is significant is that Geraldine recognized that she was no match intellectually for Ramabai, and sought the help of someone better equipped than she was to handle Ramabai's arguments as she could not cope with Ramabai's skills in doggedly sustaining her point of view. All Geraldine could do was to hit out at Ramabai, calling her arrogant and defiant, even dishonest. Worse, she was labelled a 'bad' mother who was trying to control her daughter and refusing to let her become her own person. Despite all this, Geraldine carefully compiled the collection of letters as she believed that such a collection would contribute to an account of Ramabai's life, a life that she was quite certain was worthy of recounting. When I think of what we would have lost if Geraldine had not done what she did I see a certain poignancy in her not only subjecting Ramabai to scrutiny but also subjecting herself to the critical gaze of history in which, unfortunately, she does not come off too well. For Geraldine this decision may have been part of her concern for documenting the history of conversion whereby her understanding of Ramabai would be vindicated, but for us Geraldine's account has been a way of understanding the quest of a feminist for an emotional and spiritual anchor, acceptable only on her own terms.

One aspect of Ramabai's pioneering effort in recognizing the power of communication in creating public opinion has been somewhat obscured by other issues that have dominated our concerns, and this is her critique of male domination on the one hand, and her relationship to Christianity on the other, but it is important to note that in some embryonic way Ramabai was exploring the power of photo journalism. Sabeena Gadihoke's ongoing work on zenana photography will examine Ramabai's photographic practices more comprehensively. For the moment I will point to what has struck me in the way she used writing to communicate the nature and experience of oppressive patriarchal practices, particularly in the context of widowhood and other moments of distress in the lives of women, such as famine, and the manner in which she visually documented such experiences and events, that is, her photographic practices. While Ramabai was seeking to raise funds and official and unofficial support for her work she wrote certain texts such as the well known and oft reprinted *The High Caste Hindu Woman*, and 'The Cry of Indian Women,' an appeal that she directed at Sir Bartle Frere, the former Governor of Bombay Presidency. She also wrote up narratives of widows which she sent as part of her correspondence with people in England and America, and later to Australia. She included photographs in these letters which documented, for example, the scrawny condition of widows as soon as they entered the Sharada Sadan and their transformations into healthy confident women a few years later.

These 'before and after' visual documents were meant to 'show' the world what it was like to be a widow and then what it could be, once they were in a safe and 'happy' environment. Her sense of history as events—which went beyond the notion of the politically powerful—also led to photographs of girls rescued in the famine, and of their transformation too into confident women some years later; of everyday life in Sharada Sadan and Mukti Sadan where 'her girls' performed a range of activities like food production and processing, weaving, and printing books. The printing of books itself is documented in three visuals outlining the process ending with the final product stacked up on a table behind which the printers stand proudly. There is a wonderful photograph of the hundreds of girls (sitting and standing in neat rows) that she rescued in the 1891 famine which must have required some technical skill in assembling. She photographically documented Bible propagating activities, modes of transport used and specific locations such as Pandharpur—a great pilgrim centre of the Hindus—and most amazing of all, she recorded disguising herself as a mahar woman so that no one would recognize her (she was recognizable because of her characteristic white garments and short cropped hair) when she moved in the by-lanes of Brindavan and Mathura to rescue widows who were being sexually exploited under the façade of priestly activities. This photograph is in total contrast to one taken in America where Ramabai is clothed in white with her head covered tightly, almost as if she is wearing a nun's veil. Here Ramabai and/ or her American friends were clearly evoking the chaste Indian widow for a foreign audience. From this visual journey through photographs it seems to me that Ramabai had a sense of *living* history and thus of creating and leaving behind a unique archive. I hope to explore this aspect of Ramabai's life further at some time in the future. For the moment I will end this discussion with how the specificity of the visual journey that she was 'factually' seeking to provide to her reader/viewer was transformed by a sleight of hand to lose its archival value in one case: the photograph of Ramabai disguised as a Mahar woman was published in Margaret Fuller's book[3] as the photograph of a low caste woman without any reference to Ramabai!

IV

There are two broad arenas into which Ramabai's writing can be classified: one is her writing on her understanding of the women's question—in which there is clearly an internal development— and the second is what I would call her 'travel' writing which was not necessarily strictly confined to travel in the conventional sense of the word but to other kinds of journeys of the self—the opening up of worlds from conversations with a large range of people, from reading widely, from participating in meetings and campaigns, either personally or vicariously. Ramabai was obviously a keen observer and fundamentally 'footloose'; she made good use of the way her life had been shaped by her father's travels and quest for truth so that, in a sense, she became a 'participant observer' who absorbed minute details of her constantly changing environment. While her early travels made a pilgrim out of her at the spiritual level they also gave her a unique advantage over others because through her travels she mentally documented and filed away images that she evoked quite powerfully in her later writing. There is an amazing photograph—again one of the wonderful documents that Ramabai preserved—of her family: the assemblage of different family members with their varying sartorial manifestations is marked by the piercing gaze of the seven-year-old Ramabai as she looks into the camera of life. She must have retained something of that piercing gaze as she looked at the world during her early travels which have, however, only marginally found their way into her later writings. But once she had learnt the value of writing as a way of documenting her experiences she actually wrote a travelogue, albeit episodically. Two works fall formally into the genre of travel writing—and both these are in Marathi because Ramabai is clearly speaking to a constituency which she thinks needs to be introduced to an alternative world. This is clear from the frequent resort to comparisons or contrasts between an unfamiliar and a familiar world. But in a sense Ramabai wrote travel pieces in reverse—to Sister Geraldine for example on worlds that Geraldine, or Miss

Beale would never go to or 'see' in the way she could, even though they were part of the 'west', unlike her. She described being stupefied with wonder at the beauty of the Niagara Falls to her 'dear friend' and teacher Miss Dorothy Beale, but she added to her own experience of wonderment by recalling for Dorothy something that she had read: the description of the Niagara is peppered with an account of the moving manner in which a native American had worshipped the Great Spirit at the Falls. According to his 'national custom' he threw all his ornaments, one by one into the water as these were the 'best things he had to give to the Great Spirit' (*Letters & Correspondence*, p.174). Similarly descriptions of nature are interspersed with descriptions of customs in her letters, the awesomeness of the Grand Canyon in one paragraph and the rise and progress of the Mormons of Utah, who in her opinion, are worse than the Shakta sect, in the next. Actual travels are juxtaposed with 'journeys of the mind', as it were, especially in letters to Miss Beale, with whom she shared an intellectual relationship and so she constantly flip flops between what she had seen and what she had read. For example, after she describes Mount Tacoma in Seattle, and the San Francisco Bay, she goes on to talk about the striking things she has read; books on Buddhism, 'the industrial idea in education,' an account of a meeting between the writer George Kennan and Count Leo Tolstoy which she found 'very interesting'. In the same letter she talks about a book by Kennan on the sufferings of political prisoners, and the 'fiendishness' of the Russian government. Ramabai makes clear where her own sympathies lie: with the Nihilists and the 'revolutionists' even though 'they may have their faults', as she puts it. She also bemoans not having enough time to read because of her 'active life' and yet she promises to read some book which Dorothy Beale has suggested in an earlier letter! On her way back to India after her years in America, when her ship berthed in Japan Ramabai wrote a colourful travel piece on the incredible beauty of the country—Mount Fujiyama and the sunrises sent her into raptures — and on Japanese culture, its beautiful temples, its statues (the fifty foot high Great Buddha in bronze and the thirty foot high camphor wood Kannon, the God of Mercy, benevolence and love), of its political institutions, its 'hurtful feudal system' and the deep patriotism of its people. The status of women features, as always, in her account which she describes as not so 'free' as in the West but not as cloistered as in India. While Japanese women were not barbarically loaded with jewels as Indian women were, they blacked their teeth and shaved their eyebrows after they married! She also notices that there was a caste system in Japan in the form of the Shogunate, but writes that it is 'now' abolished. Back in India after years of travel in England and America she also wrote an inspired and nostalgic piece on her brief visit to her native village and neighbouring forest where the Tungabhadra rose and her father ran an ashram for many years (pp.252-54). The place was hallowed with the memory of her parents, and she was delighted to see plants that her mother had planted filling the air with their scent.

Within travel writing she adopted different modes at different times: for example some accounts of her travels in America, in particular, are written in the 'manners and customs' genre of the old colonial writer, the difference being that now it is an *Indian woman* who is doing the documenting and that has an interesting feel to it because her observations are at all times impressed by her concerns and interests. Her travels in America opened up a whole range of issues such as slavery, women's organizations, the temperance movement, educational systems, and the working of the churches to name only a few. Her capacity to link her interests and concerns with those of her readers is particularly significant so letters to Manorama are specially designed for a little girl. One of these has a long account of slavery as personified in the life and work of Harriet Tubman, whom she met twice, and was given a vigorous handshake and huge bear hug by at least on one occasion! The account is an engaging mixture of little details required for a child reader and the larger issues represented by the institution of slavery—of how they were bought and sold like cats and dogs and had no rights, and why it was 'right' to run away from such cruelty. The account of Harriet's running away includes the dangers of doing so, of how the masters kept hounds to hunt down runaway slaves, and of Harriet's success in crossing the border into Canada where she could be safe. Harriet's repeated returns in disguise and the subversive ways used by her and others to mobilize the slaves to escape make for interesting reading even for adults. Ramabai describes strategies used by Harriet and others to plan their escape: the slaves could not read, and letters to be read to them were vetted by the masters. To get round this policing, the slaves sang hymns—no one could suspect them in that — which evoked the condition of slavery and made plans for meetings in appointed places. After this Harriet would 'lead' the runaway slaves—more than 300 of them over many years— into Canada. Finally when slavery was abolished and all the slaves were free, and Harriet could legally go back to America, she continued to work with orphans and old people and it was during this phase that Ramabai met her. Obviously there was a point to the telling of this story to little Manorama which Ramabai reveals through the concluding homily in the letter:

> You know, my dear child, there are thousands of little children like you and women like me in our dear India who are as badly treated as the slaves of olden times. I hope my child will remember the story of Harriet and try to be as helpful to her own dear countrywomen as Harriet was and is to her own people (pp. 206-208).

There was much to be done in her own country and through the account of Harriet Tubman, the sisters in Wantage were politely dissuaded from thinking that Manorama, who was with them at the time she wrote this letter, could stay on in England and be a substitute for Ramabai in their scheme of things (which would make of her an obedient member of the Anglican Church), unlike the mother who had refused that role. Travel and journeys and the writing that flowed from them were themselves part of a set of concerns that her writing never lost sight of.

As is well known by now— thanks to the increasing interest on Ramabai and the growing body of work on her— the most sustained concern in Ramabai's writing was expectedly focused on women. However, because her best known work *The High Caste Hindu Woman* dwelt so powerfully on the condition of women in upper caste Hindu society, and critiqued the social and structural dimensions of their oppression, an earlier work titled the *Stri Dharma Niti* has been disappointing to feminists looking for a radical stance in all her work. I would instead like to provide a context for her positions by examining the development of Ramabai's understanding on the 'women's question', from her first writings to the later writings, through different genres of writing including letters to individuals, to the newspapers and petitions to the British authorities.

The *Stri Dharma Niti*, [4] written in a sanskitized Marathi, is a product of the 19th century construction of the new conjugal household and addresses a growing middle class in newly-opening avenues like the bureaucracy, judicial and legal services, teaching and journalism. It is unmistakably stamped with the marks of the new patriarchal codes of 'schooling' women to enable them to better administer the conjugal household, and therefore has something of the appearance of a commissioned work, even though that may not be strictly true in terms of the original motivation in writing it (to pay for her passage to England). The fact that the book was picked up by the educational authorities suggests that the work conformed to the ideologies of a class dominating public culture, and the educational policies catering to that class. As the book unfolds, the ideologies of reform so prevalent in the second half of the 19th century on the women's question are unmistakable to any reader. These are clearly new forms of the traditional *stri-dharma* propagated from the time of the Shastra writers to turn women into pliable agents. who reproduce caste and class structures through appropriate schooling practices; now additionally the ideologies were to perform the function of turning women into class socialisers for the upper caste-middle class segments of society. However, while sharing these ideologies which the male reformers—who surrounded her both in Maharashtra and earlier in Bengal— were propagating and seeking to practise in their personal lives, Ramabai's reflection on them is marked by her own specific experiences and her ways of thinking. These are as yet unformed and inchoate but they are there: in the preface to the first edition she refers to the lack of a work through which women could understand 'their essence' and act accordingly to improve their own condition. It is because of this she says, despite her own limited intellect, and the inconsistencies in formulation due to limited understanding, heightened by her 'currently disturbed state of mind,' that she was writing this work. The disturbed state of mind could well be an allusion to being in a situation where she was still working things out in terms of a developed understanding on the state of women in the country, which she clearly regards as 'unfortunate'.

The book begins with a dedication to 'my countrywomen with love': the dedication also states that the 'small' book was written in the memory of her very 'dear late husband' by the grieving widow of Babu Bipin Behari Das Medhavi. This sets the stage for the focus on women as part of a conjugal duo, the home created by the duo, and the importance of a consciously parented and managed home. In this, the book is not very different from the manuals for *stri siksha*—women's education— the ideology behind the parables for women so popular in the *devrrani-jethani* stories about bad women and good women in Hindi literature, and the *Beheshti Zevar*, written by Maulana Ashraf Thanavi, given to all brides in a Muslim household. But what runs as a thread through the work is the emphasis that Ramabai places on the importance of education in the cultivation of a personality—one can see the beginnings of the educationist already—and the relationship between education and morality. Education is the key to true knowledge, to self reliance and ultimately to the country's progress and the individual's welfare. Knowledge is the capacity to reason and therefore Ramabai rejects parables as a way of convincing women for, in her view, they can be misread. Women must strive to climb out of the dark well of ignorance. Further education is the only capital a person can have which will always remain, while other forms of wealth can disappear overnight. Education, however is no hollow thing: without it one is deprived of the inner eye, the capacity to see beyond the outer eye, which everyone has. Education here clearly stands for knowledge and wisdom in what Phule called the *traittiya ratna*. Rote learning does not lead to understanding, which is the meaning and essence of learning. In her formulations on the importance of education for women Ramabai is not merely rehashing what male reformers were saying about women's education but going beyond it to describe its importance as a woman speaking from the inside— a woman who has been witness to its importance through the personal experiences of her own family.

Beyond the importance of education, which in her view will lead to independence, the heart of the *Stri Dharma Niti* is the code of conduct for women to ensure harmony in conjugality and marriage, and the moral training of children, all of which are *conscious* acts that are contingent upon a cultivated wife and mother. This positions Ramabai as a staunch opponent of child marriage. While this was a position some of the male reformers were also taking, what marked Ramabai's stand as unique was her advocacy of marriage by choice on the part of both partners—conjugality was about mutual love and had to be based on consensual relations without coercion of any kind. Ramabai advocated a marriage age of 20, so that both men and women could pursue their education without hindrance and domestic diversions: a human existence without knowledge was, in her view, inferior even to an animal existence; further if men and women produced children at an early age both they and their progeny would be weakened, unformed bodies creating 'useless' progeny in her view. She echoes discourses on bodily health circulating in the 19th century here and prefigures Gandhi's strong indictment of child marriage and 'child' reproduction – children producing children as he put it. In both Ramabai and Gandhi there could be a discomfort with child sexuality which at least in part informed their indictment of child marriage. But, most notably, Ramabai was against child marriage because it violated the principle of informed choice on the basis of individual personalities leading to congeniality and mutuality as the basis of the new affective household. In an amazing turn of argument she says: given that even animals have the freedom to establish a male female relationship *according to their own wishes*, why should human beings not have that freedom? This choice should not be hampered by social customs or considerations of wealth and should not be based on what is perceived as 'good appearance' because both are ephemeral. Mutual conjugal love is the most comprehensive form of love encapsulating all others, writes Ramabai in *Stri Dharma Niti*:

> Love has numerous manifestations. The love which parents feel for their offspring is called parental affection. The love that offspring feel for their parents, teachers and God is called devotion. The love of siblings and friends is called friendship. The love which the generous hearted person feels for the poor is called compassion. The love between two spouses who have two bodies and one soul, who share equally in each others joy and sorrows is known simply as love. It has no other name because it has the completeness of love. Other types of love are partial, not complete. The ultimate love is between equal and virtuous spouses (p. 68).

What is significant in Ramabai's construction of conjugality in *Stri Dharma Niti* is that perhaps for the last time in her works she evokes both conjugality and the traditional mythological female iconic figures like Sita, Anusuya, Arundhati, Damayanti who left their stamp upon 'Bharatavarsha'. Rama and Nala are also held up as icons for conjugal love. The relationship of Rama and Sita is drawn from Bhavabhuti rather than Valmiki and eulogised as the highest form of love—one where Sita chooses to accompany Rama to the harsh forest. Her abandonment is assigned to Rama's fear of public censure (by implication therefore she does not censure Rama) but Ramabai's sympathies lie firmly with Sita. She quotes from Bhavabhuti, writing that 'even a stone would burst into tears and the heart of a diamond break asunder with sorrow' at the piteous condition of Sita. And despite all this, the beauty of her conjugality was such that Sita's devotion for Rama did not diminish; instead she sent him a message from the forest full of moral and religious advice (p.74). Sita's birth in a country like Bharatavarsha thus made it unique and meant that, while it could be inferior to other countries in other qualities, no other country had saintly women like Sita. Partly such formulations seem to be part of the public sphere in the 19th century which Ramabai was not as yet critiquing, partly it was the construction of a selfless conjugality which she seemed to personally subscribe to, and partly it was an attempt to

reach a constituency steeped in such formulations with its strong
ideological requirements which she shared through her leading
role in the Arya Mahila Sabhas in western India. These shared
positions also explain many of her formulations on modesty where
there are deep anxieties about sexuality, and motherhood. Women
are divided into good and bad in her understanding and there is a
latent and running opposition between prostitutes and 'good'
women, and prostitutes are seen to 'infect' other women through
their presence in public spaces like theatres or even *harikathas*!
Motherhood and conscious parenting is regarded as crucial in
shaping children—bad behaviour, lack of character and virtue are
consequences of faulty parenting whether it is Siraj-ud-daula on
the one hand, or Napoleon and Shivaji who had good parenting!

Stri Dharma Niti is thus clearly the product of a moment in
history and a certain phase in the life of Pandita Ramabai. Because
I read it after I had already come across the better known *The High
Caste Hindu Woman* it comes through as a stark contrast to her
understanding of the women's question. When seen chronologically,
it tells us something about women's writing on schooling women
for their roles as wives and mothers, when they work within the
dominant reformist discourses, and of the more radical direction
in which Ramabai moved on in her thinking on women, almost
within the year.

Stri Dharma Niti was published in June 1882, just before
Ramabai set sail for England. A year later Ramabai wrote an earnest
plea to Sir Bartle Frere who had been Governor of the Bombay
Presidency and the tone of this plea, aptly titled *The Cry of Indian
Women* [5] makes a case for intervention by the authorities on the
abject condition of women in India. From a position in which
Ramabai had argued that women could lift themselves from their
fallen condition she now finds herself seeking urgent assistance
and support from the British. The grounds on which she sought
assistance are interesting: since India had made Britain wealthier
it is incumbent on the government to support the reforms being
advocated by organizations such as the Arya Mahila Committee.
Specifically, support was sought for an end to child marriage, a

ban on male bigamy, providing help to destitute women—
suggesting widows perhaps— and the encouragement of female
education. Concrete support was sought for financial assistance for
a widow's home. Notably, now the oppressed condition of women
was the focus of her passionate plea for action, and it was delineated
in powerful terms in this essay:

Ramabai begins her account of women's oppression with
discrimination against the female child—although not universal it
is general, and ironically no value is attributed to the girl child as
she is not regarded as serving any useful purpose to the parents.
This gives her an opportunity to pass a comment on the work/
utility of women in/to the household and how society readers them
invisible. Education is denied to the girl; even reformers are
lukewarm about it 'from fear of sacrificing their own interests'.
More learned parents too are inhibited from rescuing their daughters
from the 'well of darkness' through fear of being outcasted by the
conservative community. Thus people quickly marry off their
daughters and that pushes them into a miserable life at the hands
of their in-laws; many wives are driven to suicide. Few women
have congenial partners, and though men can and do remarry
women have no exit—their husbands regard themselves as having
'sovereign' rights over them. Husbands 'own' their wives who are
like female slaves treated in the same way as 'Spaniards treated the
native Indians'.

Widowhood increases the oppression of women; the widow is
regarded as a substitute for a servant girl. Abused sexually by family
members, they pay the penalty for the 'sin' by being 'outcasted'
whereas the men involved can pay a small fine and live 'happily
within the community'. Having travelled throughout the country
Ramabai regards herself as a unique witness to the deplorable state
of Indian women, especially the widows. She demands financial
help from England in return for the riches acquired by 'millions of
foreigners' from India even though her own daughters remain
without shelter. Here Ramabai regards the price of colonial
exploitation as being paid by women rather than men. Further,
Ramabai positions herself as better informed on the state of Indian

women through her travels than the ex-Governor, and exhorts him to facilitate her attempt to raise support from England for her mission to set up a home for destitute women.

Nothing concrete seems to have come of Ramabai's passionate plea for help from Sir Bartle Frere, or from anyone else in Britain. The stay in England, even the conversion into the Anglican Church yielded no tangible gains. If anything, England ended up as a traumatic period for Ramabai. She was witness to the painful suicide of her friend Anandibai Bhagat, found that she could not be admitted to a medical course because of a hearing disability, had severe financial constraints as she owed money, probably to Anandibai Bhagat's brothers, for her passage to England, she could not teach as she wanted to because of objections from the Church hierarchy, and she became embroiled in a controversy and a theological dispute with her mentor, Sister Geraldine. Nevertheless in this plea she made to the ex-governor she outlined her newly developed understanding of the women's question: this included the various stages in the lives of women and its differing nature in terms of discrimination suffered by them. It also became the model for the way she developed her analysis of women's status in *The High Caste Hindu Woman* which was an expansion, elaboration and refinement of the detailing of women's oppression of the 1883 work that she penned to Sir Bartle Frere.

The High Caste Hindu Woman was published four years later: by this time Ramabai had travelled extensively in America—over 3,000 miles—covering more distance than she did in her travels in India during the pilgrim years which she regarded as a critical input into her understanding of the condition of women in India. Travels in America, with her amazing capacity to observe and absorb the minutae of life, and the circle of women and men that she interacted with are likely to have sharpened her understanding of male domination and women's subordination—which was not unique to India. No wonder that the Canadian, Cecil Maud Cayley, described her as giving a most interesting lecture but as being 'very hard on the male sex', and as having 'very extreme views on the subject of women's rights' (*Letters & Correspondence* p.181).

Ramabai's interactions with women like Frances Willard, Rachel
Bodley, Harriet Tubman, and hearing of events like the Seneca
Falls meeting, and the anti-slavery and temperance movements
would have honed her analytical skills. *The High Caste Hindu Woman*
was written with the intention of moving the American public
and was admittedly a fundraising text to address a constituency
which could be more generous than England had been. More than
that, the tension that Ramabai had experienced as a colonial subject
with the power that ruled her country, so evident in her reaction
to the Anglican Church's demands for total loyalty, was countered
by a more fraternal relationship with her American supporters. At
roughly the same time that she published *The High Caste Hindu
Woman* she wrote sharply to Dorothy Beale on the Rakhmabai
case; the tone of her reaction suggests that Dorothy had been
disapproving of Ramabai's criticism of the British government's
handling of the case. Be that as it may, the judgement gave her an
opportunity to hit out bitterly at the collusion of the colonial
government and the male population of India in crushing women's
rights. She argues that even though the civil and criminal courts
need not have acted in the case since there were caste or customary
rules which could have settled things, and there was no need for
the British government to imprison Rakhmabai for refusing to
comply with the court order on the restitution of conjugal rights.
The British government had thereby given its 'sanction to an
injustice revolting to every right thinking mind. ' The logic of the
order was such that the imprisonment of Rakhmabai could be
repeated every six months as she would continue to be liable to
repeated rounds of prosecution till either 'her spirit was broken
into submission or death (came) to end her sorrows' (*Letters &
Correspondence* p. 176). She accused the English government of
resorting to double standards by claiming that they could not
interfere in religious matters when it came to providing relief to
women but of doing precisely that when an issue affected 'their
own interests'. She wrote:

> I wonder if such outrageous acts of the English government will be
> excused in heaven simply because they have promised to please the
> males of our country at the cost of women's rights and happiness and
> they do rightly give their decisions in men's favour! But what of the

over one hundred million of women? Were the promises given to women? And what a beneficial government it is that does not care in the least to defend nearly half the inhabitants of the country from the tyrannical lords whose marital property women are said to be! (*Letters & Correspondence* p. 177)

Ramabai goes on to state that having studied the Hindu law she believes that the English government is misinterpreting the law as there is nothing in it that warrants such an order of the government. The logic of profit and the unseen patriarchal contract would, she suggests bitterly, have led to the government 'winking at the custom of suttee' if Raja Ram Mohan Roy had not shown that it was 'not the religion of the country'. She concludes her letter by giving vent to extreme disappointment at the order in the Rakhmabai case:

> It is false to expect any justice for India's daughters from the English government for, instead of befriending her, the government has proved to be a worse tyrant to her than the native society and religion. It advocates on the one hand the education and emancipation of Hindu woman, and then, when the woman is educated, and refuses to be a slave in soul and body to a man against whom her whole nature revolts, the English government comes to break her spirit allowing its law to become an instrument for riveting her in chains (*Letters & Correspondence* p. 178).

The connections Ramabai made between governments, patriarchies and colonialism were rare for her time and rare even in Ramabai's writing. But it is an important indication of the way women were at least making connections, far beyond anything men were saying at the same time. The distance between the ideological framework of *Stri Dharma Niti* and the later Ramabai is striking to say the least.

The Peoples of the United States [6] is an entirely different kind of work. Begun while Ramabai was still in America it was completed and published in India in 1889. The work is less of a travelogue, more of a set of observations on a number of themes around which Ramabai arranges her descriptions and analyses of institutions, people and debates, all of which are informed by an eye for detail and acute observation. The book needs to be read in full to get a picture of its richness and complexity; From the point of view of the focus of *Rewriting History* I will dwell here mainly on her chapter on 'The Condition of Women' which is one among others on the system of government, social conditions, domestic conditions, education and learning, religious denominations and charities, and commerce and industry.

This chapter continuously engages with biases against women in America and in India, and looks at how individual women and women's collectives in America have fought back to wrest a place for themselves in society. Education for women, a running concern of Ramabai's since the days of *Stri Dharma Niti*, forms an important part of the chapter where she also deals with common arguments such as the assumption that women's smaller brain size means that they have an absence of intellectual ability, the dangers to domesticity and womanly roles through education, and the ultimate loss of livelihood to men. The terms of the debate are set in the oppositions that are made between women's natural sphere of domesticity and the public sphere of employment. Certain sectors are particularly taboo such as medicine: in India even someone like Keshub Chandra Sen had argued that a medical education would put an end to the 'womanliness of women' (p. 59) and in America men were saying that if women entered this field they would lose their innate delicacy, engage in 'unnatural' conduct and also destroy life on a large scale! According to a 'learned statesman' education for women was extremely dangerous also because it would have *material consequences*; it would take women away from their domestic duties and that would be very pernicious for both state and society. But the brave attempts of women had succeeded in turning the tide from a position where it was argued that culture for women should never develop into learning, to the argument that the spirit of the new institutions was that women 'shall be treated as self determining beings' (p. 176). In the 1880s women were not only being educated but were employed in fields such as education, law, medicine and scientific establishments. Ramabai attempts, in the chapter, to set women's learning and achievements within a feminist legacy on the one hand and the recognized and unrecognized contribution of women to knowledge; for example the kindergarten method of education that did not resort to corporal punishments was an achievement of women teachers. Other innovators and inventors had been erased for public consciousness because of male biases; Ramabai effectively dispels the oft-cited argument that women have never been inventors because they lack imagination. Instead she counters that nobody had given women scope to develop their inventiveness; she then cites a number of women who innovated in their own fields like music and astronomy but where their male relatives, including the great Beethoven, appropriated these achievements as their own!

Ramabai also writes about political and legal rights; she describes the stand of the erstwhile president John Adam's wife Abigail who refused to pay taxes as women did not have the right to vote, and the extreme case of a woman whose husband was taking away her children as women did not have a natural right of custody. Desperate to keep the children the woman denied in open court that the children were not her husband's (p.188) and so succeeded in getting a judgement in her own favour. Alluding to the Seneca Falls declaration that was made at the first women's convention to protect women's rights Ramabai details the hysterical reaction from certain male quarters against the women—they received curses, abusive epithets such as 'immoral', 'heretical', 'evil', and were labelled witches, messengers of Satan and so on and they were the subject of vicious cartoons and tirades in the yellow press. The women however pressed on with their agenda and Ramabai is deeply appreciative of their mobilization and the campaigns against slavery, for political rights, and in the Temperance Union led by women. It is in these large national campaigns, one of which she personally attended, that she heard an address by Frances Willard who described the 19th century as a unique century because of its scientific discoveries, but the most wonderful of which was women's discovery of herself. Ramabai saw this as a consequence of the collective effort put in by women during the decades after 1840 to promote their own welfare. The establishment of women's Sororis—

women's clubs— had led to many campaigns for education and a reform of women's working conditions (long working hours and exploitative treatment at the hands of factory owners). Some of the women's clubs had a special 'thinking class' to update women on abstruse subjects like philosophy. Through all the details that Ramabai puts into *People's of the United States* it is evident that she is strongly impressed with the agency of women and their power to act on behalf of themselves, despite severe opposition from men.

Two aspects of Ramabai's analysis of the condition of women in the United States deserve special attention from the point of view of a feminist understanding of established ways of thinking: one is dealt with at the beginning of the chapter on women and the second almost at the end and I would like to conclude this discussion of Ramabai's varied writing with these formulations. In Ramabai's view the task of emancipating women from their present condition was more difficult than abolishing slavery because the harm done by slavery is *visible* to all. However the harm done by the slavery of women is generally not noticed. It is like a 'mysterious heart disease that is invisible even as it destroys the heart of human society.' She says:

> Most people think that women are living not in slavery but in a state natural to them. The belief that women are not oppressed and that their condition need not be different from the present one, is so deeply entrenched in everybody's mind that it is impossible for anybody to even imagine how wretched their condition really is. What is worse, even women themselves believe that their condition is as it should be. In the past when African Negroes were slaves in America, many of them held similar beliefs....This state of mind is the ultimate in slavery…it destroys self respect and the desire for freedom: the two boons that God has given to humanity (p.168)

This is a very nuanced understanding of women internalising their oppression so fully that they do not even recognize that they have no autonomy and no freedom. Their minds have been 'crippled' and so they believe that they have whatever they should have—in sum they consent to the conditions that they live in.

NOTES AND REFERENCES

[1] Ram Bapat, 'Pandita Ramabai: Faith and Reason in the Shadow of the East and West,' in Vasudha Dalmia and H. von Stietencron, eds., *Representing Hinduism: The Construction of Religious Traditions and National Identity,* Delhi, Sage Publications, 1995.

[2] Gauri Vishwanathan, *Outside the Fold: Conversion, Modernity and Belief,* Princeton, Princeton University Press, 1998.

[3] Marcus B. fuller, *The Wrongs of Indian Womanhood,* Edinburgh & London, Oliphant Anderson and Ferrier, 1900

[4] *Stri Dharma Niti,* tr. by Meera Kosambi, in *Pandita Ramabai Through Her Own Words: Selected Works,* Delhi, Oxford University Press, 2000, pp. 35-101.

[5] *The Cry of Indian Women,* Ibid., pp.105-114.

[6] '*United Stateschi Lokasthiti ani Pravarasavritta*' tr. as 'The Peoples of the United States', by Meera Kosambi in Meera Kosambi, *Returning the American Gaze: Pandita Ramabai's The Peoples of the United States,* Delhi, Permanent Black, 2003.

SOAS LIBRARY

As Ramabai analyses the dependence of women on men in a note in her original text—which she regards as a vestige of ancient barbaric conditions— she takes up for scrutiny the position that men take on the 'burden ' of work and of maintaining their wives by slogging for hours on end. She points out that while men work for 10-12 hours at the most, women put in 16-17 hours daily to serve the menfolk. Labouring women on farms do both farm labour and household labour. In spite of this the wife has no right to the family income and must cajole or beg her husband for anything she may need. The husband then will tell her how much she is obliged to him for feeding and clothing her, forgetting that she too works. In Ramabai's words:

> In the absence of the wife in the house at least two or three servants would be employed to do the work she does single handedly. Servants are not fed for nothing, nor can they be said to be obliged to their master. But a wife, even if she does the work of ten servants, is under an obligation to her husband because *he feeds her*! (p. 214).

This is a brilliant analysis of the unpaid household labour that feminists like Christine Delphy have written about and all feminists have been trying to get the world of economics and the census to recognize. More than that, this is an embryonic delineation of the basis of the patriarchal social contract where women exchange unpaid labour for maintenance, so succinctly described by the feminist historian Gerda Lerner in *The Creation of Patriarchy* (1986) about a hundred years after Ramabai.